Growing up I᠎
and British ᠎᠎᠎ ᠎᠎᠎᠎᠎᠎

and in Washington, Moscow, Rome and Sydney

Sir Patrick Duffy

Published by Jeremy Mills Publishing Limited
www.jeremymillspublishing.co.uk

113 Lidget Street
Lindley
Huddersfield
West Yorkshire HD3 3JR

First published 2013

ISBN: 978-1-909837-04-1

Cover image:
Chasing Light: The Mystery of the Moor
© Ashley Jackson

To Mam and Dad.

Contents

Preface and Acknowledgements   7

Chapter One   Childhood in Lancashire and in Yorkshire   11

Chapter Two   The First Stirrings of Irishness   29

Chapter Three   World War Two   41

     Appendix 1   57

     Appendix 2   58

Chapter Four   Wartime Service in Northern Ireland   59

     Appendix 1   67

     Appendix 2   69

     Appendix 3   70

Chapter Five   Arrival at Westminster   71

Chapter Six   Anglo-Irish Relations   81

Chapter Seven   Conflict in Northern Ireland   95

     Appendix 1   123

Chapter Eight   Navy Minister   125

     Appendix 1   149

     Appendix 2   150

     Appendix 3   151

Chapter Nine   Death of Sheffield Steel   153

     Appendix 1   169

Chapter Ten   Lurch to the Left   171

                     Appendix 1   191

                     Appendix 2   192

                     Appendix 3   194

Chapter Eleven   Fighting for the Soul of the Labour Party 221

Chapter Twelve   The Militant Tendency   233

Chapter Thirteen   A New Realism   241

Chapter Fourteen   Demonising of the Irish in Britain   265

Chapter Fifteen   The Hunger Strikes   281

Chapter Sixteen   Changing Perceptions of the Irish   299

Chapter Seventeen The Peace Process   307

Chapter Eighteen   The NATO Assembly   317

Chapter Nineteen   Missions to Moscow, Rome,
                     Westminster and Sydney   333

                     Appendix 1   363

                     Appendix 2   364

Chapter Twenty   Reflections   365

Preface and Acknowledgements

Recalling a life dominated by industrial, military and political strife calls for a multifaceted account rather than a mere political memoir. I was born shortly after my father returned from active service in World War One. He was engaged shortly afterwards in another struggle for survival, as a coal miner in the turmoil of 1926. I was soon volunteering as a teenager for call-up in World War Two, and was joined later by my two brothers and my sister. Wartime service in Northern Ireland brought awareness of a divided community, and stirred my political involvement after arrival at Westminster. After a painful war experience, I was entirely concerned with conflict resolution whilst in official capacities in Whitehall and Brussels during the Cold War; although I was always conscious of the lurking presence of the final arbiter – the force option. For all my 25 years membership of the House of Commons, 19 years were spent on the Opposition benches. Economic, social, cultural and religious elements filled gaps in that limited political environment.

My most enduring memories start with the loss in wartime of courageous school friends and the resolution, and neighbourly decency, of outstanding fathers and mothers despite the bitterness left by the General Strike. I was still resentful of their treatment whilst under training as a Royal Navy ordinary seaman in 1940. I am immensely thankful to the Royal Navy for its tolerance and understanding of a nursed radicalism, for the medical care and attention it gave me long into peacetime and for my privileged membership of the Board of Admiralty long afterwards. I have remained so grateful also to those fine people who campaigned with me in the Tiverton, Colne Valley and Attercliffe constituencies. They know who they are, bless them. I remain full of admiration for those brave friends across the city of

Sheffield who rallied during the political strife that accompanied the startling decline of the local steel industry. I am especially anxious to place on record the distinguished roles of Sidney Dyson, Alan Wade, Ron Burford, Joe Sheedy and Rob Murray in the heroic defence of traditional values and behaviour in face of relentless pressure.

I wish to thank Dr Kevin McNamara for the unrivalled insights that he exercised at Westminster on the problems of Northern Ireland. I am also particularly grateful to all the members of my private office at the Admiralty for their unfailing helpfulness during ministry. I hope they will allow me to mention Gloria Franklin, my first Private Secretary, for her initial schooling and later guidance during difficult times. I am pleased to be able to claim Geoffrey Howland, who was my Assistant Private Secretary, as a good and valued friend to this day. And I cannot imagine any minister could have been better served and cared for than I was by my driver, Colour Sergeant John Williams of the Royal Marines. Captain P. R. D. Kimm OBE RN (Rtd) generously handled my naval queries: no better authority. The wide experience and expert knowledge of the staff of the North Atlantic Assembly in Brussels was a huge benefit at a crucial time during my presidency. Peter Corterier, Secretary-General, was unfailingly wise and helpful.

That I ventured to undertake such a long autobiographical haul is due to John Kennedy CBE and Andy Rogers. For their persistent encouragement and support I owe an incalculable debt. I am also anxious to commend Ashley Jackson for the distinction his singular artistry has brought to Yorkshire, as well as thank him for the warmth of his friendship and support over many years. I owe enormous debts of gratitude also to four Patricias: my sister Patsy, who is unsparing in her care of me; to another Patricia Duffy, my cousin in Co. Mayo, who, along with Patricia Morris of Co. Roscommon and Patricia Wilson of Goole, Yorkshire, have overcome with fortitude and skill the arduous task of transcribing bundles of pencil-scribbled notes and the evolving chapters. I cannot hint at the responsibility of behind-the-lines researchers and associate writers – for there have been none. Any errors or omissions are entirely mine. Happily, I am blessed with a good memory. Helpfully, I retained all my papers.

Chapter One

Childhood in Lancashire and in Yorkshire

On returning from school one afternoon in the autumn of 1927 in Yorkshire, and seeing my father, James, shaving at the kitchen sink, I asked my mother Margaret, 'Why isn't Dad down pit?' At seven years of age I was already familiar with his shift pattern. When he was on the afternoon shift, I would listen to the radio in the evening and tick the horse racing results in the *Daily Herald*. He and a mate, Bert Royle, had just won £29 on the 'Pools', hence the unexpectedly rare acquisition of a wireless and a bicycle.

'Because', Mam replied, 'he is going to Ireland to arrange your Grandad's funeral.'

'But who is Grandad?' I asked Dad, when he reproached me for not mourning him and asked, 'can I go with you?'

Already I had vivid memories – but none of Ireland, wherever it was located – of living alongside Wigan's tram sheds in Platt Bridge outside Wigan; of shopping for Mam at the Co-op, when she needed to tend to my younger brothers; of Dad bathing naked in his pit-black in the kitchen; of walking with Mam along a terrifyingly vast stretch of water that I later came to know as the Liverpool-Leeds canal; and of the lorry carrying our scant possessions breaking down on the journey over the Pennines after Dad transferred from the Lancashire to the Yorkshire coalfield in 1925.

In the new mining township of Rossington, south of Doncaster, I had experienced at five years all the excitement of the 1926 General Strike. With other children I had marched alongside the strikers and learned the words of a rousing song called 'The Red Flag'. I attended daily demonstrations and cheered window breaking at the homes of the few strike breakers. I protected Dad's small haul of coal as he scavenged the colliery's spoil-heap and crouched in a ditch when the striking miners were scattered and battered by police dressed like storm troopers. Alongside such events any family mention of a place called Ireland seemed irrelevant. Mention of America would soon make more sense. For Aunt Margaret and a young cousin, Jimmy O' Brien, travelled from Philadelphia to visit us in Rossington after the funeral of Grandad. Only then did I begin to realise that it was over there where most members of the family actually lived. Not in the remote place called Ireland. Nor anywhere else in Britain.

News of Ireland came to us in letters from America. That was how Dad serving in the trenches in France in 1917 had learned of the death of his mother, Julia Dunleavy, in the village of Raith in the parish of Aughamore, Co. Mayo. For all their family isolation, Dad and Mam were neither lonely nor ill-equipped socially, however, as they adjusted to living in Britain. They sorely missed the life of the Irish village they had left behind. Yet its communal values actually stood them in good stead in the working-class culture of Wigan and Rossington. But they never viewed Ireland through a sentimental prism or tried to cling to their roots. They had no time to stand and stare as they grappled with immediate problems. They simply had to face them with hard-headed practical realism and, above all, recognise their duty and obligations to their new country.

From the age of twelve years, Dad had accompanied his father, Patrick Duffy, to England for seasonal work. This was essential to sustain the older sister, three younger ones and a baby brother at home in Co. Mayo. Dad may have been only a child, but he was expected to do a man's job in England. Happily he was strong, like his father, who had been known to walk across Ireland in his early days – with neighbours – to Drogheda. They would board a cattle boat for Liverpool and then walk via Bury to the distant hiring fair at Skipton. Dad was soon left in England as a teenager to take up permanent employment in the coal mines, first in St. Helens and then in Wigan. At an early age he became a reservist in the Lancashire Hussars and was in France within a month of the outbreak of World

War One. When his cavalry regiment was stood down in 1916, he was transferred to the Oxford and Buckinghamshire Light Infantry and involved in the bitter fighting around Arras. His first cousin, Sergeant Brian Dunleavy, was killed in action quite close by.

It was very difficult to draw him on that experience. He was naturally quiet, reflective and devoted to the daily Labour newspaper the *Daily Herald*, along with the *Empire News* and *The Sunday Dispatch* at the weekend. That was when he also enjoyed a good drink of beer and a three or a sixpence bet on the horses, but never at the expense of family housekeeping. I never saw him handle a book. He was much influenced by the October Revolution in Russia in 1917, and the cloth-cap image of Lenin. If he wasn't a Labour man, I once overheard, he said he would be a communist. Apart from rejoicing over the success of Irish racehorses, he fitted perfectly into the lifestyle of the British coal miner and most working men. But he privately scorned absenteeism and never missed a shift, even when the pit worked six days weekly in wartime and afterwards.

There were no pithead baths in those days, nor hard hats, reflective jackets, oilskins or gloves. The men simply carried a water-duddly and snap-tin from home, collected a pick and shovel underground and worked in an old shirt and short pants. There were no face-masks either, and when coal-cutting machinery was introduced it filled the tunnels with coal dust like a blanket in the air. The miners developed pneumoconiosis as the dust built up in their chests and attacked the lung tissues.[1] Dad spent fifty-three years down the pit and only came out at seventy-three years when the National Coal Board (NCB) introduced an upper age limit. By this time he was being supervised at work by my schoolboy friends, who had been appointed to various levels of management – under a quite different regime, of course.

---

1 After a prolonged and noble campaign by Lord Geoffrey Lofthouse, a government compensation scheme was introduced. It was much too late, of course, for the older generation and was shamelessly exploited by certain lawyers.

Mam was also born in Raith. She was one of ten in the family of John Higgins and Helen Cunnane. Helen successfully reared all her children in a two-room, thatch-roofed, whitewashed cottage, without basic amenities. But she was actively assisted by her mother, Bid McLoughlin, who lived on the hill of Casheltourley a mile away.[2] That is where Mam was reared by her grandmother, as were her four sisters. The shrine at Knock is visible across the fields a few miles distant.

Following demobilisation, Dad had returned to Aughamore from France in 1919, and married Mam. They left immediately for Wigan, where Dad resumed work at his old pit – the Maypole Colliery in Abram. They entered lodgings with a Mrs Roberts on Warrington Road, Abram, where I was born. They often recalled the kindness and assistance extended to them generally at that time. They never saw Abram and Wigan in the same light as George Orwell. He saw in Wigan in his classic work, *The Road to Wigan Pier*, published in March 1937, only 'the real ugliness of industrialism', with its 'foetid alleys' and 'filthy hovels'. They remembered instead the dear friends they had left behind when they moved to Yorkshire.[3] They always saw more to Wigan than piers and sneers. Dad missed his 'local' in Abram, 'The Bucks Head' pub, immediately across the road from Mrs Roberts, and its splendid bowling green. Mam missed her Holy Family Church, with its parish hall and club a mile down the road in Platt Bridge, alongside which she was able eventually to rent a two-

---

2   Bid was a teenager during the Great Famine in the 1840s, and her survival remains a mystery for, apart from casual employment by the landlord, the family was without land of its own.

3   Sharon Lambert (nee Deehan) has recorded memories of the women who moved from Ireland to Lancashire. Her main themes of family, religion and the homeland were all mentioned by the respondents as important influences on their lives. Those themes certainly identified Mam, though she was quick to adapt to her new urban life and neighbours. *Irish Women in Lancashire, 1922–1960. Their Story*. Published by the Centre for North-West Regional Studies, University of Lancashire.

room terraced house, since demolished. Its proximity to the church and the Cooperative Society store compensated for the clanging from the nearby tram sheds. It had been long empty, because the previous occupant, an old gentleman – her new neighbours told her later – had hanged himself under the stairs.[4] She would never have been given a tenancy otherwise, they added, because all the local landlords were 'Orange' – as they put it. It was many years later before Mam asked me what 'Orange' meant and revealed that she had already experienced such anti-Catholicism at the clinic when I was a baby.[5] Mam and Dad never held that against the Lancashire people, to whom they remained firmly attached. They were glad to leave behind the dark shadow of the Maypole Colliery disaster of 1908. But I became aware of it from the frequent mention of Dad and his workmates' narrow escape and of its poignant Irish connection.

In August 1908, nearly all the afternoon shift of seventy-six men and boys were wiped out in the worst tragedy in the Lancashire and Cheshire coalfield. A large number of them were Irish, from Co. Mayo and one was named Patrick Duffy. The coroner heard many stories at the inquest that an explosion had been caused by gas. The coalowners and their officials argued that the Wigan pits were free of gas. Yet, there had been distinct warnings by government agencies about the presence of gas and it had been actually reported on the day before the tragedy. But the pit manager was on holiday. He was

---

4 My earliest memory at two or three years is of struggling to keep awake whilst awaiting Dad's late-night return from his afternoon shift; presumably Mam felt the need for company.

5 The Orange Order is a legal semi-secret organisation to which one of three or four Protestant men in Northern Ireland used to belong. Peter Robinson may be the province's first Leader not to be a member. Founded in 1795 as a 'bastion of civil and religious liberty' its record suggests it exists to preserve the Protestant hegemony and privileges in Ulster. It long considered any break with Britain as treasonable, even though the British government viewed the partition of Ireland as a temporary expedient, which would eventually be followed by peaceful reunification.

therefore open to the charge of gross negligence for failure to ensure that a safe system of working was in place. The company would then have had to answer seventy-six counts of corporate manslaughter. Instead the coroner confined himself to the ruling that the explosion was the result of shot-firing which ignited gas that had collected due, perhaps, to undue care. The unfortunate shot-firer, who was very experienced, was not alive to defend himself. Accidental deaths were recorded, with no mention of the manager and the coalowners and their crucial responsibility for proper ventilation and safe working conditions.[6]

There were 105 collieries working in and around Wigan in 1900. Despite the appealing names of some, such as Daisyfield, Horse Pasture, Ladies' Lane, Lovers Lane, Paradise Farm, Pear Tree and Yew Tree, along with Maypole, of course, there was the same disregard for health and safety. They were really hell holes at that time. Dad and his mates were considered expendable and easily replaced.

Parts of the underground workings of the Maypole Colliery were sealed after the disaster. Because of restricted coal-face workings by the early 1920s, there was a growing pressure on the workforce to look elsewhere. Dad was attracted to South Yorkshire because an important extension to its coalfield was being developed around Rotherham and Doncaster. The exploitation of this 'concealed' coalfield was providing access to the thick Barnsley seam, though at a depth approaching 2,000 feet. These new mines were far from gas-free, but their generous seams of coal appealed to Dad.

Doncaster was ringed by a girdle of such mines by the 1920s. Their sinking had called for skilled and very dangerous work. It was usually performed by elite gangs of Irishmen. The new mines

6   Immediately after the explosion the Mayor of Wigan organised a Memorial Fund Committee to help the dependents, some of whom – wives and children – were living in Ireland. Members of the Committee and the Lancashire Miners Federation continued to help – unlike the coal owners – and often visited Ireland.

quickly gave rise to housing, shops, schools, churches and inevitably, a huge pub. For the brewers no less than the railway companies and landowners – all privy to 'inside information' – were quick to seize their opportunities.[7] Dad opted for Rossington Main Colliery, six miles south of Doncaster, because of the number of Lancashire friends already at work there. The first turf had been cut in preparation for its sinking on 10 June 1912. People from various parts of England were invited as representatives of the capital invested. No invitation was extended, however, to the representatives of the men who would risk their lives mining the coal – members of the long established and far from militant Yorkshire Miners Union. Although the new colliery became part of the Denaby and Cadeby Colliery Company[8], it was a joint enterprise with the Sheepbridge Coal and Iron Company and John Brown and Company. They were all notoriously anti-union.

The first shaft of the Denaby Main Colliery was sunk in 1864. As the men fought for better working conditions, conflict with the owners was frequent. When the men went on strike, they were repeatedly evicted from their company-owned houses. They had to find shelter in churches and chapels and with relatives and friends, or in tents in open fields. One old lady who refused to leave her home was lifted in her chair and dumped outside on the road. A considerable Irish community was deeply involved throughout. Undaunted, it was prominent in the construction of St. Alban's Catholic Church and its convent and primary school.

In 1892 the Denaby company opened a new deeper colliery at nearby Cadeby. That pit was shattered by a terrible explosion in

---

7   A fascinating network of railways, though no longer worked, is still visible.

8   As well as the mines at Denaby and Rossington the Denaby and Cadeby Collieries company owned Dinnington and Maltby collieries. In *The Forgotten Irish*, (Black Tree Publishing, 2012), Sean Carney provides a valuable account of the sinking of the pit at Maltby and the history of its Irish mining community.

July 1912.[9] A local newspaper described the scene underground as a 'subterranean slaughterhouse'. It happened just a month after the same company had begun to sink the new pit at Rossington with such complacent indifference to the presence of the men's representatives.

Whilst awaiting the allocation of a house in Rossington, Dad lived in lodgings before summoning my poor Mam and her three small boys. She was fortunate to travel by a rickety lorry, for some of Dad's friends, including the Smith family, actually walked a hundred miles over the Pennines. She was met a mile out on the road from Rossington by many of her former neighbours in Wigan who had preceded her. If the welcome was organised by Kate Grogan, soon to be my sister's godmother, it included English women to whom Mam was already closely attached. But for their warmth, Mam would have been more unhappy at leaving her Lancashire friends. Most of the women greeting her had worked at the Maypole Colliery 'pit brow' sifting and sorting coal. But mention of that in Rossington was strictly forbidden.

Demobilisation had brought Dad a renewal of the industrial warfare in the Wigan coalfield that he had experienced before going to France. It continued to dominate his working life because of the notoriety of his new employers. Always upholding solidarity and trade unionism among fellow workers, Dad despised the Denaby and Cadeby company's anti-union practices. Foremost among them was the notorious 'Butty' system; centred originally in the person of a 'butty' who contracted with the colliery company over the delivery and price of a volume of coal. He was enabled thus to determine the numbers, the conditions and safety of the men he employed, which he exercised rigorously with the assistance of hated acolytes known

---

9   It claimed eighty-eight miners and three rescue workers. The worst accidents in the Doncaster pits were caused by explosions, for the Barnsley seam could produce gas which was very inflammable. *Mines and Miners of Doncaster*. February, 1977. Christine Heap.

as 'pufflers'. It had been declared illegal in 1870, but still lingered in various forms. Dad avoided anything approaching the practice, even though its shadowy survival in Rossington would have given him preferential treatment in the allocation of coalface working and housing, as well as membership of Rossington's first social club. As a consequence, he was always marginalised on the minimum wage of ten shillings a shift. More sinister, he was at risk of further discrimination by a company that completely owned and ran the village and could have blacklisted him right across the coalfield.

Tennessee Ernie Ford was so resonant of the captive plight of Dad and men like him in his country and western ballad, 'Sixteen tons':

> You load sixteen tons, what do you get
> Another day older and deeper in debt
> Saint Peter don't you call me 'cos I can't go
> I owe my soul to the company store.
> Well, I was born one mornin' when the sun didn't shine
> I picked up my shovel and I walked to the mine
> I loaded sixteen tons of number nine coal
> And the store boss said; 'Well a bless my soul'.

Before the introduction of underground transport and coal cutting machinery, the working life of the Yorkshire miner in the inter-war years, even in Dad's new pit at Rossington, was dominated by heavy and hazardous work. Diseases such as nystagmus of the eyes caused by poor lighting and silicosis of the lungs caused by coal-dust crippled many Yorkshire miners. Deaths from falling roofs and runaway coal tubs were all too common. In the 1920s about 80 miners died each year as a result of such accidents in Yorkshire collieries. There were other coal owners as well as the Denaby and Cadeby company who callously strove to maintain dividends at the expense of wages and improved working conditions. It required the intervention of Parliament in 1912, when it passed the Coal Mines Minimum Wages

Act, to effect a real improvement. A sharp drop in the demand for coal after WWI, however, due in part to the policy of German reparations, caused short-time working.

During the 1920s and up to the mid-1930s, Rossington colliery often worked only three shifts a week. Whenever I heard the pit buzzer sound in the early afternoon as I made my way back to school after dinner – and Dad was 'on afternoons' – I knew that later I would find him at home. Dad was often reduced to taking home thirty shillings a week. Yet the coal owners reacted in 1926 by offering smaller wages for a longer working week. It was an impossible situation for the men and they brought about the General Strike with the cry, 'Not a penny off the pay, not a minute on the day'. There was a shameful lack of sympathy generally for the miners, even though their attitude throughout was neither ideological nor violent. They fought magnificently, but their timing and leadership were poor and the other trade unions tamely surrendered after a week. After seven months and with the onset of winter they were starved back to work. They never forgave the coal owners.

Family support was a critical factor in surviving the strike. But Dad and Mam had not a single relative in Britain. Personal savings were unknown. Strike pay was exhausted after a month. There was just no money and all our mothers had no income whatsoever in the months that followed. Two people went to prison as a result of protests – both women. Previously apolitical and undemonstrative, they slipped back into their former anonymity on release. But during the crisis they stood firm, as did most of the women. Mam was not alone in refusing what passed as poor law relief during the strike and similarly spurned any form of charity. When the inevitable do-gooders rushed in afterwards, she instructed me to reject the free shoes on offer. I was also instructed to refuse the free milk introduced at school for those children assessed as malnourished. I asked her often how she had survived such privation. She would only laugh, and say that none of her neighbours and friends had much, but no matter how small they shared it. They had struck a critical balance in surviving between self-reliance and mutual help. When every penny mattered, it was the moral courage of these women, not the loudmouths among the men, which provided an essential strength of such mining communities.

The General Strike had brought to the fore in mining communities the values of mutuality and co-operation. Nurse Munday was invaluable as Rossington's midwife, supported by Nurse Carlton. Along with Doctor Kane, an Irishman, and Doctor Ritchie, a Scot, they were the totality of Rossington's health service. Together they arranged for treatment in the small hospital in Doncaster before it was replaced, and organised their own clinics in the Miners' Welfare Hall. When mothers were confined to bed with their new born, such as Mam, their neighbours nursed them, baked their bread, took in their washing, did their shopping and supervised the housework. Realistically, Winston Churchill was prepared to take on those women − including Mam, with her month-old baby and three little boys − along with their husbands on strike. Yet it was not uncommon for those men, most of whom had fought in WWI, to preface their remarks at strike meetings with a personal reference to the trenches and when they 'went over the top'. At the same time, as Chancellor of the Exchequer, Churchill was overlooking conspicuous consumption in society elsewhere.[10] He was only restrained by a wiser prime minister, Stanley Baldwin.

The solidarity engendered by the strike did enable the Rossington miners to win trade union recognition, however. Their first union secretary was Jack O'Malley, uncle of Brian O' Malley, later Member of Parliament for Rotherham. He was succeeded by Ernest Jones, who headed the Yorkshire Miners before becoming general secretary of the Miners Federation of Great Britain. Jack O'Malley, a Catholic

---

10   At exactly the same time Cecil Beaton was mixing with the famous in society and photographing them for *Vogue* magazine. At one of their parties he recalls 'tables groaning with caviar, oysters, pate, turkeys, kidneys and bacon, hot lobsters and meringues. The guests included Ivor Novello, Gladys Cooper, Tallulah Bankhead and Oliver Messer.' *The Daily Telegraph*. 12 June 2010.

and Irish, and Ernest Jones, a Methodist lay preacher from Derbyshire, represented men who were mostly churchgoers. That undoubtedly steered them towards the nascent Labour party version of socialism and curbed the appeal of the Russian revolution, which remained a major topic of conversation. Socialism in Rossington at that time was about social justice, social decency and social harmony, about the Christian ethic of the strong and fortunate helping the weak and needful. The men did not need the spur of ideology, for they knew what poverty was. I witnessed it myself. Not the popular notion of an ever varying bespoke poverty, but the reality of friends and neighbours begging food from each other. There were few streets in Rossington after the strike in which there were not early morning scurries by some children as they begged for food from neighbours before going to school. The families of some men who were no longer fit for arduous work underground were even reduced to chopping up their own scanty furniture and the inner structure of their new houses for firewood. I was often a bearer of scanty food and scavenged coal as Mam and some neighbours did their best to help.

Pay for those miners on the dreaded 'Minnie' in most of the inter-war years averaged no more than thirty shillings a week, roughly equivalent to £70 a week today. That was for those still strong enough to withstand underground work. Whilst rent for the company-owned houses claimed a quarter, our mothers had to budget in half pennies, and the farthing was still in circulation. Injury down the pit could be a disaster. Dad worked for six weeks with a broken thumb. A chest ailment, an abscess, a boil or carbuncle were common afflictions among his mates, and all dreaded tuberculosis. There was no legal right to sick pay or holidays. You could only look forward to the state pension of ten shillings a week – equivalent to £22.50 today – if you were of 'sound and sober character', and aged seventy years or over. Life expectancy for men was just fifty-seven years and for women sixty-one years. Someone fit and strong like Dad, along with his Irish workmates, was in keen demand by the various groups competing for men to join their particular section of the coal face, or 'stall' as it was described. The best collier by repute at Rossington Colliery was Jimmy Durkin, a Mayo man.

The callousness of the coal owners apart, Dad and Mam were never bitter. They never complained, never cried poverty, never shirked the hard option. There wasn't a book in the house, not even pyjamas or a toothbrush, but as children we never felt deprived. Mam made us small trousers out of Grandad's corduroys, and we wore the clogs that we brought from Wigan. We never missed pocket money and were quite excited to receive the solitary gift of an orange in our Christmas stocking. Mam taught us our prayers and a lively song called 'The Soldier's Song' that we only identified long afterwards as the Irish national anthem. Mam grew herbs in the garden that I carried from door to door for sale. When Dad and his friends erected the highest radio mast in Rossington for reception from the new Irish broadcasting station at Athlone, we felt enriched.

Mam was accustomed to hard work from childhood, and used to walk half a mile daily at Casheltourley for buckets of water. She had clearly inherited the sturdy self-reliance and personal virtues of her mother and grandmother in Co. Mayo. She never borrowed from neighbours. She never touched hire purchase and would only buy when she had saved the money. She checked her children's progress in school – to their dismay – and attended evening classes in cookery and dressmaking. Her watchword was 'respectability'; what will the neighbours say? Her driving belief was that if there were jobs to be done, whatever the conditions or hardship, we should 'get on with it'. She firmly believed in keeping Sunday special. Apart from Mass in the morning and Benediction in the evening, it was a day of rest and quiet. She was at pains to see us all dressed in our Sunday best, our only available change of clothing. She would not apply for a free bus pass in old age and forbade me to do so later on. She would have been sceptical of the accumulation of welfare benefits. However, she had acquired some first-hand knowledge of people's budgeting, spending habits and genuine need long before the Beveridge Report of 1944. For she collected weekly payments for over forty years for the Quaker-owned and Bradford-based Provident Clothing Company. Her weekly collections took her into countless homes in Doncaster and the surrounding mining villages. She was the first woman in Rossington to go out to work as opposed to undertaking fieldwork for local farmers. When one of those farmers tried unsuccessfully to sell his potatoes by the bag, Mam advised him to try weekly payments. She offered to help with customer selection – which was vital – and would help with the weekly collections. It worked, and that is how she started collecting. She was quite a woman, small and quiet in demeanour, but with unquenchable energy.

The growth of Rossington in the 1920s was largely due to intakes from Derbyshire, Staffordshire, Wales and Lancashire. Durham and Northumberland miners arrived after the General Strike. The least welcomed and favoured were the 'Lancs'. They brought with them not only bitter memories from the Maypole Colliery disaster but insistent calls also for the public ownership of all coal mines. Many new mining villages in South Yorkshire soon bore evidence of discrimination by the colliery companies in the segregated 'Little Wigans' with their remoteness from the pit, church, shops, schools, pub, bus terminal and, indeed, every available public amenity. The attachment of Rossington's miners at that time to spiritual and traditional values was reflected in the strongly supported ministries of St Luke's Anglican Church, the Methodist Chapel and the Salvation Army. They were soon to be joined by the newly-built Catholic church of Christ the King. Whatever divisions existed in religion and status, Rossington was united in a moral consensus that has since partly evaporated.

Shortly after the General Strike, Dad and his Catholic workmates started contributing to a Church Building Fund through weekly stoppages at the pit, based on a sliding scale according to shifts worked, from three pence to six pence. It sounds modest today, but such a contribution at a time of short-time working, hardship locally, and high unemployment nationally, must have amounted to sacrifice by men on the lower end of the pay spectrum.

Rossington only required policing by a sergeant and a constable on their bicycles. Crime and anti-social behaviour were relatively unknown, but severely dealt with by the local magistrates – one became notorious – when committed by miners. I can recall only two boys being sent to Borstal. Although more than one scout master, it was vaguely reported, had to be replaced, which puzzled me at the time.

Despite disparate geographical origins, all with their own cultural features, the newly arrived in Rossington had become quickly integrated into a peaceful community with a remarkable 'togetherness' and vibrant social life. Public notices were made, unaided, by the bell-man, Mr Price, who would announce them street by street. There had emerged a cricket club, four football clubs, a tennis club, an athletics club, a choral society, a brass band, a theatrical company, a British Legion club, a variety of 'sick and divided' clubs, a profusion of church activities, an allotment society, pigeon lofts in most streets, branches of the Labour Party and Cooperative Society, and packed meetings of the Miners Union in the Miners' Welfare Hall.

Whatever the temptation of every generation to view its childhood with nostalgia, the lifestyle of children in Rossington's rural setting in the 1920s – compared with today's – can only now be viewed as a lost paradise. The children still enjoyed freedom of access to the surrounding fields, woods and river. Play only required the simplest equipment: marbles, conkers and homemade skipping ropes and cricket bats. Together with the marvels of the countryside and the River Torne, it made for an unrestricted and safe childhood. In the absence of a secondary school and public library, the role of the new elementary schools was all-important. Happily, they attracted some good teachers, although others were indifferent to local needs and some even brutal and predatory in their conduct. Outstanding and subsequently legendary were Tom Power – from Killorglin, Co. Kerry, and Miss Muriel Eyre. After they married they became the first teachers to take up residence in the village. They were thus powerfully instrumental in the building of a peaceful, decent community and were much-loved.

A price was paid, however, and it can be seen in two poignant memorials. The first is a roll of honour in the Memorial Hall containing the names of the young men who valiantly gave their lives in WWII. They were my school friends, mostly drawn from the scholarship boys enjoying secondary education in the nearby town of Doncaster and not protected from call-up by reserved occupation at the pit. The second, in the Miners' Welfare Club, contains the names of those men and boys who also sacrificed their lives – ninety-two in all – in the development and working of Rossington Main Colliery. One is John Grogan, teenage son of my sister Patricia's godmother.

In defiance of the colliery company and its tough management policy, the men had also succeeded in creating a viable branch of the Yorkshire Miners' Union. Its first public act was to arrange for annual outings to the seaside, when it seemed that the entire village boarded a dozen trains for either Cleethorpes or Skegness. It entered also into an early agreement with the colliery company to jointly finance and administer impressive welfare and sporting facilities. The Welshmen were active in education, politics and the union locally, whilst the Lancashire men were more interested in workers' rights and the public ownership of the coal mines. They were united in their hatred of the private ownership of the industry and its nationalisation after WWII was celebrated joyously.

A deeper resentment was reserved for Winston Churchill because of his confrontational role during the General Strike. In the 1945 general election, Dad was entitled, along with his own, to the proxy votes of his three sons serving overseas. He informed us later that 'they had all been cast against Churchill'. Whilst Prime Minister in the early 1950s, Churchill had a horse running in the Doncaster St.

Leger Stakes and stayed overnight with the Earl of Scarbrough in nearby Sandbeck Hall. His route by car to the racecourse took him around the outskirts of Rossington and much of the village turned out to boo him as he passed.

Growing up Irish in Britain

Chapter Two

The First Stirrings of Irishness

A most significant development opened before me in the late 1920s. Father Charles Flynn had arrived in Rossington before the construction of church and presbytery. Mam informed me shortly afterwards that I was to be his first altar boy; he soon introduced me to Latin at his lodgings. It had a profound effect, for it helped me acquire at an early age a taste for reading and an understanding of language, literature and history. I served Sunday Mass in the local school and accompanied Father Flynn elsewhere on Sunday mornings when he celebrated Mass in the schools of other mining villages. I attended baptisms, christenings, weddings and funerals and was envied for my frequent travels in Father Flynn's Austin Seven, which was totally funded by his WWI disability pension. It was one of only half a dozen cars in Rossington.

I was much admired also by my school friends for energetically swinging the thurible during our outdoor Corpus Christi processions and producing clouds of incense, to the disapproval of Father Flynn's housekeeper, Miss Cook. She had the reputation of a martinet. I only came to appreciate long afterwards how much he probably needed some protection, though I actually witnessed unwittingly the need for it myself. Late on Saturday evenings after confessions at our new church, no matter how anxious I was to depart, Father Flynn would always detain me to lock up. He would never venture from the vestry himself, especially when I would report parishioners still lingering in the semi-darkness. When I once reported Mrs Amy Connolly complaining once again of not feeling well, he instructed me angrily to take her home. Mam was very amused when I complained later of such unsympathetic treatment of Mrs Connolly. Only a very long time afterwards did she explain the need for strictness by Miss Cook, and how Father Flynn was prey also for others.

If Mam had cultivated my Irishness so discreetly in the 1920s as to leave me quite unaware of it, she became much more overt towards their close. She informed me one day to report after school to the home of Miss Finnegan – a teacher, and the pride of the parish. There I learned that I was to be instructed in Irish dancing, together with another boy. I learned also, despite protests and pleadings, that I was to perform on the stage of the Miners' Welfare Hall at the approaching St. Patrick's Ball. Worse was to follow. Two little girls soon joined us to complete the group. I came in for endless teasing from school friends.

Watching the Irish dancing at the St. Patrick's Ball from the caretaker's private entrance was one of my teachers, Mr Llewellyn. He was friendly with the daughter of the caretaker. From thence, Mr Llewellyn always referred to me in class as 'Irish Jig'. Curiously, I experienced similar treatment in the secondary school in Doncaster from another teacher, Mr Bramley, who would address me as 'General O'Duffy'. It was only later that I learned that a General Eoin O'Duffy was a former commissioner of the Garda Siochána.[11] It did not occur to me to complain, or mention the matter at home. Nor did it mitigate my affection for either teacher. It did introduce an Irish awareness, however, which was strengthened annually by gifts from Co. Mayo of shamrock from Aunt Mary and a goose at Christmas from Aunt Agnes.

---

11   He had been dismissed by Eamon de Valera on taking power in 1933, and founded the Blueshirt party. My mother's brother in Co. Mayo became a member. He showed me his uniform. He explained that Eamon de Valera had abandoned the annual payment of annuities to the British Exchequer, which led to the imposition of tariffs on Irish exports. This crippled the trade in livestock, which outraged him and his friends. Some unsold cattle, he said were abandoned by their owners on the roadside as they travelled home from the fair.

The promotion of a St. Patrick's Ball by Catholic communities in aid of church building funds was practised in all the mining townships around Doncaster. Such a celebration was probably exercised universally. During a visit to the preserved Park City Silver Mine outside Salt Lake City, Utah, I spotted on display a century-old poster advertising St. Patrick's Ball for precisely the same reason. It listed the names of the local committee, many of which were identical with those similarly engaged later in Rossington. I also encountered evidence of the same observance and fundraising by Irish communities in Australia.

Mam dramatically completed her cultivation of my Irishness on my twelfth birthday. She revealed the maturity of a Cooperative Society insurance policy that she had taken out in Wigan when I was a newborn. At one penny weekly it was intended to finance my visit one day to that faraway place called Ireland – by myself. As did my brother Jim a year later, for Mam made similar provision for him. Dad planned the journey in almost loving detail, even to the designation of railway stations where he considered it safe enough for me to leave the train for refreshment. I sensed that emotionally it was he who was going home. He put me on a Friday afternoon train from Rossington to Doncaster. Then I boarded a train for Manchester London Road via Sheffield Victoria; both stations have since disappeared. After finding my way across the city to Manchester Victoria and the right platform, I found myself surrounded by people with accents just like my parents, and waiting for the Irish boat train to Holyhead. A journey repeated often afterwards in nostalgic fantasy. We sailed at 2.30 am and arrived in Dunlaoghaire at 6 am. That is when I first encountered the unforgettable aroma of the peat fire. A train of small carriages took us to Westland Row station in Dublin, which has also gone. So has the stretch of line which took my westbound train from Mullingar to Athlone, as well as the old railway station opposite the military barracks in Athlone. I arrived in Ballyhaunis that evening, still ten miles from my destination. The railway platform was thronged with people bound for Westport and the nearby pilgrim mountain of Croagh Patrick, which they would climb during the night. My journey was at an end, however, after travelling alone by train and boat for thirty hours.

I was not only embraced and welcomed 'home' by all the family, but seemingly by everyone I met. I found myself living with grandparents in the picturesque thatched cottage where Mam was born. It was an experience that I can only recall with the deepest nostalgia. The oil lamp, the soda bread, the turf or peat fire, the evening recital of the Rosary, the rick of turf to the rear and the spring just a small distance away. I eagerly joined journeys for fresh loads of turf, tried to help with the harvesting of oats that used to make for such beautiful scenery before the ranching of cattle, and sometimes walked through the night to fairs in the neighbouring towns of East Mayo. For both Jim and myself, those school holidays spent with the family were joyful and illuminating. We counted ourselves so fortunate. As well as meeting the family, we had caught sight of a communal lifestyle, along with its traditional farming life, that have both sadly passed away.

Jim and I sensed in our grandmother an attachment to an ancient fabric of living. She frequently addressed us in her native Irish tongue, and probably believed in fairies. We were deeply touched by the warmth displayed by young cousins as well as aunts and uncles, all of whom behaved towards us as if we had never been away. We were captivated by the mutual neighbourliness, the significance of the postman, Saturday bath night, the fairs, the annual race meetings at Tooraree outside Ballyhaunis and in Swinford, the mobile shop, the travelling people, the donkeys, the visiting to each other's homes of an evening, the storytelling, the ghost stories, the music, the singing, the dancing, the domestic 'wakes', the communal grief, the universality of prayer and mass-going. House sprees were numerous, highly valued and invariably organised to mark or celebrate some event or homecoming. Young men would never need or expect an invitation. They would simply turn up, whatever the distance. We witnessed also an astonishing rural self-sufficiency by family, neighbours and friends that yielded locally their own self-trained vet, the midwife, the butcher, the mechanic, the undertaker and a communal response to any distressed family. A voluntary supply of turf to an old couple or the disabled and the gathering of their harvest were commonplace. It was far from idyllic, but there was no Limerick 'misery'.

It is conventional nowadays by some Dublin-based journalists to mock Eamon de Valera's presentation of 'The Ideal Ireland' in a St Patrick's Day address in 1943 and misrepresent the text. Some appear to rejoice in what they perceive to be the transformation of a traditional Catholic, nationalistic, insular and narrow-minded society. It never struck Jim and myself as boys and afterwards that such a description ever approximated to life in the cosmopolitan society that we experienced in the parish of Aughamore. We encountered a great diversity of experiences among its people who had travelled extensively in Britain or America, or had family members who were thus domiciled. They could not be other than outward-looking.

Times were certainly hard for those people, when cash flow, such as it was, was minimised. We could not mistake their anxieties and emotions in the wake of the Anglo-Irish tariff dispute in the early 1930s. But there was no resentment towards the English people. Many of the old men became quite animated when they recalled working and living in England: haymaking outside Skipton, harvesting around Hull, picking potatoes in North Lincolnshire, before heading home for Christmas. Martin Finn recalled working with my grandfather near Westwoodside and Haxey in the nineteenth century. My maternal grandfather worked in Leeds before travelling to Philadelphia, where he took out US citizenship, before returning home. Owen Finn sighed for his much-loved Bentley Colliery, even though he had endured the explosion in 1931 that had killed more than thirty men. Hardly an insular or narrow-minded outlook, and typical of most families. Further afield of Aughamore I was more likely to be taken for an American than English.

As for the transformation of traditional Catholicism, there have undoubtedly been changes. There may be marginally fewer mass-attendees, but no longer the exodus before the last Blessing. People are there because they want to be there. They fully engage in meaningful parish gatherings. There is now a sense of belonging and a deep conviction. Their priests are disposed towards understanding and compassion. The weekly bulletins of my own parishes of Aughamore and Roscommon town reflect local communities of clergy and laity, sharing leadership and undertaking a wide range of secular as well as spiritual activity that probably leaves them closer than any other organised group to hearts and minds locally.

After a romantic jaunting car had transported me back to Ballyhaunis to begin a tearful return rail journey to Yorkshire, I was impatient for reading material on the parish of Aughamore. Apart from the early discovery that a papal bull was issued on 18 July 1492, uniting it with the adjacent parish of Knock, I gathered that little documentary evidence had survived. Nor was I successful in delving into the history of the village of Raith and particularly its development following Gladstone's land reform legislation in the 1870s. But I was assisted by a series of five articles published in the *Western People*, February-March, 1990. They were based on an address by Mr Nollaig O Muraile to the Knock Historical Society. In suggesting certain areas for investigation he provided me with a helpful framework of reference encompassing the role of local people in the rising of 1798, the Great Famine, the campaign of proselytism waged locally by evangelical protestants – the 'soupers' – and the rapid decline of the Irish language.

What caught my eye, however, was his specific mention of the practice of Irish lords (both Gaelic and Norman) in the later middle ages and right down to the late sixteenth century of employing Scots mercenary soldiers. For the most noted of such mercenaries, 'known to the Irish as galloglaigh (and anglicised 'galloglass' and even 'gallowglasses') were the MacDonnells, based in the Western isles of

Scotland and in North Antrim'. He refers to one such family who settled in Coogue, a townland within the parish and adjacent to Raith. But, 'alas, there is no one of this historic name registered as living in the parish,' he concluded. This recording was of direct, personal interest, because Mam's paternal grandmother, the original resident, whom she remembered, was Mary MacDonnell. It confirmed Mam's oft repeated claim of part Scottish ancestry, which I always regarded as unlikely.

There was no library in Rossington or at school, but I frequented the good public library in Doncaster. Aware of such a need and because brother Jim had joined me at secondary school, Mam moved the family into a rented terraced house – with no bathroom or indoor toilet – in Doncaster. This required Dad to cycle six miles daily to the pit, and then trudge underground, which he did uncomplainingly. In Doncaster he was back among an Irish circle of friends of Wigan origin. It enabled my younger brother Bernard and sister Patricia to attend the town's Catholic schools. Along with the other adjacent mining townships, Rossington eventually acquired its own Catholic primary school, which achieved national distinction, as did one in Doncaster.

The history of Catholic education in Doncaster illustrates the experience of the Irish who arrived in the town after the Famine, and their ultimate acceptance by initially hostile townspeople. In her book *Echoes in the Playground*, Anne Whitehead movingly describes the struggles of the Catholic communities against the most appalling poverty, disease and discrimination. Following Catholic Emancipation, Doncaster's first Catholic Mission came into existence in the 1830s when a chapel and tiny school were established. Apart from a small government grant, the school relied on voluntary aid and fees of one penny a week for the under-sevens and two pence for older children.

An influx of Irish migrants after the Famine imposed such pressures that a new site had to be found for the school. The selection was hardly an ideal location; it lay alongside a network of yards and squalid tenements where lived the very poorest of the poor. However, the location did have a saving grace in a supply of piped river water and an open sewer. Two adults and three adolescents attempted to teach 180 children in its two rooms. Even as late as 1897 a school's inspector discovered a seven year old child in charge of thirty-five babies. She was trying to teach them arithmetic. Nevertheless, writes Anne Whitehead, 'a picture emerged of a small but growing Catholic community which slotted comfortably into the economic framework of Victorian Doncaster, because it provided an increasing supply of labour to meet the demands of increasing industrialisation … the mainly Irish Catholic community was the bedrock upon which Doncaster's industrial prosperity was being founded.'[12]

'We should not forget it,' points out Alan Berry, one of Doncaster's foremost journalists, now retired, in his review of the book.[13] I could not do so. For me it was Wigan, Abram and the Maypole Colliery disaster all over again. It was yet another epic story of the endurance, courage and enterprise of the Irish men and women clinging to their faith in appalling conditions, doing their absolute best educationally for their children growing up in Britain. Above all they were quietly achieving both with an admirable display of self-reliance and harmony with their neighbours and the host community whilst helping develop its modern infrastructure. Britain has never had finer immigrants.

Two Sisters of Mercy arrived in Doncaster in 1887 in response to an appeal from Father Charles Bourke, of the newly established St. Peter's Church. Father Bourke was Doncaster's first Catholic parish priest since the Reformation, three centuries earlier. Remarkably, the Catholic faith was secretly maintained throughout that time by the Anne family of Burghwallis Hall, a few miles north of the town. According to their own records concerning the school, the Mercy Sisters found on arrival that 'Everything was absolutely poor and

---

12 *Echoes in the Playground. A History of St. Peter's Catholic School in Doncaster.* Anne Whitehead. Bogdanovic Books. 2000.

13 *The Star.* 19 December 2000.

struggling. The school's condition was as bad as could be and the Sisters stood it so bravely.'

The town's Medical Officer (a non-Catholic) remarked, 'These ladies are wonderful – they meet every difficulty with a smile.' Conditions around the school had become so bad that the Town Council declared the school unfit. But the school's logbooks describe happy outings in the countryside, even in its darkest days, notably Christmas festivities and the celebration of St Patrick's Day. Another new site was eventually found, the third, on the site of a former Franciscan Friary and alongside the historic crossing of the River Don. However, its surroundings were still unhealthy, as I knew at first-hand from the experience of my own secondary school, which lay alongside. A chemical manure store stood nearby, as well as an electricity generating station, a tram depot, a tannery, a flour mill and the town's public baths. The main east coast railway line and a canal were quite close, as was the Great North Road.

Yet it was here that education thrived, thanks to the teachers, as Alan Berry observed. It was such a heroic and cherished tradition that my sister Patricia inherited when she joined its crowded classrooms. Anne Whitehead herself recalls a happy childhood there, despite overcrowding. She writes, 'There was just enough room to accommodate sixty of us in a classroom.' Eventually the school was obliged to move, and this resulted in the establishment of two new primary schools elsewhere. They have come in for noteworthy praise from inspectors given their maintenance of high standards, though non-selective and still preserving a religious ethos.

The events surrounding the General Strike in 1926 stirred my political feelings. I never missed a political rally or meeting afterwards, indoors or outdoors. As well as recording the racing results in Dad's *Daily Herald* I had started leafing through its other pages – the only reading material in the house. And when my junior school headmaster, Mr Wealthall, asked at morning assembly around 1930 what great conference was taking place, my hand was the only one raised. I could not pronounce 'Disarmament' properly, to the amusement of the other children, but the headmaster swiftly acknowledged that I was right. Thus, I had caught a glimpse of the political agitation surrounding the general elections of 1929 and 1931, and the current concern about naval disarmament, the economic depression and the public sector pay cuts, of which certain of our school teachers were insensitively loud in their complaints. I was active shortly afterwards along with the other scholarship boys at the request of the senior school headmaster, Mr Fawcett, in the distribution of literature in Rossington favouring the League of Nations. It was cynically received, however, especially by men who I knew had served in France in WWI, though none were pacifists.

For most Rossington people the 1930s was a pivotal decade. It started with economic depression and the fall of a Labour government; it was interspersed by a royal abdication and coronation; and ended in another World War. It also marked a social revolution for them, as living was relieved by the arrival of the wireless, a newly built cinema and Littlewood's Pools. For my parents those years were especially welcome as the wireless popularised Irish melodies and generously covered St Patrick's Day. It also opened the minds of many neighbours. As did the cinema, with films about a Father Flanagan in *Boy's Town* and *Little Nellie Kelly*, starring Judy Garland. They were well received, and quickly followed by films with Bing Crosby as a priest in *Going My Way* and Ingrid Bergman as a nun in *The Bells of Saint Mary*. Much-loved and influential Irish actors such as Jimmy Cagney, Pat O'Brien, Spencer Tracey, Gene Kelly, Tyrone Power, Bing Crosby, Maureen O'Sullivan and Maureen O'Hara, together with brave Jewish film producers in Hollywood were significantly instrumental in easing historic prejudices towards the Irish and Catholics generally.

Social relief in local mining communities could not conceal social divisiveness in the town of Doncaster. Class consciousness lingered, even if it was no longer acute. A gulf separated the miners and many townspeople. An emergent middle class of people was employing the daughters of miners as domestics in their new £500 houses, but they rarely offered a good word about the miners themselves. Even the railway and engineering trade unions in Doncaster, which had deserted the miners in 1926, discriminated against them in the town's Trade and Labour Club, on the Trades Council and in the selection of candidates for the local elections.[14]

Coal output and shifts worked by the miners did pick up in the mid-1930s, however, because of re-armament, which enabled many families to pay off debts incurred during the General Strike. Because of severe unemployment, any kind of legitimate work was now prized. Jobs were all that mattered; welfare was not on the political agenda. As for benefits, their very suggestion would have caused derision.

For me the 1930s were initially years of increased Irish awareness personally that was gradually overtaken by political involvement, starting with membership of the Labour League of Youth. I observed the Spanish Civil War with close interest, and brought it to the attention of my local branch. But it did not attract much interest in Rossington or in the town of Doncaster. And mine was considerably dampened after reading Orwell's *Homage to Catalonia* and reports in Mam's newly acquired Catholic weekly, *The Universe*.[15] The rise of Hitler, Germany's occupation of the Rhineland and its increasingly adventurous foreign policy caused real concern, however. It led to widespread discussion of whether Britain should re-arm, and how soon. The Doncaster Labour party, in common with the Labour Party nationally, was opposed to re-armament. It confined its public demonstrations to open-air meetings outside Doncaster's racecourse. They attracted little attention from Sunday strollers. In sharp contrast,

---

14   I complained about this on arrival at the London School of Economics (LSE) in 1946 in a letter to my tutor, Professor Harold Laski, who was then chairman of the Labour Party.

15   Both amply confirmed by Anthony Beevor's later study, *The Battle for Spain, The Spanish Civil War*.

the British Union of Fascists held thronged meetings on Saturday evenings in Doncaster's marketplace. A mass meeting in the adjacent Corn Exchange, standing-room only, was addressed by its leader, Sir Oswald Mosley. He could not have staged such a rally in any of the surrounding colliery villages. It would have caused a pitched battle. The organised labour movement in Doncaster was feeble in its attitude towards the growing crisis.

There was a general feeling nationally against war. There was none of the jingoism of WWI. Sensing it, no doubt, Prime Minister Neville Chamberlain did his best to save the peace. Yet he has been saddled ever since with the charge of misjudgement in his appeasement of Hitler. His Ambassador to Germany, Sir Neville Henderson, seriously questioned in *Failure of a Mission* whether he really had any choice. Unhappily, Chamberlain's sudden decision in March 1939 to guarantee Polish sovereignty created conditions that made war more likely. But providentially he had given Britain breathing space to be a little better prepared for war. Chamberlain resigned in May 1940 and died six months later.

Yet on the outbreak of war in September 1939[16] all the people locally had risen as one to the challenge of Hitler. Their conduct throughout WWII remains a source of undying pride. All my friends unhesitatingly joined the armed services in combat roles as their fathers, still working down the pit, had done in WWI. Most died bravely on active service, many of them flying in Bomber Command. Women also played a full part. Girls who would never have contemplated manual work poured into the factories. They were magnificent in every way: a wonderful generation, and of imperishable memory. Special trains ran around the clock from West and South Yorkshire through Doncaster to take them to their dangerous work at a huge armaments plant to the south at Ranskill.

---

16   Father Flynn made the announcement from the altar at Mass on the Sunday morning. He had delayed his entrance long enough to hear Neville Chamberlain's broadcast at 11am.

Chapter Three

World War Two

I volunteered immediately for service in the Royal Navy. My call-up was deferred as I was still a teenager, so I promptly registered under the National Services Armed Forces Act 1939, submitting a false age. I was called up early in 1940, and summoned to *HMS Royal Arthur*, the former Butlin's holiday camp at Skegness, for initial training. I received further shore-based training in the spring at the naval barracks in Devonport, *HMS Drake,* where I was officially enrolled as JX 189036. Soon the barracks were subject to constant bombing alerts, with personnel sometimes spending the night in shelters. We trainees had not yet heard of Dunkirk, given the news blackout, or heard Winston Churchill's historic broadcast. But we knew that momentous events were taking place elsewhere and about to engulf us, as we witnessed damaged British and French warships limping into harbour daily. We rushed to assist, and actually came across the dead still manning guns, or found them strewn around the upper decks.[17] Remarkably, morale in the barracks was unaffected. But it was a shock. They were dark days and the severe bombing of the city of Plymouth was still to come.

Soon, however, my name was piped in the middle of the night to report to the Master at Arms, and I learned that I was on draft to the battle-cruiser *HMS Repulse.* The train journey to the Home Fleet anchorage in the Orkney Islands was prolonged due to bombing. Sometimes the special train – without corridors – would

---

17   I noted the arrival of the renowned French submarine *Surcouf.* I had departed before she was boarded by British soldiers on 3 July to prevent her leaving harbour. A French engineer and three soldiers died in an exchange of fire. The first bloodshed between France and Britain since Waterloo.

be shunted into sidings for many hours. Ladies would throw bags containing sandwiches through the carriage windows. Troop trains packed with exhausted, dishevelled soldiers would pull up alongside. On recognising our naval uniforms they would shout thanks for their deliverance from the beaches of Dunkirk.

On arrival at Scapa Flow in the Orkneys, I learned that my ship was at sea and that I would be berthed temporarily in the Fleet depot ship *HMS Iron Duke* – Admiral Jellicoe's WWI flagship. The upturned vessels of Germany's former navy, still afloat, immediately caught my eye. As did the buoy marking the sunken battleship *Royal Oak*, torpedoed by a U-boat the previous autumn at its anchorage, with the loss of 833 men. A school friend had survived by swimming a half-mile to the shore. He told me afterwards that he was terrified that in the darkness he might be 'swimming the wrong way'.

My first problem on joining my new ship was to find a place to sling my hammock. Not even the fourteen inches of space standard in Nelson's navy was available anywhere. There was no personal welcome at the gangway either; you just had to shift for yourself. I spent some nights on an exposed section of the upper deck, before finding room on my mess-deck – No. 49, fo'c'sle, starboard. I was quickly briefed on my specific duties, which included peeling potatoes and acting as 'cook to the galley' for my mess-mates, as well as a daily scrubbing of the mess table. My mess-mates attached the highest importance to personal hygiene and cleanliness. So I had to be absolutely scrupulous in the performance of my duties, for they kept a keen eye on newcomers. Some were surprisingly well-read, and a few subscribed to book clubs ashore. The protest at Invergordon on 15 September 1931 against the cuts in lower-deck pay, some of which exceeded ten per cent, was often recalled. Their resentment was always directed at 'their lordships', as they described them – the Admiralty Board – and never at their own officers.[18] My membership of the fo'c'sle starboard watch generally determined my timetables for meals, church, mail, pay and rum-issue (for which, underage, I received three pence a day in lieu of 'grog').[19]

Rise and shine in harbour was at 6.00am, with breakfast – after cleaning the fo'c'sle upper deck – at 7.15, and dinner at 12 noon.[20] My general duties arose from allocation to various working parties. They ranged from scrubbing decks[21], carrying stores inboard – prominent among which, I noted, were frozen rabbits from Australia – painting the ship's side and working ashore on the construction of a new canteen at Flotta, one of the islands that ringed Scapa Flow. My most taxing and sometimes frustrating daily task was to clamber the 120-foot foremast to scrub out the small chamber occupying the summit from which the six fifteen-inch guns were controlled. The challenge was to survive a dangerous climb in all weathers of the ship's superstructure as well as the foremast, much of it exposed, and arrive with sufficient water in the bucket. Sometimes it would disappear in a fine spray, and I would have to start all over again. I felt it a minimal hardship in rough seas in the North Atlantic as I viewed the screening destroyers pitching and tossing and sometimes disappearing completely as they plunged into deep troughs of the tumultuous waves.

18 Some men of the Atlantic Fleet refused duty in protest. The Admiralty Board hastily promised a revision, and the more extreme cuts were in fact reversed. But the damage had been done.

19 That was in addition to my pay of one shilling per day, of which I had already allocated half to Mam. By the end of the war my daily payments were nineteen shillings as a Lieutenant, three shillings flying pay and a further four shillings – which was described as a War Excess payment. After allotments to Mam and income tax of five shillings and three pence per day, I received a net sum of fifteen pounds each month.

20 See Appendix 1.

21 Periodically I had to help 'holystone the decks, scrape the cable' Hornblower fashion and tackle the gigantic links of her anchor cable.

The chamber at the top of the foremast – or 'spotting top' as it was called – was also my defence station and my action station. From there I was able to observe the control of the ship's main armament.[22] Even a practice 'shoot' at sea was an unnerving experience at the top of the mast as the large ship heeled over on recoil. The experience shattered a sailor who had joined the ship with me and he was sent ashore: his name was Nelson. As a teenage ordinary seaman, however, I felt privileged to join the ship's gunnery officer and his team. Although my duties never exceeded cleaning and the fetching of cocoa from the galley during the night watches. We would be four hours on and four hours off at sea. That meant very little sleep. Yet there was no more exciting moment than the Commander's tannoy announcement that 'the ship is at two hours' notice for steam'. That meant that we were going to sea.

Repulse was a good ship, impressively structured with fine lines for its size. She embodied more than a ship's company. She was really a township afloat and well run. She had a complement of 1200 officers and ratings and was commanded by Captain W.G. (Bill) Tennant. He had just arrived after impressively supervising the evacuation of thousands of troops from the harbour mole – as opposed to the beaches – at Dunkirk. I was especially taken with him because of his manner and practice of regularly clearing lower-deck for pep-talks. He arranged also boxing competitions on the upper-deck mid-ship, which were very popular. There was a worry, however, on the part of some of my mess-mates and it was huge. *Repulse* had been designed and built for action in WWI. She had the main armament and the speed of a capital ship, but grave doubt remained about her protective armour and durability. The early fate of the battle-cruiser

---

22   *Repulse* displaced 32,000 tons, had a speed of 32 knots, a range of 3650 miles and a main armament of six fifteen-inch guns. Each of the gun's shells stood taller than myself, and weighed in the region of a ton. In action *Repulse* could fire full broadsides at a rate of twelve a minute.

Hood in action against the formidable German battleship *Bismark* in the North Atlantic in May 1941 gave us the answer.

After the outbreak of WWII, *Repulse* operated in various groups hunting German capital ships and commerce raiders seeking transit to and from the Atlantic. In December 1939 she performed escort duty for troop carriers between Canada and Britain. The start of the allied campaign in Norway in the spring of 1940 saw her protecting mine laying warships. Towards the end of the campaign she was switched to Icelandic waters because of the danger of a leap-frogging German invasion. If that was an unproductive time for *Repulse,* it was hardly surprising. For the Germans were then breaking British naval codes. The threatened invasion of Britain in the autumn put Scapa Flow on high alert. On its relaxation *Repulse* and other capital ships such as *Nelson* and *Rodney* sailed to Rosyth to allow a week's leave. What struck me most as we lay alongside those ships after arrival was the intense rivalry between the ships' companies and the vituperative name-calling they exchanged.

I was well aware by this time that I was under close surveillance. I seemed to come in for the dirtiest and most demanding tasks in my part of the ship. They reminded me of the extra duties imposed on me in Devonport barracks by my petty officer. I recalled a surprising interview with my divisional officer, a lieutenant commander, in barracks. He revealed that I was under consideration for officer training, and that a CW (standing for Commission and Warrant) paper had been issued in my name. This would follow me as I was about to go to sea, recording my progress or lack of it. A kindly man, he offered his best wishes.

Now that I was at sea, I found myself subject to periodic interrogation by a new divisional officer. Ultimately I was summoned to meetings with the Commander and the Captain. Finally, I was taken by motorboat across Scapa Flow to the cruiser *Naiad* to appear before a Fleet Selection Board. One after another the senior officers comprising the board asked me questions which seemed irrelevant at the time. On reflection, however, I realised they were very pointed. My extensive reading stood me in good stead under persistent probing. Although I was left feeling at a disadvantage when revealing that my father was a coal-miner. I was also perplexed when asked how I would feel about leaving behind my crowded fo'c'sle mess and the menial tasks assigned to me. Though tempted, I was already sufficiently insightful of the Navy's ethos, its history and sense of caring. I stated a reluctance to leave, explaining how much I admired my longer serving messmates from whom I was learning so much. The candidate who followed, an ex-public schoolboy, admitted afterwards to giving a different reply to that particular question. We learned subsequently that he had failed, and that I was destined to appear next before an Admiralty Selection Board ashore. As a result I had to leave *Repulse* and start the long journey from the Orkneys to Portsmouth and to the naval barracks, *HMS Nelson*.

On arrival, clothing, kit bag and hammock were deloused, and I was placed in the hands of a petty officer. Prior to my Board interview some days later and, quite against my personal inclinations, he insisted that I take the evening off and 'go ashore'. No drinking, he warned, but something relaxing such as dancing at Southsea Pier, for which he provided directions. I had no sooner found the place and grasped that there would be very little dancing that evening for there were only two girls and another five sailors present, than there was an air raid. Though we evacuated the building quickly, bombs were falling close by as we threw ourselves painfully on to the pebble beach. One of the girls asked me to take her home, where we were met by a hysterical mother who begged me to stay as they were otherwise alone. I had thoughts only for the welcoming portals and security of the barracks and my early morning interview, however. But I could only make a very slow return, with an Air Raid Precaution warden on every corner screaming at me to 'get off the street'. Then I found the barracks main gate closed because of the air raid. As the wardens were still active, I had to go away and find a place of concealment in an alleyway. There I spent the night, anxious not to be late for my morning appointment and, equally important, that I would pass the inspection of my petty officer.

The Board comprised a rear admiral and two captains whom, I suspected, had been briefed on my earlier plight. In addition to helpful questions relating to my sea-time, they appeared to be taking a close look at me; at my bearing, confidence and manner. The interview over, I stayed in a waiting room while they conferred. A bell rang and I went in again to be told … 'We have decided to recommend …'. Whereupon I was under instruction to report immediately to the shore-based *HMS King Alfred* situated on the seafront at Hove. For the following few weeks – after physical training before early breakfast – I was required to study, drill and exercise with the utmost intensity.[23] Weekly examinations called for extra classes in the evening and still more private study, against the looming spectre of final examinations. Some CW candidates failed and were sent back to sea.[24]

For myself, the unexpected reality of having progressed from bell-bottoms to gold-lace was a very proud moment. It was only then that I revealed to bewildered parents that I was now a naval officer, if only a temporary sub-lieutenant. My father could not believe it. Nor could his WWI battle-hardened workmates down the pit. My brother, James, followed me a year later as an engineering officer, also in the Royal Navy.

I opted for flying duties, and briefly served with coastal forces whilst awaiting call-up by the Fleet Air Arm. I served in the escort carrier *Biter*, the fleet carriers *Formidable* and *Implacable*, and filled staff appointments. Finally, I was given command of the Naval School Air Radar. My experience of naval aircraft covered the Swordfish,

---

23 Memorably relieved one evening by a concert headed by a relatively unknown Vera Lynn.

24 One companion who suffered that fate was the son of a stage celebrity. He went down with his ship in the Mediterranean shortly afterwards.

Albacore, Barracuda and Firefly. *HMS Biter* – among the first converted merchantmen – was remarkably cost-effective, despite being limited to 400 feet of landing deck.[25] But without protective armour and full of high-octane fuel, she was very vulnerable. She shipped an excellent Swordfish squadron, no 811, which was among the first to deploy the homing acoustic torpedo. Our own ship was its first victim, unhappily, when the new weapon became detached from an aircraft that had pitched over the side and homed in on the propellers. That put the ship into Rosyth dockyard over Christmas 1943. We were present therefore when the flagship *Duke of York* steamed into the Firth of Forth following her sinking of the German battle-cruiser *Scharnhorst* in Arctic waters. We lined up that evening in the officers' club to congratulate the victor, Admiral Sir Bruce Fraser – truly the most modest and gracious of men.

The Swordfish aircraft has been laughed at, sneered at, condemned as clumsy, too slow and become known as the 'string-bag'. By this time it was the oldest plane in active operational use in the world. But with the exception of the Spitfire it had become the best-loved and most successful plane of the war. Flying from the carrier *Illustrious* it attacked Italy's Home Fleet at Taranto in November 1940. Flying from the carrier *Ark Royal* it went in at noon in a clear Mediterranean sky to attack the Italian battle fleet off Spartavenia. Those operations were a major factor in the demoralisation of the Italian navy. And the interception of the *Bismark* in 1941 was due to a Swordfish strike, as is well known.

Biter would steam in the middle of a convoy in the North Atlantic, whilst her Swordfish aircraft provided air cover day and night. They were effectively reinforced by a small detachment of Hellcat fighter

---

25   She was responsible for the destruction of U-Boats and enemy aircraft on convoy protection in the Atlantic, and on the Russian run. She was engaged also in U-Boat hunting in the Bay of Biscay in the company of Captain Walker's famous 'Black Swan' class of sloops – a most dangerous assignment.

aircraft. The introduction of such pocket-handkerchief carriers multiplied our seaborne squadrons. Parallel with the expansion of fleet carriers they helped seal the air gap in the dramatic phase of the Battle of the Atlantic. Thus in a new sphere – though not in a new role – the Swordfish was making a further contribution to its imperishable fame. So were the men who manned them. Operating over the emptiness of the oceans day and night, with no landmarks, no navigational points, in radio silence, finding the target in all weathers, then locating the carrier and landing on its heaving deck called for the most highly trained personnel: pilot, observer and telegraphist air gunner.

Formidable [26] also engaged in Russian convoy support whilst I served in her. But she was principally engaged in anti-shipping operations along the Norwegian coast and, in particular, strikes on the battleship *Tirpitz* lurking in Alten Fiord. My sea duty in *Formidable* following my appointment to its air staff early in 1944 was in marked contrast to my duties in *Biter* and the protection of Atlantic convoys. I was back with the Home Fleet at Scapa Flow, and that represented a momentous change. Nothing exemplified the change of scale more than the attack on *Tirpitz*. For I witnessed in Operation 'Mascot' the greatest concentration of maritime firepower since the outbreak of war. Its three carriers embarked several squadrons of bombers and covering fighters, supported by a battleship flying the flag of Commander-in-Chief, Home Fleet, several cruisers and many destroyers. Prior to the attack the aircraft seemed to fill the sky for miles around. It was an exhilarating sight and the air-crews performed with incomparable skill and bravery. The mission was successful. But I entertained and recorded reservations about its execution at the time. I pondered afterwards on its planning and management, and remained saddened over the loss of the Home Fleet's air ace, Lieutenant Commander Roy Baker-Falkner.

---

26   See Appendix 2.

After the sinking of the *Scharnhorst* late in 1943, the *Tirpitz* remained the greatest maritime threat to the Fleet. Displacing more than 50,000 tons, with 15-foot guns and formidable armour, she was the largest warship in the world. Churchill declared that the 'destruction or even the crippling of the *Tirpitz* is the greatest event at sea at the present time'. She had been damaged by naval midget X-Craft submarines in September 1943 but repaired by early 1944, according to Intelligence. Once again she posed a potential threat to Atlantic shipping, Russian convoys and preparations for the imminent D-Day invasion. The best option, it was finally agreed early in 1944, was to attack her in a carrier-borne aircraft daylight raid at its heavily protected mooring in Kaafiord at the head of the Alten Fiord. The aim was to deploy two waves of dive-bombers flanked by fighters in Operation 'Tungsten'.

On 30 March 1944, the carrier *Victorious* left Scapa Flow with the main battle fleet, Force 1, together with the battleships *Duke of York,* flying the flag of Admiral Sir Bruce Fraser, and *Anson,* flying the flag of Vice-Admiral Sir Henry Moore, with the cruiser *Belfast,* five destroyers and two Canadian warships. In the evening the carrier *Furious* also headed northwards along with the second battle fleet, Force 2, which included four escort carriers. As the task forces rendezvoused off the coast of Norway, it was reported that *Tirpitz* was weighing anchor to start post-repair trials. Two strikes were launched in rapid succession early on 3 April. The Germans admitted fifteen direct hits and two near-misses along with 'heavy damage to the upper deck, leaving it on fire'. Because of failure to press home at least a further strike, only limited success was achieved. This was soon confirmed by Intelligence, which reported that *Tirpitz* was moving again and testing her guns following repairs. It was decided at the Admiralty in June, therefore, to carry out another attack in mid-July in Operation 'Mascot'. The carriers *Formidable, Indefatigable* and *Furious* would be led by the flagship *Duke of York* and supported by the cruisers *Belona* and *Jamaica* along with screening destroyers.

The strike force was commanded by Lieutenant Commander Baker-Falkner and comprised forty-four Barracuda dive-bombers, which, along with eighteen Corsairs of 1841 squadron led by Lieutenant Commander Tony Bigg-Wither, were concentrated in *Formidable*. Escort and cover were provided by squadrons of Seafires, Hellcats and Fireflies aboard the other two carriers. To avoid German radar, no aircraft was to fly above 150 feet. The three Barracuda squadrons, which formed an efficient and professional fighting arm of the Navy, skimmed the waves on their approach to the Norwegian coast before climbing to attack height. However, a German submarine had detected the strike force and given *Tirpitz* fifteen minutes' warning. Consequently, smoke was already obscuring the target when the strike force arrived. The aircraft had to dive blind, aiming at the red glow of the ship's gunfire. They were supported by some of the fighters attacking gun emplacements on the surrounding hill and mountain sides, whilst the remaining fighters provided top cover. Soon *Tirpitz* and the shore batteries were putting up a box barrage around 5,000 feet, and so it was difficult to judge the success of the attack. But the squadron diary of 1841 squadron recorded that 'the raid doesn't seem to have been amazingly successful'.

After *Formidable* left Belfast in the spring of 1944 prior to her deployment in Operation 'Mascot', the expectation on board ship was that she would soon sail for the Far East to join the British Pacific Fleet. She embarked three Barracuda aircraft as a '*Formidable Flight*' to assist in her work-up. Among their crews were Sub-Lieutenant Gilbert Clark and Sub-Lieutenant John Smith, later Sir John Smith and MP for the City of London and Westminster. Dr Gilbert Clark and I often reminisced in the years afterwards about Operation 'Mascot' and the extraordinary drama in which Gilbert, quite unexpectedly, found himself prior to the take-off of the strike force. Whilst manoeuvring on the flight-deck, Baker-Falkner damaged his aircraft, immediately jumped out, and replaced Gilbert's pilot, Sub-Lieutenant Donald McLachlan, and took off in their aircraft. Thus, from merely following the strike force in the '*Formidable Flight*', Gilbert suddenly found himself in the lead aircraft and acting as the strike commander's navigator. Meanwhile, McLachlan, after inspecting Baker-Falkner's damaged aircraft, persuaded the crew, Lieutenant Guy Micklem and Chief Petty Officer Arthur Kimberley to return. He then raced up to the bridge and requested permission to take off in the abandoned aircraft. Captain Ruck-Keene pressed Rear-Admiral Rhoderick McGrigor to agree. McLachlan took off five minutes after the main body, which he passed through on its return. The crew were decorated for such outstanding bravery.

The Barracuda air crews embarked in *Formidable* compared its deck-handling unfavourably with that in *Furious.* Dr Clark and I sympathised, but knew that other factors were involved. Notably the hurried work-up of *Formidable* before she rejoined the Home Fleet. Her policy of ranging large numbers of Barracudas on deck so as to achieve an early airborne mass unit – American style – was also a factor. We were also aware of the difficulties involved in the handling of aircraft, for no part of a warship is so exposed to the weather as the landing deck of an aircraft carrier.[27] The aircraft handler ratings were brave. Theirs was a dangerous and demanding role, and there were many casualties, some fatal. Yet, I understood the squadron's complaints about damage to aircraft, for they had to be remedied by their own overworked maintenance teams. Ruck-Keene went so far as to replace the deck-handling officer, Lieutenant Commander O'Rourke – quite unfairly, I thought. Then he drove the deck-landing parties to the point of serious unrest, as he acknowledged to me personally. There was concern also about morale among the ratings manning the radar plot in the Aircraft Direction Room

---

27   Commander Anthony Kimmins, in a telling BBC broadcast described the serious hazards facing the flight deck parties. He cited the driving rain or a snow blizzard, and even the chunks of ice that would occasionally hurtle towards them at 40 mph when the carrier turned into the wind for take-off.

(ADR). But if Ruck-Keene was to effectively deploy combat-ready squadrons at such short notice, he felt that he had to galvanise his ship's company as best he could and try and strike the right balance. Not easily accomplished, for he was very pro-Fleet Air Arm and, like McgGrigor, adored the air crews. This was strikingly and unhappily borne out during the return passage of the strike force to Scapa Flow.

The *Tirpitz* strike aircraft had already been serviced, refuelled and bombed-up in readiness for the anticipated second strike which was cancelled due to fog from seaward. Inevitably, U-Boats had been instructed by this time to converge on the Fleet's forward line of advance as it set its return course. Their numbers and location were confirmed by code-breaking operations at Bletchley Park and conveyed to the task force by the very discreet 'Ultra' code. Admiral McGrigor on board *Formidable* was then persuaded to consider anti-submarine patrols by aircraft. Actually, three crews had been standing by on the flight deck since the strike. McGrigor now arranged in collaboration with the Commander-in-Chief for a normal anti-submarine patrol ahead of the Fleet to be carried out by Swordfish from *Furious*. Lieutenant-Commander Baker-Falkner proposed instead that he and his senior colleagues in *Formidable,* Lieutenant-Commander Richard Kingdon, who commanded 830 squadron, Lieutenant-Commander Bigg-Wither, who commanded 1841 squadron, and his senior pilot, Sub-Lieutenant Harold Mattholie, should carry out two patrols of square searches ahead of the Fleet – effectively one Barracuda and one Corsair to port and one Barracuda and one Corsair to starboard. The Corsairs accompanying the Barracudas were intended to give close fire support against any U-Boat engaging the Barracudas. Clearly, Ruck-Keene was influenced by Baker-Falkner and Micklem who, unbelievably, were still wearing dinner mess kit together with bow tie under their flying gear. Ruck-Keene in turn influenced McGrigor and both completely ignored the operations staff.

Kingdon and Bigg-Wither safely completed their patrols. But Baker-Falkner failed to return, despite the *Duke of York* making smoke and firing high altitude shells and star shells from her 5.25-inch calibre guns and *Formidable* sending up star shells. It was a catastrophic loss and aroused deep resentment among members of the Home Fleet's squadrons. They blamed the carriers' senior officers rather than their own commanders. Mattholie crash-landed in Norway and was taken prisoner. He later concluded, 'What an inexcusable loss of lives, on a pointless sweep, after a failed attack, and Baker-Falkner such a highly respected wing leader.'[28]

I had viewed much of the tactical direction and decision-taking with increasing misgiving. Ruck-Keene was an inspiring leader and good captain. But he was so admiring of his air–crews, as was McGrigor, that both were too indulgent of them. They were much more disposed to listen to the squadron commanders rather than the ship's staff. That affected the management of operations. It could have shaped early planning. Thus a burden of responsibility was falling on certain squadron commanders well beyond the required coordination and the leadership of their own squadrons. It could have affected the judgement of Baker-Falkner and Kingdon, who was another strong personality. It was unlike Baker-Falkner to have proposed such a 'pointless sweep' in the words of Mattholie, and to have insisted on manning it himself. His loss and that of his colleagues was keenly felt beyond the Home Fleet. A commemorative mention of Guy Micklem in the *Observer* every mid-July for many years afterwards was a haunting reminder.

I was obliged to leave *Formidable* when she left for the Far East soon afterwards because of a three-monthly medical check imposed on me by the Air Medical Board at Lee-on Solent, which effectively confined me to home waters. This was the result of a crash that left me lying overnight on a Scottish mountain in mid-December. I was fortunate to escape frostbite, and fortunate also to come into the care of Sir Harold Gillies, the leading plastic surgeon. His patients appeared

---

28   *Wings over the Waves*. Graham Roy Drucker. Pen and Sword Aviation. 2010.

to be drawn largely from tank crews and naval aviators, whereas his son-in-law Sir Archibald McIndoe looked after Royal Air Force personnel at East Grinstead. I managed to persuade the Air Medical Board to allow me to return to frontline squadron work, however, and I served with naval air squadrons 817 and 822. I also received a draft chit for 'air duties in Malta' but experienced such difficulty in getting there that I was switched elsewhere.

I nearly made it to the Far East in the summer of 1945 with 822 squadron. A good unit, well manned and motivated, it was due to leave in August to take part in the coming campaign in South-East Asia. Its designed role was an attack on Singapore, for which it had worked up in Northern Ireland over Lough Foyle.[29] The squadron's Barracudas and stores were already embarked in *HMS Campania* moored in Liverpool Bay, with its personnel on embarkation leave, when the atom bomb was dropped.

It was not possible for many post-war years to avoid periodic corrective surgery from Sir Harold Gillies at his clinic in a pavilion in the grounds of the Hampshire Mental Institution, at Park Prewitt outside Basingstoke. Neither was it possible to secure an official discharge from the Navy whilst the surgery lasted. I was only released when my 100 per cent disablement status had been reduced to thirty per cent, though amended since to forty per cent. By that time, and several years after the war in the early 1950s, I had taken a degree and a doctorate at the London School of Economics (LSE) and Columbia University, New York, fought two parliamentary elections and started lecturing at Leeds University. Post–traumatic stress syndrome had

---

29   It was only subsequently when Navy Minister and in a position to call in the papers from the archives at the Admiralty that I fully appreciated how hazardous were the orders that awaited us – to dive-bomb the docks and naval installations at Singapore. For I learned also just how heavily defended were the intended targets. The squadron was subsequently rearmed with the Firefly aircraft. It was a dream after the Barracuda, which was critically underpowered and unforgiving in flight, particularly in the dive.

not then been invented, and if depression or a bad back had been officially designated as disabling, we would have lost the war. At the urging of mothers as well as fathers, we simply 'got on with it'. But my parents shared the general expectation that I would be subject to an invaliding discharge. After the loss already of several school friends, I could not consider such a soft option.

Before seeking extended leave to join the first post-war term at the LSE in October 1946, I had participated as commanding officer of the Naval School of Air Radar in airborne radar trials at sea in *HMS Implacable*. Those trials pointed to exciting developments in detection, surveillance and target acquisition. It was a revolution in naval warfare; it was thrilling to be part of it. It made me realise that in terms of naval technology, my service span over just six years measured a greater advance on Admiral Jellicoe's *Iron Duke* – where I started afloat in 1940 – than the *Iron Duke* represented over Admiral Nelson's flagship *Victory* a century earlier.

Appendix 1

DAILY PROGRAMME FOR MONDAY, OCTOBER 27th, 1940.

FLEET DUTIES. Guard, M.G. & D.S.B. - "Nigeria".

MOVEMENTS. 0745.. Weigh & Proceed for Full-calibre Firings.

EVENTS. A.M... A.A. Firing.
P.M... Catapult Aircraft. (1300 Approx.)
15" & 4" Full-calibre Firings.
1320.. (Approx) Fire 3 single 15" Full charges to mats obturators.

DUTY LIEUT.CMDR. Williams.

DUTY PART. 2nd, Port.

ROUTINE. 0600.. Call the Hands.
0630.. Both Watches of the Hands, Secure for sea. (breakfast,
Cable Party of Port Watch & Nav. Party of 1st, Port to
0640.. Up Guard & Steerage Hammocks.
0715.. Hands to breakfast.
0720.. Cable Party of Port Watch muster on Fxle, Nav. Party of
1st, Port close up.
0755.. Cable Party of Starboard Watch muster on Fxle, Nav.Party,
A.A., Lookouts & Triple Guns Crew of 1st, Starboard close u
0815.. Quarters Clean Guns.
0830.. 1 G - Anti-Aircraft Bugle - 1 G.
0840.. Approx. Starboard Watch of the Hands stand by to stream
P.V's. After P.V's are streamed - Both Watches of the Hand
Cooks of Messes carry on below.
0915.. G - Anti-Aircraft - 3 Gts. H.A. Recorders to muster.
1100.. (Approx) Close Range Harbour Crews & Oerlikon Crews of
Both Watches close up.
1130.. 15" Personnel, 15" Recorders & A/C Handling Party of Port
Watch to dinner.
1245.. 15" Turrets Crews & Control Parties close up, 15" Recorder
to muster, A/C, Handling Party of Port Watch close up.
1300.. 4" Recorders to muster.
1315.. Exercise Action.
1430.. (Approx) Starshell Night Action Control Parties close up.

SPECIAL PARTIES. Time. Fx. Top. A.D. R.M.

Flour Party, 0650.. 3 3 3 1&3.

BOATS. Duty Boats:- On Anchoring - 2nd,P.B., 2nd, Launch.
Special Trips:-
0715.. Drifter to take our Mail to Hood; & prisoner & escort to
Dunluce Castle. Then Drifter to report to Hood to take
her Stewards to Scapa.

NOTICES. Long Range A.A. will close up from 1745 until 1900 daily
until further notice. The two Guns Crews of the Part of the Watc
ashore will stand fast, the other six crews closing up.

Preliminary Examination for L/S, & P.O. will take place
tomorrow, Tuesday.

Commander's Office.   (Signed) J.M.F. GROMBIE.
26th. October, 1940.   COMMANDER.

Appendix 2

H.M.S. "FORMIDABLE"   —   DAILY ORDERS   —   THURSDAY 25TH MAY, 1944

Duty Officers

Duty Lt-Cdr	Lt-Cdr O'Rorke		**Duty Petty Officers**
O.O.D.	Lt. Duffy.	Fxle P.O.	PO Grafton.
Standby O.O.D.	Lt. Ellison.	Q.D. P.O.	PO Quinn.
Duty W.O.	Mr. Lawrence	Discip. P.O.	PO Mortimer.
Duty Cypher Officer	Pay Lt. Griffiths.	Gunners Mate	PO Cooke.
		T.G.M.	PO Waite.

Tides   H.W. 0217; 1436.   L.W. 0758; 2031.
SUNRISE 0603   SUNSET 2244   UNDARKEN SHIP 0615   DARKEN SHIP 2000.
ARMED SENTRIES   to be posted from 2200 until 0640.
PATROL   Embarkation
DUTY WATCH   Starboard (2nd)
DRESS OF THE DAY   Overalls or No.3's — Dutymen No.3's.

ROUTINE   Daily Dockyard.
        SHIP WILL BE AMMUNITIONING.

0740 & 1315   Both cranes and for'd winch drivers close up.
        Ammunitioning Parties fall in in "A" and "B" Hangar as
            detailed. Remainder of Both Watches of the hands fall in
            in "C" Hangar
0855   Captain's Requestmen to clean.
0915   Captain will see Requestmen.
1015   Ceremonial Piping Party muster in Port After Pocket.
1030   F.O.I.C.N.I. will visit the ship.

SPECIAL PARTIES
        Attention is drawn to the notice giving details of Revised
        Ammunitioning Parties,and positions for falling in, posted
        in the Petty Officers Flat.
0900   Canvas Store (2 Radar)

TRANSPORT
0815   Jeep to Belfast S.T.C. with two ratings.
0900   Bedford for Canvas Stores Party.
1030 & 1430   Jeep for D.S.B and Postman.

CHURCH
0710   Holy Communion Service.

NOTICES

1..   RATION CARDS - Commander's Memorandum No. 133 dated 24th May
        For the purpose of issue of personal Canteen Ration Cards,
        Pay and Identity Books are to be collected by Presidents and
        Leading Hands of messes as follows:-

Thursday May 25th	Messes 1 to 14
Friday May 26th	Messes 17 to 38
Saturday May 27th	Messes 39 to 56
Sunday May 28th	Messes 57 to 95

        Cards will be collected and given to canteen by 0800 and will
        be returned by 1300 the same day.

2.   FOUND.
        On the Flight Deck - one large key.
        Claimants apply to S/Lt. Davies.

3.   Attention is called to Commander's Memo 134. concerning the
        visit of F.O.I.C.N.I. this forenoon.
        Gangway staff are to be particularly careful about dress.

4.   Yesterdays Ammunitioning Results:-

	Target	Achieved
4.5"	1,900 rounds	2,400 rounds.
Pom-Pom	400 cases	700 cases.

                N i c e   W o r k.

Chapter Four

Wartime Service in Northern Ireland

Those wartime experiences left me disappointed in the Irish government's declaration of neutrality on the outbreak of WWII. It is all too easily overlooked, however, that as many as fifteen European countries had adopted the same policy at its outbreak. So did the United States in both world wars, until forced to abandon it. Nevertheless, I soon became aware of the Irish contribution in Britain's armed services. I was conscious of the Irish presence in *Repulse* when shipmates assembled on the upper deck on Sunday mornings in Scapa Flow for trans-shipment to *Hood* for Mass. I never served in ship or squadron afterwards without similar reminders. When I journeyed to Co. Mayo in wartime on crutches due to injuries, I boarded ship in Holyhead by a gangway reserved specifically for His Majesty's Forces and marked accordingly. It is estimated that 150,000 Irish people, North and South, volunteered to fight and at least 10,000 of them were killed. Among the Irish who served were some of the war's greatest heroes. Wing Commander Brendan 'Paddy' Finucane, of a staunchly republican family, was outstanding in the Battle of Britain.[30] Another was Lieutenant Commander Eugene Esmonde of Wexford, who had studied for the priesthood. He was killed leading his Fleet Air Arm squadron of Swordfish – which was decimated – in attacks on major German warships attempting passage of the Dover Straits. He received a posthumous Victoria Cross (VC), making two awards to the Esmonde family. Eight Irishmen were awarded VCs in WWII; seven came from the South, and one from the North: Leading Seaman J.J. Magennis from Belfast.

---

30   A Requiem Mass was celebrated in his honour at Westminster Cathedral.

On the other hand, my first wartime visit to Northern Ireland severely jolted my 'Britishness'. For I soon encountered evidence of special problems in the province. I had joined *Formidable* in Belfast in 1944. It was lying alongside the Victoria Wharf in the Harland and Wolf shipyard. One evening I was assigned the duties of Officer-of-the-Watch, and found myself in possession of a Confidential Notice for the briefing of sailors going ashore. It contained, to my astonishment, 'Directions for Travelling Belfast by Naval Ratings'.[31] The 'Prohibited Areas', the 'Areas to Avoid', and those defined as 'Out of Bounds' made for such extensive coverage as to prompt queries from liberty men as to where they could actually go.[32] In conversation initiated later by a uniformed guard who was patrolling the wharf, I was secretly informed that 'things were not as appeared on the surface in Belfast'. I was told of the deliberate concealment of discrimination and segregation, as well as a brutal denial of civil rights; that different standards of justice were applied locally; that men like him could only get a job from the Navy – not from Harland and Wolf. In his own words, 'Catholics were trampled on in Northern Ireland.' My own experience as Officer-of-the-Watch had already aroused suspicions that policing in Belfast was quite different to that I had experienced elsewhere. For I found myself witnessing and logging late-night injuries suffered by sailors returning from shore leave at the hands of the Royal Ulster Constabulary (RUC).[33]

Subsequently, whilst my 822 squadron was temporarily based at the Royal Naval Air Station, Maydown, outside Derry/Londonderry, the camp hairdresser whispered similar complaints of the oppression of Catholics in that city. Restrictions on movements by servicemen

31   See Appendix 1.

32   See Appendix 2.

33   When I tried to recall that experience subsequently in the House of Commons, I was shouted down by Loyalist MPs.

were also in force, but by no means as severe as in Belfast. Yet, socially, I never met a Catholic in either city. Neither did my brother Jim when his frigate sailed into both ports. The invitations that found their way to us through official channels came exclusively from Protestants. Again there was a marked difference with Belfast. Our Derry hosts were altogether more relaxed and friendly and not in the least affected by our Catholicism. They were shirt manufacturers, with second homes across the border in Donegal. They were devoted to Dublin, its theatres and, in particular, its international rugby games. They disarmingly explained why they referred – like most local people seemingly – to their city as Derry, rather than by its official title Londonderry. They also explained the absence, in confidence, of a friend at one social gathering we shared with them early in 1945. He was busy at the Town Hall, they said, amending the electoral register and ward boundaries because of occupation by homeless squatters of abandoned US army camps. They described it themselves as 'gerrymandering' – the first time I had heard of it – and said it was done on the insistence of the 'Orange' people. Again I was baffled, until told that such people were determined to deny political control to the city's predominantly Catholic population.

That such a thing should be happening in a British city astounded me. Such disclosures moved me to question for the first time the 'Britishness' in which I had been nurtured. I found it difficult to reconcile also with the anomaly of Leading Seaman Magennis, who had received Northern Ireland's only VC, yet lived in that part of Catholic Belfast which I declared out-of-bounds to sailors going ashore from *Formidable*. Nor could I reconcile it with the absence of conscription in the province, despite the proclaimed attachment to the British way of life that I had often heard expressed in the Officers' Club in Belfast.[34] For there could hardly have taken place a rush of local volunteers to defend it whilst the Harland and Wolf shipyard was crowded with around 30,000 workers.

---

34   See Appendix 3.

Like most British people then, and perhaps still, I had only the vaguest awareness of Irish history. There were still no books at home, apart from school prizes. There was no mention by my parents or their families in Co. Mayo of the problems in Northern Ireland, and of the apparent malign part Britain had played in bringing them about. No Irish history was taught in my Yorkshire schools in the 1930s. None was taught either in the schools of Joan Lingard – best-selling author of *Across the Barricades* – when she lived off the upper Newtownards Road in Protestant East Belfast. 'Not a word about Irish history was ever breathed, nor were we encouraged to read Irish writers apart from a few poems by Yeats,' she wrote.[35]

For my own part, I was more familiar with the life of John Milton than that of Oliver Cromwell, for all his notoriety. Though I had been mystified that Milton of all people had recommended draconian action in Ireland. I was also puzzled by the view taken by MacCauley of the wars in the late seventeenth century. He treats the Scottish James ll and Catholic Ireland as villains and the Dutch William lll and the Ulster Presbyterians as heroes, even though both had arrived in Ireland uninvited. Puzzled, because I was not entertaining a personal change of stance, much less of identity. I deeply valued my anglicised upbringing, my family background, my dearly loved school friends, some of whom were already war casualties, as were some valued mess-mates I had left behind in *Repulse*. Clearly, I needed to undertake more serious reading, and quickly, if I was to preserve my 'Britishness'.

It was only then that I became aware of the displacement of the native Irish by a plantation policy. That is, the colonising of the north of Ireland with people from Scotland, loyal to the Crown and the Protestant faith. It was only then that I learned that the sequestration of Catholic-owned land had reduced Ireland's Catholic Irish indigenous to a ragged tenant class. The 1641 Rising, the Siege of Derry, the Battle of the Boyne and the 1798 Rising all duly followed. It was

---

35   *Across the Barricades.* Joan Lingard.

only then that I understood the impact of the malicious penal laws; the persecution of people who could not conform to the Protestant religion; the plundering of their monasteries; the deprivation of their language and literature; the flight to the continent and its armies of potentially able leaders and commanders. It was only then that I read of the Great Famine of the 1840s, when Mam's grandmother, Bid McLoughlin, was a teenager. Studies of its complexities since the publication of Cecil Woodham-Smith's *The Great Hunger* continue to make compelling and heartbreaking reading.[36] According to Sir Shane Leslie, a cousin no less of Winston Churchill, millions died whilst plenty of food was available. The Famine 'calls England to the judgment bar of history', he wrote, in a severe indictment of British government policy.[37] The government's indifference or ineptitude was by no means confined to that social disaster. German travellers to Ireland in the early nineteenth century were shaken by the poverty and degradation they witnessed.[38]

I quickly caught the significance of the first general election in Ireland after WWI. It was fought on the single constitutional issue that had been put aside on its outbreak in 1914. What followed has been told often. It bears repetition, however, because of its implications for the paramount issue that has so long divided the Irish – South and North – the issue of consent. The election results were quite sensational. Sinn Féin swept the board with seventy-three seats; the Unionists won twenty-six and the Nationalists six. The triumph of Sinn Féin was soon confirmed by the local elections of 1920. Much of the British media, ignoring the earlier settlement of Home Rule

---

36   Notably *The Graves are Waking: The History of the Great Irish Famine*, John Kelly, 2012, and the *Atlas of the Great Irish Famine* published by the Cork University Press, 2012.

37   *The Irish Tangle for English Readers*. Sir Shane Leslie.

38   *Poor Green Erin: German Travel Writers Narratives on Ireland from before the 1798 Rising to After the Great Famine*. Edited and translated by Eoin Bourke, 2012.

that was to be implemented at the end of WWI, were now enraged at the notion of Sinn Féin setting up an Irish parliament. But Sinn Féin went ahead and Dail Eireann met for the first time in January, 1919, in the Mansion House in Dublin. London declared the Dail 'a dangerous association', however, and banned it. Thereafter, a democratically and constitutionally elected parliament of the whole of Ireland was forced to go underground. In casting such a democratic voicing of consent in a vicarious light, London had planted a time-bomb at the heart of Ireland.

During the unrest that followed, General Sir Neville Macready arrived as the new commander of British forces in Ireland.[39] So did the 'Black and Tans'[40] and the 'Auxiliaries', who were recruited in Britain from among demobilised soldiers. They quickly acquired notoriety for unofficial reprisals, to which there was soon a measured response. For violence was now met with violence on a growing scale. The famous Kilmichael ambush in which the notorious West Cork Flying Column wiped out a force of Black and Tans indicates how fierce had become the exchanges and the guerrilla warfare that characterised them. The wanton destruction of Knockcroghery, situated a short distance from Roscommon Town, deeply affected my grandparents nearby in Co. Mayo. They always enquired of me on arrival about the state of its railway station, through which my train had passed.

Despite the might of the British Empire, the overwhelming majority of the people of Ireland had opted constitutionally for a united Irish republic, and had accordingly established a de facto

---

39   Among his officers was Major Bernard Montgomery, whose mother lived in retirement in the Irish Republic. Major Arthur Percival was another; it is recorded that he was especially ardent in the performance of his duty in Munster. Twenty years later as GOC in Singapore, he displayed much less ardour in shamefully surrendering the huge garrison without a fight.

40   They were kitted out in the dark green (almost black) tunics of the Royal Irish Constabulary (RIC) with khaki military trousers.

government. What they received instead was the partition of their country, with the border drawn on the basis of a crude sectarian headcount to protect a minority still protesting loyalty to the British Crown. This was a minority, moreover, that threatened in 1912 to defy the strivings towards the quite different outcome of such as William Ewart Gladstone – whose papers at the British Museum I had pored over – and Herbert Asquith. Lord Randolph Churchill had laid down an ominous marker on 22 February 1886, with the declaration that 'Ulster will fight and Ulster will be right'. It was followed by the mass signing in 1912 of the Ulster Covenant which threatened to use 'all means which may be found necessary' to defeat the Home Rule Bill. A modest Home Rule Bill had been introduced at Westminster in 1912, but delayed by the outbreak of WWI. By that time a minority of self-styled Loyalists were preparing to oppose it at the point of the gun. And the nationalist reaction led to the rise also of armed resistance and Easter Week 1916. The gun was back in Irish politics.

After 1922 Ulster ceased to be a province, and became a state. A state founded on coercion, with discrimination[41] and bigotry[42] ruthlessly practised by leaders – reliant on a Special Power Act – right down to local councillors. Why did Britain remain indifferent to its Catholic minority, I asked myself, when it had gone to such lengths to protect the Protestant minority in the south of Ireland – the old

---

41   Short Bros. and Harland and Wolf, the two biggest employers, were long bastions of job discrimination.

42   Seamus Mallon, MP for Newry, and founder member of the Social Democratic and Labour Party (SDLP), was very much involved with the civil rights movement from the early 1960s. What really brought him into politics, he records, was the experience of the family of one of his pupils when he was teaching. They were trying to get out of a horribly dilapidated home and into a council house. At that time councillors had the power of allocation. That family was turned down by a councillor who said: 'No Catholic pig and his litter will ever get a home in Markethill while I am here.' *The House Magazine.* 16 July 1990.

Ascendancy class? I could only conclude that in its handling of the issue of consent, Britain had used different criteria in relation to the northern situation. Thus partition would remain a divisive issue. And the historic readiness of Loyalists to employ the force option in its defence had set a fearful precedent for all in Northern Ireland. How to reconcile an inevitable minority response with an implacable, though contrived, majority, protected and sustained by Britain, and persuade both sides to seek a constitutional and peaceful settlement was nevertheless the way forward. But would a government in London prove equal to the task? Henceforth, my acquaintance with that part of Ireland for which London was responsible and, indeed, my 'Irishness', would be shaped at Westminster by my own minor involvement in the search for such a peace process.

Appendix 1

CONFIDENTIAL NOTICE

DIRECTIONS for Traversing Belfast by Naval Ratings, giving routes taken
And areas PROHIBITED from being used.

Ratings to and from Canning Street, Pollock Dock & Custom House or coming into Belfast, are to use York Street to Royal Avenue, avoiding Donegall Street and Waring Street; then down to Castle Place to Custom House.

Ratings proceeding between Custom House and Quays where Liverpool and Heysham Steamers berth are to proceed along the Quay.

PROHIBITED AREAS;   York Street area ... between York Street and the river. West of Donegall Place and Royal Avenue Area between York Street and North Queen Street.

AREAS TO AVOID;   West of Donegall Place and Royal Avenue. Area between York Street and North Queen Street. If going To Victoria Barracks, Upper Donegall Street or Antrim Road district, Clifton Street is to be used.

OUT OF BOUNDS   Adjacent areas North, East and West of Victoria Barracks are OUT OF BOUNDS.
The Market area, bounded by Chichester Street, Donegall Street, Adelaide Street, Ormsan Avenue to River Lagan, East Bridge Street and Oxford Street, is OUT 0F BOUNDS.
ALBERT BRIDGE is OUT OF BOUNDS.
Falls Road and entire district is OUT OF BOUNDS.
Princes Street is OUT OF BOUNDS.

PROHIBITED AREA   Between Grosvenor Road and Divis & Mill Street, College Square North, Durham Street.

Springfield Road   & adjacent street to Cupar Street on East, Mackies Foundry on West is a PROHIBITED AREA.

To cross the River Lagan, Queens Bridge only is to be used. East side of River Lagan PROHIBITED AREA between Short Strand, Bryson Street & between Madrid Street and Newtownards Road.

The Ardoyne area, Crumlin Road, bounded by Flax Street, Butler Street, Kerrer Street & Crumlin Road is PROHIBITED. Also the areas between Woodvale Road, Bray Street, Chief Street, Crumlin Road and to North-East of Crumlin Road.

MARROBONE DISTRICT   The small area bounded by Antigun Street, Glen Street, Oldpark Road to Ardoyne Ave. & Ardiles Street, to Flax Street, & Crumlin Road. The small area bounded by Newington Street, Limestone Road, Atlantic Ave. & Newington Ave., is PROHIBITED.

In future the following premises are to be considered as OUT OF BOUNDS to all Naval personnel:
No.7 Amelia Street, Belfast.
Elephant Bar - Corner of North Street & Winetavern Street.
The Red House - Corner of North Street & Union Street.
Deveny's - Junction of North Street & Peter's Hill.
The Palace Dance Hall, 49 York Street, Belfast.
The Gibralter Bar, 174 York Street, Belfast.
Quinn's Public House, Lough Shore.
Nelson's Club, Frederick Street, Belfast.

Page 2

The area enclosed by the following streets need not be considered as out of bounds, but Service personnel are warned that they enter it at their own risks:

Clifton Street - from Carlisle Circus		
Donegall Street	Royal Avenue	Upper North Street
Old Lodge Road	Carlisle Street -	to Carlisle Circus

The above-mentioned streets themselves <u>and the buildings fronting immediately on to them</u> are not affected by this order.

Appendix 2

CLUBS AND CANTEENS IN BELFAST FOR RATINGS

Y.M.C.A. WELLINGTON PLACE About
200 yards to right when facing front of City Hall.
Sleeping accommodation (about 300) 6d per night
Open all day until 0100.

POLLOCK DOCK NAVAL CANTEEN
Dufferin Road.
Open all day. Meals and games. Separate reading
And writing rooms for C.P.Os & P.Os & other
Ratings. Generally a concert on Thursdays.

BRITISH LEGION. 7/9 VICTORIA STREET
Open 2.0 p.m to 10 p.m. Games, tea room etc.
On Sundays, tea is followed by a concert or cinema
Entertainment at 7.30 p.m.

BRITISH LEGION, ROYAL NAVAL BRANCH'
184 Upper North Street.
Open all day. Billiards, Darts and other games.

THE LARGE ASSEMBLY HALL, Howard Street.
Canteen open from 4.0 p.m. Concert every Sunday
(vocal & instrumental). Doors open 6.0 p.m.
Admission free. Community singing from 6.0 p.m.
Sleeping Accommodation for 20 men.

VICTORIA MEMORIAL HALL
(Corner of May Street & Up. Arthur Street
Open 7.45 p.m. to 10.0 p.m. on Sundays only.
Community singing and light refreshments.

CHURCH OF IRELAND YOUNG MENS' SOCIETY
& BRITISH RED CROSS SOCIETY.
20, Donegall Square, East.
Canteen open weekdays 9.0 a.m. to 10 p.m.
Sundays 4.0 p.m. to 10 p.m.
Billiards, Games, Magazines etc.

68 TEMPLEMORE AVENUE, NEWTOWNARDS
ROAD.   CANTEEN
Open 8.0 a.m. to 11.30 p.m.
Refreshments. Games, etc.

STRANDTOWN SERVICES CANTEEN
Gelston's Corner, Belmont Road
Open 6.0 p.m. to 11.0 p.m.
Sundays 3.0 p.m. to 11.0 p.m.
Games, Billiards, Refreshments.

SANDES SOLDIERS HOME   CLIFTON S.
All men in H.M. Forces welcome
Recreation & Billiard rooms.
Sleeping accommodation 1/- per night.

CATHOLIC WOMEN'S LEAGUE CANTEEN &
CLUB. 63 VICTORIA STREET
Open weekdays 4.30 p.m. to 10.0 p.
Sundays 3.0 p.m. to 10.0 p.m.

MALONE SERVICES CLUB, RANGERS HALL
Malone Avenue, (Lisburn Road end)
Open Thursdays & Sundays, 2.30 p.m. to 10.30 p.m.
Table Tennis, Billiards, Darts & other games.
Refreshments at nominal charges.

SUNDAY CONCERTS
In Co-operative Hall, Frederick Street, (off York Street)
For men in uniform at 7.30 p.m.
Light refreshments.

Appendix 3

OFFICERS' CLUB,
69 HIGH STREET, BELFAST
TELEPHONE 22196.

Club Hours : 10 a.m.—11 p.m. (Sunday : 7 p.m.—10.30 p.m.)

MORNING COFFEE   LUNCHEONS   TEAS   SUPPERS
Served Daily except Sundays.

———

ILLUSTRATED AND DAILY PAPERS.   WRITING FACILITIES.
Cards and Markers available for Bridge.   (Table Money, 6d. per Person.)

———

DANCES.

FRIDAYS   SUPPER DANCE   7.30—11.30 p.m.
(Including Supper (3 Course), served from 7-30 p.m.)
SUBSCRIPTION 5/-.
BAND: SOUTH WALES BORDERERS.

SATURDAYS   DANCING   8.30—11.30 p.m.
BAND: MEDICOR MELODY MAKERS.
SUBSCRIPTION 2/6.

SUNDAYS   EVENING PARTY   7—10.30 p.m.
SUBSCRIPTION 2/6.
Including Light Supper.   (Meat dishes extra.)
BAND: MEDICOR MELODY MAKERS.

———

N.B.—To conform with the licensing laws of N.I., alcoholic liquor may only be served to Club
Members.   (N.B.—Membership Subscription 5/- for duration.)

———

A Member introducing a friend must sign his name and unit, also name and address of his
friend in visitors' book.   Only a Member may introduce a lady to the Club Dances.

Chapter Five

Arrival at Westminster

There was great competition for entrance to the LSE when it returned to Houghton Street, Aldwych, in the autumn of 1946. I had to attend for interview and sit an examination along with a host of other applicants, even though I had adequate academic credentials including London matriculation with a first division pass. I had resisted being invalided out of the Royal Navy in wartime. With the cooperation of a very sympathetic Air Medical Board at Lee-on-Solent I had even taken on frontline squadron assignments. I could not ignore the reality of a lingering post-war 100 per cent medically disabled category, however, and an instruction from Sir Harold Gillies to attend his clinic outside Basingstoke every three months. This unusual arrangement had been fulfilled by the Navy in wartime so long as I was serving in home waters. Now it had to involve the LSE, who turned out to be just as understanding and accommodating. I was not their only war casualty, of course.[43] I was granted official leave on full pay and allowances by the Navy in order that I could attend the LSE, and not officially discharged until after graduation. My sponsoring hospital was Haslar, across the harbour from Portsmouth. By that time I had also been awarded a grant by the Education department, which I could not possibly accept. I experienced considerable difficulty in persuading the Ministry to withdraw it whilst students elsewhere were still clamouring for their grants.

---

43   One was Alan Milne, who had lost his sight whilst crossing the Rhine in 1945. It did not prevent him achieving a 'first'. A most appealing person, fellow students readily assisted by reading to him. None more so than David Bennell, whose kindness and ever-practical response were boundless.

Now that I was ostensibly a civilian I renewed membership of the Doncaster Labour party. I raised immediately those unexpected briefings I had received in Northern Ireland, but without stirring up any interest among its members. Only the first of many reminders of how selective the Left was in relation to human rights, especially when it came to Ireland. I attended meetings in London of the Anti-Partition League addressed by Eamon de Valera. I was intrigued by the visit that Prime Minister Clement Attlee made to Co. Mayo in 1948,[44] for it followed the repeal in Dublin of the External Relations Act, which indicated a recasting of British–Irish relations. Mr Attlee went then to a meeting with Sir Basil Brooke, Prime Minister of Northern Ireland. It was not for the purpose of reform, surprisingly, but precisely the opposite – the consolidation of the partition cleavage that divided the country. Accordingly, I tried to interest certain faculty members at the LSE in the Attlee mission, and appealed also to its Students' Union, but in vain. They were not interested. They were indifferent also to the voiced concern of such Leftish Labour members in parliament as Hugh Delargy, Geoffrey Byng and J.P.W. Mallalieu, who had already raised the alarm.

My failure left me wondering why, in a variety of ways, the Left in Britain – whether Fabian, Labourist, Marxist or trade union – could be so insensitive to a man like Brooke, who wasn't spared even by his own kind at his memorial service in 1973. 'It can be argued,' said Bishop Arthur Butler, preaching on that occasion, 'that if he had

---

44   He and Mrs Attlee and two young daughters stayed in Malcolm House, Newport, as guests of Mr and Mrs Bevir. Mr Bevir was a former professor at Queen's College, Cork. Mrs Bevir was related to Major D.A.S. Browne of Breaffy House near Castlebar, a few miles distant. I was also holidaying in Mayo in the same month of August, and presumed a wide gap existed between the exposure of the Attlees and myself to contemporary Irish society and, perhaps, our domestic briefings.

thought differently and acted differently, Northern Ireland would not be in the state in which it is today.'[45]

Whilst still a student at the LSE and following my appointment as a lecturer at Leeds University, I fought parliamentary elections in 1950, 1951 and 1955 in the Tiverton constituency of Devon. Even in that unpromising, though beautiful, countryside I tried to spark interest in Northern Ireland. But again without success. My Conservative opponent was Derek Heathcote-Amery, later Chancellor of the Exchequer. Fortunately, I had the lively assistance of fellow students at the LSE and the impressive support of Shirley Catlin, later Baroness Williams, who was then at Oxford. It was a joyous campaign in 1950. We near doubled the Labour vote on 1945, and lifted it into second place above the Liberals.

Totally dedicated members of the local party further strengthened the Labour vote in 1951 and in 1955, by which time they were able to employ a full-time agent and acquire their own premises. Aside from my studies at Columbia University, from which I returned for the 1951 election, I gave them unstinting support, undertaking monthly weekend visits from Yorkshire. All became prominent in their rural communities, either as councillor, mayor, magistrate or honoured otherwise. They were fine people and remained lifelong friends, though some confessed later to initial doubts when I was selected because I was Irish and Catholic.

I was no more successful in engendering interest in the affairs of Northern Ireland in the Colne Valley constituency in West Yorkshire. I had become involved politically following the demise of the Labour MP, Glenvil Hall, in late 1962 and the need for a by-election early in 1963. Some of the towns and villages of this widespread rural constituency, that straddled the Pennines with its rolling hills and picturesque scenery, provide the setting for scenes in the BBC's

---

45   Bishop Butler was as critical as *The Times* of the exclusion of Catholics from responsibility and participation.

much-loved series *The Last of the Summer Wine*. In his distinguished work, Ashley Jackson, a leading watercolour artist, has captured the spirit of its moors and 'Wuthering Heights' landscape.

In the Colne Valley itself and over the Pennines in Saddleworth were mill towns largely characterised by their Methodist and evangelical chapels. They had been the scene of past Liberal-Labour battles which the Liberals had won as late as 1935. It was one of the very few constituencies with boundaries unchanged since the nineteenth century. That presumably strengthened its self-contained character, its social stability and enduring Liberal tradition. But it had also developed unusual socialist connections. There was no constituency in the UK remotely like it. The history of the Labour movement has flowed through the Colne Valley. The Colne Valley Labour League was founded as early as 1891. In a sensational by-election in 1907 the constituency elected Victor Grayson, the first man to be elected on a straight socialist ticket. Yet the political breakthrough could not be sustained. Grayson lost the seat, fell out with his parliamentary colleagues, took to drink and was linked with dubious characters.[46] Eventually he disappeared in mysterious circumstances. Meanwhile the political character of the constituency was changing under the impact of rapid industrial development and prosperity.

By the 1930s, with its mills working round the clock, the Colne Valley had become the powerhouse of the textile industry. By the early 1960s, however, most of those mills had closed. The industrial character of the Colne Valley was giving way to residential development for commuters. Labour was losing strength on the local urban district councils. For all the historic militancy locally, I found no abject poverty such as I had witnessed in the mining areas of South Yorkshire. The Huddersfield jobless figures were below the national average. Nevertheless, I issued a warning at the selection conference I attended to determine the Labour candidate at the

---

46   *Victor Grayson. Labour's Lost Leader*. David Clark.

coming by-election. 'Though the retention of the seat at the coming by-election was important as a morale-boosting win for the coming general election,' I said, 'it should be borne in mind that the three staple industries of our Yorkshire region – steel, coal and textiles – were now in decline.'

I was selected from a long list of distinguished nominees, all of whom subsequently entered parliament.[47] Among them were Merlyn Rees and Bryan O'Malley, who were selected for by-elections that arose shortly afterwards in Leeds and Rotherham.

I campaigned without a break from the New Year onwards through the long cold winter of 1963 and experienced severe conditions in the high Pennine valleys between Huddersfield and Oldham. For this had become a crucial by-election for the major parties. The Liberals had just won several by-elections in normally safe Conservative seats. This by-election would show whether they could also win a Labour seat.[48] My essential task in the characteristic Tory constituency of Tiverton had been to woo those working-class voters who were still traditional allies of the 'county' people, the middle class and the retired military. I had to cultivate the 'conservative' working man; always a potent figure, however much Labour tries to ignore him. My tactics in the Colne Valley would not be dissimilar, though my target now would be those working-class voters who remained supporters of the Liberal party and its nonconformist origins. Even my few remaining coal miners at Emley Colliery still cherished the Liberal-Labour ties fostered a half-century earlier by their Yorkshire Miners' leader, Ben Pickard of nearby Kippax.

---

47 Safe seats in the region in those days were in the tight possession of the trade unions, notably the Yorkshire Miners.

48 A changing electorate in the constituency had now marginalised Labour's hold on it, as the secretary of the constituency Labour party, Councillor Jessie Smith, had warned in the previous year's annual report.

My Liberal opponent, Richard Wainwright, public-school educated and a Leeds accountant, was a Methodist. There were few chapels in the constituency which he was not visiting as a lay preacher, according to *The Guardian*.[49] He was also a wartime conscientious objector and only my own war record deterred some of his aides from making an issue of my Catholicism. The Liberals then had few political scruples in a tight finish, unlike the Tories. That had been my experience earlier in Tiverton and repeated later in Sheffield.

Richard Wainwright's more aggressive colleagues focused on the Conservative candidate, Andrew Alexander, a leader writer at the *Yorkshire Post*. They were well aware that the Conservative vote was key to the outcome. The Conservative party had never won the seat. Its vote was fragile and prone to swing to the Liberals to get Labour out. Tactical voting was exercised locally long before it became fashionable elsewhere. It had to be the prime tactic of the Liberals. Therefore they left me alone and Andrew Alexander came in for rough handling instead, unfairly, for he was a good candidate. He records that he encountered a lukewarm reception when canvassing normally Tory voters. Some thought he would be 'pleased to know they were switching to Liberal … anything to keep Labour out'.

By the campaign's closing stages it was reported that the political temperature had risen markedly 'as the Conservative and Liberal candidates went at each other like a couple of Kerry Blues'.[50] Andrew Alexander complained that Mr Wainwright seemed 'hell bent on injecting a note of personal insult into his election', and had inferred 'that he was a liar'.[51] On the following day it was reported that Andrew Alexander 'had issued a writ for slander', and it had been served on

---

49   'Some of his local organisations are more or less coterminous with Methodist chapel committees'. *The Guardian*. 21 March 1963.

50   *The Daily Telegraph*. 13 March 1963.

51   *The Huddersfield Examiner*. 13 March 1963.

a former Liberal candidate 'who is helping Mr Wainwright ... in his campaign'.[52] I was not spared myself by Andrew Alexander, who rightly pointed out weaknesses in my campaign literature, notably the sections relating to public ownership. Richard Wainwright paid me little political attention. Along with his appeal to the many chapels, he was content to rely on the carloads of supporters and canvassers who flooded in from all over the country. Despite the severe weather, the tempo of campaigning was maintained. Turnout on polling day was seventy-nine per cent, thanks to my agent Harold Sims, and his equally impressive regional colleague Baroness (Betty) Lockwood – sensationally high for a by-election. Labour held the seat, but not decisively.

I was staying afterwards at Flamborough on the Yorkshire coast, without a telephone, when Harold Wilson was forming his first government. The Chief Whip, Ted Short, located me eventually via a neighbouring farm and invited me to become the Yorkshire Whip. The appointment required a covert role that I dared not risk with a highly marginalised constituency, and I declined. He rang again the next day 'at the request of the prime minister' he said. But I still felt that my unusual constituency called for a more prominent parliamentary profile. I then received a call from Patrick Gordon-Walker, the newly appointed Foreign Secretary, inviting me to become his Parliamentary Private Secretary (PPS). Unfortunately Patrick had lost his seat at the general election, failed to win the hastily arranged by-election and was obliged to step down as Foreign Secretary. I felt as disappointed for Patrick as I did for myself. He had immense charm and appeal on all sides and must have distinguished himself in the new post. The 'Ocean View' farm on Lighthouse Road, Flamborough, must have been bewildered by the succession of calls from Whitehall.

The Colne Valley constituency was now distinctly marginal, as forecast. That was confirmed the following year at the general

---

52   *The Daily Telegraph*. 15 March 1963.

election, though the seat was held. The election was fought under the new leadership of Harold Wilson. The 1964 result suggested an emerging pattern of voting which was confirmed in turn at the general election of 1966. Thus I found myself campaigning, yet again, for the third time in just three years and this time Labour lost the seat. But the Labour vote did go up in each of my three campaigns and, expressed as a percentage – the only valid yardstick – was never surpassed within those constituency boundaries. Tactical voting had put me out, of course.

The outcome in the Colne Valley now depended on the Tories at Westminster. A serving or incoming Conservative government firmed up the Conservative vote in the constituency just enough to deprive the Liberals of some of their electors and see Labour home, as in 1963, in 1964 and later in 1970. But a serving or incoming Labour government tempted enough Conservative electors to resort to tactical voting to 'get Labour out', as in 1966 – when the Conservative candidate lost his deposit – and twice in 1974, long after my departure. Despite the pattern, David Clark (my successor and later Lord Clark) and I helped to maintain the Labour vote. We could do no more. Because of tactical voting, however, a serving Labour government put us both out at the general elections in 1966 and 1974.[53]

Harold Wilson was born just outside the Colne Valley and fully understood the unusual campaigning difficulties. He invited me to go to the House of Lords after the general election of 1966. The invitation was repeated by John Silkin when he became Chief Whip and coupled with that to Lord (Terence) Boston. Again I was driven

---

53   A hint of fundamental change occurred in 1979, when the Conservative vote had become unusually assertive following the arrival of Margaret Thatcher. It enabled the Conservative candidate Councillor Holt to break the mould in 1983, and achieve second place for his party for the first time since 1959, and ultimately led on to victory for the first time.

to explain another preference: to make an early return to the House of Commons, which I accomplished at the next election.

Apart from my maiden speech on arrival at Westminster in 1963 that was devoted to a changing regional economic scene, my inner thoughts focussed on Northern Ireland. I felt that such failures as I had experienced thus far to publicise its state of affairs could surely be met now. Since WWII certain Labour MPs had already tried to do so. They had raised specific questions about the abuse by local councils in the allocation of houses and jobs and the drawing of electoral boundaries. Such probing was always resented on the floor of the House of Commons by the Ulster Unionist MPs, notably by a Professor D.L. Savory, who represented the Queen's University, Belfast, of all places. They were assisted by successive Speakers who discouraged such interventions and actually blocked the tabling of questions. But I was now armed with the contemporary remark of the prime minister of South Africa, Mr Vorster, that he would exchange all his own country's repressive legislation for one clause of Northern Ireland's Special Powers Act. Now, surely, I had the constitutional right to question the record of civil rights in the province. I was mistaken. The Table office would still not accept any such questions. Stormont was a closed shop. I was soon to be joined in parliament, if briefly, by a formidable ally in Kevin McNamara, who was returned at a by-election in Hull two years later. On my re-election in 1970 for the Attercliffe constituency in Sheffield, we linked up in the Campaign for Democracy, in which he and Paul Rose were doing outstanding work.

Chapter Six
Anglo-Irish Relations

The most important development in Western Europe after WWII was a collective approach to both security and trading. The North Atlantic Treaty Organisation (NATO), underpinned by the US, had quickly emerged in response to the domination of eastern and central Europe by the Soviet Union. A Common Market of six nations followed, inspired by the wish of France and Germany to buttress that collective security. Its members were intent also on moving towards freer trade. A European Free Trade Association of seven nations also emerged. Both organisations focused on competitiveness among and protection for their members. Their development was a challenge to Britain, Northern Ireland and the Republic of Ireland. In the Irish Republic it forced a reappraisal of the economic policies of self-sufficiency pursued by successive Irish governments since 1932.[54]

The likely impact posed acute problems, politically and economically, for my own regional economy of Yorkshire, where the run-down, and possibly the demise, of its staple industries of textiles, coal and steel was already casting a shadow.

Roy Mason – outstanding chairman of the powerful Yorkshire group of Labour MPs – and I worked closely together in the promotion of a regional response.[55] We persuaded our parliamentary colleagues in Yorkshire to investigate the implications for their own

---

54   They had been advocated by Arthur Griffith, who founded Sinn Féin and led the Dail delegation to London that signed the Anglo-Irish Treaty, the founding document of Irish independence. His anti-Treaty opponents in Fianna Fail adopted his 'economic independence' ideas on coming into government in the Thirties.

55   We had become so close that in his reports from Westminster for *The Guardian*, Ian Aitken used to refer to us as the 'old firm'.

constituencies in a manner that would enable us to present a report to Parliament. The campaign acquired such political momentum that we actually secured a full day's debate in the House of Commons on our regional economy. Roy Mason opened the debate from the front bench and I wound up. It had the sanction of a three-line whip, which was without precedent at regional level.

The plight of Yorkshire's regional economy reminded me of the condition of the staple industries of Northern Ireland. Shipbuilding was a major concern by 1970, even though the shipbuilders had constructed the largest building dock in the world in which a ship of one million tons could be built. The Harland and Wolf yard, which built my aircraft carrier *HMS Formidable* prior to WWII was now facing liquidation with the loss of 10,000 jobs.[56] I linked up with Ian Paisley MP on more than one occasion in late-night debates in Parliament appealing for financial assistance to save those 'Protestant' jobs. It was an uphill struggle given the moribund state of industry in many other regions in the UK. Furthermore, Northern Ireland was no longer paying its way, and the deficit was structural. For there were no defence or diplomacy costs, nor was there a contribution to the National Debt. It is difficult to quantify how much the province was getting from London. But even at that time the real total of its annual budgetary support from London (quite apart from government loans) was rising significantly.

Whilst I was struck with the growing need of Northern Ireland for financial support from Britain, I was equally taken with the contrasting economic relationship the Irish Republic was developing with Britain. The Irish Republic had found itself on the edge of a vast community that was moving towards free trade. It had been 'left out in the cold' in the negotiations that were producing new trading blocs. It had been such a shock that under the drive of Sean Lemass a sustained

---

56   Belfast was famed for its ship-building during the nineteenth century. Many consuls-general were located within the city.

and novel attempt had been undertaken to wean the economy away from protectionism. It focused generally on supply-side economics and started with the launch of development programmes in 1957. It led to the introduction of the successful Industrial Development Authority (IDA) and a new economic policy framed largely by Dr Kenneth Whitaker. Corporate tax on foreign multinational companies was cut, freer trade with Britain entered into in the 1960s and education reformed. Whilst the changing financial relationship of Northern Ireland with Britain was pointing to growing dependence, the Republic's changing and expanding pattern of trade was actually opening up a larger market for Britain.

I took an early opportunity on returning to Westminster in 1970 to draw attention in an early-day motion to the significant shift in Ireland from that of a rural agricultural society to one that was becoming industrialised and urban.[57] It reminded MPs that since the Anglo-Irish trade agreement of 1965, the Irish Republic had become the UK's third biggest customer. It was a hint to the Government to revise its policy of regional aid generally. It was also a hint to both Dublin and London of the growing importance of the mutual economic benefit – and the interdependence that would stem from it – of the continuing shift in Ireland from that of a rural, agricultural society, to one that was becoming industrialised and urban, rather than the irredentism that had so long plagued Anglo-Irish relations.

I had been re-elected chairman of the Parliamentary Labour Party's (PLP) Economics & Finance committee on my return in 1970. Its membership was still small, but selective. None, happily, were ideologues. Some had a business background. Like myself, they were less and less inclined to allow current Labour party doctrine to

---

57   The signatories of the motion included Kevin McNamara, Roy Hattersley, Maurice Foley and Merlyn Rees. I was puzzled, however, that I could not persuade Joel Barnet, Robert Sheldon and Edmund Dell, all specialists in this business sector, to support it.

stifle fresh thinking on the economic processes that ultimately yielded jobs. I considered it urgent as I pondered on the fundamental shift in employment in my own industrial constituency. If I still saw a role for state intervention and funding, however, I was no longer wedded to Keynesian economics. Unlike the bulk of Labour party activists, I no longer believed in the remedial affects of pump-priming the economy. That the state could borrow and spend willy-nilly without those responsible looking over their shoulders at private-sector creditors struck me as unrealistic. That industrial strife could be permanently staved off by government subsidy, moreover, as with certain collieries I was aware of in the Yorkshire coalfield, seemed to me to be less and less likely given the growing competition from overseas suppliers. That jobs generally would not be eventually threatened by a contagion of inefficiency and inflation also struck me as unavoidable, as I listened to employers and trade union officials in my constituency. They, like myself, now recognised that self-induced burdens elsewhere in the UK economy would inevitably affect employment in our city of Sheffield. We were now well aware, from hard-won experience, that change, leading to innovation, was the key to the rebirth of declining industry.

Recalling the teachings of the distinguished economist Schumpeter whilst I was at the LSE, I was now inclined to believe that the way ahead for the ailing industries of Northern Ireland, as well as in Sheffield, was not to rely too much on financial handouts from London. The more rewarding approach was to adapt, invest and, above all, remain globally competitive. That seemed to me to be Dr Whitaker's objective in the Irish Republic. In a novel approach he was searching for inward investment with tempting rates of corporation tax associated with choice of location. Even though the lure of corporation tax flexibility was not available in Northern Ireland, I could not identify anyone on its industrial scene with the imagination and vigour of Dr Whitaker. I wondered if its traditional enterprise was now being stifled by a growing dependence on London.

Nor could I see an adequate level of competence in the government of Northern Ireland, with the exception of Brian Faulkner. Least of all could I seriously entertain the Ulster Education Minister, Captain (*sic*) Long, when he visited Sheffield in January 1972, and officially hosted a luncheon. I refused his invitation, despite criticism in one local newspaper, the *Morning Telegraph*. I appealed publicly to others to do the same. Alderman Sir Ron Ironmonger, Leader of the council, and my constituent, responded, along with others. In an extraordinary speech Captain Long laid the blame for their problems 'squarely at the door of outside revolutionary influences'. He defended the newly-introduced policy of internment, that is, dawn raids on the homes of people and locking them up without trial. He forecast that the security forces in Ulster, having broken the back of the problem, would now see an end to it 'in months rather than years'. That was just two weeks before the events of Bloody Sunday in Derry, for which David Cameron as Prime Minister later apologised. It indicates how remote both this Ulster Cabinet Member and Sheffield's *Morning Telegraph* were from reality. Yet, given the Army's lack of general guidance, power was now returning to Stormont and presumably to men like him. At a time, moreover, when the fear of a Protestant backlash and the need of the control of firearms remained uppermost in the minds of many.

Contrary to the optimism of Captain Long, security in Northern Ireland was now on a knife-edge. Edward Heath's Conservative government was no longer deceived, however, for it abolished Stormont.[58] Henceforth it was to be direct rule from London, with a new office of secretary of state. The first holder was William Whitelaw. Up to Bloody Sunday, Edward Heath had insisted the North was none of Dublin's business. Afterwards he sought meetings with the

---

58 Which Grey Gowrie, Second Earl of Gowrie and a very thoughtful minister, who served under secretary of State Jim Prior in Margaret Thatcher's administration, later considered a mistake. *The Daily Telegraph*. 20 January 1993.

authorities in Dublin as his government devised the Sunningdale Agreement, which embodied a formula for power-sharing. It was abandoned soon after he lost power in the early months of 1974, however, for the Labour administration that followed capitulated to the threat of revolt from Loyalists. Merlyn Rees, who succeeded Whitelaw as secretary of state, never displayed any sense of authority in his exercise of the historic Agreement.

The 'spongers' speech of the new Prime Minister, Harold Wilson, infuriated the Loyalists and they threatened to revolt. Rees all too easily accepted the Army's advice that they could not fight on two fronts and the IRA were the main enemy. What a change from 1969. Despite festering problems resulting from the denial to Catholics of such basic rights as housing, electoral representation, employment and the widespread civil rights protests earlier, a Labour government had once again adopted a 'head in the sands' attitude. Such neglect in a British colony in Africa would have caused uproar among some Labour MPs.

Kevin McNamara concluded from his own rigorous research later that thirty years of bloodshed could have been avoided if the Wilson government had acted sooner to enact a timetable of reform that essentially met the demands of the civil rights protestors.[59] They were not alone. Documents released by the Public Record Office under the thirty years rule reveal that during the decisive moments of conflict between 1968 and 1972, neither the Wilson nor the Heath administrations knew what to do. Yet Kevin McNamara had often reminded them that the Catholics in Northern Ireland 'merely wanted British standards for British people'.

I had met such civil rights leaders as John Hume and Gerry Fitt in their homes. I had come to know some of the impressive people they rallied under the civil rights banner. I was especially taken with Austin Currie, Ivan Cooper and Paddy Devlin, who were to become well-

---

59   2008 John Kennedy Lecture, Institute of Irish Studies, University of Liverpool.

known minority leaders. The brutal treatment they suffered at the hands of Loyalist authorities led them to form the Social Democratic and Labour Party (SDLP). Their experience could not fail to stir apprehension in Catholic neighbourhoods and heighten interest in those people who were prepared to fight to defend them.

After the return of a Labour government in 1974, I became chairman of the Select Committee on Trade and Industry. I succeeded Bill Rodgers (later Lord Rodgers of Quarry Bank) following his ministerial appointment at the Ministry of Defence (MoD). His prime concern had been to help bring about the reinvigoration of British industry in order that it could become a globally competitive powerhouse once again. That remained the exclusive mandate of my committee colleagues and myself. The motor industry immediately caught our attention, for it seemed to us to be a spectacular example of our industrial decline. Once the thriving heart of British manufacturing, it now appeared doomed to a slow death. Poor demand, crippling over-capacity and increasing competition were striking features of that decline. Yet, there was no shortage of innovative skills and engineering ability. It had once dominated the home market and had the vast potential export market of the Commonwealth nations. By 1972 car production had peaked at no more than two million cars, however, whilst Japanese and European car makers were already outpacing us in productivity, quality control and sales. More disturbing was the evident explanation for Britain's pain – self-inflicted wounds. Britain was no longer providing the car industry with a steady flow of investment, inward as well as domestic, the low inflation essential for a stable business environment and modernisation. To compound such failures, the car industry was plagued with weak management, restrictive practices and wildcat strikes. Derek 'Red Robbo' Robinson, the communist convenor for the Amalgamated Engineering Union (AEU) at Longbridge in the Midlands, was linked with numerous walk-outs. In a single year during the 1970s hundreds of wildcat strikes were called. The same was happening at Cowley, Oxford, where the workforce was dominated by the Transport & General Workers' Union (TGW). The workers at each plant had become so militant that even their own union leaders could not control them. The problem became acute by the mid-1970s when the Cowley shop stewards attempted to collaborate with Robinson. Whereupon the union leaders – unable to agree on countervailing action – turned on each other. If the issue was not so serious the situation would have been seen as farcical.[60] It amounted to a state of anarchy in a key industry, with too many of its workers – led by Robinson – engaged in what they perceived to be a class struggle rather than the production of cars for sale in an increasingly competitive global market. Meanwhile I viewed anxiously the deleterious effect on the supply chain, from component manufacturers right down to the foundries and commodity steel production in my own constituency.

The government's reaction was to bring together the various producers and their distinctive brands into the British Leyland Motor Company (BLMC) in 1968.[61] The hope that this new critical mass would make the industry more competitive and play a central role in modernising British industry was dashed by the recession which followed the quadrupling of world oil prices at the end of 1973 and by the Three Day Week early in 1974. British Leyland was badly hit by the fall in car sales and had to turn to the government for financial support.

----

60   Although it did prompt some derision, notably the production of the notorious Boulting film *I'm Alright Jack*.

61   It was a merger promoted by the Industrial Reorganisation Corporation (IRC). With car, truck and bus manufacturers, the group at one time held some 40% of the British car market. But despite the introduction of the best-selling Mini and the continuing appeal of such prestigious marques as Jaguar, Rover and the Land Rover, the group had an incoherent product range and had been slow to develop new models to cope with international competition. The IRC was succeeded by the NEB, set up by the incoming Labour government of 1974. It was a body with wide powers to invest in companies so as to enable funding for new product development, and to create new ventures in sectors that were thought to be of strategic importance.

That is where my select committee came in. It was entitled to delve into government expenditure and thereby question policies relating to trade and industry. Thus, through the right kind of inquiries, my colleagues and I were in a position to prod the government towards greater value for taxpayers' money. In selecting the car industry as a subject of inquiry, we hoped to improve its effectiveness. For BLMC was on the brink of bankruptcy by the end of 1974. The economic consequences of such a collapse were appalling. One hundred and fifty thousand people were employed by the company in the UK. There was an equal number of jobs in the component industries dependent on BLMC. It was calculated that the closure would cost Britain's balance of trade £2 billion a year. In consequence the government agreed to guarantee BLMC's growing overdraft with the banks in exchange for a hand in running the operation. This would be handled by the National Enterprise Board (NEB). Its newly appointed chairman, Sir Don Ryder, was tasked with reporting on the company and listing recommendations for its future to the responsible minister, Tony Wedgwood-Benn.

Our select committee spent the first eight months of 1975 investigating the motor industry. I opened the inquiry with a warning to witnesses called before us, whether captains of industry or trade union leaders, that I expected them to show an acceptable standard of transparency and responsibility. I was very mindful in that regard when the AEU leaders Hugh Scanlon and Reg Birch appeared, for they had been responsible for allowing Robinson, their own communist convenor, to forge militant and irresponsible trade unionism at Longbridge. We awaited the publication of the Ryder Report.

The Ryder Report appeared in April, and pulled no punches. In brief, it recommended the replacement of much factory machinery as a matter of urgency, the introduction of a cohesive model strategy and the eradication of industrial relations problems. It pointed out that it would take an enormous amount of investment to make the company 'viable and fully competitive' by 1981. It proposed capital expenditure of no less than £1,264 million – which would have to come from the Government – along with £260 million worth of working capital. The Labour Government gave the plan its full and unconditional blessing, and it went forward. BLMC ceased to exist as an independent company and in June it became known as British Leyland Ltd. (BL). This signified that the company was now fully under government control. The NEB was given the task of overseeing it and charged with allocating large sums of money over the following four years in order to guarantee the company's survival. We were not convinced.

In recommending the expansion of BL – to build it out of its financial mess – my colleagues and I thought Ryder was painting a rosy image of what shape it would be in by 1981. He was basing a great deal of his forward projections, we thought, on his prediction that BL would maintain a 33% share of the market in the UK. That seemed to be making no allowance for either the unpopularity of the company's products, or the need for some plant closures. Instead he proposed sweeping organisational changes in the management structure. We were agreed that the proposed financing of BL was based on 'fundamental mistakes' and was a 'bad bet' for the taxpayer. We accused Ryder of treating 'public money as confetti'.[62] If 'lame ducks' are no answer, neither are uncontrolled state hand-outs, we told the Government. The truth was BL now had too many workers producing too few cars that they had difficulty in selling. The Ryder plan was not going to cure that.

Along with my colleagues, I had had no hesitation in coming down against Ryder's actual proposals. A difficult and politically dangerous decision for a Labour chairman to take against a Labour government and a popular minister. The report caused a sensation,

---

62   We pointed out that the amount of taxpayers' money he was demanding was precisely the amount needed to pay pensions to all men at sixty years instead of six-ty-five years and, ironically, become a permanent pensioner itself.

as I feared, which is why I delayed its launch until early August after Parliament had gone into summer recess. Even so, only two members of my committee were present. Holiday plans detained some; others were plainly fearful of the reaction. Not that I was spared the anger of my Labour party colleagues for long. I was condemned from the platform of the Labour party conference a few weeks later by the TGW assistant general secretary, Ron Todd.[63] At the first meeting of the PLP after Parliament resumed in the autumn, I was singled out for attack by Norman Atkinson MP, a member of the AEU.

On the other hand, the *Financial Times* thought my team had 'done more to assert the authority and status of the House of Commons than a thousand political speeches'. It made me 'Man of the Week'.[64] But I had already left for Co. Mayo to escape the press coverage and continuing furore.

Unlike today's select committees, mine had accomplished its mission without the powers to send for papers, people or ministers. But we knew how to ask and direct the right questions. Select committee work was never the same again. It attained a new standing, status and penetrability. It seemed to me then to be an entirely appropriate instrument for probing policy on Northern Ireland. I said so, and it was later adopted.

Two years later Prime Minister Jim Callaghan cautioned the Labour party conference against the longstanding belief that the Government could spend its way out of recession. In so far as it ever did exist, he warned, it worked 'by injecting a bigger dose of inflation into the economy, followed by a higher level of unemployment as the next step'. Just prior to conference, the government had been rescued

---

63   He and I were to clash later over his stand on unilateral nuclear disarmament whilst he was serving on the Labour party national executive committee (NEC).

64   *Financial Times*. 16 August 1975. I was enormously assisted by our parliamentary Committee Clerk, later Sir Robert Rogers, Clerk of the House of Commons and our Special Adviser, Professor D.G. Rhys.

by the International Monetary Fund (IMF). After years of industrial subsidies and Keynesian policies, Britain had been unable to service its debts.

As for the fate of BL, its share of the UK car market slumped from 35% to 16% and was in danger of a forced liquidation. On becoming Prime Minister, Margaret Thatcher admitted in her memoirs, 'The political realities had to be faced. BL had to be supported … and, most painfully, we provided £900 million.' A restructuring plan was finally agreed, and some jobs were saved, for a while. But did the British taxpayer get value for money? After various re-configurations the BL Group, by then renamed MG Rover, went bankrupt in 2005. That brought to an end mass car production by British-owned manufacturers. MG became part of a Chinese group. Jaguar and Landrover were sold on by Ford in 2008 to TATA Motors of India.

At their first face-to-face meeting following the setting up of the power-sharing executive set up under Sunningdale, Brian Faulkner warned the Taoiseach, Liam Cosgrave, of his political difficulties, notably arising from border security. In consequence, I was delegated by Roy Hattersley, Foreign Office Minister, in February 1976, to pursue the matter through the medium of a three-day visit to Dublin by a parliamentary group of ten, which I would lead.[65] It was a powerful group of strong-minded MPs who would need careful handling to maintain unity. The group entered into full discussions with members of the Dail, the Senate and the Foreign Minister, Garrett Fitzgerald. It paid courtesy calls on the Taoiseach; Liam Cosgrave, Opposition Leader; Jack Lynch, the Minister for Justice; Patrick Cooney, Dr Conor Cruise O'Brien and the Speaker of the Dail. We were also briefed by the British Ambassador, Sir Arthur Galsworthy, and his Defence Attache.

---

65   The delegation included Martin Flannery, Bruce Grocott, Peter Hardy and Alec Woodall from the Labour benches, Michael Mates, Ian Gow, Tony Nelson, Norman Miscampbell from the Conservative side, and Stephen Ross, who was Liberal.

Discussions ranged during the course of our visit over economic matters, the emergent European community, oil exploration, fishing limits and especially the Northern Ireland problem, with particular reference to border security. The object of the visit I stressed again and again in public to offset offensive reporting, was to strengthen friendship between both countries. It was reported, however, that our mission 'was prompted by a growing feeling in the Commons that Dublin is back at its old game of dragging its feet'. We were urged to 'plead with the Irish government for tougher anti-terrorist laws'.[66] Relations between Dublin and London have never been better, I would insist. Privately, the aims of the delegation were to further the active support increasingly available in Dublin for our policies in Northern Ireland, allaying Loyalist fears and assisting efforts to bring about a political solution in the North in which the interests of both communities were fairly represented.

We did not escape the fire of some of Dublin's press either. One comment was headed 'Silly men from London', and found it difficult, it went on, 'not to feel a sense of outrage at the cheek of a group of British MPs coming over here to examine us on security'. 'We should ask them,' it proceeded, 'about the Loyalist bombers who visited Dublin and are still free in Belfast. We should challenge them on the lies told by Scotland Yard to shield their errors. We should ask them do they condone the use of forged press passes by British soldiers in Belfast and Dublin? We should also point out to them that we did not draw or create the border.' Finally, it stated, the Justice Minister 'and the Gardai, have accomplished wonders. These MPs should be sent home with fleas in their ears.'[67]

Nevertheless, I was struck by the courtesy extended to us in all quarters, and I continued to express the hope that our visit would lead to a much closer identity of outlook. We were all impressed by

---

66   *Daily Express.* 16 February 1976.

67   *Evening Herald.* 18 February 1976.

the detailed briefing at Dundalk Barracks by the Irish Army and the frank and helpful tour that was then laid on of Irish Army border locations.

The Irish Army felt its border role was underrated and misunderstood, given that it was subject to its own police in such matters. Thus it had not the British Army's extensive powers of search and arrest; it was also bound by strict and somewhat ambiguous regulations under the Republic's Defence Act of 1954, which limited firing to exceptional circumstances. Members of the delegation welcomed such important clarification and privately wished the Dublin government had been bolder in its presentation, and sooner.

I stated afterwards, however, that the Irish authorities had been helpful and that all the delegation felt they now had a greater understanding of the security problems in the border area. I emphasised that the purpose of such an exchange visit was to listen to one another's views, and see how they might help to find a solution to the Northern problem. 'We would not be here,' I said, 'if we were not friends of Ireland.' The visit concluded with lunch at Dublin airport, when our return flight was delayed because of the genuine warmth of the parting hospitality and presentation of gifts by the secretary of the Irish Transport & General Workers' Union. After the burning of the British Embassy in Dublin only a few years earlier and the subsequent tension, I felt our visit had eased Anglo-Irish relations, as did my colleagues.[68]

68 An immediate result was a 'softening' in the attitude of Martin Flannery on the 'Troops Out' issue.

Chapter Seven

Conflict in Northern Ireland

On returning to Westminster, I was invited by Jim Callaghan, then Opposition spokesman for Northern Ireland, to a chat one Sunday evening at his home in Greenwich. I was joined by Merlyn Rees, Roy Hattersley, Bruce Millan and Brian Walden. I quickly gathered that they knew little of Northern Ireland, though Roy Hattersley quickly learned. Drawing on his former experience as Home Secretary, Jim offered a fascinating glimpse of the morass in that strange corner of the UK. He praised the Dublin government for its sensitive handling of events in the North since 1968. But he criticised the RUC for its early obsession with the belief that the conflict stemmed from a massive Irish Republican Army (IRA) plot. Whereas, Jim explained, until the crucial policy changes in 1970, the IRA was lacking in organisation and had no real plans to launch an offensive. Following conversion to Marxism in 1968, the IRA had been on the point of forsaking violence and opting for politics. After the curfew in the Catholic area around the Falls Road in Belfast in 1970, it split over the issue of how best to respond to such armed discrimination. One faction, which became known as the 'Provisionals', wanted to go on the attack, whilst the 'Officials' favoured defence. The younger 'Provisionals', moreover, were not so much interested in ideology as action here and now. They were also disgusted with the lack of leadership from Dublin.

In the Falls curfew the Army initiated full-scale raids in the Catholic neighbourhoods in search of arms. Incredibly, the raids involved the use of tear gas, free use of their own firearms by soldiers, indiscriminate arrests, looting and the destruction of homes, including unforgivably, religious objects. There were no such Army deployments in Protestant neighbourhoods, despite worries at the highest level of the number of weapons held by loyalists. Indeed, the first policeman to be killed at this time, Victor Arbuckle, was killed by a loyalist on the Shankhill Road on 11 October 1969. The Provisionals then were anxious to take on the defence of Catholic areas. Their emergent role soon escalated into open warfare and spread to the Border areas.

Jim revealed that CS gas was first used in Belfast in a desperate hope that it would enable the RUC to control the situation and obviate the need to call in the Army. But his hand was forced by the assaults on Catholic districts in Belfast by the armed Protestant paramilitaries, the B-Specials.[69] In consequence, the Army's arrival was welcomed warmly in those areas as protectors. Jim thought he was then making headway. Given the right circumstances and general acceptance of all concerned, he said he would like to see the whole of Ireland 'come together'. But the guns must be put away, he insisted, and complete reforms carried out first in Northern Ireland.

That was the position of my father who was making his final visit to Ireland at about that time. Still a Lancashire Hussar at heart, he was shocked in February 1971 by the first killing of a soldier by the IRA, Gunner Robert Curtis. He feared that in consequence, the Catholic cause had lost the moral high ground in Northern Ireland and public support in Britain. He was quite right, of course. But how significant was that public support, I asked him? Had the situation in Northern Ireland ever concerned his fellow-workers in Britain, I asked? He was in a position to judge given his long working life in Britain and his family's close ties with Ireland, north and south. Since our wartime service in the province, brother Jim – whose last warship operated from Derry – and I had often diverted to Belfast and Derry in the course of our travels to the west of Ireland. I came to observe

---

69   They were phased out in 1972. The Ulster Defence Regiment (UDR), 9,000 strong, mainly part-time militia, was formed to back up the Army and controlled by the MoD. But it admitted many former B-Specials, whilst the few Catholics who did join were under constant pressure to leave.

at first hand, therefore, some of the developments Jim Callaghan had described at Greenwich.

I would book into a hotel discreetly at about the same time, go walkabout in Belfast and in Derry, guided by wartime memories, and never failed to witness some form of protest. I encountered very early on some of the civil rights groups that sprang into prominence. My financial contributions to their welfare funds – posted at Westminster – were detected later and brought to my attention in the Ministry of Defence (MoD). During many private and official visits to Belfast, I usually stayed at the Europa Hotel. In face of competition only from Saigon and Beirut it became known as the 'world's most bombed hotel'. More than once my sleep was interrupted by a bomb-blast, sudden darkness, falling plaster and the sound of running people shouting all manner of instructions. That was the fairly common experience of some uncomplaining journalists.

Jim Callaghan's successor in 1970 in the new Conservative government, Reginald Maudling, appeared to give up after his first visit. Voicing the memorable judgement that it was a 'bloody awful place', he became more of an observer. He was in a difficult position. The Downing Street Declaration of 20 August 1969 had fatally compromised the British Army. It was henceforth committed to uphold a regime dependent on 'special powers', whilst the grievances of the Catholic community were largely unaddressed. Such political guidance, or lack of it, led inevitably to power drifting back to the old order at Stormont. It confused the Army's rules of engagement, led inexorably to the Army's disastrous involvement in such tragic events as the Falls curfew in 1970, internment, the tragedy of Ballymurphy in 1971 and Bloody Sunday in 1972. Together with the 'not an inch' and 'no surrender' thunderings of Ian Paisley, founder of the Democratic Unionist party (DUP), the apparent preparations for armed conflict by William Craig, leader of the Ulster Vanguard, and the posturings of the Ulster Defence Association (UDA), such developments were moving aggrieved communities in Catholic areas to see the IRA, but only the Provisional IRA, as their protectors.

I was in Belfast when internment – or imprisonment without trial – was introduced in August 1971. It was badly handled by the Army, given its role, because of incompetent intelligence-gathering by the Special Branch of the RUC. I sat in afterwards at protest meetings in people's homes and in community halls. I received personally many eyewitness accounts of the raids by soldiers on homes in Ballymurphy, the rounding up of men – some mistakenly – and of the attacks on Catholic homes by loyalists. I heard that over the next three days the paratroopers (paras) killed eleven unarmed civilians, including a Catholic priest, Father Hugh Mullan, and a woman, Joan Connnolly: most of them shot in the back. The priest, I was told, had taken the precaution of phoning notification to the Army barracks before going to a field where Bobby Clarke lay dying. After annointing Bobby, he waved a white flag, went to phone for an ambulance and was shot in the back. The MoD claimed that the casualties were armed, just as they did in Derry six months later on Bloody Sunday. Indeed the accounts I received at the time from the Ballymurphy families suggested greater brutality by the paras than occurred later in Derry. Those families have been tireless since in their unrequited demands for a public enquiry.[70] Unprecedentedly, some 7,000 refugees actually fled from the UK. They were housed in old army bases in the Irish Republic. Such events had quite simply made inevitable the strengthening of the new IRA.

---

70 A twenty-one year-old man was shot dead at the same time elsewhere in Belfast. He was innocent, unarmed, had no paramilitary connections, no criminal convictions and posed no threat, a report by the North of Ireland's Historical Enquiries Team disclosed recently. He was Billy McKavanagh, a Catholic. The report found that he was shot dead by a soldier from the Royal Green Jackets in Catherine Street in the Markets area in the early hours of 11 August 1971, two days after the introduction of internment.

I returned to Westminster as soon as possible after internment to support Jock Stallard MP in his attempts to initiate the recall of parliament. I found a disconsolate Michael O'Halloran MP sitting in the Members' lobby, bent on the same mission, but reporting failure. However, some of us did succeed in arousing enough concern among colleagues after the Labour party conference in the autumn to justify a special meeting of the PLP to reconsider the party's bipartisan policy on Northern Ireland.

Kevin McNamara, John Smith and I were the most prominent speakers. We were singled out afterwards by Harold Wilson and the party's Chief Whip, Bob Mellish, for positive, constructive speeches and the avoidance of declamatory language. Mine was directed towards compromise and constitutional reform. Although I pointedly reminded colleagues that 'no nation can use large-scale imprisonment without trial and leave its moral standards unimpaired.' John Smith described the complex situation regarding Northern Ireland that existed in parts of Scotland. Kevin McNamara appealed for more understanding of Protestantism in Ulster, and presented the most sympathetic portrayal of the Orangeman that I have ever heard. That was the man that Tony Blair decided later was unfitted, after the most distinguished and effective service in a 'shadow' role, for appointment as Secretary of State for Northern Ireland, as he was considered too 'green' – by whom?

Such apparent indifference to the festering problems resulting from the denial of basic rights in employment, in housing and in electoral representation by Catholics had roused little concern within Labour's parliamentary party. Apart from some on the left of the party, however, and others among whom there still lingered surprisingly an imperial mindset – 'what we have we hold'– there could no longer be blissful ignorance among the bulk of Labour MPs.

For thanks to the initiative and courage of Brendan MacLua, the *Irish Post* had begun publication in Britain in February 1970. It provided factual, objective and much-needed coverage of the events in Northern Ireland that were spilling into Britain. Such as the incident in 1970 in the House of Commons when a CS canister was lobbed down from the public gallery in protest at the treatment of its Catholic communities. It almost landed at my feet, but did engulf me in smoke. The *Irish Post* covered huge rallies in Trafalgar Square, which I attended, and in Birmingham in July 1971. It covered the arrival of Bernadette Devlin at Westminster and her remarkable maiden speech. It covered Bloody Sunday in Derry, as a result of which the British Embassy in Dublin was set ablaze and the Irish Ambassador in London recalled. It described Bernadette Devlin's assault of Reginald Maudling in the House of Commons. Hugh Delargy and I took her downstairs immediately afterwards for a soothing drink in the Members' bar. I asked her what she was saying as she was punching Maudling. 'I could murder you,' she replied. Brendan MacLua's independent line of reporting would prove invaluable to the Irish community in Britain as they came under increasing pressure in the Seventies.

Contrary to the optimism of Captain Long, security in Northern Ireland was now on a knife-edge. Edward Heath's Conservative government was no longer deceived after Bloody Sunday in Derry, however, for it quickly abolished Stormont. Henceforth it was to be direct rule from London, with a new office of secretary of state. The first holder was William Whitelaw. Up to Bloody Sunday, Edward Heath had insisted that the North was none of Dublin's business. Afterwards he sought meetings with the authorities in Dublin as his government devised a formula for power-sharing embodied in the Sunningdale Agreement. That is why I was concerned at such a critical time in October 1973 by news reports, however bizarre, of the Littlejohn brothers and, in particular, the role of Kenneth Littlejohn acting as a British agent in the Irish Republic.[71] I raised the matter with Prime Minister Edward Heath on 13 August 1973, expressing concern about 'the future of Anglo-Irish relations'. He assured me in a letter dated 28 August 1973 that his government was 'seeking to ensure that our relations with the Republic of Ireland should not suffer as a result of the wild allegations which have been made by the Littlejohns and others.'

After Ballymurphy I could not understand why the paras had been deployed at all in Derry. I raised this with the General Officer Commanding (GOC), General Tuzo, when I met him the following summer. That they killed innocent civilians there in contravention of their orders, and then lied about it, was a very dark moment for all concerned. For the chain of guilt eventually went right up to General Tuzo, and beyond to the top. General Sir Mike Jackson, who went on to head the Army, was involved in recording the military version. Thus Reginald Maudling told the House of Commons that the paras in Derry had acted in self-defence. Prime Minister David Cameron in admissions and apologies later set aside the official report of Lord Widgery. It was all undeserving of the proud county regiments, such as my father's Lancashire Hussars – in which he took such pride – that comprised the bulk of the British Army.

General concerns were admitted by the GOC and the RUC Chief Constable, Sir Graham Stillington, at a meeting on 7 June 1972 with MPs representing the Northern Ireland Labour group at Westminster. The delegation comprised Kevin McNamara, Jock Stallard, Stan Orme, Russell Kerr and myself. It was the first of several meetings we attended in Belfast and Derry. We met also the Irish Trades Union Congress (TUC), the Northern Ireland Labour Party (NILP), the

---

71   'For it now seems probable', reported *The Sunday Times* (7 October 1973), 'that among the undisclosed jobs which … Littlejohn performed for Britain was to kidnap a prominent IRA Provisional in the South and drive him at gunpoint over the border to a waiting Security Forces ambush in Northern Ireland.'

Association for Legal Justice in Belfast,[72] Ulster Unionists in Derry
and groups on its Creggan estate. When I queried the presence of the
paras in Northern Ireland, General Tuzo explained the difficulty he
was experiencing in the transfer of NATO assigned troops, which I
readily understood later on arriving at the MoD. General Tuzo insisted
that he was 'endeavouring to restore goodwill with Catholics', but it
was a 'race against time' given 'mounting Protestant anger'.

Echoing him, the Chief Constable said the 'Protestant backlash
had to be taken seriously'. In that case, we asked, what 'are you doing
about privately-held licensed weapons?' The Chief Constable replied
that he was only concerned about the private possession of guns 'by
7,000 to 8,000 over the province, including vigilantes and those who
drill, as well as those who will take up arms – which are ancient for
the most part.'

Shortly afterwards, on 29 January 1973, following an upsurge in
sectarian murders, Ritchie Ryan, then the Irish Shadow Minister for
Foreign Affairs, asked William Whitelaw to call in all arms. This may
have led to an order which came into effect on 15 March 1973 in
Northern Ireland, calling in licensed weapons for ballistic tests and
the submission of photographs of their holders.

The NILP representatives also expressed 'apprehension about
the state of the Protestant mind'. They requested us to ask Whitelaw
to establish the 'medical examination of internees before and after
release'. They wished to see direct rule working, and policing resumed.

The leaders of the Association for Legal Justice went much further.
They were of an entirely different persuasion and mostly concerned
about imprisoned republicans: their political status, visiting hours (half
an hour a month), heating in cells, food parcels, free association, access

---

72   Non-sectarian, though mainly Catholic in membership, it was set up in 1971
to campaign against the Special Powers Act and internment without trial. Its panel
of lawyers gave free advice, and catalogued cases of alleged brutality by the security
forces.

to their own lawyers and doctors and the acute danger of loyalist assassination on release.

The Irish TUC admitted a 'tremendous polarisation' among its members, and a 'lack of confidence' in local government and its personnel. It was concerned about rising unemployment, especially 'west of the Bann, in the border counties and in Derry'.

The plight of the unemployed in Derry was not among the concerns of a group of local Ulster Unionists whom we met next. They wanted Stormont back, still regarded it 'as constitutional', and now did 'not believe Whitelaw, Westminster and any politician'. A Major Glover and the Reverend Dickinson insisted that there was 'nothing wrong with Northern Ireland before 1968', rejecting direct rule and 'any peace moves'. Recent public demonstrations in which they had been involved were 'necessary', they said, for people to 'express themselves'. They were defiant in face of our probing, rather than hostile, but decidedly flummoxed on our departure when Kevin McNamara revealed that Russell Kerr and Stan Orme had been engaged in combat missions with the RAF in WWII, and that I had been based briefly at the naval air station at Maydown outside Derry whilst working up over Lough Foyle with a Fleet Air Arm squadron.

The meetings we attended on the Creggan estate, in St Mary's Club and St John's School, were sharply contrasting exposures. They could be summed up by one person present who said 'life for them in Derry was unreal'. Their concerns were internment, the status of political prisoners, the imminent danger of hunger strikes, discrimination, unemployment and school attendance down from 94% to 76%.

Such findings in Derry were of much less interest to a section of the media than our experience on return to Belfast. Gunmen hijacked our car, but returned it quite courteously later on. According to one news report, we got a 'taste of terror'.[73] It happened during a further visit arranged by Gerry Fitt MP to meet the wives and

---

73   *Daily Mirror.* 7 June 1972.

families of internees in the headquarters of the Central Citizens Defence Committee[74] on the Falls Road.

The Labour MPs who fulfilled this programme represented the core group of those most active at Westminster in the affairs of Northern Ireland, together with Maurice Miller, a founder member, and Martin Flannery who joined following his arrival at Westminster in 1974. Kevin McNamara and I always deferred to colleagues in the election of officers so as to ensure the group conveyed the widest possible basis of concern and was free of the suspicion of sectarian tinge.[75] It resulted in the prominence and ministerial appointment later of Stan Orme, whom I judged to be the least equipped among us. He clung to the myth of a non-sectarian trade union movement in Belfast that had kept political strife off the shop floor, and the role of a certain Sandy Scott MBE, a fellow-member of the AEU, as a peacemaker. He overlooked the relative absence of Catholics on the shop floor and their total absence in many places of work because of job discrimination.[76] He must have been disappointed by the significant involvement of 'non-sectarian' trade unionists with the Ulster Workers Council (UWC) in their revolt later against the Sunningdale agreement. As well as their total lack of response to the appeal of Len Murray, general secretary of the TUC in London, when he headed a poorly attended march of some twenty-five people, mostly women and members of peace groups in Belfast and, notably, the absence of Sandy Scott.

---

74   It was formed in Belfast in 1969 as vigilantes to defend Catholic areas against sectarian attack. Non-military, it drew support from all Catholic classes, and after the Provisionals moved in, it became a relief organisation.

75   A practice long favoured by another group within the party – the Labour Friends of Israel.

76   Harland & Wolf, Belfast Ropeworks, Sirocco Engineering, Rolls Royce, Standard Telephones, to mention just a few?

Kevin McNama and I were constantly in and out of Northern Ireland from the early Seventies onwards, always scrupulously maintaining a balanced approach. That entailed separate meetings with members of the IRA. Mine took place late at night after a circuitous and prolonged drive in Belfast. My hosts and others present, like those who had met me initially and then driven me to the meeting, were all professional people. Whereas the IRA member was clearly a working man. He told me he was a carpenter and had a family of 'several little boys'. Otherwise, he had very little to say: impressive in demeanour, without any bravado, determined and impervious to my entreaties. Others present were friendlier, voluble even, but would accept no payment in return for their hospitality. I understand that the IRA member was dead within the year. I often wondered what became of his 'little boys'.

I visited Long Kesh prison – later named The Maze – in 1973 with Kevin McNamara and Jock Stallard, to meet loyalist and republican prisoners. We were met by the Deputy Governor, who informed us that the prison population numbered 1,469, of whom '571 were detained', as he put it. We encountered difficulty in meeting the loyalist prisoners. Unlike the republicans they had not succeeded in establishing a credible political wing, only political spokesmen. Thus I only made practical contact with Billie McKee[77] and with Gusty

---

77   He complained of 'draughty huts in compounds 12 and 13, and disturbance by night Army patrols'. Otherwise, he reported, 'the cook house was too small', which resulted in such a slow service that 'sometimes a few meals are short and often the men affected may wait a half-hour or more … when they would be cold'. He described the 'meat buying as questionable, especially ham, for each week three meals on average were rejected.'

Spence[78] on whose behalf we made representations to the Secretary of State concerning accommodation. Gusty Spence thanked us for 'raising the many and varied questions with the Secretary of State', and said results had 'been quick in coming. After so many months of hard slogging to move Long Kesh on the slightest of grievances your success is all the more astonishing.'[79]

Gusty Spence and I got on increasingly well in follow-up correspondence. He was well aware of my wartime background and referred to it admiringly. He was fascinated by the disclosure that my father had been a reservist before WWI, and went to France as a Lancashire Hussar. 'Hussar, Hussar', I can still hear him murmuring. And my father was a Mayo-man, I pointed out, always 'loyal to both', and that he had also fought bad employers as a coal miner and as an unflinching trade unionist devoted to the ideal of the solidarity of all working-class movements. Gusty Spence was most interested. Perhaps I had helped to set him thinking. After the breakdown of the Loyalist ceasefire later that year, he publicly renounced violence and from prison preached accommodation between Northern Ireland's working-class communities. He entered into closer contact with republican prisoners and even learned the rudiments of the Irish language. In correspondence he appeared to be increasingly disposed to the view that working-class loyalists had been as much the victims of misrule as had Catholics. After serving his sentence he helped to form the Progressive Unionist party in an effort to divert the UVF into political channels.

---

78   Gusty Spence, who died in 2011 aged seventy-eight, was the founding father of the modern Ulster Volunteer Force (UVF). He was born in Belfast and brought up in the Shankhill, the heartland of Ulster Protestantism. His father had been a member of the original UVF, formed to oppose Home Rule. He left school at fourteen years, and in the late Fifties joined the Royal Ulster Rifles. As a sergeant in the Military Police, he served in Germany and Cyprus until leaving the Army in 1961 on account of ill health. He was convicted of a sectarian killing in 1966.

79   See Appendix 1.

Kevin and I visited Armagh Jail, where sixty-five republican women, five loyalist women and 12 'detainees' were confined. We received complaints about the lack of bathrooms and toilets, and the lack of 'visits to detainees by detained brothers'.

Finally, Kevin and I called on Cardinal Conway. He raised the case of the Price girls in Brixton Prison, and suggested a 'little reasonableness in their handling might deprive the IRA of a propaganda weapon'. I promised to visit the girls in prison and raise their case with the Home Secretary.

Those IRA and Loyalist prisoners I met, including David Ervine, struck me as men who would never have arrived in Long Kesh but for the political situation in Northern Ireland. Many were articulate and well-educated, especially on the republican side, and had clearly taken full advantage of the Open University courses – some attaining degrees. The political or 'special category' status which was granted by the Conservative government in 1972 (and removed by the Labour government in 1976) was still in force. The exercise of more care in its official definition might have prevented it from becoming such an issue later. For the organisation of the prison was more relaxed because of the cooperation of the inmates, I was told. Although the IRA and Loyalist command structures were not officially recognised, they were clearly evident. Indeed, the IRA was turning their imprisonment to their own tactical and political advantage, as I pointed out at Westminster. Long Kesh did not appear to be gripped at that time by the crisis brewing over the Sunningdale Agreement. Nor did Gusty Spence mention it in correspondence. Although it was the culmination of desperate attempts by the Heath government during 1973 to check the ever-threatening situation by undertaking far-reaching change.

Most nationalist representatives had withdrawn from the Northern Ireland parliament at Stormont after internment and the controversial killing of Catholics that followed. From March 1973, when Stormont was abolished, William Whitelaw strove to replace it with a different devolution that would appeal to alienated nationalists and unionists alike. It would move forward on two distinct, but related, fronts. The restoration of devolution would take place, first, on the basis of a coalition of both communities in executive or decision-making and power-sharing government. However, it would be linked with a constitutional settlement embracing the moderate Northern Ireland parties and the Irish coalition government in Dublin under Liam Cosgrave. This departure implied political and institutional recognition of what was long described as the 'Irish Dimension' of relationships within Northern Ireland. The SDLP had insisted that all-island relationships were integral to the proposed developments and could only be expressed by an all-Ireland council.

Whitelaw had set himself a huge task. The republicans and the loyalist paramilitaries posed a severe challenge to begin with. But he soon decided that they were not for turning. His new policy was not well-received by the unionists either. Its reception in the South of Ireland mirrored a wide spectrum of feeling, ranging from support for the pursuit of power-sharing by John Hume and the SDLP to sympathy and even active support for the IRA's defence of Catholic communities. The memory of Bloody Sunday and the sacking of the British Embassy in Dublin in its aftermath was still fresh. The extradition of IRA suspects to face trial in Britain or Northern Ireland was also a thorny problem prior to the Sunningdale conference. The Irish government argued that to do so would be contrary to international law and also inconsistent with the Irish constitution.

Great concern was also being expressed at Westminster at this time over the refusal of the Cosgrave government in Dublin to drop the case under the European Convention on Human Rights, taken by its predecessors, alleging inhuman and degrading treatment of detained persons by the security forces in Northern Ireland.[80] The run-up to

---

80   The European Court of Human Rights found that the British Government was guilty of inhuman and degrading treatment, but not torture.

the Sunningdale conference was hardly an opportune time therefore to meet the Unionist demand that had also arisen for the collateral amendment of Articles 2 and 3 of the Republic's constitution. These articles claimed jurisdiction over Northern Ireland. Nevertheless, in the concern and industry he displayed in connection with all these proposals, Garret Fitzgerald, Irish Minister for Foreign Affairs, matched the strivings of William Whitelaw for an acceptable devolution.

Fitzgerald proposed, for example, some 'common form of policing' for the island to fall within the remit of a Council of Ireland, together with trans-jurisdictional courts to try specified offences. It could conceivably have eased the problems of both extradition and border security. The British Government, however, preferred an improvement of existing extradition arrangements, together with the establishment on the border of 'four square' cooperation between the RUC and the Garda Siochana on the one hand, and between the British and Irish armies on the other. The Irish government pushed also for agreement on the proposed Council to be settled in advance of the formation of a new executive. And Fitzgerald tried very hard to get London to agree to Dublin acting as co-chair at Sunningdale. Otherwise the Irish delegation was at risk, it was felt, of appearing to obey an 'imperial summons'. In the light of subsequent events, Fitzgerald was exercising a surer touch than the commendable Whitelaw.

Brian Faulkner was initially opposed to power-sharing. He came to favour it eventually, despite a shrinking of support within his Unionist party. But when elections were held in June 1973, Unionism split, leaving Faulkner dependent in the new Assembly on remaining colleagues, the SDLP and Alliance parties. No other party or group was yet ready to support the notion of sharing power with political opponents. The three who were still talking remained divided on fundamental issues, however. These had emerged primarily as internment, the role of the police, rent or rate strikes and a possible Council of All-Ireland. Both the reduced Official Unionists and the

SDLP had to keep looking over their shoulders at the reaction of their supporters. But Mr Faulkner's problems were the more acute. He and his colleagues had to compete with Mr Craig and Mr Paisley, with former colleagues who now declared themselves the Unofficial Unionists and with the Orange Order.

After secret talks with the Irish Government at his home in Co. Down in September on the future role of the Council, he quickly formed a power-sharing Executive together with the SDLP and Alliance parties. The announcement of its members, notably the appointment of prominent SDLP members to serve as senior ministers under Faulkner as Chief Executive, produced violent scenes at the first meeting of the new Assembly in November. Faulkner and his supporters were assailed with shouts of 'Traitors out' by Ian Paisley and his newly emergent DUP supporters.

It was against that background that power-sharing representatives of the British and Irish governments met at Sunningdale in Berkshire in December to consider the Council of Ireland and agree the Northern Ireland Constitution Act, 1973. Ominously, those unionists who had broken away from Faulkner had formed a new alliance – the United Ulster Unionist Council (UUUC) – under Harry West, together with the supporters of Ian Paisley MP and William Craig MP. And Faulkner suffered a severe blow on 4 January 1974, when the Ulster Unionist Council rejected the new Council of Ireland. Faulkner had no choice now but to resign as Unionist leader. To compound his difficulties, Prime Minister Heath called a general election in February. Prompted by confrontation with Arthur Scargill and the miners, he had declared the issue was 'Who governs Britain'. The results in Northern Ireland were catastrophic for the newly installed institutions. The UUUC won 51% of the vote, and eleven out of the twelve seats at Westminster.

The incoming Labour Government in March, led by Harold Wilson, reassured the Executive of its support. But the Executive lost its mandate in mid-May, when a motion against Sunningdale was passed at Stormont. The Ulster Workers Council then swung into action. Though trade-union based, it was not a trade-union type organisation. It was actually a sectarian association of various paramilitary groups, some of which were held responsible for the murder of around 200 innocent Catholics and would go on to double that number.[81] But crucially, they controlled electricity. From 16 to 29 May the UWC, backed by the leaders of the UUUC, staged a coup against the institutions set up under the recent Act. The alleged objective of the stoppage of all essential services – electricity, gas, water, sewage and deliveries of food – was the defeat of the agreement at Sunningdale.

It was very soon evident in the turmoil, however, that those leaders were bent on the destruction of the new Constitution and all its works. Stan Orme, who was now Minister of State for Northern Ireland, pressured the SDLP to soften its stance on the Council of Ireland. Thirty-three persons died from bombings in Dublin and Monaghan, in which two of the three cars involved had been stolen in Northern Ireland. Unionist Executive members were in dread of sewage on the streets. By the end of the month Faulkner and the Unionist ministers resigned. Power-sharing was at an end. Direct Rule was restored. So was Protestant supremacy.

Was Sunningdale a 'Bridge too Far'? Not so according to Seamus Mallon in the light of his memorable comment on the Good Friday Agreement (GFA) in 1998, that it was 'Sunningdale for slow learners'. Or was it 'An Agreement too Soon', as suggested by Dr Sean Farren, a leading member of the SDLP, in a meritorious presentation in

---

81   Kevin Myers, distinguished Dublin journalist, born in England, later reflected on the calibre of such Protestant paramilitaries. 'In my life', he wrote in *The Irish Times*, (23 April 2003) 'I have not met such stupid brutes.' There were exceptions, he added, but for the most part, 'loyalist terrorists were witless thugs, for whom the killing of papists was a recreation and an end in itself.'

University College, Dublin, in 2006.[82] Judgment calls, of course, for an evaluation of the roles of the various protagonists. They included not only major stakeholders such as the rival governments in London and Dublin, the contending political parties and the concessions and compromises generated by the key issues of power-sharing and the proposed Council of Ireland, but also the armed groups. Such a judgment is a function of actual experience or involvement as well as standpoint or research. Although an outsider, mine derived in part from a longstanding personal, military and political experience in Northern Ireland. But it stemmed also from a close acquaintance with some of the major players handling the new policy. It was informed also by the access provided by my appointment as Navy Minister because of devolved responsibility for the Royal Marines' involvement in Northern Ireland.

That ministerial appointment gave me access to classified and intelligence reports at the MoD, from the intelligence and security organisation at Cheltenham, the Government Communications Headquarters (GCHQ), but in Belfast also, and at the many Army outposts which I visited and found most instructive. They provided a clearer picture of the relative strengths and activities of the IRA and the various paramilitary groups drawn into the UWC. They afforded glimpses of shadowy groups of highly armed men in country districts without sinister titles, but probably more effective as killing machines. Such groups contributed significantly to the vicious murders of many unarmed and innocent Catholics in their homes and on the streets. One such gang that came up repeatedly in briefings was the Glennane gang, a coalition of RUC and UDR men who joined forces with loyalist paramilitaries in the mid-Ulster area to carry out atrocities. The farm of James Mitchell, a reserve RUC policeman, was regarded as its hub. According to the 2007 Barron Report, the farm

---

82   Paper presented at the conference 'Assessing the Sunningdale Agreement', Institute for British-Irish Studies, University College, Dublin. 15 June 2006.

was involved in the Dublin-Monaghan bombings. Yet Mitchell was only convicted of keeping a major UVF arms dump as late as 1978. His punishment was a one-year sentence, suspended.

Susan McKay, who has delved deeply into the shrouded activities of the Glennane gang, has written that such treatment of Mitchell suggests collusion, not just in the security forces but in the prosecutions arising as well.[83] The conduct of such official services and their management was in sharp contrast at times with the official treatment accorded the IRA. Might a more balanced approach have led to less reliance on the IRA in Catholic areas? Would that have paved the way sooner for John Hume's brave attempts to lure the IRA into political and institutional channels, rather than encourage the growth of Sinn Féin?

Perhaps Sunningdale was too soon for British ministers to nurture such a development. But the stance of Irish ministers was also very much bound up with the here and now. And in the outcome it was distinctly more purposeful, considering the vulnerability of their coalition government. They clearly meant business. Nevertheless, the British ambassador in Dublin, Sir Arthur Galsworthy, called them 'timorous'.[84] Garret Fitzgerald's push for co-chairmanship at Sunningdale clearly indicated an awareness of the mutual responsibilities involved. For he had undoubtedly recognised that he would have to put Articles 2 and 3 of his country's constitution on the table. His proposal of some 'common form of policing' also sprang from a deeper appreciation of the institutional difficulties surrounding such hot problems as border security and extradition. But the British ambassador merely viewed such proposals as a reflection of the 'shallowness of Irish thinking'. He sneeringly described the co-chairmanship proposal as 'a bee ... buzzing in Dr Fitzgerald's bonnet,

---

83   *Irish Times*. 13 June 2008. See her book *Bear in Mind These Dead*. Faber & Faber.

84   See the British state papers for 1973 at the National Archives in Kew, London.

very excitedly, as his always do'.[85] Unhappily, the demeaning references to Fitzgerald would have been consigned to the official record and reappeared in the briefing material prepared for Margaret Thatcher prior to her fateful meeting with him ten years later. Perhaps they explain the contemptuous manner of her rejection of his proposals? Whereas Fitzgerald's approach throughout, including his wish for the proposed Council to be settled in advance of the formation of the Executive, hardly justified such a dismissal.

As for compromises, it was inevitable that the Unionists would be very sensitive of concessions. Given their historic supremacy and discrimination against Catholics, they had much more to give. Was that why support for Brian Faulkner among his Unionist colleagues dwindled so dramatically and caused some to abandon him? Where was the willingness to give and take when the SDLP actually stood back from the proposed Council? Their key demands of the maintenance of the Union and consent to change were secure and altogether more generous than the stark option, for example, that Charles De Gaulle gave to the French settlers domiciled in Algeria since the invasion of 1830. They were certainly more flexible than the economic necessity imposed on my father when he left his beloved Co. Mayo, however much he came to value his new-found Anglo-Irish status in Britain. Or did the prospect of a peaceful, tolerant and inclusive society lose its appeal for the unionists generally, if it brought them closer to such people as my father had left behind in Co. Mayo? Yet London and Dublin had just signed on to the growing inclusiveness of the European Community. Could the unionists indicate, as a matter of fact, any feature of public life in the South of Ireland as anomalous or as threatening to civil and religious liberty as the dominant political

---

85   By this time fellow foreign ministers in the European Community were quite enchanted with Fitzgerald.

roles of the Rev. Paisley, Rev. Bradford, Rev. Beattie and the Rev. Smyth in the North of Ireland?[86]

Where were the moderate Protestants, then, during the February 1974 elections? Why did identifiable groups of Protestant professional people, such as doctors, nurses, industrialists and even the clergy, urge negotiations later with the UWC? They must have known that it was not normal industrial action they were supporting. They must have realised that it was an act of insurrection they were endorsing and therefore illegal. What did they want? There was plainly a lack of moderate Protestants and trade unionists prepared to step up to the line on the key issue, which John Hume summed up quite bluntly: 'Protestants do not want to share power with Catholics.' Dr Farren, in his searching and comprehensive Paper reveals that in a personal letter in 1976, Brian Faulkner wrote, 'The real objective was the sharing of power. The Council of Ireland was only a red herring.'

Perhaps social conditioning was still too keenly felt for such a unifying step. From a Presbyterian standpoint, Dr John Dunlop reveals in his book the 'frightening intensity' of some Protestant hostility to Catholicism, which 'goes deeper than rationality and cannot be separated from the political issues and the associated violence' in Northern Ireland.[87] Susan McKay discloses that she did not set out to write a damning testament of Orangeism in her insightful book. Yet the record of her conversations at kitchen tables, in church halls and

---

86   Such figures found on arrival at Westminster that their concern for moral and ethical issues generally was always supported by Kevin McNamara and myself. And I was thanked personally by some Ulster MPs for my leading role in the fight to 'Keep Sundays Special'. I even opposed Sunday racing, though I was vice-chairman of the All-party Racing & Thoroughbred Industries group.

87   *A Precarious Belonging: Presbyterians and the conflict in Northern Ireland.* The Black-staff Press. 1995.

on marches served to reinforce the image of a paranoid, intransigent and deeply unlovable people.[88]

The UWC and its supporters had brought off a spectacular coup. But it was an illegal act. Yet the RUC arrested none of the law-breakers. Indeed they openly fraternised and cooperated, re-routing traffic away from their barricades. Former ministers Paddy Devlin and Ivan Cooper alleged that they actually set them up for an ambush on the main Belfast-Dublin road near Dromore, Co. Down.

The British Army also kept a low profile and stayed in the background for many days. Soldiers did not raid any homes in Protestant districts, nor did they arrest or detain any of the so-called strikers and law-breakers. I was told that at Milltown, near Belfast, they refused to come to the assistance of some Catholic families who were being intimidated. After the Army had taken control of petrol supplies they actually watched, it was reported, as UWC members gave out petrol at the notorious filling station on Tate's Avenue, Belfast. The Army maintained a low profile only briefly, however, for it soon became active in Catholic neighbourhoods on and around the Falls Road and in Anderstown in West Belfast.

Merlyn Rees was now Secretary of State for Northern Ireland. Roy Mason, who had been appointed Secretary of State for Defence, would succeed him in 1976. I was close to both. I had been a fellow student at the LSE with Rees, and I had just been appointed parliamentary private secretary (PPS) to Mason. There wasn't a more decent person in the House of Commons than Rees, but he had little grasp of Irish affairs. His PPS, Dr Edmund Marshall MP, was going around telling colleagues – in an echo of Captain Long – that the problem in Northern Ireland was essentially one of 'gangsterism'. Rees was not equipped for the problems that awaited him, even though he had been shadowing Whitelaw as Opposition spokesman and received therefore a multitude of briefings. Neither was Mason,

---

88   *Northern Protestants: An Unsettled People.* Blackstaff Press. 2000.

despite an impressive ministerial record hitherto. I was very close to both, and felt deeply for them. I was well aware from my wartime combat situations of the severe demands of crisis management and individual reactions. Brian Faulkner was unimpressed by the reaction of Rees.[89] Garret Fitzgerald went further in his memoirs, alleging that the British administration 'spectacularly failed to tackle the extreme loyalists'. Both complained that Rees refused to talk to strikers or to move decisively against them, and dithered about orders to the security forces. Mason was privately contemptuous of Rees's handling of the crisis and refused invitations afterwards to enter into joint discussion in public.

I reminded both that if they were firm on power-sharing as the only prospect for reform and peace – quite apart from the insurrection against a constitutional Act – then they had a mandate to take on the rebellious UWC. Their stock reply was fear of the 'Loyalist backlash', explaining that the groups comprising the UWC had 100,000 guns and many more unlicensed. I pondered on the source and quality of such intelligence, given the different picture presented in 1972 by the GOC and the Chief Constable.[90]

When Roy Mason invited me in 1974 to become his PPS, I agreed only after a week of pressure. Ordinarily, I was pleased to work with him. I had demonstrated that during our successful working relationship within the Yorkshire group of Labour MPs. But I was anxious to retain so far as possible a balanced view on Northern Ireland and therefore remain detached, whereas Mason was bound to be heavily committed. My first task, on his request, was to compile

---

89   He 'just seemed to have gone into a flap', he wrote, adding that 'Rees's information appeared to be largely inaccurate and he kept producing maps and pointing out roads claimed to be free of obstruction but which I knew to be blocked.'

90   Yet as late as May 2005, during the peace process, the number of such weapons, including shotguns, held on license by loyalists was reported to be up to 144,554. License holders usually offered 'vermin control and clay pigeon shooting' as the reasons.

a glossary of acronyms relating to Northern Ireland, though I was well aware that he had been officially briefed. He asked me to brief him also on political parties north and south. He was familiar with the record of the SDLP, for whose leaders he never demonstrated any warmth. But he was anxious to meet Gerry Fitt, who refused to meet him, however. When I pressed Fitt, he told me that he regarded Mason's appointment 'as a disaster', because, as he put it, he is a 'little John Bull'. That is probably the key to an understanding of Mason's conduct in Northern Ireland. He was intensely patriotic and supportive of the armed services. His dearest wish in wartime was to serve with the Royal Air Force, which was ruled out by his coal-mining occupation.[91]

Furthermore, Mason was now Defence Secretary at a critical time in the Cold War. He had to balance scarce security resources for Ulster against assigned force obligations within the Western alliance. That was a basic problem also for General Tuzo, as he had reminded me in 1972. But at the same time Mason had to fulfil a Labour party conference decision to cut defence spending. Soon he was engaged in Cabinet in a desperate fight to save the Sea-Harrier, which would prove vital in the approaching battle for the Falklands. He was heavily burdened, under severe pressure around the Cabinet table on defence spending and unsure of support on the consequences for security in Northern Ireland.

The different standards Labour continued to apply to Northern Ireland were brought home sharply also to Jock Stallard and myself early in the life of the Labour Government in 1974, when, as we saw it, we tried to help the new Home Secretary, Roy Jenkins. In March 1973, car bombs went off outside the Old Bailey in London. Among those arrested were Dolores and Marion Price. They were sentenced to twenty-five years' imprisonment, which they wished to serve in

---

91   I attended the British Tattoo in Berlin with him at that time and his enthusiasm and admiration for the troops matched that of the GOC, who sat alongside.

Northern Ireland. They were soon on hunger strike and being force-fed. Stallard and I visited them in Brixton Prison. We were anxious to avoid a repeat of the famous hunger strike by the Lord Mayor of Cork, Terence McSwiney, also in Brixton Prison in 1921. We asked the sisters to call off their protest, and give a new Home Secretary time to handle the issue in view of its historic sensitivity. They refused, insisting that they were not criminals: they were 'not comparable to Myra Hindley, they were political prisoners', they said. 'Death would be preferable to force-feeding.'[92] I reported to Jenkins, and stressed the danger of political escalation if the sisters remained on hunger strike in Brixton of all places. He did not appear interested, displaying yet again – it seemed to me – Labour's preference for irresolute politics on Ireland, and the risks of ambiguity. He did not even wish to meet us. For all his eminence as a historian, Jenkins was even unmoved by my warning of the earlier Irish hunger strike at Brixton, even though that event was still being commemorated annually in London.

Stallard expressed the same frustration about Jenkins as he did about the girls themselves. 'Why did we bother?' he asked. Because, I pointed out, whatever the conflicting viewpoints at the Home Office and in Brixton, the girls see themselves at war and therefore prisoners-of-war. Whatever the apparent indifference of Jenkins and the scarcely disguised hostility of some parliamentary colleagues, we must continue to engage in conflict resolution. We have a plain duty to do so, whatever the risks we run in our constituencies and in Parliament. But we are in good company, I said, for we have like-minded colleagues, however small in number, and must remain positive and constructive.

I reminded Mason on his appointment as secretary of state in 1976, as I had reminded him earlier, of the formidable history of Irish republicanism, its historic mission, its traditional factions and the

---

92   I noticed that Marion took the *Guardian* newspaper daily, and Dolores *The Irish News*, 'to read the deaths', she explained.

political as well as the security hazards he would encounter. I urged him to encourage political movement. He was not interested. Just as he had been scornful of the attempts of Merlyn Rees, he now viewed John Hume in the same light. He was intent on 'smashing the IRA', coupled with an earnest endeavour to tackle discrimination against Catholics, it needed to be said. Unhappily, his anxiety to alleviate unemployment in Catholic areas influenced him no doubt into his ill-fated venture into the declining motor industry.

By the 1950s the UK was the second-largest manufacturer of cars in the world (after the US) and the largest exporter. Subsequently, however, the UK car industry experienced considerably lower growth than competitor nations such as France, Germany, and Japan. Many British car marques were passing into the ownership of foreign companies. By the 1970s productivity and industrial relations were giving cause for grave concern. In 1973–74 the giant BLMC faced collapse. That was when my select committee on Trade and Industry decided to delve into every corner of the industry. After close scrutiny we rejected the proposed Ryder plan for recovery. No-one could say they had not been warned. Yet an even more questionable prospectus for a motor plant was promoted by Mason at a packed press conference in Belfast in August, 1978. It was to produce the 'dream' car of John Delorean. Despite my recent in-depth and extensive inquiries into Britain's motor industry, I was not even consulted. Four years and £84m later, Delorean was exposed as a fraud and crook and went to prison. The Dublin government had earlier seen through his web of myth, deception, spin and disinformation and turned him down. Again I pondered on the quality of administration available first to Rees and now to Mason in the Northern Ireland office in London and at Hillsborough in Belfast.

Yet conditions did improve otherwise during Mason's term of office, with fewer troops visible, partly because there were fewer border attacks. The police now controlled security – similar to the practice encountered by my group's visit to the border areas south of the border in 1976. Random attacks, however, still reflected a greater daring by loyalist gunmen and bombers to venture further afield than their republican counterparts. Which pointed to the suspicion at least, I reminded him, of passive if not active support from the Army and the Police. Roy waived aside such a suggestion, as he did many other complaints that were now coming the way of both of us. In particular he rejected complaints about the ill-treatment of prisoners interrogated at the Castlereagh holding centre, despite my own reminders of the police brutality I had personally experienced and officially logged in Belfast in wartime. However, he was obliged to act promptly on the Bennett report on police interrogation procedure released just before he left office.

Bennett was a reminder that after ten years of a mini-civil war during which 2,000 people had been killed, more than 20,000 injured and millions of pounds of damage done, Northern Ireland was no nearer a solution to its problems than it was when the civil rights movement began. Those all too few MPs who had sought a constitutional settlement from the beginning were now strengthened in their belief that the situation could only be tackled by an ending of the political stalemate. There was no evidence of moderate Protestant opinion, however. Protestants were still held to be loyal, whilst Catholics were generally regarded as disloyal. The divisions between the two communities had deepened, and after the UWC insurrection over Sunningdale, the IRA was inevitably still in business.

Roy Mason was hampered in addressing that central problem by his isolation inside a compound. He and his ministers and their closest advisors commuted between RAF Northolt to the west of London and Belfast. They moved only outside the compound when surrounded by a security screen that made any casual or discrete contacts impossible. They hosted many meetings with dignitaries, businessmen and trade unionists, as well as politicians and journalists. They would only go out for the most part to attend political, mainly unionist – though not discriminatory – gatherings. Although Lord

Melchett and Don Concannon MP in their ministerial capacities did try hard to break through such barriers to reach ordinary people. But my suggestion to Mason that he try fishing, for which he had a passion, in Co. Fermanagh, as a preliminary to venturing a little further south, to the Moy river, was greeted with horror. We did manage to break loose one evening when I was on an overnight stay at Hillsborough and visit a jazz club in the city of Belfast. But that was an isolated event. Inevitably, Mason acquired the reputation of a unionist, and was much lauded in Loyalist circles. He was much exercised by the prospect of 'someone', as he put it 'called O Fiaich becoming Catholic Primate' and asked me for a brief.[93] But he was not anti-Catholic, and we were always together on ethical issues at Westminster.

Following authorisation of public financial support for Chrysler, my select committee came under pressure in 1975 to investigate its activities in Iran. James Callaghan, as Foreign Secretary, warned me off. He told me that he had enough problems in that area, without my committee getting involved. When I resisted, he went further, pointing out that my first duty was to the Labour government and to the Labour party that had combined to put me into parliament in the first place, and not to my committee. Harold Wilson, as Prime Minister, then sent for me, promptly understood my position as chairman of an all-party select committee, and accepted my assurance that I would do my best. Indeed, my committee members were most helpful ultimately. But Jim still remained angered, which led to a stand-up row later in the dining room of the House of Commons. Roy Mason was so concerned by now, given the need for Jim's support in Cabinet, that he asked me to have a placatory word later on in the division lobby. Totally unexpected, Jim was to have a different word with me shortly afterwards, when he spoke to me on Skynet whilst I was in the Far East accompanying Mason on visits to Hong Kong and South Korea.

---

93   There was no need to worry, I told him, unlike others who were worried, I gathered – and in London.

Appendix 1

FROM: Gusty Spence
Long Kesh Prison
N. Ireland.

2/2/74

Dear Mr Duffy,

Many thanks for your kind letter. We are grateful to you for raising the many and varied questions for us with the Secretary of State, Mr Frances Pym, and results have been quick in coming.

I had a meeting with the Camp Governor, Mr Truesdale, and very soon we shall have our first Camp Council meeting with official blessing. The issue of TV sets is almost resolved and we have been promised our quota within the week. Mr Truesdale has undertaken to see each spokesman at least once a month at Compound level to expedite matters on which the Assistant Governors have no powers. We have had no results as yet on the Camp parcel service but I have no doubt that they too shall improve soon. The inter compound land contact between the various organisations still seems a very thorny question and the official attitude still appears to be that this will not take place. However, with a maximum of goodwill I am confident that commonsense will prevail and it shall be put into practice.

Your deputation, above all deputations, has proved the most successful in relation to achievement and we congratulate each of you in the presentation of our various points. After so many months of hard slogging to move Long Kesh on the slightest of grievances, your success is all the more astonishing

I hope that you took back with you a deeper understanding of the Loyalists confined in this camp as we unquestionably have reappraised our opinions concerning the motives and sincerity of you as visiting members of the Labour party. You certainly got our vote for your obvious concern with conditions in the camp, interest in our opinions on various matters and speedy manner in stirring Long Kesh to movement.

Thank you on behalf of all the men.

Sincerely,
(Signed)
Gusty Spence

Chapter Eight

Navy Minister

I accompanied Roy Mason to the Far East shortly afterwards on a programme that included visits to Hong Kong and South Korea. During tea with the Governor of Hong Kong, his secretary entered to say that the Prime Minister, who by now was James Callaghan, would be coming through at 8pm on Skynet and wished to speak to me. Speculation about a possible appointment was rife. Roy warned me to accept whatever Jim Callaghan proposed and not to fall out with him again. It was a much friendlier Jim who later invited me to 'follow him as Minister for the Navy' in the Ministry of Defence (MoD). He mentioned also a number of notable figures who had similarly 'started their ministerial careers as Navy Minister'.

Jim advised me to 'get on top of the admirals' or they would dominate me and then I would be no use to him. They had 'awesome responsibilities' he explained, and he had to 'have the best'. I was able, after taking up my appointment, to reassure him not only of the quality of the membership of the Board of Admiralty but of the flag officers I had met elsewhere.

I had met the First Sea Lord, Admiral Sir Edward Ashmore, in the course of my duties as PPS before arriving at the MoD in March 1976. I was very much attuned to his thinking and he now became an admirable guide and mentor. I had not met the Vice Chief of the Naval Staff (VCNS), Admiral Sir Raymond Lygo. But with his background in naval aviation, along with an earlier command of *HMS Ark Royal,* I felt an immediate rapport. His briefing and advice in dangerous times were most instructive. As was the recent experience of his successor, Admiral Sir Andrew Morton, who had successfully commanded an important global task group deployment. I was looking forward also to meeting Admiral Sir Peter White, Chief of

Fleet Support (CFS), for our paths had crossed repeatedly in wartime. He was the first supply officer to become a member of the Admiralty Board.[94] Whilst PPS I had met his successor, Admiral Sir James Eberle, when he was Flag Officer Sea Training (FOST) at Portland. Our chief worry when he joined the Board was the poor productivity and through-put of ships at Devonport Dockyard. Any improvement became an uphill struggle, despite warnings about its future to the trade unions, who remained entangled in their demarcation disputes.[95] The chief concern of Admiral Sir Richard Clayton, Controller of the Navy, was the inadequacies of the Type 42 destroyers, largely resulting from Treasury constraints. Those inadequacies were unhappily borne out in the Falklands conflict. Only one MP, Robert Rhodes James, was alive to their shortcomings and often reminded me of them. I became deeply interested from the outset in the personnel responsibilities of the Second Sea Lord, Admiral Sir David Williams and his successor, Admiral Sir Gordon Tait.

I was sorry to miss Vice Admiral Sir Louis Le Bailly, whose final appointment as Director-General of Intelligence, 1972–75, I learned, he performed with distinction. He was also a distinguished naval engineer and made an immense contribution to remedy the technical shortcomings of the Fleet which had been revealed during WWII. The improvement in the mobility and operational capacities of ships was critical to their success in the Falklands War. I did benefit from his continuing forward-looking approach to strategic matters in defence

---

94   As well as a dramatic and action-packed career in WWII, Admiral White was central to the rationalisation of the Navy's shore assets globally in the 1960s and 1970s.

95   During the general election of 1983, when back in opposition, I spent a day in the dockyard as shadow defence minister. After my final meeting with the shop stewards committee the chairman called for a vote of thanks. He was unable to find anyone present prepared to either propose or second the motion. 'We know Mr Duffy' was one comment I distinctly recall. The fundamental changes of which I had warned, did come about eventually, however.

affairs. I became aware also at that time that he was serving in the cruiser *HMS Naiad* when I joined her briefly late in 1940 for my Fleet Selection Board.

As a former First Sea Lord and Chief of the Defence Staff, Lord Mountbatten was an ever-ready, but not always welcome presence in naval circles – until I banned him. I was present on a Friday evening in Amport House in Hampshire, in my early days as Minister, for the annual dinner of Anglican Naval Chaplains, when Lord Mountbatten made the address. He made a clumsy attempt at bawdy humour, exclusively at the expense of Catholic chaplains, mostly in the Far East. That gave me less offence than his apparent disregard of the presence of one female, the WRNS officer daughter of the Chaplain of the Fleet, Archdeacon Basil O'Farrall. When the top table diners filed out for coffee, I remained. I then left by a patio door at the rear. It was only intended as a gentle protest. I was not going to proceed otherwise. But despite my assurances, the Chaplain of the Fleet, who had joined me almost immediately, remained concerned. As an indication of the speed with which such information was disseminated in the MoD the first utterance of Roy Mason, as Secretary of State, after we were seated on our usual London-bound train from Yorkshire on the following Monday morning, was 'quite right'. And at an early meeting after arrival in the office, Edward Ashmore was equally terse. 'He was definitely off-side,' he said, and we agreed that Mountbatten should no longer be permitted to address naval personnel. He clearly held it against me and distanced himself thereafter.

During the following Spring, together with Sir Peter Whitely, Commandant-General Royal Marines (CGRM), I battled successfully to persuade the Cabinet to hold on to 41 RM Commando. Lord Mountbatten had attended its decommissioning in Malta. So he was astonished when Jim Callaghan broke the news of its reprieve at the reception in the Royal Yacht in Portsmouth on the eve of the Queen's Silver Jubilee review of the Fleet. Mountbatten searched immediately to thank me. In Portsmouth Town Hall the next day, during the Queen's official visit – following which it was intended that I should make the public announcement – he told my mother that I 'was such a good chap'. She was quite bemused, not knowing what it was all about.

Prime Minister Callaghan continued to take a close interest in naval matters. My daily intelligence brief on ships' movements was available to him first, of course, and he would often follow up an item with me later.[96] In contrast, he would sometimes query matters closer to home and catch me out. He once enquired as to the number of offenders held in the Naval Detention Quarters in Portsmouth, particularly on the first floor where the more serious offenders were confined. Given his naval family background, he was genuinely interested and well briefed. He would sometimes raise such naval domesticities with me in the dining room of the House of Commons – unless I had spotted him first and taken avoiding action. He was very concerned about proposed defence spending cuts and instructed me to monitor their impact on the Fleet.

The Labour party Manifesto at the October 1974 election had called for the 'widest ranging defence review' to bring our contribution 'into line with that carried by our main European allies'. The specific cuts proposed for the Navy were of the order of 15%, and upwards, in the planned number of vessels. Frank Allaun and other members of Labour's National Executive Committee (NEC) relentlessly pursued such defence cuts – irrespective of the fluctuating demands of the Cold War.[97] Illogically, they clamoured simultaneously for the

---

96   Notably with regard to the unexpected access of Soviet submarines to the Atlantic, and a growing anxiety about our systems and their security, generally.

97   To me, the all too familiar phrasing and persistent campaigning for defence cuts pointed to Frank Allaun MP as the source. His ploy of posing an average NATO contribution for our European allies had no regard for the structure, performance and force levels of the Alliance. It overlooked the influence of geography in determining the specialist contributions of some members and the assigned roles of others. It ignored the UK's special position, second only to that of the US, and carrying therefore corresponding senior appointments as well as sharing special missions.

abandonment of nuclear armaments which, by throwing greater reliance on more expensive conventional arms, would unavoidably lead to greater defence costs and expenditure. Repeated pleas to them to meet and clarify such issues were always ignored. They also bypassed the parliamentary party's back-bench defence committee.[98]

Labour's electoral commitment – which was not a burning public issue in 1974 anyway – was followed by a Defence White Paper in March 1975, confirming wide-ranging cuts in inherited forward estimates over a ten-year period. But when the Chancellor, Denis Healey, came to Cabinet in November 1975 for agreement he was already burdened with the recent loan from the International Monetary Fund (IMF) and was driven to seek additional cuts. Yet the earlier review had indicated how small was the margin for further cuts. Most of the non-NATO commitments, as I was well aware, had already gone; some of the NATO proposals – reinforcement of the Northern and Southern flanks, for example – went with the White Paper. There were real fears that if the Treasury were to insist on further savings then commitments as well as equipment programmes would have to go. The reaction in defence circles, and on the part of the press, was sharp. That was Jim Callaghan's legacy on becoming Prime Minister in 1976 and, insofar as it affected the Navy, what awaited my arrival at the MoD.

The Government could hardly touch the strategic deterrent: amortised, the cost was sharply reduced. Neither could it abandon the security of the UK and its immediate approaches. That left the Central Region and the Eastern Atlantic. It was not thought feasible to cut the British Army on the Rhine because of its central importance to NATO. Supported by Jim Callaghan, as Foreign Secretary, and

---

98   Later, in my shadow defence capacity, attendance at the NECs defence group was still a revelation. A bored Jo Richardson MP occupied the chair and conducted proceedings at such a juvenile level as to actually allow discussion of a proposal – by a co-opted person, of course – that the 'Royal Navy should be reduced to coastal forces'.

Merlyn Rees as Northern Ireland Secretary, Roy Mason had been quick to warn cabinet colleagues of what else was at stake. Amid a bitter row over priorities he pointed out that if defence spending was slashed indiscriminately Britain would not only be unable to fulfil its commitments to NATO, but that tens of thousands of jobs would also be lost in the aerospace and shipbuilding industries. That fairly illustrates how ill-thought out was Labour's recent electoral commitment on defence and the typically negative role of certain members of its NEC, who remained unmoved.

Roy Mason's other pressing concern was the Eastern Atlantic and the urgent need of naval air cover. He was afraid that among the first victims of the cuts would be the Harrier jump jets. I had become aware as his PPS that Russian 'Bear' long-range reconnaissance aircraft were regularly tripping the reflexes of our defences. They could loiter high over our task forces in the Atlantic and transmit information to Soviet ships and missiles over the horizon. Hence the need of the Sea Harriers. I had accompanied Roy and his Private Secretary, John Maine, to an impressive demonstration at Dunsford, Surrey. It was arranged by Captain Alan Leahy RN, a much experienced and admired member of the Fleet Air Arm. When asked afterwards for my impressions, in the light of my own acquaintance with naval aircraft in wartime, my single word was 'miraculous'.

Together with the First Sea Lord (1SL), and in the most unfavourable circumstances, Roy Mason presented the case for the Sea Harrier to Cabinet. In the teeth of opposition led by the Chancellor and to the point of threatened resignation by Roy, the fight was won. Otherwise the Navy's remarkably successful deployment to the Falklands in 1982 would not have succeeded.

This episode marked a turning point in a long decline in the Fleet Air Arm. For the Sea Harrier would be deployed from a new class of vessel quaintly named 'through-deck cruisers'. This was done to avoid any suspicion that the Navy was trying to get round the decision taken by Denis Healey in 1967, when Defence Secretary, to do away with aircraft carriers. It was accepted at the time, though always seriously in question, that the Royal Air Force and its access to land air bases would continue to provide the kind of cover the Navy had been used to, both in range and availability. Now it was recognised that a new class of small carriers, the 'Invincible' class, was needed to provide maritime air cover in the mid-Atlantic. They would carry the Sea Harrier aircraft and Sea King helicopters; the latter equipped with sonars which they could lower into the water to detect submarines. The Invincible class – a sister ship had been authorised and a third planned – would be the Navy's backbone in the 1980s.[99] Like other important carrier developments introduced by the U.K. since WWII – mirror landing systems, angled decks, steam catapults – it incorporated yet another striking change in air-at-sea techniques. It had a 'ski-jump' ramp on the bow to facilitate Harrier take-offs.

My first questions to 1SL on arrival were how well equipped was the Navy after past defence cuts and how would it operate after the further threatened cuts.[100] Did the historic preamble to the 1652 Articles of War conferring pre-eminence on the Royal Navy – 'It is upon the Navy under the good Providence of God, that the health, prosperity, and safety of this nation does chiefly depend' – still stand? The Navy's WWII strength of 790,000 men and women had inevitably shrunk, I was informed, and now numbered 75,000, including 8,000 Royal Marines. Only two carriers, *Ark Royal and Hermes,* remained in service and would soon be phased out. The rest of the Fleet consisted of just nine nuclear and nineteen conventional

---

99   Whatever its size, the Invincible class of carrier, for example, signalled new air-to-sea techniques, and was pointing the way to future sea power. Significantly, the Americans were making an advanced Harrier under special license.

100   Before I left the Navy in 1946, after six years' wartime service, it was a formidable force with fourteen battleships, fifty-two aircraft carriers, sixty-two cruisers, 259 destroyers, 131 submarines and 9,000 smaller vessels.

submarines, two cruisers, two amphibious ships, sixty-nine destroyers and other escort ships and about a hundred smaller vessels. In support of the Fleet were some forty Royal Fleet Auxiliary (RFA) tankers and store ships, all manned by civilians. The naval dockyards at Chatham[101], Devonport and Rosyth were in process of modernisation. A covered-in frigate re-fitting complex was nearing completion at Devonport. Britain also had four Polaris ballistic nuclear submarines, with enormous destructive powers.[102] So numbers did not convey a true picture. Nevertheless, it was clear that the Navy was not what it used to be. And to 'try and squeeze it much more would cost bone and muscle', said 1SL. Matters had now been reduced to such a state that ships' commanders had become careful of cruising speeds, for example, to conserve fuel. Yet they were still required to keep sea-lines open and protect the UK merchant fleet which, after Japan, was then the second largest in the world.[103]

The Navy's roles and objectives were now limited, but still vital. Its principal function, broadly, 1SL explained, was to operate within the NATO alliance (to which it contributed some eighty per cent of the maritime strength in the Eastern Atlantic) and provide defence for trade in key areas. Its prime contributions, apart from the Polaris

---

101   Where Nelson's flagship *Victory* was built, but the dockyard was soon to be decommissioned.

102   Between 1955 and mid-1969 Britain's strategic nuclear weapons were carried by the so-called V-bombers. As doubts grew about their survivability against improving Soviet air-defence systems, a sea-based strategic nuclear deterrent became an attractive alternative. At Nassau, Bahamas, at a meeting between Prime Minister Harold Macmillan and President John Kennedy in 1962, it was agreed that America would transfer Polaris missiles to Britain. Thus Britain's nuclear deterrent was transferred from the RAF to the Navy.

103   We are a trading nation and still depend very much on countries overseas both for raw materials and for markets for our exports, I was reminded. Historically, use of the sea has always been vulnerable to military action or the threat to our trade routes or security.

deterrent, covered mine clearance to keep open our harbours for trade and nuclear submarines, an amphibious force for landing in Northern Norway, protection of fisheries, oil and gas rigs[104] and, above all, the capability to keep the Eastern Atlantic and the channel ports open until the American Fleet could reinforce us. Viewed in both a domestic and international context, the tasks and responsibilities of the Navy were far beyond the comprehension of Labour's NEC.

With the many demands now being made on fewer ships and men, was the Navy fast reaching the stage, I asked 1SL, where it would not be able to maintain the very important biennial global task group deployment[105] or even fulfil all its various NATO commitments? He remained confident about the Navy's size and ability to carry out its modern role. He did admit, however, to deepening anxieties about manpower retention, amphibiosity, the Sea King helicopter replacement, mine countermeasures and possible inadequacies in the eight Type 42 missile destroyers – of which the first two, *Sheffield* and *Birmingham,* were already in service – compared with the superior armament of the latest Russian *Krivak* missile destroyers. We both lamented the phasing out of the 43,000 ton fleet carrier *Ark Royal.* For we were painfully aware that we were losing a mobile airfield capable of covering 600 miles in 24 hours, together with its fixed-wing supersonic Phantom and subsonic Buccaneer aircraft. I had

---

104   Along with CGRM I was instrumental in setting up the first quick reaction force of Royal Marines for their protection in the North Sea.

105   I once joined such a task group in the Eastern Mediterranean. Though ostensibly observing NATO exercises, my mission was to secure access to the Suez Canal of a nuclear-powered attack submarine that was in covert company. Inevitably, that entailed meetings with such Egyptian authorities as the naval C-in-C Alexandria, the chairman of the Suez Canal Company and the War Minister (*sic*) in Cairo. Whilst the talks were progressing, I received a call from Prime Minister Callaghan, who graciously asked if I could 'spare the submarine'. It was that Swiftsure class vessel that was then switched to the South Atlantic and deterred an earlier threatened invasion of the Falklands.

visited her with Mason in September1974 for a demonstration during night exercises. I had been left deeply impressed. She had figured in the sophisticated television production *Sailor* which became a smash hit and put the 'Ark' into millions of homes. She would be decommissioned at a time, moreover, when the Russians were building their own *Kiev*-class carrier, with its fixed-wing aircraft.

On the other hand, 1SL pointed out that with its 150 ships the Navy was still, after the United States and the Soviet Union, the third biggest in the world. But given that the Soviets had twice the number of warships at sea as NATO and their rate of growth, especially in nuclear-powered submarines, was twice NATO's, I was obliged to ask if the NATO navies could hold them in the Eastern Atlantic until the Americans arrived. He admitted that the margins were tightening. Other Board members were more pessimistic, I gathered. We were well aware that in their last big exercise during the previous year the Russians had deployed 200 ships worldwide. The Russian Fleet of 848 warships and smaller fast attack craft was now seen by some to be as modern as our NATO total of 668 warships (including the US fleet). The Warsaw Pact countries and the Soviet Union in particular had now achieved force levels far larger than would be needed for defensive purposes. Their military capability was rapidly increasing both in numbers and quality.

Most remarkable was the development of the Soviet Navy and its closure of the technology gap. It could not be justified against the threat of attack from the West. If the balance of maritime power were allowed to shift so far in favour of the Warsaw Pact that it had the evident ability, in a period of tension, to isolate Europe by sea, the effect would be profound. NATO's maritime forces therefore had to be equipped and organised to counter all forms of Soviet naval action at any level. The Russians were now commissioning, for example, deeper-diving and quieter submarines. The US provided the largest maritime contribution to NATO. Britain, by virtue of her geography and expertise, also played a major part. Among the countermeasures undertaken by the Royal

Navy was a new and powerful wireless station at Crimond, north of Aberdeen, which I officially opened in July 1978.

I was struck during my early visits to ships at sea by the immense changes wrought since I left the Navy in 1946. Bristling with modern technology, advanced weapon systems, sonars, radar and other communication links, the first impression was of ships that were now part of the space age. Nevertheless, Edward Ashmore and I thought that a 'Way Ahead' conference at Whale Island, Portsmouth, would be timely. It was agreed by the Admiralty Board at that conference that the continuing modernisation of electronic equipment, weaponry and the use of helicopters and aircraft should be prioritised to offset the growing disparity in force levels.

The special relationship in intelligence, maritime capabilities and missions made for close ties between the navies of the US and the UK. The onus in the most hazardous and successful missions fell directly on the Royal Navy. It called for regular visits to the headquarters in Norfolk, Virginia, of Admiral Ike Kidd, Supreme Allied Commander Atlantic, with whom I developed close ties.

Sometimes I would be accompanied by Admiral Sir Henry Leach, Commander-in-Chief Fleet, based at Northwood. As midshipmen, both lost their fathers following the Pearl Harbour attack. Ike Kidd's father died on the bridge of his flagship *USS Arizona*. Henry Leach's father went down shortly afterwards off Singapore in the flagship of Operation Z, *Prince of Wales,* along with my first ship *Repulse.* Admiral Kidd and Admiral Leach were very concerned about the patrol patterns of Soviet ballistic-nuclear submarines (SSBNs) and the rate of growth of their hunter-attack submarines (SSNs). As the Cold War intensified, Soviet submarines grew into the largest such force in the world – and became quieter. Detecting and tracking them globally became an acute problem. It was the quick-essential analogue of 'finding a needle in a haystack'.

The Bell Laboratories of AT&T in the US had been foremost since WWII in research in undersea surveillance and the detection and tracking of submarines. The programme was named SOSUS or Sound Surveillance System. Those pioneers realised that low-frequency sound impulses could travel vast distances under water due to the existence of a deep sound channel. In a classic demonstration, a 200-pound charge of TNT was detonated by a research vessel off the west coast of Australia. The sound impulses were picked up by hydrophones off Bermuda, having travelled 11,000 nautical miles on a great circle southern path around South Africa. About the same time it was discovered that submarines radiate distinctive sound signals associated with their propulsion systems as well as on-board pumps and machinery. Every class of submarine releases a unique signature – a kind of maritime fingerprint. Bell Laboratories in New Jersey experimented with a sound spectrograph that led to collaboration between the US Navy and the Royal Navy at the Bahamas in *HMS Alert*. Thanks to fibre-optic technology, an underwater system was designed to distinguish submarine sounds and identify the class of submarine. It straddled the Atlantic Ocean bed from South Wales to the Carolinas, and also covered the Greenland–Iceland–UK gap.

At the invitation of Ike Kidd I listened to French SSBNs leaving port on patrol. Yet, despite SOSUS, air and naval patrols that started at the North Cape of Norway, some Soviet SSBNs, Ike Kidd informed me, were taking up patrol assignments undetected off the US coast. There was speculation that the intruders may have succeeded in 'navigating' gaps in SOSUS at the Greenland ice-cap and in coastal waters further south. Concern focussed on security, however. It had been voiced by 1SL at our first meeting. Both he and Ike Kidd feared that it might be due to in-house failure. For neither had much confidence in counterintelligence. Ike Kidd would invite me into his inner sanctum after formal briefings – to the fury of his staff, and mine, who were excluded – for further private exchanges.

It had also become depressingly clear that Soviet attack submarines had begun to operate on different routes and that communication channels generally had been changed.

Those security fears were publicly exposed in the mid-Eighties by the biggest US spy scandal in decades. It involved four retired or active members of the US Navy. Active and undetected for many years, they were headed by John Walker and included two other family members – one, Michael, a young sailor aboard the carrier *USS Nimitz*. Walker retired from the US Navy in 1976 after twenty years' service. During his naval career he had Top Secret Crypto clearance and access to classified information pertaining to the encryption of naval communications. He was latterly stationed under Admiral Ike Kidd's command in Norfolk, Virginia. His continuing activity on behalf of the spy ring led to his arrest in May 1985, but only because he was betrayed by his estranged wife and not by counterintelligence.

Admiral J.D. Watkins, Chief of Naval Operations (CNO) told a Pentagon briefing a month later that the loss of information to the Soviet Union was 'very serious'. My immediate concern was that the monitoring of the Royal Navy's antisubmarine work by a secret body known as the Strategic Systems Performance Analysis Group, which was passed to the Americans, may have found its way to the Russians, thus revealing how we and the Americans detect and track their own submarines and disguise our own.

At the time, following assignment to the North Atlantic Assembly and membership of its Military Committee, I had entered into close working relationships with members of the US Congress who had been similarly assigned. They shared with me reports they were receiving on the spy ring. The disclosures suggested such disturbing implications that I felt bound to raise them in a letter to the then Prime Minister, Margaret Thatcher. I received a reassuring reply (See Appendix 1).

Damage limitation apart, it was obvious that counterintelligence had failed lamentably. Spy-catching in the US was mainly the job of the Federal Bureau of Investigation (FBI), which had a traditionally edgy relationship with the Central Intelligence Agency (CIA), which in turn remained suspect.[106] Walker was given away by his estranged and outraged wife when their son, serving in the *Nimitz,* was recruited by his father. Aldrich Ames, another notorious traitor, only came in for attention later on following a tip from a KGB defector.

Not that either could be held against the Americans in view of the disappearance from the Foreign Office in London of Guy Burgess and Donald Maclean in 1951, before turning up in Moscow, whose interests, it turned out, they had been serving for twenty years. They were tipped off by Kim Philby, the notorious 'Third Man', who followed them several years later. For years afterwards, rumours persisted that there was a 'Fourth Man', which were confirmed by Margaret Thatcher in 1979. She disclosed to the House of Commons that he was Sir Anthony Blunt, a distinguished art historian and Keeper of the Queen's Pictures. Perhaps Admiral Ike Kidd and Admiral Edward Ashmore had an inkling when they were sharing with me their anxieties about in-house security. They knew that shared intelligence and any threats to it lay at the heart of the 'special relationship' and especially that of their own navies' close ties.

The First Sea Lord explained that, for a considerable period in the 1950s and early 1960s, it was thought that the threat of a nuclear war was an adequate deterrent in Europe, and that it was sufficient to maintain a tripwire of conventional forces to identify aggression before resorting to nuclear weapons. The tripwire strategy succeeded, despite the close shave of the Berlin airlift crisis in 1948 and the Cuban missile crisis of 1962. But as Soviet nuclear power grew, and as the Americans became enmeshed in Vietnam, doubts about its viability grew. They led to the formulation of a new strategy, based on the linked concepts of flexible response and forward defence.

---

106   It continued to be charged with incompetence. It overplayed Soviet military capacities in the 1950s, then underplayed them before overplaying them again in the 1970s. As late as 2007, Tim Weiner complained in *Legacy of Ashes: The History of the CIA* that the US had yet to develop 'a first rate spy service'.

These two concepts involved the development by the West of a range of forces, deployed throughout the territory of all members of the alliance, to provide an adequate deterrence to aggression, whatever form it might take. This policy was rather more expensive than the tripwire strategy. But once the initial massive investment in nuclear technology and delivery systems had been made, nuclear weapons were relatively cheap, while conventional weapons, with their increasing sophistication, grew ever more expensive.

I was then introduced by 1SL to the seminal notion of Field Marshal Michael Carver, Chief of the Defence Staff (CDS), that peace depended on the balance of risk rather than the balance of force in Europe (See Appendix 2). The fundamental question, he argued, related to America and the strength of the American relationship with Western Europe: how far she was satisfied with burden-sharing in forward defence, for example, and how far Europe could be relied upon therefore for her to deliver an appropriate nuclear response. The First Sea Lord shared Michael Carver's thinking on the governing policy of the balance of risk. A key element within it that affected us, he often reminded me, was the Navy's duty to keep open the sea lanes of communication to the Eastern Atlantic and channel ports. He never ceased to remind me either of the crucial role, as he saw it, of those twelve German divisions on the north German plain, and their large well-trained reserves. He believed that it was a land force which the Russians feared above all.

I was Navy Minister from March 1976 until April 1979 when the Labour government fell. Throughout that time Royal Marine detachments undertook tours of infantry duty in Northern Ireland and there was always a naval presence in Carlingford Lough for which I was responsible to Parliament. That gave me a stake in the province: frequent visits and entitlement to classified briefings in outposts and command centres. It gave rise to further insights into the work of

GCHQ at Cheltenham,[107] including its role in Northern Ireland. I was aware of the shared intelligence penetration of the IRA we had with Dublin. I entered fully into the commitments that arose, including night patrol participation with the UDR. Those links with the province were strengthened by the appointment of Roy Mason as Secretary of State for Northern Ireland in 1977, for he personally welcomed my company.

Fred Mulley, who succeeded Roy Mason as Defence Secretary, was my constituency neighbour in Sheffield. We shared the same agent in the redoubtable Alderman Sidney Dyson. Fred confided an increasing worry over Ulster, not only over security but because it had become a drain on assigned NATO forces. Operation Banner tied down as many as 28,000 troops at a time for more than a generation. Though assisted by thousands of locally recruited forces in the UDR and the RUC, they had to contain an area 120 miles by eighty. Following an enquiry I made at a ministerial meeting about the latest IRA threat assessment, we were informed in 1978 of a significant Army intelligence report. This made clear that a victory against the IRA was unlikely, due to the border and problems arising from extradition. Such difficulties regarding the border did not accord with the findings of the earlier visit by my parliamentary group in 1976.

As well as the problem of force numbers in Ulster and its relevance for assigned NATO roles for the Army, nuclear policy had also become a major concern of the Prime Minister and ourselves at the MoD. At a time of strengthening support within the Labour party for nuclear disarmament, we were suddenly faced with the Soviet introduction in Western Europe of the SS20s – a new generation

---

107   It was Britain's largest intelligence agency. Tasked with listening in on global communication, it intercepted communications – phone, fax, e-mail and internet – and enabled MI6 to gather human intelligence (humint). It was heir to Bletchley Park and its great achievement in cracking the German Enigma code. It was kept under wraps until the trial of Geoffrey Prime in 1982, who had worked at the agency, when he told the Soviet Union that Britain had cracked its codes.

of intermediate range missiles. Acting on behalf of the Alliance, Jim Callaghan, German Chancellor Helmut Schmidt and US President Jimmy Carter held a meeting in Whitehall at which Jim asked me to be present. Their decision to respond with Pershing and Cruise missiles produced protest rallies in Britain, and across the Continent. It also gave rise to the notorious Greenham Common women's encampment. Moderate Labour MPs had responded in the early Seventies to nuclear unilateralism through the Manifesto Group. But at the MoD we felt badly in need of a rigorously thought through and utterly compelling rationale for nuclear deterrence.

I mentioned to my colleagues at a weekly ministers' meeting that because of his expertise, Michael Quinlan, a very promising deputy under-secretary at the MoD, should be invited to draw up such a statement. His submission was outstandingly successful, and has endured morally as well as politically to the present day.[108] He was a most formidable intellectual opponent of the CND. The Russian Chiefs of Staff once paid him the compliment of inviting him to lecture them on the subject. On leaving office and becoming Leader of the Opposition, Jim Callaghan looked to me for certain defence briefings, and was particularly anxious to be kept abreast of Sir Michael Quinlan's thinking on nuclear deterrence. Michael and I shared the same background to some extent, of course. We agreed in private conversation that the nuclear dilemma affected the whole western world, and Ireland was avoiding its responsibilities. I encountered the same feeling within the NATO Assembly.

On average I would be out of the office one day a week. I would be visiting a shore establishment or a ship. In addition I had regular engagements around the Alliance that varied from visits to command headquarters on both sides of the Atlantic, in the Mediterranean, to naval bases and defence manufacturing corporations in the US.

---

108   He was later Permanent Under-Secretary, and became our most distinguished defence analyst.

They extended each February to sharing the rigour of sleeping in the snow with the Royal Marines during their midwinter annual training within the Arctic Circle in Norway. A familiar routine would be an early departure by helicopter to Portsmouth or fixed-wing aircraft to Plymouth, where a helicopter whisked me to a frigate or destroyer in the Channel or Western approaches. After an eventful day at sea, I would return to London and the private office at the MoD in which I would have to try and compress a day's business into an hour. For I would soon have to head to the House of Commons. There I would collect constituency mail – I had no secretary – deal with the many messages awaiting me and rarely leave before a vote at 11.30pm. As the Government had no parliamentary majority of its own, I would sometimes be detained all night before presenting myself once more in the Department at 8.00am, very much in need of a bath and breakfast (See Appendix 3).

On visits to ships at sea I was always impressed with the training and leadership of commanding officers. I was fascinated by the competence in their varied specialisations of the officers and with the youth and skills of the ratings. I sensed a slightly less formal relationship and a more relaxed standard of discipline than I had known in wartime. I encountered everywhere distinctly better living conditions, much improved and varied food, generous recreation space and bunks instead of hammocks – but no rum. Sea-time was now very often prolonged, however, and conditions were severe in heavy weather. Yet there was a constant striving for a happier balance between sea-time and shore-time. Pay and the abandoned pledge of comparability became a serious issue in the stagnation that characterised the economy in the late Seventies. I was given a real drubbing on that account on many a mess-deck, despite the best endeavours of 1SL and myself.

Yet morale ashore and afloat was high, according to 1SL, as was recruiting – fourteen out of fifteen applicants were turned away. Entrants could take a university course at the Navy's expense, and obtain release later if they became inclined to another profession.

More than seventy countries were sending officers and seamen to the UK for all types of training, including the Irish Republic, whose entrainees I observed at Dartmouth. It was all in sharp contrast to the headlines that appeared sometimes in newspapers like The Daily and Sunday *Telegraph* such as 'Britain's Crumbling Defences' and 'Air Forces: the pathetic truth'. Similarly, Michael Holloway in three reports in the *Sheffield Morning Telegraph* starting on 21 March 1977, wrote that, 'The Royal Navy (is) not what it used to be.' He concluded that, 'the Royal Navy is fast reaching the stage where she cannot or will not be able in the future to fulfil her commitments to NATO.'

The hostility of certain defence correspondents was obviously intended for the Government rather than the Navy. It was in striking contrast also to the tone and warmth of the annual naval debates in Parliament. In June 1978, for example, I assured the Commons that 'the Fleet Her Majesty reviewed last year may have been smaller than the one at her Coronation – but it packed a much greater punch.' Michael White reporting in *The Guardian* (20 June 1978) said that 'the two front benches were awash with mutual goodwill.' And, 'with patent sincerity, nods and smiles they' – Sir Patrick Wall leading for the opposition, and myself – 'both declared themselves anxious' to hold a debate 'worthy of the Senior Service' for which they 'all had a deep unswerving love – Mr Duffy's phrase.' Such Navy debates were reported elsewhere as 'love-ins'. That was how my naval accountability was received by MPs, some of whom had, like myself, served in wartime unlike most of those defence correspondents. Malta was prominent among our wartime connections and memories. We were saddened therefore by the run-down of its historic naval facilities as

Prime Minister Dom Mintoff increasingly challenged the authority of Britain and NATO.[109]

My first official visit as Minister in 1976 was to Portsmouth Naval Base. I was promptly shown on arrival the space where I slung my hammock in 1940. During the inspection I queried the absence of the chaplain, who was quickly summoned. I informed the Commodore that I expected the chaplain to be present and prominent on such occasions. I had already decided that one contribution I could attempt, so far as it fell to me, was the maintenance of the Navy's traditional standards. I came to appreciate and value subsequently the chaplains of all denominations[110] and learned from them much about

---

109   For all his irascible and troublesome reputation, Mintoff and I always got on well together during my visits. On one unforgettable occasion I was invited to Sunday dinner, 12.30 for 1 pm, alone – without the British ambassador. When I arrived, I learned that Mintoff was swimming, but would soon return to prepare the meal himself. We sat down at 5pm. He and his wife Moyra, a charming lady and a distant kinswoman of the Duke of Portland, were seated at either ends of a long dining-table and myself midway. As they were not speaking at the time, I was the medium of all communications. I was assisted and guided throughout most impressively by Flag-Officer, Malta, Rear-Admiral Sir Nigel Cecil, from the Villa Portelli. His tactful and skilful handling of events brought the Royal Navy's historic tenure to an honourable close.

110   Later I spent two days at sea in the Mediterranean in the aircraft carrier the *USS Kennedy*. My briefings, along with the hospitality – I occupied the Admiral's quarters – were generous. Yet I learned much more about life in that vast ship with its huge complement from conversation with the chaplain.

the Navy's current ethos and its pressure points.[111]

My first request on my initial visit to the Devonport Naval Base must have puzzled the Commodore. It was to see the redundant railway platform from which I had departed at midnight in mid-1940 – kit-bag under one arm and hammock under the other – on draft to *HMS Repulse*. I expressed the wish to be left alone with my memories of those lost lads who had accompanied me at that time, as well as the other friends I had made on board my first ship, *Repulse,* which had gone down in the South China Sea. I remembered the bitterness that still lingered on its mess-decks from the events at Invergordon a decade earlier, and the oft repeated hatred of 'their Lordships down at the Admiralty'. It never occurred to me that I might one day be a member of the Admiralty Board myself. But I sensed also among my old shipmates a special brand of comradeship. That is why I was anxious to return to that railway platform and pay tribute. So many of them were lost the following year. And a few moments' stillness alone was more evocative for me than any other wartime memories of action stations and conflict.

I spent my annual leave each summer in Co. Mayo, a custom which the Prime Minister always queried. On one occasion he suggested I take Scotland Yard personnel with me because an IRA training camp had been located close to my destination. However, I had full confidence in the exemplary twenty-four-hour cover provided by Ireland's Special Branch, who would meet my boat on arrival in Dun Laoghaire and put me back on it later. I was well served by official

---

111   I was quick to respond when the Catholic Bishop of the Forces announced his retirement. I enquired as to procedure governing his replacement, and learned that it was customarily left to the Archbishop of Westminster and the Duke of Norfolk. In collaboration with the Second PUS at the MOD, Sir Arthur Hockaday, I intimated to them my wish to make the appointment, for I had in mind our own excellent senior naval Catholic chaplain, Francis Walmsley. They agreed immediately, and thus paved the way for the appointment of the first naval Catholic Bishop, which was warmly welcomed also by Admiralty Board colleagues.

Intelligence and close personal surveillance on both sides of the Irish Sea. Threat assessments always remained high, however, and I was constantly reminded of my risk exposure. When staying in Sligo, I shared 'cover' with Lord Mountbatten who also stayed locally. We both came in for the close personal attention of Inspector McMahon of Garda Siochana. He and I were aware that the local IRA unit always knew when I paid my annual visit – and of my movements.[112] Inspector McMahon called early each day on Lord Mountbatten and myself to verify our intended movements. He always conveyed enquiries as to my welfare from Lord Mountbatten and his good wishes. Even an unplanned visit to a restaurant or pub would find Inspector McMahon standing opposite afterwards alongside his car, though my twenty-four-hour Special Branch team would be also parked discreetly close by. He was painstakingly concerned also for the security of Lord Mountbatten and rigorously conscientious in the performance of duty.

Acting on official advice, I did not go to Ireland during the summer that Lord Mountbatten was murdered. Inspector MacMahon complimented me the following year for observing that advice. He was extremely disappointed that Mountbatten had not done likewise, for he had received the same warning and advice, explained the Inspector. But Mountbatten waved it aside, saying, 'They won't touch me.' Every possible precaution had been taken against the tragedy, he insisted. So I was puzzled by the report – released under the thirty-year rule – of the British Ambassador in Dublin, Robin Haydon, with whom I sometimes stayed. It was critical of the Garda Siochana for not being 'more vigilant and conscientious' and the 'level and

---

112   I had only been in the public bar of the Station Inn opposite the railway station a few minutes, tucked discreetly in a corner with Margaret Holland, wife of the owner, when Tony Holland rushed down from an upstairs lounge shouting, 'Get out. Get out. The IRA have asked if they can speak to you.'

adequacy of Garda security.'[113] My personal experience was absolutely the opposite. Inspector McMahon was deeply affected afterwards and, I believe, took early retirement.

On taking the chair of the historical Board of Admiralty at my first meeting, I murmured regret that my father, who had just passed away, could not share my pride in the great honour now conferred on me. He would have been all the more sensitive of it as a former cavalryman, then infantryman in World War One. My father would have been astonished, however, by the changes my appointment brought about in my mother's lifestyle, accustomed as he was to her unstinting support. She always got up for him at 4am when he was on the 'day' shift at Rossington Colliery, and before that at the Maypole Colliery. She sustained me also – as a bachelor – in all my work in Parliament, and was always waiting up for me when I returned from London, however late the hour. She was at my side when our new St Peter-in-Chains church was opened in 1973 by Cardinal Heenan. She accompanied me on many of my ministerial duties, notably at the Silver Jubilee Review of the Fleet by the Queen at Spithead in 1977. On the following day the Queen paid an official visit to the city of Portsmouth, and my mother was accompanied by Lord Mountbatten in the official party that eventually went into lunch in the town hall. At the Silver Jubilee Review of the Royal Air Force at Finningley, held a little later,[114] Prince Charles singled her out – in front of a distinguished gathering in the Officers' Mess – to ask if she would look after Prince Edward, then twelve years old.

She launched her own ship, *HMS Lindisfarne,* at Aberdeen and attended its rededication and decommissioning at Rosyth many years later. She attended my knighthood investiture at Buckingham Palace with my sister, Patricia. She was by my side at St. Joseph's

---

113   *The Times.* 30 December 2009.

114   Where, I observed, that Marshal of the Royal Air Force Arthur Harris, who had commanded Bomber Command in wartime, was strikingly neglected. He had travelled from South Africa for the occasion.

Church, Handsworth, in my constituency, for the Memorial Mass of Thanksgiving held at my request for my agents and dear friends in Attercliffe who had passed away prior to my retirement from Parliament. Quite a transition for the barefoot girl who started life in Co. Mayo, accustomed to carrying several buckets of water daily a half-mile from a spring well, then getting Dad off to work in Wigan at 4am before undertaking weekly collections on her bicycle in South Yorkshire for so many years. Finally, launching her own ship in the presence of the Bishop of Aberdeen, now Archbishop Mario Conti of Glasgow, brought me great joy as well. The late Queen Mother could not have been more considerate and caring of her on the occasions they met. We were all so proud of Mam. As I was, indeed, also of my Attercliffe constituency in the east of Sheffield. For generations it had produced the guns and protective armour for the warships of the Royal Navy. To represent such special people in Parliament also filled me with pride.

Appendix 1

I wrote to the Prime Minister, Margaret Thatcher in early July asking if she was being kept fully informed by Washington, whether she knew now the full extent to which the Navy's undersea role and its strategic forces had been compromised, and raised finally the current 'need to know' basis of access to secret information relating to security and the practice of Positive Vetting. She assured me in a letter (5 August 1985) that 'we are being kept fully informed by the United States'; that 'there are no grounds for supposing that the viability of the UK deterrent has been called into question'; that it was a 'fundamental principle that 'need to know' is drawn as tightly as possible', and we had recently adopted more rigorous minimum standards of Positive Vetting.

Following further spy revelations within the Alliance I wrote again to the Prime Minister later in the year. I drew attention to President Reagan's recent statement that espionage was a growing threat. I mentioned also its changing culture. As the stakes grew, motivation for treachery appeared to becoming downright frivolous.

This highlighted, she replied, 'the necessity for constant vigilance', and assured me that a great deal more information from the Americans since she last wrote to me was assisting damage assessment 'caused to the Royal Navy, and of devising further corrective action'.

'Spies seem to work less for ideological reasons than for kicks and money, and a disturbing proportion appears to be detected less by counterintelligence than by defection and even by accident.' (Letters 3 December 1985).

Appendix 2

He found it difficult to envisage a realistic scenario in which Russia could conceivably imagine that she would gain anything from military operations which involved her in direct hostilities with the US, certainly as long as the link of escalation from conventional action through tactical nuclear to strategic remained credible.

The peace of Europe and of the world would depend, therefore, upon the risk to Russia remaining high, he concluded. The two elements which had kept and continued to keep the risk high was the direct involvement of the US in the defence of Europe, and the possibility, indeed the probability, that she would use nuclear weapons against Russian forces involved in aggression in Europe and in the North Atlantic, with the risk of escalation to targets in the Soviet Union. Europe's fundamental defence problem was how to ensure that those two elements were maintained. This called for the right balance between nuclear and conventional forces. It also called for the naval planners to provide for the possibility that the nuclear deterrent was not exercised or otherwise failed, and to be ever vigilant at sea.

Navy Minister

Appendix 3

A not untypical weekly programme.

On MONDAY 15th May 1978, the House will meet at 2.30 p.m.

PRIVATE MEMBERS' MOTIONS until 7.00 p.m.

PARLIAMENTARY CONTROL OF THE EXECUTIVE : MR EDWARD DU CANN.
IMPROVEMENTS TO THE A66 : MR RICHARD PAGE.

Afterwards

Motion relating to the TOWN AND COUNTRY PLANNING (WINDSCALE AND CALDER WORKS) SPECIAL DEVELOPMENT ORDER.

HOUSING (FINANCIAL PROVISIONS) (SCOTLAND) BILL : CONSIDERATION OF LORDS AMENDMENTS.

DIVISIONS WILL TAKE PLACE AND YOUR CONTINUED ATTENDANCE FROM 9.00 P.M.

AND UNTIL THE BUSINESS IS CONCLUDED IS NECESSARY.

On TUESDAY 16th May, the House will meet at 2.30 p.m.

Ten Minute Rule Bill : Government Contracts – Mr John Cope.

FINANCE BILL : PROGRESS IN COMMITTEE.

DIVISIONS WILL TAKE PLACE

YOUR CONTINUED ATTENDANCE FROM *3.30 P.M. PROMPT IS ESSENTIAL.

On WEDNESDAY 17th May, the House will meet at 2.30 p.m.

Ten Minute Rule Bill : British Leyland (Dismissal of Directors) – Mr Tom Litterick.

TRANSPORT BILL : REMAINING STAGES.

DIVISIONS WILL TAKE PLACE AND YOUR CONTINUED ATTENDANCE FROM 3.30 P.M.

AND UNTIL THE BUSINESS IS CONCLUDED IS ESSENTIAL.

* ALL MEMBERS ARE REQUESTED TO INFORM THE WHIPS OFFICE IN THE LOBBY (EXTNS. 4333 & 4401) OF THEIR ARRIVAL IN THE HOUE.

151

On THURSDAY 18th May, the House will meet at 2.30 p.m.

Supply (15th allotted day)

Debate on INDUSTRIAL RELATIONS IN THE NEWSPAPER INDUSTRY.

Motion on the BREAD PRICES (AMENDMENT NO.5) Order.

DIVISIONS MAY TAKE PLACE AND YOUR CONTINUED ATTENDANCE FROM 9.00 P.M.

AND UNTIL THE BUSINESS IS CONCLUDED IS NECESSARY.

On FRIDAY 19th May, the House will meet at 11.00 a.m.

GOVERNMENT BUSINESS WILL BE TAKEN

HOMES INSULATION BILL : 2ND READING.
SOLOMON ISLANDS BILL (LORDS) : 2ND READING.
INDEPENDENT BROADCASTING AUTHORITY BILL : REMAINING STAGES.
DOMESTIC PROCEEDINGS AND MAGISTRATES' COURTS BILL (LORDS) : REMAINING STAGES.

DIVISIONS MAY TAKE PLACE AND YOUR CONTINUED ATTENDANCE FROM 11.00 A.M.

AND UNTIL THE BUSINESS IS CONCLUDED IS NECESSARY UNLESS YOU HAVE

REGISTERED A FIRM PAIR.

On MONDAY 22nd May, the House will meet at 2.30 p.m.

Supply (16th allotted day).

Debate on THE PAY OF THE ARMED FORCES.

DIVISIONS WILL TAKE PLACE AND YOUR ATTENDANCE BY 9.00 P.M. IS ESSENTIAL.

MICHAEL COCKS.

Chapter Nine
Death of Sheffield Steel

In 1969 I was selected to succeed John Hynd, former Minister for Germany, in the Attercliffe constituency of Sheffield. I was elected the following year. A name of considerable antiquity, Attercliffe appears in the Domesday Book as Atective. Sheffield figures as Escafeld, and both villages were mentioned within the great manor of Hallam. From such beginnings Sheffield became one of Europe's main manufacturing cities, with its industrial heartland located in Attercliffe. Its industry acquired a reputation for quality because of the distinctive combination of ingenuity and skills of management and workers.

A boldly designed and controversial city centre had met the devastation of wartime. Industrial atmospheric pollution was being overcome, and the popular image of grime and smoke was being replaced by that of a city anxious to attract commerce as well as manufacturing. The city became famous for its two football clubs – United and Wednesday. By the 1970s, Sheffield Wednesday's stadium was reckoned to be the best outside Wembley. The Bramall Lane cricket ground staged Yorkshire county matches. Other national pursuits were speedway, greyhound racing and wrestling. Sheffield had a morning newspaper in *The Telegraph*, later the *Morning Telegraph*, which was strong on business, commercial and industrial matters. *The Star* aimed at an all-round news coverage in the evening.[115] But soaring above such strengths was Sheffield's unrivalled reputation for the production of high-quality steels.[116]

---

115   Saturday nights were not complete for my father without *The Star*'s sports edition, The Green 'Un.

116   Razors used by participants in the famous 'OK Corrall Shoot-out' and deposited in the museum in Tombstone, Arizona, signify 'Made in Sheffield'.

The city had long been noted for its plate and cutlery. But much of its wealth was based on steel used for larger-scale projects, as in the construction of railway systems and ships. The Royal Navy was especially dependent on the city for its guns and protective armour. Thirty per cent of the employed population worked in steel or related metals. Most of the secondary industry and service activity was directly related to the prosperity of steel. As late as the closing Sixties unemployment was far below the national average. Effective local administration, in which the city's Labour party played an important part, had been a contributory factor.[117] After gaining thirteen seats in 1978, the Labour party gained its largest council majority in years – eighty seats to twenty-seven. That was my political inheritance. I felt it a rare privilege to represent in Parliament the bulk of the city's industry situated in my constituency.

I was well aware on arrival of the problems awaiting the Yorkshire region's staple industries of steel, coal and textiles. In the case of steel it was soon apparent that the problem was fundamental rather than cyclical. Along with other manufacturing cities, Sheffield was already struggling to become a service centre as well.[118] For storm clouds were gathering over its steel industry as economic growth now needed less extra steel. Steel producers everywhere faced the same basic problem: how could they bring that shrinking demand into line with capacity?[119] The collapse of industrial output in the UK in 1979–81 followed a long period in which the manufacturing share had steadily

---

117   Sheffield became the first large municipal borough to return a Labour majority – as early as 1926.

118   In the mid-1970s it acquired a large Midland Bank office and the headquarters of the Manpower Services Commission.

119   Within the Organisation for Economic Cooperation and Development between 1973 and 1984, consumption of steel as a percentage of gross national product fell annually by an average of 3.7%.

reduced.[120] The contraction in output and employment were without parallel and evident in other industrial countries.[121] Such a downturn boded ill for Sheffield and its steel industry.

I learned during annual visits to the firms in the constituency – see Appendix 1 – of their growing difficulties. Operating at reduced capacity by the mid-Seventies, most had been affected by the stagnation in the UK economy. Cutbacks in the motor industry, I was warned, could soon cost thousands of jobs in the forging industry. Rising energy costs, crippling interest rates, a strong pound hitting exports and growing import penetration were increasingly affecting Sheffield. New rules on competition and subsidies faced its steel firms on arrival in the EEC, and called for close monitoring. Unemployment was on the increase; about 7.7 per cent of the working population were registered out of work by 1980, with widespread short-time working. Even so, this was still marginally below the regional and national average.

But by 1980 the British Steel Corporation (BSC) was losing nearly £2m a day, and Ian MacGregor had taken over as chairman. He took an early opportunity to invite all Sheffield MPs to meet him. He was trying to give Britain new structures in forging and engineering steels capable of facing the best in Europe, he explained. He was particularly anxious to preserve the River Don steelworks and Firth Brown, for he admired them and their workers. But it could only be done at the cost of redundancies, he admitted, even though their productivity was at an all-time high and matching the best in Europe. He aimed by merging them to create a formidable UK company capable of competing with other international forge masters and foundries. Similarly with the historic private sector plant

---

120   While gross domestic product increased by 19% between 1966 and 1979, manufacturing output grew by only 11%.

121   Europe lost 240,000 jobs over the previous seven years, with BSC alone accounting for 140,000 of them in just five years.

of Hadfields and its future in a restructured engineering steels sector: although it had slimmed down to a shadow of its old size, it still continued to operate at a profit. Now MacGregor was attempting, according to his Phoenix proposals, to fit it into a tightly-manned, highly modern group capable also of facing the best in Europe. On inviting comment, deep anxiety was expressed by the assembled MPs about the scale of redundancies and the plight of individual workers, which he was quick to share. But on his corporate plans for both sectors, there was no comment. As one colleague whispered on leaving, 'What more could we say?'.

MacGregor's plan to save steel had cut the losses back to an average of just £70,000 a day by early 1982. There seemed every prospect that his corporate survival plan had overcome the country's most serious industrial crisis. But not without severe pain for BSC. A main problem by now was its lack of operational autonomy. Sometimes it had to heed conflicting commands from Brussels as well as Whitehall. Nevertheless, there were grounds for hope that the steel industry's long night was almost over. Six months later those recovery hopes were no more. MacGregor admitted in a message to the steel trade unions that the downhill slide had not been checked. He warned that further painful decisions and sacrifice might yet have to be made. A sorry, sad situation was how the Iron and Steel Trades Confederation (ISCT) general secretary, Bill Sirs, afterwards described Sheffield's steel industry. The bottom had fallen out of steel throughout Europe. Too much steel was now chasing too few customers.

In the US and Japan as well as the UK and the EEC, customers disappeared, orders evaporated and steel generally had to slash production to less than half its capacity. Steel had become cheaper to make in the Third World. Countries like Brazil, South Korea and India had invested in new plants. Their wages were low. In a straight fight for basic steel they would always win. The steelmakers of Europe and America, despite their recent draconian measures, were compelled to reduce capacity further and move upmarket to offset growing competition from other materials. As for the UK economy, the disappearance of about 20% of manufacturing industry since 1979, and the dismal outlook for the four key sectors of shipbuilding, engineering, construction and the car industry had led to MacGregor's bleak reappraisal. For example, along with a growing number of foreign-made cars came a growing number of foreign transmission assemblies in such cars. There was soon a wider use at home of such foreign assemblies by Ford, Vauxhall and British Leyland. That affected the component manufacturers as well as BSC in South Yorkshire. Yet a growing wave of Toyota, Nissan, Hondas and Fiestas could be seen on Sheffield's roads and also in the underground car park at the town hall.

Special steels and heavy engineering had dominated the east end of Sheffield for 100 years. Their collapse and the faltering attempts to rationalise the remnants for survival, wrought havoc in the lower Don Valley. Employment in steel fell from more than 54,000 to less than 18,000 Once the proud powerhouse of the national economy, one-third of my constituency was now either derelict or underused. Despite enormous efforts to cope with market forces and world-wide recession, Attercliffe was now the scene of social as well as industrial devastation. For the collapse of steel and the loss of thousands of jobs enhanced the programmes of so-called slum clearance. The demolition of those homes destroyed close-knit working-class communities and the quenching of an unmatched community spirit that had defied wartime bombing.

I sought every means of redress for Attercliffe. I explored every avenue of succour and protection. I wrote to ministers and led delegations to their ministries. I raised questions in parliament, tabled early-day motions and requested debates on the adjournment of the House of Commons. I explored every possible parliamentary device with the support of local MPs. It is all on the record. One commodity not in short supply in Sheffield, I informed the House when opening a debate in June 1981, was spirit. Rather than licking their wounds, local industrialists were going out looking for business and not simply relying on the government. Promotional effort was mainly directed at Germany, the United States and Japan. Recovery could have been assisted, I suggested, by more government help. But there was no begging-bowl mentality. Such appeals were now seriously hampered in the early Eighties, however, by the emergence locally of a political instability that affected the credibility of the city's administration. I was no longer able to appeal on behalf of the close working relationship that had previously united political and business leaders in the city. That mattered in Whitehall.

Until 1979, Sir Ron Ironmonger, Leader of the council, and John Hambridge, Director of the Sheffield Chamber of Commerce, shared a stable partnership – sustained by George Wilson whilst briefly the next Leader. Such a valuable unity was sustained by an effective consultative body, the Industrial Development and Advisory Committee.[122] Speaking later at his election as president of the Sheffield Chamber of Commerce at the Cutlers' Hall in 1985, Peter J Ford recalled that during the period from 1945 to 1979, 'the foundations were laid for a sensible and realistic adjustment to the post-steel era, and an excellent working relationship was formed between [the] political and business leaders in the city. The motto was 'Sheffield first and foremost', and the people living here were prepared to bury their differences in the greater cause of promoting the city to the outside world.' He believed that the private sector still had the will, and was confident that it could meet the challenge posed by the Industry Act of 1972. It provided a framework, in his view, in which self-help policies designed to modernise steel as well as the local business environment could receive necessary government help.

---

122   A unique feature, it was run by the Council, comprising the city's MPs, councillors, officials, trade union and business representatives, and regional officers of the departments of Industry and Environment.

By 1980, however, there had emerged on the city council a new Labour group under the leadership of David Blunkett. It contrasted sharply in style with the previous group. The practice of that group had been to meet after council elections to elect its executive. This 'inner cabinet' then discussed and framed policies. It shared an interface with the district party, which also elected its own executive and officers. Within its structure were the ward parties, which selected candidates for the local elections. The function of the district party, according to Labour party rules, was to lay down broad policy guidelines and draw up the election manifesto. Inevitably there were different views, both among the councillors and between the group and the district party. But there had existed understanding, tolerance and compromise. Those in disagreement usually went off and had a pint together. That was now much less in evidence. The new faces of power grumbled now about the old guard; some despised them.

Shortly after taking over the new regime reported sweeping changes, such as rebuilding the party from the bottom up. Despite Blunkett's claim of 'tolerance',[123] the vetting was introduced of councillors who had been sitting for more than ten years. A significant change in the composition of the Labour group was also taking place. The blue-collar trade unions, which had helped form council policy and provided many a councillor, were in decline by 1980. They were being replaced in the district party by delegates from public sector trade unions. More significant was the changed relationship of the district party with the Labour group. 'The city party makes policy,' admitted Blunkett, 'and the group implements that policy as a section of the party.'[124]

That proved to be a crucial and fateful departure from past practice by the Labour group. The Attercliffe party would soon be in the line of fire of the district party. The old partnership of the Labour group with

---

123   *The Star.* 26 May 1982.

124   *The Guardian.* 7 May 1985.

the private sector symbolised by the Ironmonger/Hambridge axis had gone. That partnership had been sustained by hard-won awareness that short-term problems could still be overcome, as in the past, by Sheffield firms working harder and smarter to overcome competition. But it was an awareness that obliged Labour in its concern for jobs to recognise certain basic truths, such as the centrality of entrepreneurial activity in driving economic growth in order to provide savings for more investment to generate further expansion and, hopefully, more jobs and – given productivity increase – more income, which could then properly raise questions of distribution. A quite immutable sequence in economic development and growth, although Sir Ron Ironmonger and Councillor Isidore Lewis and I were nervously aware of its pejorative interpretation in some quarters. With the right attitude and mutual confidence, we always believed that we could tackle any such misunderstandings that might arise within the Labour movement. But now that the old partnership had gone, it appeared doubtful that the new Labour group would any longer entertain such perceptions. For example, many of its new members saw public sector spending as an answer to Sheffield's problems, creating public service jobs and stimulating regeneration. They also felt that they could do it by themselves.

A city traditionally proud of being one of Britain's best governed had clearly changed political complexion. If it now presented a challenge to Sheffield's business and former political leaders and their joint policy of 'Sheffield first and foremost', it also presented an early challenge to Michael Heseltine, Secretary of State for the Environment.

He had quickly undertaken certain encroachments on local government autonomy. I protested in a debate in November 1981 that a battery of weapons was already available to handle any local authority disagreeing with central government policy. I followed it up in a letter and a personal approach one night in the Members' lobby of the House of Commons. I explained that the Council was now exploring a range of resources to help sustain its steel industry in crisis. It was also anxious to stimulate the development of new industries, new enterprises and new technologies. I referred to his important speech at the recent Tory party conference, where he had outlined the problems of the inner cities and focused on Liverpool. I pleaded with him to help restore entrepreneurial endeavour in Sheffield as well as Liverpool. He was unmoved, and feelingly reeled off many administrative shortcomings of the Sheffield council. One, citing 15,000 surplus school places, he repeated to me ten years later on his return as Environment Secretary. He left me in no doubt that Sheffield was one of his least-loved local authorities. Why did he entertain such feeling when he was prepared to take a chance on Liverpool?

He would be aware that Sheffield's new council had questioned the scope of the Industry Act 1972, which had been introduced by the previous Conservative Government. It was now viewed as narrow in its provisions by the Council, which was critical also of the Labour Government that followed the Heath Government from 1974–79. That Labour Government had introduced the concept of a strategy for industry which, in my view, was imaginative and bold considering the desperate state of the economy.[125] Carefully shaped, its main features were in sharp contrast to the more market-oriented approach of Margaret Thatcher's Government in the early Eighties.[126] But despite persistent questioning, her ministers insisted there remained wriggle room within the early Act for local authorities such as Sheffield. I was also reminded that enterprise zones were also on offer. If selective

---

125   It included support for undertakings in trouble, deals struck with foreign firms over choice of location, along with an Accelerated Projects Scheme, a Selective Investment Scheme and various sectoral modernisation schemes for particular manufacturing industries.

126   It reduced regional spending, for example, along with existing controls over business through industrial development certificates, before abolishing them.

financial assistance under Section 7 of the 1972 Act had become subject to rather stricter criteria, it was now up to Sheffield to make its case. How did the new Council respond to that challenge?

It launched a new initiative in 1982 with the formation of a new employment department. A radical departure in local government, it presented radical ideas about its role in the jobs market, calling for a far greater degree of social and economic planning. It produced a report also in 1984 – 'Steel in Crisis' – which, along with criticism of management and the serving Conservative Government, blamed previous Labour Government for not nationalising enough of the industry. Moving closer to home, the Council's solution was to abandon privatisation, move towards a fully integrated steel industry, and expand capital investment on projects which would provide demand for Sheffield steel. It followed up with an appeal to potential investors the following year with the launch of two high-quality brochures. All of which I dutifully signalled, whenever possible, to the Environment and Industry Ministers. By now, however, the Council was allowing the rates issue to divert it from the steel crisis. Labour councillors were also redefining the image of the city by proclaiming the 'people's republic of South Yorkshire'. The red flag went up over the town hall, and so did the rates – to the detriment of Sheffield's steel, according to the major stakeholders.

As early as June 1980, management at the River Don plant revealed that they had called a halt to key forging work because they could not meet the rates bill – topping a million pounds. The following year local engineering employers claimed that 'massive local rate rises' had led to fourteen firms cancelling, or delaying, investments that 'could accelerate city job cuts'.[127] During visits to Hadfields, Derek Norton, its chief executive, repeatedly warned me of the threat posed by 'unbearable' rates to the plant's brave fight to survive. By 1982, management at the River Don works complained of facing a rates

---

127   *The Star.* 11 March 1981.

bill of about £2m a year. David Clark, general manager, stated that 'high rates affected profits so seriously that buildings were now being urgently demolished to avoid paying rates on them. River Don received so few benefits from local councils,' he added, 'that rates amounted to a tax on the works' existence.'[128] Councillor Alan Billings, the Council's budget chairman, sympathised with the problems of heavy industry, but rejected Mr Clark's claim that the River Don works received little from the Council. Towards the end of the year, however, John Pennington, BSC Special Steels managing director, also warned that further heavy rate increases could threaten steel jobs in Yorkshire. 'We can understand the situation of the BSC' said *The Morning Telegraph*. 'They cannot sell their steel for any more than they could three years ago, yet they see local authority rates rising by 20, 30, even 40 per cent a year. Neither we nor industrialists want to see wholesale redundancies among council workers. But is there not a case for the reduction of the Town Hall workforce through natural wastage?'.[129]

The Council was now the largest single employer in the city, with a workforce still rising to 35,000. It was increasingly made up of non-jobs, its critics alleged. The appointment of a 'peace' officer was indicated as just one example, whereas a proper response, it was pointed out, would have been to shed 10,000 jobs.

The refusal of the Council to rein in spending despite rate capping did have a dramatic impact on the rates. Since 1981, domestic rates rose from 135p in the pound to 323p during 1986–87. Yet the Council had been unable to balance its books, despite the unusual tolerance of the District Auditor,[130] as well as borrowings from unlikely

---

128   *The Morning Telegraph*. 6 February 1982.

129   *The Morning Telegraph*. 19 November 1982.

130   For him to say that the Council were 'not guilty of wilful misconduct', protested *The Star*, [6 July 1987] 'is stretching it a bit'. For 'they had surely been advised by officers that what they were about was illegal.'

sources. For a time Sheffield councillors had been able to ignore government guidelines on rates, provided they were willing to take the consequential cuts in grants. But by 1985, with new rate-capping legislation on the statute book, things were difficult. If councillors chose to levy a rate in excess of the Government's maximum, or levy no rate at all, they would find themselves in direct confrontation with the law.

I continued to do my best on their behalf in Parliament. I pointed out repeatedly to ministers that by depriving Sheffield of intermediate status, for example, they had deprived it of EEC funding. I reminded them that through the grant-related expenditure for 1983–84 it had cut the city's spending and placed it in twenty-ninth position in the league table of thirty-six metropolitan districts. I pointed out, furthermore, that they were punishing it through the grant penalty system, despite its inner city problems. But seeking protection for the Council's programme of self-help, which was now controversial, and generally defending it, was becoming an uphill struggle.

Meanwhile Blunkett – by now elected to the Labour party's NEC – was active in assembling a united front of Labour rate-capped councils against the new legislation. The Environment secretary of state, Patrick Jenkin, wrote to Blunkett on 27 February 1985, assuring him that he would 'continue to behave moderately and reasonably notwithstanding the determination of the council you represent to seek to undermine the operation of the Rates Act as approved by Parliament.' However, the number of councils holding out in support of Blunkett soon dwindled, and a specially convened meeting of the PLP on 3 April dissociated itself from the campaign.

A leader in *The Guardian* described the multi-authority campaign as a 'disastrous failure', and much of the defiance into setting a rate as a 'confidence trick'. The most culpable of councillors were those who knew all along the strategy – whether confrontation with the government or pressure on its financial reserves – would fail. But they never said so in public, 'either for opportunistic personal advancement or in order to set up a witch-hunt against more cautious and realistic Labour councillors and leaders.' Into this category *The Guardian* placed 'Mr David Blunkett of Sheffield'. There was money available for compromise deals, it went on, and the councillors knew it. 'But all too often, they were just gutless and plain bad politicians.'[131] Sheffield's own *Morning Telegraph* accused the city's Labour group of a 'destructive and pointless policy they got second-hand from Militant-led Liverpool.'[132]

As councils abandoned the no-rate tactic one by one, only Sheffield, Liverpool and the London boroughs of Camden, Greenwich, Hackney, Islington and Lambeth still maintained their stance. Such councils had gained early support for opposing rate-capping by arguing that it would cause intolerable cuts in services. But that was not happening in Sheffield, according to Peter Ford in his Cutlers' Hall address in 1985, when he described 'the idea that reduced council expenditure must mean a reduced level of services [as] thoroughly misleading and mischievous.' Nor elsewhere, reported *The Guardian*: 'The Government has called the council's bluff and most of the leaders are soldiering on for want of an acceptable fall-back position.'[133] Other newspapers shared the same scepticism as they reviewed possible fall-back positions. If Sheffield threw down the gauntlet now and risked swingeing surcharge penalties, as was frequently mentioned, the councillors could be bankrupted and lose their homes and possessions. Tory and Liberal councillors said they intended to stay within the law, however. Would they be joined by enough Labour doubters was the question. Yes, there were twenty of them, eight coming from Attercliffe and only one Attercliffe councillor against, with two sick.

---

131   *The Guardian*. 17 June 1985.

132   *The Morning Telegraph*. 13 April 1985.

133   *The Guardian*. 29 April 1985.

As Blunkett headed the campaign remnant determined not to set a rate, Sheffield was becoming increasingly associated in the media with such controversial local authorities as Liverpool and Lambeth. That boded ill for Sheffield's public image, and suggested trouble for the Attercliffe party. It was also becoming clear that the motives of the rebellious authorities had been mixed. They varied from the ideological to the tactical, ranging from pressure on current ministers to a lingering hope of ultimate relief from an incoming Labour government. There was also undoubted opportunism on the part of certain players who were mindful of their careers. *The Guardian* mentioned that 'Mr Blunkett would be disqualified from running for Parliament', along with Councillors Roger Barton and Clive Betts.[134] But there was also a large group within the Sheffield district party that was set on confrontation at whatever personal cost to some councillors.

The bitterness that developed was intensified 'by the fact that many left-wingers on the district party are actually employees of the city council.'[135] It generated also more personal hatred across the city than at any time since the Bevanite years of the Fifties. There has always been a seam of ugliness in the Labour party. It flared now in the Sheffield district party as revenge was meted out to those Labour councillors who had voted to set a legal rate and thus saved the entire city from grave trouble. They were accused of betrayal, which was rejected in the Attercliffe party. At one such meeting, the accusers themselves were charged with betraying the standards of the old guard. Nevertheless, a disgraceful vendetta was exercised against senior and experienced councillors. Some were stripped of positions and others subject to de-selection procedures within their ward parties. Those responsible should have been present at that particular meeting of

134   *The Guardian.* 7 August 1985. Blunkett would soon be selected to succeed Joan Maynard as MP for Brightside.

135   *The Star.* 2 September 1985.

the Attercliffe general management committee (GMC) when Gerald Marshall, the most decent, honourable and able of councillors, presented his report.

The current confrontational tactics with the government had risked placing the council in an illegal position, he explained, whereas the Council could have avoided a head-on confrontation, ridden the storm, and waited for the return of a Labour government. Instead the district party had emerged as the real controller of the city council's policy. It had forced the Council to go on refusing to set a rate, despite reminders that the tactic had been exhausted. 'Responsibility for the council's actions no longer rested with elected members. It now rested with political opportunists,' he concluded. He broke down in tears. There was a stunned silence. There was absolutely no defence of the group or the district party. The meeting was adjourned.

All my Attercliffe councillors, apart from one, complained to me of the undermining of their responsibility by the left wing of the district party. It was no longer down to elected councillors, but to 'strutting peacocks' in the district party who could actually be Council employees, declared an editorial in *The Star*.[136] Labour councillors were no longer being treated as elected representatives of the people, it added, but as delegates mandated by the district party. Its joint deputy chairman, incidentally, was Dan Sequerra, full-time official of the then Association of Scientific, Technical and Management Staff (ASTMS).

Given its rich political legacy, what had brought Sheffield's Labour group to such an impasse? The London borough of Islington was already a pointer. The dominance of radical white collar delegates within its Labour district party had given rise to lurid press reports. I briefly shared a room in Parliament with its MP, Michael O'Halloran. In his absence, I sometimes received messages intended for him. They gave me an insight into the vicious and relentless pressure to which

136   *The Star*. 2 December 1986.

he as well as some of his councillors was subject. Certain London boroughs were demonised in the media, of course. But given published reports, they did ask for it as they acquired an unfavourable image.[137] Sheffield's councillors did not stray thus far. But they did become associated with such 'loony' councils – together with Liverpool – because of the rate-capping campaign.

Such developments led to an inquiry by the Labour party in 1985 into charges that in Liverpool its district party had made a practice of interfering in the day-to-day management of the city council. The report published early in 1986 found that the district party had taken decisions on issues which ought to be the prerogative of councillors. It described it as an 'extremely unhealthy development', particularly when meetings were dominated by shop stewards and members of the Council's trade unions. Most disturbing of all, the report indicated an organisation that was secret, widespread, well organised and seeking to determine the line taken at all such meetings – the Militant Tendency. The Attercliffe party could hold up its head high after the rate-capping crisis. Not so well publicised was the brave fight already being waged by its officers along with its battle-hardened councillors in tackling infiltration by this same sinister organisation, the Militant Tendency.

---

137   *The London Evening Standard.* 21 October 1986.

Appendix 1

CONSTITUENCY PROGRAMME - SEPTEMBER, 1981

1	Tues	11 a.m.	Sheffield University (accompanied by Mr Trotter)
		7.30 p.m.	Mosborough ward
2	Wed	11 a.m.	Bone Cravens
		7 p.m.	Public Meeting on Unemployment AUEW House (accompanied by Mr Alan Wade)
3	Thrs	11 a.m.	River Don Steelworks
5	Sat	10.30 a.m.	Surgery, Labour Hall
8	Tues	11 a.m.	Sanderson Kayser
9	Wed	10.30 a.m.	GMWU Retired Members (accompanied by Mrs Jessie Hamlyn)
		7.30 p.m.	Handsworth ward
10	Thrs	11 a.m.	B.S.C. Tinsley Park (accompanied by Mr Alan Wade)
11	Fri	8 p.m.	Birley Women's social (at the home of Brian and Jean Stewart)
12	Sat	10.30 a.m.	Surgery, Labour Hall
		8 p.m.	Miners' Welfare Hall, Rossington
16	Wed	11 a.m.	Firth Brown (accompanied by Mr Alan Wade)
		7.30 p.m.	G.M.C., Labour Hall
17	Thrs	a.m.	Royal Hallamshire Hospital (accompanied by Mr K. Curran)
		7.30 p.m.	Firth Brown Labour Party Branch
18	Fri	11 a.m.	Whitbread Brewery (accompanied by Mr Alan Wade)
		3.45	Michael Foot. Town Hall.
		4.15 p.m.	Industrial Development Advisory Committee, Town Hall
19	Sat	10.30 a.m.	Surgery, Labour Hall
20	Sun	2 p.m.	Seminar, Royal Victoria Hotel
22	Tues	11 a.m.	Record Ridgeway (accompanied by Mr Alan Wade)
23	Wed	11 a.m.	David Loewy (to be confirmed)
		6.30 p.m.	Attercliffe Parish Church
		7.30 p.m.	Darnall ward
		7.30 p.m.	Birley ward
24	Thrs	10.30 a.m.	Hadfield's (accompanied by Mr Alan Wade)
25	Fri	12.45 p.m.	Mr John Pennington, Managing Director, B.S.C.
26	Sat	10.30 a.m.	Surgery, Labour Hall
27	Sun	-----------	Labour Party Conference Brighton

Chapter Ten

Lurch to the Left

Against the backdrop of social change in the Sixties and the economic shockwaves that had buffeted the outgoing Labour government in 1970, some political reaction was inevitable. It was especially manifest among those rank-and-file party members who now felt deprived of power. I was not prepared, however, for the turbulent times that lay ahead in Attercliffe for its industry, for my party and for myself. A drastically changed membership of the party's GMC was the starting point. Since my original selection in 1969, Sheffield had taken in a chunk of Derbyshire and amended its own boundaries. This had led to the reorganisation of my four ward parties.[138] So I had to face a further conference to confirm acceptability by this new membership. Not easy: as a reconstructed left-winger, I had changed my stance on major issues such as Europe – with a referendum in the offing – as well as public ownership and defence. I was becoming involved in the conflict in Northern Ireland, with no local encouragement apart, significantly, from an up-and-coming Rob Murray in my constituency and local MPs Martin Flannery and Joan Maynard. I held unflinching views on moral and ethical issues such as abortion. I had been totally transparent at my original selection in 1969. I concealed nothing, nor resorted to populism, which had become fashionable at selection conferences. When asked, for example, if I would live in the constituency, if I was selected, I said no.

---

138   One was closed down due to house clearance, a second was transferred and I received two new ward parties from the north-east Derbyshire constituency. One was largely representative of Sheffield housing overspill and the other covered small townships in the Derbyshire coalfield.

In defying the Attercliffe party over the Common Market in 1971, however, I had to face a sacking motion shortly afterwards. I survived by five votes at a crowded meeting.[139] After that early clash I was at pains subsequently to discuss major issues thoroughly with the membership, although my early position was justified by the referendum of 1975, when two-thirds of South Yorkshire's electorate voted for the Common Market.[140]

I realised that I could only continue to carry my party with me, which I did henceforth, apart from ethical issues – when the executive and I agreed to disagree – by a consultation that was properly arranged. Accordingly, from then onwards, I organised an autumn conference for the Attercliffe party. Together with an agreed agenda reflecting contemporary issues and the distribution of prepared papers, there was ample scope for discussion in seminar-like conditions during two sessions (See Appendix 1). Such annual 'seminars' – as they became known – were always well-attended in the comfortable surrounds of the Royal Victoria Hotel on Sunday afternoon, interspersed with a proper tea.[141] I arranged a similar consultation in 1974 in collaboration with my neighbour, Fred Mulley, then Secretary of State for Education, on the economic policy of the incoming Labour government. When the Conservative government announced earlier its controversial changes in industrial relations law, I proposed immediately a conference of Sheffield's trade unionists, for which I prepared papers. This was welcomed by Councillor Will Owen of

---

139   It was proposed by Councillor Dot Walton, who chaired the new Mosborough ward party. It had been drawn up, she later revealed, by Tom Swain, MP for the north-east Derbyshire constituency. He was anti-Common Market, so he said, but really resentful of losing two of his ward parties.

140   *The Star.* 9 June 1975, which observed: 'The Left are not as close to the British working man as they led us to believe.'

141   I met the cost wholly and personally, which eventually approached £500 annually.

the Transport and General Workers Union (TGW), who offered his city centre premises as the venue. It was so successful that Will Owen adopted the practice permanently. Henceforth, such consultation became a common practice of the city's trade unions as well as the Attercliffe party.

None of that prevented my future in Sheffield becoming the subject of speculation after the sacking of Eddie Griffiths in the Brightside constituency next door, because the media then became active in head-hunting Labour MPs considered at risk. The proscribing of organisations, which had been introduced in 1930, had been abolished in 1972 by Labour's NEC. It also allowed moves against sitting MPs, so long as the rules on dismissal were followed. My tough chairmanship of a select committee's enquiry into the car industry in 1975 did not go well with – as *The Economist* put it – those 'left-wing activists who think every ailing industry should have an open-ended meal ticket.'[142] Even in Sheffield there were some who could not see the connection between a successful motor industry in Birmingham and its continuing demand for Sheffield steel.[143] For those so-called activists, the action of the *Financial Times* in making me 'Man of the Week' on the publication of the select committee report was the kiss of death.[144] As was an editorial in *Quality*, the journal of the Sheffield Chamber of Commerce, praising my 'wise remarks' on the importance of profit in industry. I braced myself for trouble ahead.

In September 1975, however, there was a welcome development. Sir Ron Ironmonger, Leader of the Council, proposed to the

---

142   *The Economist.* 16 August 1975.

143   Unbelievably, Derek Robinson – or the infamous 'Red Robbo', communist convenor of the British Leyland trade unions – was invited to address a meeting in Sheffield soon afterwards.

144   The *Financial Times.* 16 August 1975.

Attercliffe party that it should silence any such critics. I received an overwhelming vote of confidence. 'Thank goodness common sense has prevailed in Attercliffe,' said the local press.[145] Sir Ron explained that, 'if we go on as they are, this time next year there will be no Labour Party as we know it.' He hoped Attercliffe 'would provide the lead to other constituencies who fear they may be under attack from what he [saw] as totally unrepresentative minority factions.' There must be 'no party within a party, no faction', which fairly expressed the consensus of the meeting. My officers, always close friends, were also insistent that their party must always reflect mainstream politics. Otherwise, they pointed out, the gap between what the party nationally preaches and what large numbers of its traditional supporters actually want will continue to widen.

On the other hand, the arrival of Joan Maynard in Brightside and Martin Flannery in Hillsborough indicated that elements elsewhere in Sheffield were taking a turn to the left. It was also clear that this new Left was operating within a different political spectrum. Less tolerant, even of the right to 'conscience' on moral issues, it was becoming increasingly impatient with moderate Labour MPs. My concern then was not so much for the new policies, as for their attainability given the changing mood of voters. The Labour party was undoubtedly in need of new thinking. But I was anxious that it should not get out of step with the electorate again, as happened between 1951 and 1964. I warned my party that the Bevanite experience was a contributory factor, and expressed the hope that it would serve as a salutary warning to the new Left in Sheffield.

Aneurin Bevan had captivated Labour's Left in the 1950s, including myself. I remember him addressing a packed Corn Exchange in

---

145   *The Star.* 19 September 1975. The motion cited my 'excellent work in the constituency, diligent and painstaking efforts in attacking general problems both in the constituency and in the city', and my 'unfailing help to the city and county councils in forging a link with Parliament.'

Doncaster on a Sunday afternoon of all times, before going on to speak in Sheffield to another massive turnout. After dividing Labour on the issue of nuclear armaments, he suddenly changed sides – to my consternation. I came to appreciate his empiricism, eventually, in the context of his new responsibilities and confidential briefings. I then valued him all the more for his flexibility. I said so to his wife, Jennie Lee, on arrival at the House of Commons. She wept.

I learned also from his experience that in policy differences we must preserve some sense of proportion and some respect for the opinions of others. Nor must we risk cutting ourselves off from our roots or a changing electorate, warned Jim Callaghan in addresses to Labour regional rallies. Otherwise the gap between what Labour preaches and what our supporters actually want will continue to widen. Labour's support, which was at a record level of turnout in 1951 had slipped to 31% by 1970. It was still slipping in the early Seventies, to the apparent indifference of some in Sheffield.[146]

For example, at a Communist party meeting organised by the AEU in the Memorial Hall in Sheffield in the mid-Seventies, Joan Maynard warned that the newly-elected Labour Government's 'attempts to patch up the capitalist system [are] doomed to failure', and called for a 'long overdue' cut in defence spending. Her remarks were echoed precisely at about the same time by Jo Richardson, writing as secretary of the Tribune group of Labour MPs. She called for the implementation of 'bold socialist policies, implicit in Clause Four of the Labour Party constitution.'[147]

I had shared their passion for wholesale nationalisation once upon a time. But the early impact of the nationalisation of coal in the South Yorkshire coalfield had already moved me to grave misgivings, as had other pointers. On arrival in Parliament in 1963, I noted the absence

---

146   Labour's share of the total poll at the two general elections in 1974 was lower than at any time since 1935.

147   *Tribune*. 12 September 1975.

of one serious economist in the formidable Tribune group. I quickly became chairman of Labour's parliamentary Economic and Financial Affairs committee and found myself looking in vain for the attendance of many, if any, Tribune MPs. Nevertheless, among those who did attend were some of the ablest members of the PLP. I noted also the failure of George Brown's interventionist policies in his Economic Affairs department created in 1964. I was leaning more and more to the role of the market rather than the command economy, but within a mixed economy. Where to strike the balance I saw as a looming question for Labour.

When my father died in the early Seventies, I found myself pondering once again on the benefits of nationalisation. He was a coal-face worker for fifty-three years, and only absent once on the single occasion of a broken limb. On retirement he received a weekly pension of thirty shillings from the National Coal Board (NCB) and a few shillings monthly from his local union branch funds. But he had still been working six shifts every week when he was in his early seventies. The excessive growth in the NCB bureaucracy in Doncaster pointed blatantly to 'too much harness and too little horse'. In addition to an existing office block, five more had been built or added. One is still the town's only skyscraper. From being known as the Coal House, it is now styled the Council House. What else. A further large block of office space is still unoccupied after many years.[148] At least the senior administrative appointments within the NCB had become more credible. Unlike the choice of the post-war Labour government of a retired major-general as the first chairman. Now Joan Maynard and Jo Richardson, both members of the party's NEC, were calling for more of the same. They were also pressuring, as matter of fact, their own government – without a working majority – to undertake yet more radical policies in defiance of stark warnings

---

148   The excessive clerical staff even tried to share the miners' traditional 'free coal' concession.

from the electorate. I helped form a response within the PLP, which was called the Manifesto group. It brought together colleagues who were concerned to relate democratic socialist philosophy to current needs and practicalities.

I became concerned also by the late Seventies in Sheffield about the emergence of the new brand of Labour councillors. Some believed they were ushering in a dramatic new age for the city. They called for a socialist republic of South Yorkshire. More disturbing, given the steel crisis, was the apparent shift in the composition of the Labour group from blue-collar to white collar and the change in its political complexion. Recalling Aneurin Bevan, I warned my Attercliffe councillors of the realities of power. I appealed for a more pragmatic rather than ideological approach, especially on the part of the new Labour group. For a new regime was gradually replacing a group which had included such distinguished councillors as Sir Ron Ironmonger, Sidney Dyson, Isidore Lewis, Jim Sterland, Grace Tebbutt and some with whom I had a special connection such as Roy and Enid Hattersley, parents of Roy (later Lord) Hattersley; Reg and Roy Munn from a prominent Labour family which includes Meg Munn MP; and a young Joe Ashton, who acted as whip before becoming a Member of Parliament – as did Roy Hattersley junior, of course. Roy Hattersley senior was one of my councillors in Attercliffe, and immensely appealing.[149] Sidney Dyson (see Appendix 2) and Enid Hattersley, whose contrasting backgrounds and personalities intrigued me, were outstanding Lord Mayors. They were succeeded in the group by David Blunkett, Clive Betts, Alan Billings, Alan Wigfield and Mike Bower among others.

The Star newspaper cleared a page – ironically headed, perhaps, 'First Steps to Heaven' – for the new council Leader, David Blunkett,

---

149   Gentle, courteous, deeply conscientious and caring, I came to see him as almost priestly in manner before I learned that that had been an earlier calling.

to assess the first year in office of 'The Young Ones'.[150] Blunkett expressed in reply a desire for more self-reliance through town hall cooperation and partnership, especially with industry. There had been wider consultation already, he claimed. He would resist public spending cuts and seek to relieve local unemployment. He acknowledged the formidable responsibility which now rested with the Council, and particularly with the Labour group. That was all.

A reading today still brings to mind Hans Christian Andersen and the fable of the Emperor with no clothes. For rhetoric apart, Blunkett and his followers were offering Sheffield so little in its desperate plight. Or signposting, indeed, how they were to get from where they were to where they might want to be. It was difficult to discern among 'The First Steps to Heaven' any mandatory vision or clarion call. Or any awareness of the need to carefully handle communications, visibility and ethics. It was also difficult to detect among those most prominent in the group actual experience of commerce, industry and inter-governmental relations. They had yet to learn that a government in London, much less a council in Sheffield, could not create economic growth, though they could impede it.

On the other hand, council and government working together could at least foster a favourable environment for the tried and trusty to attempt economic recovery locally. Instead the new councillors opted for a more interventionist, even corporatist role. They behaved as if they could actually manage the local economy themselves, for control was central to their concept of socialism: control-ism rather than its social and personal content. Inevitably, they favoured the ultra course of action over the pragmatic and reformist – even to the contemplation of lawbreaking. For that had now become the litmus test of being truly left wing. 'Looking back', David Blunkett conceded later, 'we perhaps didn't fully understand the old mechanisms of Government and that we couldn't just make an announcement or

---

150   *The Star.* 25 June 1981.

pass legislation and think changes would happen straight away.'[151] More recently, he acknowledged that working with people in an 'ever-changing economic and social environment' involves 'facing down those who pretend that they have simplistic solutions and that reality will somehow go away if they shout loud enough.'[152]

There was money available for compromise deals during the rate capping crisis that followed, as the Minister, Patrick Jenkin, often reminded me. But the new regime was more concerned for its political credibility than the interests of Sheffield's ratepayers. It is unimaginable that the worldly-wise old guard could ever be prone to such hubris, and be so culpable as to sanction the witch-hunt to come. It was reported that every spring bank holiday the new Labour leaders went to their annual camp in the Lake District.[153] I don't know what they discussed, but I never detected any new ideas in their pronouncements, especially in relation to economic management. They might have found attendance at my annual seminar more profitable.

I had long since disclosed to my senior colleagues in Attercliffe that I had been seeking the Holy Grail of such new Left thinking since the 1950s. It had proved most elusive. The search was centred in Sheffield, of all places. I was accustomed to doing so together with close and such valued friends as Edward Thompson, a colleague at Leeds University, and Drs William Carr and Royden Harrison of Sheffield University. Sometimes Bert Wynn, leader of the Derbyshire Miners, would attend our discussions.[154] I travelled simultaneously to Scotland

---

151   *The Star.* 24 May 2010.

152   *The Times.* 4 April 2012.

153   *The Star.* 26 May 1982.

154   At the same time I used to visit Vin Williams, who inspired the conversion of Wortley Hall into a trade union social centre, at his home in Driver Street, Woodhouse.

to relate our findings to Lawrence Daly, who was later to become the Miners' leader, at his home in Fife, and sometimes stayed overnight.[155] We were all conscious of the enormous underlying strength of the Labour movement in Britain and the loyalty it commanded. How we could possibly influence its ideology and direction was our objective. The arrival of the *New Reasoner* publication was a guide. How far our mission could be linked with working-class organisations was assigned to Bert Wynn, Lawrence Daly and myself. It was a difficult role for me, as consumer choice was increasingly challenging central planning; incoming reports from eastern Europe on economic management were also far from encouraging. Consequently, my thoughts on economic policies generally were becoming more broadly based. My colleagues were ever tolerant of my wandering economics brief.

I had harboured more certitude when I arrived at the LSE after WWII. I had been fascinated before arrival by the analysis of Karl Marx and dazzled by the polemics contained in *The Communist Manifesto*. Professor Harold Laski, for all his fearsome radical reputation, soon diverted me. He kindly invited me to his home in Fulham one Sunday evening and presented me with a copy of his book *The State in Theory and Practice*. He advised me to read all the writings of Marx on the economy. I had already been jolted by the realisation when seated for my first lecture in the Old Theatre that it was there that a famous debate took place in 1934. It was between John Maynard Keynes and Friedrich Von Hayek. They became identified with different perspectives in their approach to such economic problems as the use of capital, its relationship with money, their influence on profits, investment, prices, markets, government policy and their consequences for innovation, employment and wages. They were reputedly in conflict with each other and with Karl Marx. In the light of such varied thinking, my thoughts on such matters were in constant revision.

---

155   Daly founded the Socialist League, which offered a flash of hope after successes in local elections.

My thoughts were exposed, moreover, to endless debate in seminars and student politics where they were threshed and threshed again. Eventually, I became wedded to Keynesian economic policies, perhaps because they were more popular at the LSE, though Von Hayek was a faculty member. But his writings and those of Josef Schumpeter could not be conveniently set aside. Nor the arguments of Marx, for I remained aware of the magnetic appeal that his basic argument must have for some workers, and remain relevant for others, especially in the light of the recent economic and financial crisis. He had insisted that capitalism was doomed because it was driven by profit, thus driving down wages and undercutting consumer demand. Too great an extension of credit brings down the entire system. Quite apart from the contradictions in his writings claimed by Keynes and Von Hayek, I wondered in my immaturity if there might be more to Marx than that.

My assigned task within the *New Reasoner* group – and ongoing concern – was to reconcile such writings with a fair deal for workers. I took my father as an exemplar. He knew nothing of the economic concepts I was now entertaining, although they could have major consequences for his job and pay, of course. Yet I had long realised that he and his mates would not be easily persuaded by any ideology that they feared would change their general lifestyle. That realisation was driven home by Labour's third successive election defeat in 1959. It was a major disappointment to all of us. We agonised over the results, as we had done so over Anthony Crosland's book on *The Future of Socialism* published in 1956. We decided to broaden our ambience. We circulated papers for wider discussion. I booked the Danum Hotel in Doncaster for consideration of the election returns in 1959. It attracted a mass gathering from all over Yorkshire. That was a notable departure from Labour's traditional meeting places, as was the thorough report of its proceedings and disturbing conclusions. It was forwarded to the regional office. I went further afield.

Whilst lecturing at Leeds University, I arranged and organised day and weekend conferences for trade unions in Yorkshire – notably with the district committee of the Confederation of Shipbuilding and Engineering Unions (CSEU) in Huddersfield – quite apart from lecturing at their national summer schools. I worked closely with the Workers' Education Association (WEA). I addressed branches of the Yorkshire Miners at the request of its general secretary, Ernest Jones.[156] He invited me to join him in Barnsley as personal aide and secretary. It was an enticing offer. We were privately agreed on the union's need of research facilities and the adoption of modern communication techniques. I was also invited twice to join the Extramural department at Sheffield University. I could not bring myself to leave Leeds University, however, and the stimulating company of talented colleagues. But arising from joint discussion with Bert Wynn and Ernest Jones I did persuade both Leeds and Sheffield Universities to authorise day-release courses at both the universities for Derbyshire and Yorkshire miners. That historic development stemmed directly from our *New Reasoner* group's activities.

As I became personally acquainted with some of the students, I saw how the courses and the academic environment were transforming many of them. They furnished the NCB with valuable personnel managers and local councils with future leaders. Sir Jack Smart, former branch secretary at Glasshoughton colliery, became the widely respected head of the national body of local authorities. Other graduates from the Leeds course distinguished themselves in Parliament. They included Lord Lofthouse, Deputy Speaker, Joseph Harper, Yorkshire regional Whip, Sir William O'Brien and Alex Woodall. I encouraged certain students to attend Ruskin College, Oxford. A rich yield also came from the WEA, covering mayoralties,

---

156   Ernest had been my father's union branch secretary at Rossington colliery before going to Barnsley. Outstanding performance at both levels assured his promotion as general secretary of the national union.

leaders of councils and committees and members of the magistracy. They were all pragmatist in outlook, though I never ceased urging them to continue seeking the Holy Grail. During that happy and productive time with the WEA, thanks to an outstanding Leeds-based district secretary in Fred Sedgwick OBE, I occasionally joined forces with one of its lecture organisers, Harry Newton, then living in Selby. Personally likeable, a good speaker, hard left, he was sometimes belligerent and confrontational. Such intransigence and militant style hampered discussion. But he became a popular figure in the Labour movement in west and north Yorkshire. It was later revealed by an employee of MI5 that he was a secret agent, and had been directed to monitor the CND.[157] Unhappily, he was not alone.

In his 'fight and fight again' defiance of the adoption of nuclear unilateralism at the Labour party conference in Scarborough in 1960, Hugh Gaitskell was addressing among others, the first shoots of the post-war generation. They were the fortunate young people who had known nothing but decent accommodation, full employment and peace. They had also become exposed, on the other hand, to lowering standards at certain new-styled universities and polytechnics. Adopting the flower power peace movements, environmental interests and relaxed moral standards, they were prone during the Sixties to challenge freedom of speech at trade union schools and universities. Visiting speakers, when allowed access, and including left-wing Labour MPs, risked humiliation when addressing students' unions. To be doused with water as a preliminary was not an uncommon experience, even at the LSE. Whilst I was once addressing the Students' Union at Sheffield University, a 'fringe' meeting was actually taking place contemptuously in the middle of my larger gathering. When I later addressed the Students' Union at the University of East Anglia, as Navy Minister, one student present confided afterwards that he was a naval midshipman on student

---

157   *The Guardian.* 28 February 1985.

release. But he dare not reveal his identity. It was tempting to recall the warning of Frederick Engels, close associate of Karl Marx, that the pseudo-learned presumptuousness of the so-called educated is a much more serious problem than 'ignorance of the masses'.

I found it disturbing that such people might become white-collar workers in the public sector as social workers and welfare rights advisers. Equally worrying was the growing replacement of blue-collar workers in the Labour movement by such think-a-likes.[158] Where such a sectional self-interest congregated in Labour's district parties, as happened in Sheffield and Liverpool, it enabled some to exercise a disproportionate influence. It led in Sheffield by the mid-Eighties to a basic shift in the relationship between the district party and the Council's Labour group. That was demonstrated all too unhappily during the rate-capping crisis. Such developments in both cities attracted the attention of the Militant Tendency movement. It focused in Sheffield on the Attercliffe party.

I had been convincingly endorsed in successive election and confidence votes, and was about to be comfortably reselected in the autumn of 1981. A certain intolerance since my original selection had persisted at two firms in my constituency, however. When I visited their premises, the AEU secretary-convenors of shop stewards at Davy-Loewy and Bone Cravens refused to meet me either separately or with management. Although Bone Cravens was located only just across from my constituency office, and Davy Loewy a little farther down the road. With reselection looming in the autumn of 1981, I decided to abandon my annual visits to both firms to avoid provocation. Nevertheless, a baffling situation arose at Davy-Loewy, which was triggered by the non-cooperating AEU secretary-convenor, Eddie Keys (See Appendix 3).

---

158   In its first newsletter in November 1986, the Sheffield LCC-Tribune group described a much-changed local trades council as 'mainly middle-class'. The Dulwich Fabian Society analysed the New Left in its 'Discussion Documents', and concluded that its activists were drawn from similar social backgrounds through shared educational experience and inter-related types of employment.

That I had been set up was the reaction of my constituency officers. They rallied immediately in support, with the exception of the constituency secretary. It had become a difficult position to fill, and was briefly occupied by Mick Elliott, a national executive member of CND and a former communist.[159] All my other officers were in no doubt that it was a contrived dispute, if only because of the timing. Labour MPs were being subject to mandatory reselection for the first time. The three local moderate MPs Fred Mulley, Frank Hooley and myself were considered to be at risk. My officers also believed it was contrived because of the role and attitude of certain members of the local district committee of the CSEU. Those particular members had saddled the committee with a vexatious and bizarre dispute at Davy-Loewy solely on the words of Keys, the AEU secretary-convenor. Worse, they introduced a taped recording of a conversation I had had with management which, presumably, had been 'hacked'. They constantly brandished it, whilst denying me sight or sound of it. I was never allowed to see it or hear it played. Which never really worried me, for I knew that it was irrelevant to the charge being levelled at me of interference in an industrial dispute. Yet they swiftly entered into a judgment from which other committee members were soon very anxious to retreat.

Hardly anyone in my Attercliffe party believed them anyway, nor anyone further afield, least of all the many shop stewards committees around my constituency. They formally notified me of their intention to challenge the CSEU, or took the opportunity to praise me.[160] I had always had very good relations with the important Firth Brown shop stewards committee, for example. Its secretary wrote to the

---

159   As a delegate from ASTMS he had represented the Sheffield Trades Council the previous year, along with George Caborn and Blanche Flannery, both communists, at the World Parliament for the Peoples of Peace in Bulgaria.

160   Notably at Sanderson-Keyser, where the shop stewards convenor had informed the Trades Council right at the outset that in view of my 'past record [he] would personally put complete trust in [me] in any circumstances or situation.'

CSEU to put that on record. I had arranged a visit by them to the naval dockyards whilst I was Navy Minister, for I also valued the relationship. Whereas the Davy-Loewy shop stewards were out on their own in this particular complaint.

Pleas for peace to my party officers came very quickly from some of the CSEU members, first privately and then publicly. A meeting was arranged with my constituency party, which was addressed by the chairman of the CSUE district committee, George Caborn, who was also district secretary of the AEU. He was shouted down, not allowed to speak, publicly humiliated and the meeting was abandoned. At a further meeting, two distinctly placatory CSEU representatives admitted that I was clear of the original charge of 'interference'. 'We want to bury this one,' they declared, 'and as soon as possible,' which was overwhelmingly endorsed by those present. Keys, who was also present, but with a different attitude, grudgingly admitted that 'the relationship between himself and Pat Duffy could have been better.' A close friend and shop steward at Davys, Kelvin Godwin, was soon elected the new constituency secretary. Within a short time he replaced Keys as secretary-convenor at Davys. Its shop stewards committee then initiated with me a long-sought working relationship.

My constituency party had given me a clear vote of confidence in the presence of those CSEU officers. On the same day, a short distance away in the neighbouring constituency of Heeley, Frank Hooley, an excellent MP, was being deselected. He was replaced by Councillor Bill Michie, who had notoriously run up the red flag over the Town Hall. *The Daily Telegraph* described the deselection of Fred Mulley on the other side of the Attercliffe constituency a month later as an 'earthquake' and asked, 'If Fred fails, who among old Labour can find a way of saving or winning back South Yorkshire for old-fashioned democracy?'[161] That will be our mission, my Attercliffe officers told me, though we might now stand alone.

---

161   *The Daily Telegraph*. 1 March 1982.

That we were at least still holding the line was demonstrated soon afterwards at the Attercliffe party's annual general meeting. Under the headline, 'Duffy's team routs the Left', *The Star* reported that its members 'delivered what was virtually a vote of confidence in their beleaguered MP Pat Duffy when … virtually every Left-winger was swept from office.' Among those mentioned were Richard Caborn MEP – soon to succeed Fred Mulley – and Ken Curran, full-time officer of NUPE. When the local CSEU committee enquired later about a private meeting to discuss better relations, London was suggested. We agreed on the Naval Club in Mayfair, which I had helped found after WWII, and where I stayed as an MP. I never found a second home in London necessary, even when I was a Minister and later whilst I was switching to and fro' to Brussels on NATO business and, at a time, moreover, when MPs were required to put in much more time at Westminster. The meeting and the lunch that followed could not have been more pleasant. I was back among good men whom I had long admired, and with many of whom I had become personally close. This general and harmonious resolution of an unjustifiable dispute was resisted by only three individuals so far as I was aware. They were Mick Elliott, soon to depart, Ken Curran, a local NUPE officer, though he was not a member of the CSEU, and Jonathan Foster, in whose name a version of the tape was published in the *Morning Telegraph*, soon to depart also.

Despite the CSEU policy that the original dispute be 'buried', an early joint report on hospital pay[162] – with which I was not involved – by Curran and Foster, indicated that both would continue to revive it, as indeed they did on every conceivable pretext. Yet his first report apart, Foster never once checked with me any of those subsequent

---

162   *Morning Telegraph.* 19 May 1982.

pieces.[163] He telephoned me twice only, never once spoke to my Agent, never travelled the short distance to Attercliffe to interview us, although he had been prepared to visit the European Parliament in Luxembourg earlier in the year.[164] Unlike David Flynn, editor of *The Star*, who dropped everything in mid-December and travelled to London to interview me. I complained to Foster's editor in 1983 about his inaccurate and, on occasion, hostile reporting. But Peter Darling was always unsympathetic.

My chairman, Ron Burford, headed the ASTMS branch at Davys, of which Dan Sequerra was fulltime officer. The day following my first meeting with the CSEU in the city centre, Ron received a call from his general secretary, Clive Jenkins, encouraging him to stand by me. That was a setback for Sequerra, if not a distinct affront. It explained, I assumed, the different tone also of a private and confidential letter I received within days from the previously hawkish Sequerra. My request to him afterwards for its release from confidentiality, in order that I could pass it round my party officers, was angrily refused. Terry Duffy, president of the AUE, rang me probing the roles in the dispute of George Caborn and his prospective successor as the union's district secretary, Derek Simpson, also a communist. It was Simpson for whom Terry reserved his venom: such language. I received many calls of support from trade union officers I had coached years earlier at their union's summer schools. They were now occupying posts of varying prominence within their organisations.

---

163   How far Foster was out of touch may be gauged by his early description of me as an 'innocent abroad in the jungle of industrial relations'. As a matter of fact I was fully conversant with the Davy dispute in all its industrial and legal implications, and more so than anyone else in Sheffield. Whilst attending trade union summer schools in the Fifties – voluntarily, and in an unpaid capacity – I specialised in arranging mock disputes so that I could coach the trade union officers and shop stewards present.

164   *Morning Telegraph*. 10 January 1981.

After my early defiance headlined in *The Star*, I complied with the advice of my officers to keep quiet, despite my obvious anxiety to place the phone 'hacking' in the hands of the police. I was guided legally by Gerry Bermingham, then a Sheffield city councillor , and later an MP. I pressed him to allow me at least to present a complaint to the Press Council against the *Morning Telegraph* for breach of its own ethical code[165] and the improper conduct of one of its representatives, Foster. Gerry pointed to the record of the Press Council, and warned against reopening the Davy dispute in any event because of its likely handling coinciding with the timing of the next election.

The year of 1981 had been climactic for me because of deepening involvement also on two other major fronts. One was the crisis in Northern Ireland arising from the hunger strikes. Alone, I challenged Margaret Thatcher on the issue in Parliament. I accused her of unnecessary intransigence. But for once the lady was for turning and there followed changes which led to new policies, the signing of the Anglo-Irish Agreement and later the unfolding of the peace process. The second front was the NATO Assembly, where I now represented the Labour party. I had been appointed to an early chairmanship and found myself meeting key players in the Western alliance – industrial and political – and eventually within the Soviet bloc. With a glimmer of change in Moscow, and nuclear agreement in the offing at long last, it was a crucial period. After the emergence of Mr Gorbachev the breakthrough came, along with the fall of the Berlin Wall. By that time I was President of the NATO Assembly.

---

165   Which ran thus: 'The Staff of *Morning Telegraph* go to a great deal of trouble to ensure that news items are accurate, fair and balanced. Over the years the paper has built up an enviable reputation as a reliable and trusted friend of the community. If ever you feel that any item in *Morning Telegraph* has not maintained this high standard, please write to the Editor...' *Morning Telegraph*. 1 July 1985.

I never allowed any one of such disparate roles to divert me from constituency needs. I always stayed close, as *The Economist* once observed. Whatever the claims of Westminster or ministerial duties or NATO programmes – even as far away as Washington on a Friday – I would fly back overnight. I was always in the constituency office in Darnall on Saturday mornings for 'surgeries', year in, year out. Whilst my first Agent, Sidney Dyson, was living, I would collect him because of his infirmity at his home on Dover Road and return him afterwards. I was loyally supported later by his successors, Alan Wade, Ron Burford and Joe Sheedy, with equally congenial and supportive constituency secretaries Kelvin Godwin and Rob Murray, who were ever present. After the 'surgeries' we would adjourn to the nearby Darnall 'Libs' club or the Horticultural ('Horty') club. That is where I would feel at home. There, like my father, I would be ready for a real pint. With the active encouragement of Kelvin Godwin I would scan the racing page of our newspapers in search of a 'winner'. He would tease me that I only backed Irish horses, and sometimes conceded that they were among the best. I was often back on Saturday nights visiting other good working-men's clubs in Handsworth and Beighton. Sunday mornings I divided between attendance at Mass and visits to the steel industry shop stewards meetings that were usually held in Tinsley, bordering Rotherham, and only sixteen miles from home.

The crisis in steel locally was now my prime concern, however, with prior claims on my attention and energies. I remained puzzled that the local CSEU had allowed certain members to divert it from the unprecedented destruction of steel and engineering capacity and jobs in Attercliffe. The situation they contrived at Davys was absurd. The Attercliffe party officers saw it as the opening round of the battle for the soul of Labour in Sheffield.

Appendix 1

Patrick Duffy MP.

HOUSE OF COMMONS
LONDON SWIA OAA

25 July 1988.

Secretaries, Ward Parties
 and affiliated t.unions,
Attercliffe C.L.P.

SEMINAR
Royal Victoria Hotel, Sheffield.
Sunday, 16 October
2.00 p.m.

Britain and the world are changing fast.   And so must Labour.   We have launched a major review to examine the problems which will face Britain in the 1990s, and to devise the most up-to-date policies to meet them.

Our annual seminar will look at the seven main policy areas.   This is YOUR opportunity to tell us what YOU think.   We are listening.

There will be two sessions, with maximum discussion, as always, and it is proposed that they proceed on the following lines:

1. Economy   – how can we ensure that Britain has the industries and services of the future?

2. Equality   – how do we tackle poverty and how should it be paid for?

3. Consumers   – how are basic services – health, education, homes, transport – best provided?

4. People at work   – how do we improve job satisfaction, the quality of management and industrial relations?

5. Britain in the world   – how can a Labour government most effectively defend and enhance the security of the British people?

6. Environment   – how can we best ensure that industrial development does not bring with it more pollution?

7. Individual Freedom   – how can we protect people against crime, and how can we get back to traditional values?

Tea will be provided, as usual, at about 4 p.m. and it would help if you would kindly notify our constituency secretary, Mr. Robert Murray, of the names of those who plan to attend.

With every good wish.

Yours sincerely,

Pat.

191

Appendix 2

As befits its standing, Sheffield has been favoured with many distinguished Lord Mayors and Lady Mayoresses. None have recorded a more memorable year of office than Sidney and Mary Dyson. None, moreover, have served their city more selflessly or from more humble beginnings.

Sidney started work at fourteen as a butcher's boy. He was an imposing figure, well over six feet, with an equally imposing stomach. He dropped his 'h's profusely and I often heard him say, 'My dear, no doors in Sheffield are barred to me.' When he appeared at banquets in his ordinary clothes no-one thought it untoward of him. He was widely popular, except in his own party.

Mary was born in Portland Place, Doncaster. It was the poorest part of town, located within a network of squalid yards. But living was relieved of some disease by the piped river water supplied by the nearby sewer. After Mary's father moved the family to Sheffield in search of work she met Sidney. They were married in the Methodist Chapel, through which Mary acquired unwavering spiritual beliefs, creativity and artistry. They believed their early industrial hardship enabled them to develop a lifestyle of service to others, despite lifelong financial penury. Mary often recalled that she only ever sampled spending power when she became Lady Mayoress. Although he acted as constituency agent to two ministers in Park and Attercliffe as late as the Seventies and became an alderman, Sidney's annual income never exceeded £1,200. Fred Mulley and I failed to secure for him the award of an OBE from Harold Wilson, when he was showering higher honours on all manner of strange and dubious people who had no acquaintance with Labour's grassroots. But even their wealth and apparent status could not match the dedication and self-sacrifice of Sidney and Mary Dyson.

Their only son, Cyril, married Sheila McDonald in 1984. Born in Ireland, Sheila completed her teacher-training in London. After Cyril's death in 1992, she travelled extensively, developed a passion for mountaineering and learned to fly. A remarkable woman, like Mary, she has published in *Here a Little, There a Little* (Northend 2005) a loving testament to Mary, who rose from being a buffer girl in the Sheffield cutlery industry to be Lady Mayoress, 1970–71.

Appendix 3

The Davy-Loewy parent company in London was planning to combine its operations with its associate, Davy Instruments, operating also on the Darnall site. Eighty jobs were at risk. I only became aware of it when local MPs – including the local Conservative MP – mentioned a circular letter they had received from Keys.[166] I wrote immediately to Keys seeking confirmation and eventually received the belated circular. Nevertheless, I sought his advice on how he wished the matter to be handled at parliamentary level, and copied my letter to the same local MPs. I received no reply from Keys. At the request of a deputation of Davy shop stewards, without Keys, a meeting did take place in my constituency office. I was urged to request local Davy management to convey to the chairman and board members of the parent company their anxiety about job retention. However, no comfort was forthcoming. But local management was anxious to maintain the best possible relations with the displaced men. They assured me of help in the setting-up of a cooperative, and promised to remember the men in the event of redevelopment. I kept the local MPs informed, in accordance with customary practice. None of this was done until I had checked and been given to understand that local trade union procedure had been exhausted. That is to say, there was no further official trade union involvement.

---

166   I had communicated with Keys earlier in the year in response to a general appeal to stave off the proposed merger of Davy-Loewy with the Enserch Corporation. The Monopolies Commission rejected the Enserch bid, but throughout the campaign Keys corresponded with me only by a circular letter which he addressed also to six local MPs, though I was the one with specific parliamentary responsibility. He ignored my invitations to meet personally either in my constituency office or elsewhere at his convenience. Yet he encouraged Joan Maynard and Martin Flannery to become involved which also led to confusion.

Late one Thursday night in December, the Yorkshire regional whip told me in the House of Commons that he had heard of a 'confed' meeting that he thought I should attend. I had to ring Ernest Johnson, secretary of the local CSEU committee for confirmation. Only then did I learn that it had been summoned to discuss – presumably in my absence – a taped recording of one of many conversations that I had had over several weeks with Brian McAteer, managing director of Davy Instruments. I rang my Agent, Alan Wade, who was equally shocked. His simple response was, 'What a set-up. We will take them on.'

Attending the meeting on the next day, Saturday 12 December 1981, we found it chaired by the CSEU district committee chairman, and AEU district secretary, George Caborn. Looking round the room I noticed that attendance was not confined to CSEU officers, but included Davy shop stewards Eddie Keys and Bill Walker, among others. The only business that morning declared Caborn, was to charge me with 'interference ... in an industrial matter that was being handled by trade union officers that undermined Mr Ernest Johnson [Confederation secretary] and Mr Eddie Keys.' Yet Johnson immediately disclosed that at an earlier meeting a sub-committee doubted that it had a remit to discuss the matter. However, Dan Sequerra, full-time officer of ASTMS had moved that 'it lay on the table'. That was why it had come to the district committee. Johnson then stated that I 'had involved management contrary to the wishes of trade union members.' That was not borne out by correspondence or minutes of meetings – which I brandished – or assurances concerning procedure, I replied. Nor did it accord, incidentally, with Johnson's own subsequent admissions.

I challenged the meeting's credibility, the lack of notice or, indeed, an invitation, the absence of an agenda, and demanded sight of the so-called tape. Where was it? Where was the evidence? How was I supposed to meet the charge? I declared the meeting out of order, likened it to a Star Chamber, indeed, and said I would leave. But I said I would stay long enough to answer questions. There were none.

So I raised some myself. How many people had prior knowledge of this business, and whom, and for how long? How many transcripts of the so-called taped conversation were in circulation, and in whose possession? Above all, I asked, where is that 'damned tape'? Again, no reply.

John Brearley of GMBATU also described the meeting as the 'wrong forum and the wrong way of going about it'. He insisted that I was 'entitled to fair answers'. He queried the ethic of making such a tape, its use at that meeting and the repeated reference to it without even a sight of it. Before I could follow up Keys said he was going to propose to the Davy shop stewards that they have nothing more to do with me. There you are, I said, that is 'essentially what I have always been up against at Davys.' Whereas, I repeated, I had always acted in accordance with procedure. In this particular case, I reminded the meeting, I had acted at the specific request of the Davy shop stewards – without Keys. Already there were signs of misgivings among some present, that were reinforced within days. But Keys remained hostile along with Sequerra, as both hastened to judgment. I reminded Sequerra that they had never had a Labour MP in Sheffield who had serviced and protected its trade unions as I had, and invited rebuttal. There was none. I left.

I learned later that a decision was taken to sever relations with me, and to report the matter to my Attercliffe party. Before leaving I gave an assurance – on request – that I would not go to the press. But I warned of a certain leak. This was confirmed three days later when the *Morning Telegraph* published extracts from a taped conversation along with a report of the Saturday meeting by a Jonathan Foster.[167] Foster, previously unknown to me personally, had telephoned the previous afternoon inviting comment. I had declined, of course, given the CSEU embargo. I still had not seen any tape, and to my bewilderment one was now in the possession of a newspaper that had been hostile

---

167   *Morning Telegraph.* 15 December 1981.

to me since my arrival in Attercliffe.[168] It had remained hostile despite repeated complaints to the editor, Peter Darling.[169] Unlike *The Star*, which I always found absolutely objective, professional and fair under the editorship of Colin Branigan, David Flynn and Michael Corner.

When David Flynn rang me after the *Morning Telegraph's* report, I readily agreed to meet him in the House of Commons. I was totally transparent at a lengthy meeting. I opened all my files and produced ample documentary evidence of non-cooperation by Keys. I indicated his repeated bypassing of me in favour of Martin Flannery and Joan Maynard, their encroachment on my constituency responsibilities and my correspondence with them. There was nothing in the reported tape transcript, I emphasised, that I would withdraw. I had acted throughout in good faith. I explained how I was pressed by Davy shop stewards in the absence of Keys to talk to management. I did so on several occasions, but only after receiving confirmation that trade union procedures had been exhausted. I found management at Davy Loewy equally concerned about the preservation of jobs and the plight of their displaced workers. They pointed to the good severance package in addition to the statutory redundancy payments, both better than any hitherto and any secured by the main plant. They were anxious that it should not be put in jeopardy. They were also anxious lest top management in London might become adversely affected by prolonged confrontation and factory-gate demonstrations such as had just occurred a mile away at the Hadfields plant, which had been needlessly besieged by miners stirred up by Arthur Scargill.

Now I had been set up at the time of mandatory reselection, and I assured David Flynn that I was going to fight it. 'As a bid to discredit

---

168   It started with the *Morning Telegraph's* criticism of my opposition to the visit of Captain Long, inept Education Minister in Northern Ireland in January 1971, two weeks before Bloody Sunday.

169   In correspondence dated 18 October 1983, 26 October 1983 and 23 November 1983.

the MP', summarised *The Star*, 'it is a sneaky move that smacks of the dirty tricks department.'[170]

My officers arranged a meeting in the Coop Hall, Manor Top, on Sunday 3 January 1982, to consider the action of the CSEU. George Caborn, as district chairman, was invited to attend and make a statement. But as soon as he began to speak – at a large meeting – he was shouted down and unable to continue. Such a strong reaction was clearly a rejection by those present of the action of the CSEU, and ruled out any further proceedings. It was decided to arrange a further meeting for Sunday 7 February. Before it took place, however, according to a full report in the *Morning Telegraph*, of course, Caborn addressed the Sheffield Trades Council after 'asking them to listen to the tape'. I was not invited to defend myself. I had not yet even seen any tape, and never did see it. The Trades Council was obviously not concerned about natural justice nor human rights, though reminded by some present.

At the second meeting of the Attercliffe party the CSEU was only represented by two officers, Ernest Johnson and Len Crossley. The Davy shop stewards were only represented by Eddie Keys. After appeals for calm, the meeting was much more restrained than the first. The CSEU officers and Keys were now clearly placatory. Indeed, Crossley stated repeatedly, 'We want to bury this in the interests of our members, and as soon as possible.' Despite persistent questioning by Rob Murray, later constituency secretary, Johnson could not say or would not say 'whether the phone conversation had an effect on the outcome of the dispute.' But he did concede that the original charge was without foundation. For he admitted, significantly, that after the external conference on 29 October, procedure was exhausted. So I was clear of the original charge of 'interference … in an industrial matter that was being led by trade union officers.'

---

170   *The Star*. 16 December 1981.

Keys admitted that the 'relationship between himself and Pat Duffy could have been better'; that there was a 'time-gap' between the dispute and him notifying me by a circular letter which went also to the local Conservative MP; and that he had absented himself from the meeting of the Davy shop stewards and myself in my constituency office. Despite repeated questioning, he would not elaborate on the statement that 'This tape fell into our hands by chance.' Nor would he be drawn on his claim of thirty years' membership of a Labour party elsewhere – which could never be verified. The CSEU officers and Keys then withdrew and a general discussion took place.

It was preceded by a warning from Councillor Gerald Marshall that 'someone in this room was going to the Press, and continues to do so blatantly.' My officers believed it was Ken Curran of NUPE, who was not even a member of the CSEU. It was a very brief discussion, helpfully summed up by Richard Caborn, son of George, who reminded the meeting that there been a 'clear conciliatory move from the Confed; Pat had answered it. Accordingly, [he] moved that Pat respond appropriately to the Confed, and that the Party should now close the matter.' Councillor Ron Burford accepted the proposal as chairman. He pointed out that the matter had been properly aired and discussed on all sides, without restriction. So he moved that the matter be closed.

A proposal by David Milsom, a Young Socialist and a member of the Militant Tendency, that 'the MP's reselection should be set on one side' was not seconded. Neither was there a seconder for a motion by Ken Curran that 'the MP be censured'. The chairman's motion was carried by sixty-two votes to five, with four abstentions. It was an overwhelming vote of confidence. It also had an interesting sequel. Martin Flannery MP and Will Owen, on whose TGW premises the early meeting with the CSEU took place, when both were present, told me separately afterwards that they 'never understood what was going on.' In fact, Will Owen promptly invited me to Sunday tea at his home.

199

Images

My maternal grandmother Ellen Cunnane,
in the parish of Aughamore, Co. Mayo,
Ireland, 1930s

With my brother Jim, late 1920s

Shipshape for Sunday Divisions, HMS
Repulse, 1940

Initial training at HMS Royal Arthur, 1940

201

HMS Biter in the middle of her convoy, 1943

Images

Sunday Divisions on HMS Biter, 1943

Swordfish torpedo aircraft on HMS Biter, 1943

My brother, Sgt. Bernard Duffy, Italy, 1944

At sea during officer training

*My sister, Patricia Duffy, WAAF,
stationed at Bletchley Park, the vital
wartime communications and code-breaking
centre, 1944*

Full complement of Naval Air Squadron 822

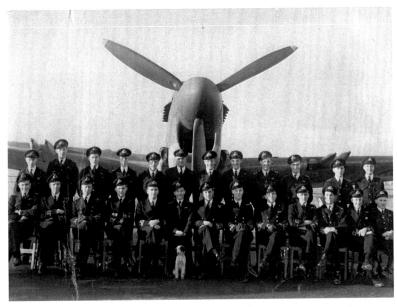

Naval Air Squadron 822 - I am seated on the front row, fifth from right

Campaigning in the Colne Valley by-election, 1963

Colne Valley by-election success, 1963

Russell Kerr MP, Kevin McNamara MP, myself, and Stan Thorne MP in front of Leinster House, Dublin, 1974

Examining a naval Puma helicopter with Miss Fleetlands, Portsmouth

With Roy Mason MP, and Alec Woodall MP, in Yorkshire during the 1975 EU Referendum campaign

With Roy Mason MP after his appointment as Defence Secretary and mine as his Parliamentary Private Secretary, after we had landed at RAF Finningley, near Doncaster, South Yorkshire, in Harrier jump-jets, May 1975

Trade and Industry Select Committee, 1975

*Holding the Official Report of the Trade
and Industry Select Committee on the
future of the British motor industry outside
the Treasury, London, August 1975*

The Board of Admiralty. Admiral Lewin, First Sea Lord, on my right 1978

My first Ministerial appointment, after Prime Minister Jim Callaghan had telephoned me in Hong Kong. I am accompanied by the General Officer Commanding Land Forces during a visit to the Hong Kong Squadron

A dinner to conclude the annual conference of naval Church of England Chaplains, July 1976. Admiral Sir David Williams, Second Sea Lord, on the left, and Earl Mountbatten of Burma on my left

The Board of Admiralty, Whale Island, Portsmouth, 1976. The First Sea Lord, Admiral Sir Edward Ashmore, is on my left

The Irish Taioseach, Liam Cosgrave, front left, myself, front right, and members of the Parliamentary All-Party delegation that I led to Dublin, 1976

With my brother Jim, on the left, at the Royal Tournament, Earls Court, London, 1977

Bishop Mario Conti of Aberdeen (now Archbishop of Glasgow), with my mother when she launched HMS Lindisfarne at the Hall Russell shipyard, Aberdeen, June 1, 1977

Pictured with Irish naval cadets at Britannia Royal Naval College, Dartmouth, 1977. From left to right: C. G. Grant, from Monaghan, G. T. O'Donohue, from Buttevant, S. Anderton, from Cork, and M.A. Mellett, from Castlebar. He is now Commodore Mark Mellett DSM, Flag Officer Commanding Naval Service, Irish Defence Forces

Images

Pictured again with Irish naval cadets G. T.
O'Donohue and S. Anderton at Dartmouth

Naval visit, July 1977

The Rt. Hon. Fred Mulley MP, Defence Secretary, hosting Sidney and Mary Dyson, the
Lord Mayor and Lady Mayoress of Sheffield, together with the president of my Attercliffe
constituency party, Alan Wade, and his wife Pauline, at the MoD while I was Navy Minister

Visiting HMS Echo in the Humber

The inauguration of the WT station at Crimond, Aberdeenshire, July 1978. Top secret at the time, this was a valuable addition to NATO's communications systems

Images

With Prime Minister Jim Callaghan at the opening of the new Covered Frigate Refitting Complex at Devonport Dockyard, 1978

Visiting a WRNS establishment with the Director, Vonla McBride

On the mess deck of a destroyer

With the Royal Marines, Lympstone, Devon

In the galley of a naval shore base

Visit to a hydrographic vessel of the Russian Navy at Shoreham, Sussex. The ship was attending the Oceanology International 1978

Taking the salute of the Royal Marines at Lympstone, Devon

Campaigning with Roy Mason MP in Attercliffe during the 1979 General Election campaign

Greeting Lord Mountbatten at a Royal Marines concert at the Albert Hall, London, February 1979. Standing behind is Vice-Admiral Veldkamp, Commander-in-Chief of the Royal Netherlands Navy

Above: Laying a wreath in Piskaryovskaye Cemetery, Leningrad, July 1989

Left: Laying a wreath on the Kremlin Wall, Moscow, July 1989

With Cardinal Josef Glemp, Warsaw, 1989

With US Secretary of the Navy Graham Claytor in his office at the Pentagon, Washington DC

Presentation to my mother by the Commanding Officer, HMS Lindisfarne, on the occasion of her recommissioning after her mid-life refit, Rosyth, August 1990

With General Vladimir Lobov, Commander-in-Chief of the Warsaw Pact military forces in Rome, October 1989

With His Holiness Pope John Paul II in his study in the Vatican, October 9, 1989

Ceremonial ending of the Cold War in Westminster Hall in the Palace of Westminster, London, November 1990

With my mother in the Central Lobby of the Houses of Parliament before leaving for my Investiture at Buckingham Palace by Her Majesty The Queen, July 16, 1991

Presentation of the 'Sword of Honour' by Vice-Presidents Jose Lello of Portugal and Seki Yavasturk of Turkey on behalf of the Nato Assembly, in recognition of my knighthood, Madrid, November 1991

A pilgrim on the Camino Santiago de Compostela

Chapter Eleven

Fighting for the Soul of the Labour Party

The Labour party has always attracted a great number of factions, been burdened with clashes of personality and beset with policy differences. It has not changed.[171] Party members have always organised in pursuit of different policy objectives ranging politically from right to left, from the practical to the utopian. Historically, the parliamentary party has favoured the Right in the party's structure, among its officers and in its policy-making. The Left has always been more active, however, assisted in recent times by the weekly journal *The Tribune*, and the Tribune group in Parliament. Their campaigning led in the Seventies to changes in the party's rules governing internal dissent. The list of 'proscribed organisations' was abolished, and constituency parties were allowed to drop their MP if they so wished. The Manifesto group was then formed on the right of the parliamentary party, focussing on the party's elections and parliamentary business such as debates, questions and committee work. It was not so much concerned with issues as with the party's structure, with elections to its NEC and with resolutions to party conference. I was glad to support such concerns in 1977 by responding to the invitation of Bill Rodgers (now Lord Rodgers) to join the Campaign for a Labour Victory.[172]

Of particular concern to the campaign was the conduct of the NEC. Instead of promoting constructive dialogue, especially with

---

171   See A.E.P. Duffy, 'Differing policies and Personal rivalries in the origins of the Independent Labour Party'. *Victorian Studies*. September 1962.

172   'Is the party facing the important issues and taking account of opinion in the country in its policy-making processes?' he asked. 'Did the NEC any longer speak for the grass-roots, and was it representative?' His most damning criticism was of the NEC's neglect of the party, finances and membership.

the Labour Government and with the trade unions on how best to achieve economic growth and the right levels of public spending and priorities, it had become preoccupied with the introduction of new reselection procedures. Not on account of the energies and qualities of Labour MPs, but only about their attitude to party dogma. Two NEC members, Frank Allaun and Joan Maynard in the guise of the Campaign for Labour Democracy, a grouping that had been formed in 1882 as a parliamentary left-wing alternative to Tribune, never succeeded in concealing their ultimate aim of a Labour party made up only of good far-left socialists. Or, in the view of another NEC member, Eric Heffer, to simply get rid of the moderate MPs. He argued initially that constituencies should be given 'greater influence on their MPs without making them delegates.'[173] But he revealed deeper feelings in the Eighties in the chair at annual conference when he jeered at a clustered group of such parliamentary colleagues and described them as 'rabble'.

Meanwhile those same moderate Labour MPs were responding to the radical reselection proposals by campaigning for local rank-and-file membership to carry an automatic vote. All the members would thus be fully involved, instead of confining voting on crucial issues to the GMC with which an MP dealt on the whole. The hard-left of the NEC led by Tony Benn repeatedly blocked such a proposed one-man-one-vote. They were determined to keep the reselection process within the sole control of activist-dominated local parties. They were well aware that such a widening of the franchise for reselection would protect moderate Labour MPs.

At the annual conference at Brighton following the election defeat in 1979, moderate MPs were left in no doubt that, for all their appeasement, the Left was now intent on taking complete command of policy, the election of the Leader and the selection of MPs The Labour party was ceasing to be Harold Wilson's 'broad church' that

---

173   *The Guardian.* 23 July 1979.

should encompass a wide variety of political convictions. It was no longer a united party either, now that it was out of office. That was unhappily confirmed by the rolling manifesto prepared by the NEC for a national conference which was held in late May 1980. It was based on an embarrassingly left-wing statement, 'Jobs, Peace, Freedom', which was intended to tie the hands of the Leader in future. The tone of the conference turned out to be markedly left-wing. Big cheers greeted pledges for unilateral nuclear disarmament and coming out of Europe. The old centrist balance which had sustained the Wilson and Callaghan governments was being undermined. Confirmation was forthcoming at a special conference held at Wembley in January 1981, when an electoral college comprising constituency parties, the trade unions and the MPs was proposed to take the election of the party Leader out of the hands of the PLP.

Despite Labour's defeat in 1979, calls were even made by some for a 'genuinely Socialist alternative'. For such people, electoral considerations came second to purity of doctrine. Yet striking testimony was available by 1979 from a series of studies of British public opinion conducted first at Nuffield College, Oxford, and at Essex University, showing how far public support for Labour's policy positions had already declined. The Observer RSL survey[174] asked voters which of a number of political leaders most nearly represented their own political views. A mere 3% named Tony Benn, compared with 29% for Jim Callaghan, 28% for Margaret Thatcher, 23% for Edward Heath and 15% for David Steel. As the Labour party and the British people were drifting apart, it was now evident that Jim Callaghan was more popular than his own party. Yet in May 1979, following the general election, he had to leave Downing Street. His administration never had a stable majority, and its fall after the 'winter

---

174   Published during the election campaign on 22 April 1979, it showed that a majority of Labour voters now supported such Conservative proposals as giving council house tenants the right to buy their home.

of discontent' was not unexpected. For a year he led the party in opposition and struggled to stem its drift. He tried to calm Labour's internal feuding by appealing for 'restraint and tolerance'. Attacked by colleagues who had served with him in government, horrified by the growing extremism, he resigned the leadership in 1980 and was succeeded by Michael Foot It was soon apparent that the mood and aspirations of Labour's activists could no longer by met even by a new Leader from the Left.

Michael Foot was a decent man. The widespread tributes paid to him on his death testified to an unusual popularity extending well beyond political boundaries. Nevertheless, his election as Leader represented a risky departure from the safe-looking public figure of Jim Callaghan. Labour candidates were soon being beaten into third place in one by-election after another, shedding two deposits in the process. The party's vote was running at half what it was in May 1979. In the Labour seat of Mitcham and Morden in London, less than twelve per cent of the electorate turned out to vote for the Labour candidate, David Nicholas. Writing afterwards in *Tribune*, Nicholas frankly declared that he was a supporter of Tony Benn. 'But as anyone who has recently canvassed knows,' he admitted, 'he is extremely unpopular on the doorstep.' The politics of this new hard Left around Tony Benn was simply not compatible with Michael Foot's leadership, much less that of Wilson and Callaghan.

I had looked elsewhere when voting in the newly-instituted electoral college. I voted for John Silkin as Leader and Roy Hattersley as deputy, against the preferences of the Attercliffe party; incidentally. I defended both as outstanding candidates, with their individual courage, political acumen, personal presence and fluency in speech and writing. Both had fathers who I much admired. I am in no doubt that the history and wellbeing of the Labour party in and out of Parliament would have been better had either become Leader. Michael Foot and Neil Kinnock were also good men and, in some respects, gifted. But they were both ill-equipped for leadership, which calls for particular qualities in any circumstances. The premature death of John Silkin was a severe blow to the Labour party, I believe. Happily, Roy Hattersley confirmed his leader-like qualities when standing in for Neil Kinnock later as Deputy Leader, notably at the despatch box in the House of Commons.

During his two years as Leader, the performance of Michael Foot, in the opinion of some, 'varied from merely disastrous to downright catastrophic'.[175] It led to a split, and the founding in 1982 of the Social Democratic party (SDP). Its appeal of a third way attracted the support of many Labour MPs and their departure left deep scars and a void. The future of the party was now at stake, and Roy Mason, Geoff Lofthouse and I devoted ourselves to its survival in the Yorkshire coalfield. Roy Hattersley and I coordinated support, also in Sheffield, for the moderate political leadership of the region's trade unions. Cyril Ambler of the Health Workers, Michael Davey of the Transport Workers, Frank Wilkinson of the General and Municipal Workers and Roy Morton of the Electricians were outstanding. It was the courage and example of those regional leaders who brought the Labour movement in Yorkshire safely through the strife unleashed by the Coal Strike of 1984. In its prime city centre site in Sheffield, facilitated by the council's Labour group,[176] the Yorkshire Miners under the leadership of Arthur Scargill were a lost cause. It was a leadership that my father, who spent a lifetime down the pit really getting at coal, would not have understood, much less supported. For Scargill achieved the impossible, given the traditional solidarity of the miners. He set miner against miner, and destroyed the unity of many mining communities. Where there was once a solid union, there was now a fragmented workforce. He spawned also a style of leadership and behaviour totally alien to the British Labour movement. I was obliged to attend many of Scargill's rallies in Sheffield, when he displayed a

---

175   *London Evening Standard*. 15 July 1982.

176   After a brief occupation, it remained empty for more than twenty years.

certain oratorical power. But there was no argument, just a rant. Then he would step forward and clap his audience in a style that I soon witnessed in Eastern Europe.

The fields around the BSC coking plant at Orgreave, on the boundary of my constituency, were the scene for the dispute's defining moment. Even with solid backing the strike now appeared suicidal. Orgreave demonstrated the total lack of leadership. I contributed weekly payments locally to strike funds amounting to £5,000. I never received any official acknowledgment or thanks from the Yorkshire or Derbyshire Miners. Jimmy Reid, who led the Upper Clyde Shipyard workers' sit-in during the days of the Heath government, predicted that the 'main casualty will undoubtedly be the democratic Left in British politics. It will also undermine the electoral fight-back of Labour, and could even mean a further decline in the party's main base among the working class.'[177]

The Left was operating within a different political spectrum. Impatient not only with parliamentary democracy, it was also disinclined to respect the rule of law as would soon become evident in Sheffield. It was vital, therefore, that for a successful electoral fight-back the moderate candidate, Bill Jordan, should be elected leader early in 1986 of Britains's second largest union, the engineers. Significantly, it was also the first AUE election for leader which would use a government funded postal ballot. Roy Hattersley and I organised a bumper meeting in Attercliffe in support of his successful bid. There was no complaint from George Caborn, with whom I always had a good relationship.[178] Nor did the engineers' national leader, Terry Duffy, ever complain to me about him, despite their conflicting political loyalties. He knew that George was an effective,

---

177   *The Observer.* 16 September 1984.

178   Although he had tried very hard to win Attercliffe at the selection conference in 1969, when one third of those present were his own mandated union delegates. Some of them had broken their mandates, of course, and voted for me.

tireless and dynamic district secretary. Terry worried only about his successor in Sheffield, Derek Simpson, a quite different personality. Together with Tony Woodley he later became a joint general secretary of the union Unite. He generated much adverse publicity on account of his change in life style. He had switched earlier from communist to Labour, and joined my troublesome Mosborough party.

In his Attercliffe address, Bill Jordan described the 'damage done to our own union with extremists in control – and on [his] own doorstep because of the work of Red Robbo.' He saw as his next quest the need to 'lead the purge on Militant Tendency within the Labour party ... to establish realism as the guiding light of socialism.' By this time in the early Eighties my neighbouring MPs Fred Mulley and Frank Hooley had been deselected and I had survived as the only moderate Labour MP in Sheffield. But I had had to beat off a spurious attempt at a coup by the Left at the firm of Davy-Loewy in my constituency. The explosive headlines it generated soon fizzled as my Attercliffe party brushed them aside. My Attercliffe councillors also came to the aid of the Labour group when it was courting disaster by defying government policy on rate-capping. It was rescued on the brink by the courage of eight of my nine councillors who refused to support such illegality. Meanwhile the battle-hardened Attercliffe party was being called upon to deal with infiltration by the Militant Tendency. For the Militant issue had now superseded rates as Labour's major problem countrywide. Sheffield, along with Liverpool, was at the heart of the crisis, as was my own Attercliffe party.

The *Tribune* newspaper was now rivalled on the Left by groups pursuing more revolutionary programmes. The most successful and well publicised of those factions was Militant, centred around the newspaper of the same name. The movement became known as the Militant Tendency, and went to great lengths to conceal its real identity.[179] Denis Healey and Reg Underhill, former national agent,

---

179   Circulating bulletins were leaked to *The Guardian*. 21 December 1985.

warned as early as 1979 of the danger of infiltration. They had called for the reopening of the report in 1977 on 'Trotskyist infiltration into the party'.[180] Frank Allaun, the party's immediate past chairman, shamefully denounced the Underhill documents as 'old stuff stale and disappointing'. A year later the NEC's Organisation committee under the chairmanship of Eric Heffer gave the Militant Tendency 'a clean bill of health'.[181] In 1982, however, following a lengthy investigation, the NEC arrived at a different view. It concluded in its report that Militant was a separate organisation with a programme that was contrary to Labour rules. This was rejected by Sheffield's Labour group, which also decided to convey its 'disgust' to the NEC. The group's chief whip, Bill Michie, said he knew of no evidence that Militant breached Labour rules.[182] Yet the chairman of the Heeley party meeting earlier in the year that preferred him to the sitting MP was Councillor Paul Green, who was most active in Sheffield on behalf of Militant.

During 1984 it had become evident that people were being directed into the Attercliffe constituency party. There was an obvious concentration of such newcomers in one particular ward, Mosborough. The intention to make it into a Militant stronghold was soon apparent. Two very active 'young socialists', David Milsom and Sharron McDermott, moved in from two other wards, as did Paul Green and Geoff Bright from Heeley next door. They were all known Militants. Alan Hartley, one of Militant's top men in the region, formerly its organiser on Humberside, even moved in from Hull together with his wife, Jane.[183]

---

180   *The Times*. 7 December 1979.

181   *The Times*. 5 December 1980.

182   *Morning Telegraph*. 22 June 1982.

183   During the Eighties Militant secretly infiltrated in Yorkshire alone seventeen constituencies, with offices in Leeds and Hull. It had a cell structure in every major city and town in the county. *The Yorkshire Post*. 3 October 1988.

Why had the Mosborough ward party been targeted? It was a new township with a mining background. The party secretary was Jim Walton. He went down the pit at fourteen years, worked underground for forty-seven years and became his union's branch secretary. Jim and his wife Dorothy, always known as Dot, who was equally tireless in serving the party, were an exemplary partnership.[184] They constituted a unique team in the public life of Sheffield. Both served as councillors in north-east Derbyshire before Dot was elected to the Sheffield city council. She filled its highest office as Lord Mayor from 1985–86. Jim and Dot Walton, along with Bill Mirfin, Harry Healings, Bill Farrar and other long-serving party stalwarts drawn from the villages of Halfway and nearby Beighton, formed the core of the newly created ward party. They were fine people, representing the best traditions of the Labour movement. All shared the humblest beginnings and had faced adversity in employment in a manner I found inspirational. I considered myself fortunate to share their company. They had contributed enormously to the sensibility of their local party over many years. Now they were being outnumbered and outgunned by an influx of new members, spearheaded by certain white-collar workers. Such an infusion was straining the party's cohesiveness.[185] The newcomers had formed an 'Action Group', with

---

184   They formed the Halfway Elderly People's Club, organising various events, including holidays; they organised Christmas tea dances and concerts, as well as the local Coronation celebrations. Together they gave distinguished service locally to the Royal National Lifeboat Institution, for which Dot received the Gold Badge and Jim his certificate. Both were awarded the MBE.

185   Rob Murray reported to the executive that he had received complaints from Mosborough party members. 'One was that a retired miner was ordered out of a meeting for valid questioning of constitutional issues. At the same meeting a disabled woman was told to shut up or be ordered out. Recently, members who have given devoted community service as school governors have found themselves removed for no good reason.' The two Mosborough councillors who had voted against illegal rate-capping were instructed to resign. The third councillor from the ward was absent ill.

records and funds more comprehensive than those of the ward party. All strongly suggestive of a 'party within a party'. Tension arose as the official minutes and rulings were incessantly queried and challenged. It resulted at one meeting in Jim Walton, as party secretary, throwing his minute book at a tormentor.

Because of such fractious meetings, an invitation was issued to the constituency party president, Alan Wade, to attend Mosborough's annual meeting in early February 1984, to adjudicate on any contentious matters. He soon had his hands full, for he was also asked on arrival to act as scrutineer. It led to an error in the counting of votes.[186] But there was no attempt at concealment.[187] Nevertheless, given the aftermath, Alan and Jim felt obliged to resign – Alan from the presidency[188] and Jim as the party secretary. The post of local secretary passed from the traditional hands of the mineworkers to one of Dan Sequerra's members in the ASTMS – Dave Hutchinson.

A perfectly genuine error in the counting of votes at the annual meeting of the ward party affected its representation at the approaching constituency party's annual meeting. The Attercliffe party officers, including a Left vice-president, accepted the advice of the regional secretary to confine the matter and its resolution to the Mosborough party. This was disregarded, however, by the Mosborough party's delegates at the constituency annual meeting shortly afterwards. With

186 If I had been stuck in a corner of that small crowded room, with no desk, and points of order flying around on which I had been expected to rule and count votes at the same time, I would have been even more confused.

187 Certain individuals called on Jim Walton the following morning and challenged the previous night's voting. There was no attempt at evasion. When contacted, Alan Wade's immediate instruction was to surrender all the voting slips to this highly unusual private scrutiny rather than await the formality of the next meeting – such was his confidence in the outcome.

188 At no stage did I doubt Alan Wade's integrity. Employed by ACASS, he was steeped in industrial relations and their disputations. He was devoted to Sheffield's 'old guard' on the city council, and to his predecessor, Sidney Dyson.

their augmented representation, they insisted also on another annual meeting, which took place six months later. By now such temper and challenges had become a feature of Attercliffe constituency party meetings. They came to a head at the second annual meeting in September.[189] However, Ron Burford and Joe Sheedy, always close and supportive of Alan Wade, were clearly elected president and youth officer respectively.

The Attercliffe constituency party had hitherto enjoyed effective, tolerant and relaxed management. There had been occasions in the recent past when delegates on the Left had attended its meetings without credentials. George Foulds, who chauffeured his wife Mary – who was implacably opposed to the Waltons – had been known to vote. Alan Wade, as president, or the other officers, never objected or attempted to make an issue of it. The very first time doubts had arisen from a reverse situation, however, there was confrontation. The main feature of the first annual meeting earlier in the year, which I attended, was the violence of the language and the ferocity of some of the exchanges by new delegates. Soon those same delegates were just as intolerant of the advice and guidance of the regional secretary.

This temper was quite alien to the custom and tradition of the Attercliffe party. Seemingly, it was becoming commonplace elsewhere. Frank Blundy, treasurer of the Woodhouse Central Working Men's Club, told me after that particular meeting that it reminded him of what he and his fellow officers were now having to endure. They could cope with the problems that were then threatening all working men's clubs, not just their own, if only some members would appreciate

---

189   At the outset, a delegate from Mosborough questioned the eligibility of a delegate present – Alan Aikin, representing the Darnall ward. Alan explained that he believed that his business premises nearby provided a basis for attendance, though he always abstained from voting – as was well known. He might have mentioned that he also gave employment to party members, including some of the newly arrived in Mosborough. A motion was carried that he be allowed to stay pending an investigation by the executive.

what they were up against. 'But one slip and you are out,' he said. 'They want blood.' Ken Livingstone was making the same complaint in London about such people on the Left. 'Granted that all of us make mistakes … the structure of the Left is such that before you've really had time to think … you've been denounced in the most bitter fashion.'

Following the September meeting some members wrote to the regional secretary raising the Attercliffe party's constitutional standing, membership and administration. David Robertson, who was a very good regional secretary, arranged such an inquiry. He stated in his report that in 1984 only two delegates were ineligible to attend the constituency meeting because of failure to pay their subscriptions and, ironically, both were from Mosborough. Only one trade union delegate – of the Communication Workers – was also ineligible. Of the Youth section's entitlement to two delegates, one did not live in the constituency. None were the intended targets of those complaining. In fact they were 'own goals'. As were the complaints about administration, none of which appeared to be valid according to the report. It did recommend, however, as a matter of routine, that a set of Standing Orders should be drawn up, based on the model contained in *How to Organise for Victory*. Significantly, the most relevant and important outcome of the inquiry was the official response of David Robertson. There 'is a need to remind the Party that factional activity is not tolerated,' he reminded everyone, although it was clearly directed at the delegates who had raised the complaints. 'Delegates should understand that they represent the views of the organisation which appoints them and not the views of a 'pressure group' or 'caucus'.' It was really game, set and match to the traditional management of the Attercliffe party by such officers as Sidney Dyson, Alan Wade, Ron Burford, Joe Sheedy, Kelvin Godwin and its new constituency secretary, Rob Murray. They were now prepared to act on the cue contained in the regional secretary's words and tackle the 'factional activity in the party' – the Militant Tendency.

Chapter Twelve

The Militant Tendency

The fight against the Militant Tendency in Attercliffe was led by the constituency secretary, Rob Murray. Acute of mind, meticulous and able, he was more than a match for their supporters in Attercliffe and, if need be, where they were skulking elsewhere in the city. First of all, however, he dealt effectively with my reselection following the 1983 election. Nominations for me outnumbered by four to one those in favour of other contenders, including Mick Elliott. That pointed to a shortlist of one, me, which was formally adopted.

In the first move to attack Militant activity within the Attercliffe party, the Darnall ward, of which Alan Wade was the chairman, struck the first blow. It put forward a resolution to go before the next general management meeting in July 1985. It asked for implementation of 'agreed national policy regarding the unacceptability of a party within a party and, therefore, precludes members of the Militant Tendency from holding any office either at ward or constituency level within the party.'

Following those meetings, Rob Murray wrote individual letters to Paul Green, Geoff Bright, Alan Hartley, David Milsom and Sharon McDermott telling them that they had been excluded from membership for one year for being 'named' as members of Militant, 'which is recognised as a Trotskyist entryist group.' Bright was chairman of the National Union of Railwaymen branch at Tinsley in the constituency. He was a key figure in the blocking of coal shipments during the recent Miners' strike. He had already been chosen by his union as a delegate to the Labour party conference in late September. He and others – Jane Hartley and Steve Wisher – were added to the list for participating in Militant protest meetings. They were all given the opportunity to cease involvement with Militant, which they refused.[190] A recommendation to expel Green, Wisher and McDermott was carried in the executive prior to the turbulent September meeting by thirteen votes to two. At the full meeting attended by some 100 party and trade union delegates, the expulsions were approved by sixty votes to thirty-eight. The remaining four, Alan and Jane Hartley, Milsom and Bright were dealt with in like fashion later on.

A regional inquiry into an appeal by Paul Green against expulsion was held in December. It was conducted by Paul Corby and Beverley Marshall, members of the regional executive, along with the secretary, David Robertson. Ron Burford and Rob Murray attended as constituency officers, assisted by Alan Wade from Darnall, and Jeff Habberjam, Harry Healings, Bill Farrar and Sheila Dootson from Mosborough. Paul Green was supported by the new Mosborough party secretary, Dave Hutchinson, Alan Wigfield as secretary of the council's Labour group and Howard Capelin as chairman of the Heeley constituency party.[191] Green drew attention in his submission to the 'decisions of support for his position from all the other Sheffield CLPS and the District Party.' He accepted under questioning that he regarded the *Militant* newspaper as part of an organisation promoting a political programme, and that when he was selling *Militant* he was promoting 'its aims and programme'. When asked if he would be prepared to cease being thus involved, he replied, 'Yes in Militant

---

190   All seven argued that they were not members of the Militant Tendency, as alleged. They conceded, however, that they supported the ideas of the *Militant* weekly paper and made donations to it.

191   The constituency officers claimed that problems with the Mosborough party dated from the time of the arrival of Green. There were complaints of harassment and intimidation. Habberjam testified that he had witnessed the active involvement of Green at the Militant rallies in Sheffield. In reply to questions, Hutchinson agreed that the Mosborough party had assisted in organising protest meetings that were partly promoted by Militant. Speaking on behalf of the council's Labour group, Wigfield stated that it had 'unanimously expressed its support' for Green.

Tendency, but I would continue to work to make donations, sell the paper and support its aims and programme.'

Despite their expressed concern for the feelings of the district party and the other Sheffield constituency parties, the regional officers pointed to their duty to base their assessment on verbal and documentary evidence. At the same time they had to have regard for the 'strong feelings of the Attercliffe CLP who have voted overwhelmingly to act in accordance with Party Conference policy and the NEC decisions …' They were 'unanimously of the opinion that the CLP was justified in its decisions' and therefore recommended that 'the appeal of Paul Green be rejected'.[192] Such consideration contrasted sharply with that of the NEC shortly afterwards.

Neil Kinnock had announced earlier at the party conference in Bournemouth that he saw no place in the Labour party for members of the Militant Tendency. His test-case was commonly regarded as the Militant-dominated Labour party in Liverpool, which was subject to an internal Labour party inquiry. Yet David Blunkett tried to get its Leader, Derek Hatton, off the hook by proposing talks to solve Liverpool's council crisis. They predictably came to nothing. But Kinnock's stand at conference had been overwhelmingly endorsed. It was supported by Michael Foot at a December meeting of the PLP. Meanwhile the NEC was considering Paul Green's expulsion by Attercliffe. His appeal had been clearly overruled by the Yorkshire regional executive only the week before. Yet the NEC only voted by the narrowest of margins – fourteen votes to thirteen – to uphold that decision. Blunkett voted against. He preferred to defer such action, he stated, until Militant supporters could be dealt with by 'political persuasion'. He was dithering once again and at a time when Kinnock was trying to present Labour to the electorate as a modern and serious party.

---

192   Report of an enquiry by the Yorkshire Regional Labour party into an appeal by Councillor Paul Green. 10 December 1985.

Blunkett offered a variety of reasons for doing so, which came as no surprise to my officers and myself. We saw his indecision as all of a piece with the prevarification that characterised his city council leadership during the rate-capping crisis. Anxious to have it both ways, he found himself increasingly ready to wound but afraid to strike. Now he was being warned by Rob Murray in a published letter of the danger of 'ambivalence ... towards expulsion ... despite the party having a clear policy deeming Militant to be ineligible for membership and a constitution that imposes an equal duty on the National Executive Committee and constituency parties to take appropriate action.'[193] Rob and my officers would have been only too glad, had we been consulted, to explain to Blunkett why we had been forced to take action. We were very anxious to expose him to the limits of 'political persuasion' by arranging a visit to a Mosborough party meeting. He was not interested. He never contacted me, either personally or by letter. Neither did Kinnock, unbelievably, for all his nervous handling of Militant at party conference. We would have passed up the ammunition. We were left entirely on our own in Attercliffe, as we spearheaded the battle to save Labour's credibility locally and, perhaps, nationally.

Blunkett had been at it once again over the expulsion of Paul Green, when he opted for a 'cooling-off' period. He admitted the need to deal with Militant, 'an organisation within an organisation', but declared that, 'Labour must resist purge-mentality' and called instead for a 'bridge-building Left'.[194] But where was his evidence anywhere of readiness to enter into such bridge-building and compromise? There was none on the part of the district party, as he must have been painfully aware when it usurped the authority of his Labour group. That was just a brutal exercise in real-politik. In the prevailing cockpit of Sheffield's Labour politics, as he also knew

193   *The Guardian.* 21 November 1985.

194   *Tribune.* 3 January 1986.

only too well, you had to purge – though properly – or be purged, simply to survive. Green answered him effectively when he said he would continue his activities in the party, despite his expulsion.[195] He claimed also that 'several other councillors could be expelled on the same grounds – by selling and donating money to the newspaper called *Militant*.'[196] Why did Blunkett fail to react to such a serious charge, and so close to home?

The district party also answered Blunkett when it condemned Green's expulsion, as did Green's trade union, the local AEU. Blunkett's own Labour group 'told the NEC that the expulsion of an 'exemplary' councillor would be 'short-sighted, malicious and very much against the party's interests.'[197] Not the language of 'bridge-builders'. The district party grudgingly accepted the expulsion only on the basis that 'rules are rules'. And the Labour group did so only by a majority of four votes, after a heated debate lasting more than three hours. The Brightside and Central constituency parties passed motions calling for Green's reinstatement. The Hallam party failed to do so only by one vote. The Heeley went further, and adopted him as the official candidate in his former Intake ward.[198] Where was Blunkett looking in Sheffield when he called for 'bridge-building' and had called earlier for 'political persuasion'?

Yet Blunkett continued to scorn Green's expulsion by describing it as using 'a sledgehammer to crack a nut'.[199] George Fisher, a member of Labour's old guard on the city council, did not think so. He was still the most senior and respected member of the Birley ward party

195 *Morning Telegraph*. 20 December 1985.

196 *The Star*. 20 December 1985.

197 *The Observer*. 22 December 1985.

198 *The Star*. 27 January 1986.

199 *Morning Telegraph*. 16 January 1986.

that was also sheltering members of Militant. But he had had enough, he told me. He was resigning because he was 'so hurt by the way the Party is going in Sheffield ... it had become a 'rabble'.'[200] Nor was the mammoth protest rally by Militant in the city a few weeks earlier addressed by Tony Mulhern, president of the Liverpool Labour party, and David Nellist, a Labour MP, suggestive of a 'nut'–sized problem. Or the call of Derek Worlock and David Sheppard, respectively Catholic Archbishop and Anglican Bishop of Liverpool, to 'Stand up to Liverpool's Militants'.[201] Blunkett had also been publicly reminded by Rob Murray that the Party had a policy; accordingly, the NEC and individual constituency parties had a duty to carry out. He warned him as well of the inadequacy of 'fancy footwork'.[202]

Blunkett's failure to face up to reality in Sheffield and on the NEC was matched in Liverpool by Eric Heffer, MP. The Labour party investigation into the Liverpool district party revealed a 'level of systematic abuse and breach of party rules'.[203] Yet Heffer complained that the NEC was staging an 'attack on the people of Liverpool and that is unforgivable.'[204] I had challenged him more than once about the intrusion of Liverpool Militants into my constituency, which he always denied. It led eventually to a stand–up row in the tea–room

---

200   'I find that after long and soul searching thought', he wrote in a letter, 'I must resign my membership of the Labour Party.' though he held its Certificate of Merit.

201   *The Times*. 1 October 1985. 'Our Christian teaching is that we are members of one another,' they explained. 'The dogmatic, divisive policy of the Militant leadership reject this.'

202   *The Guardian*. 21 November 1985.

203   *The Guardian*. 27 February 1986.

204   *The Guardian*. 27 February 1986.

of the House of Commons.[205] Unaffected by the findings of the official inquiry, Derek Hatton and Peter Taafe, editor of the *Militant* newspaper, were back in Sheffield in the spring of 1986 to address a rally at the city hall. Referring to that inquiry in an interview with *The Star*, and dealing with the accusation of acting irresponsibly in Liverpool in the rates-battle, Hatton stated, 'All we did was manage to get through exactly the same thing that was proposed in Sheffield, but they couldn't get it through.'[206] Then he challenged Blunkett to a public debate on the matter. Along with Taafe he shared the rally platform with 'half a dozen recently expelled members of the city's Attercliffe constituency Labour Party.'[207]

For some months the shadow of a court battle hung over my officers and myself, as Militant threatened to go to law. In early March 1986, Rob Murray was exchanging with me letters from John Peysner of Peysner and Foley, solicitors in Sheffield, demanding reinstatement for Green. The letters, which were copied to David Hughes, the National Agent, alleged breaches of Labour party rules and of natural justice, together with the threat of an injunction to make the decision void. Despite our appeals to London, neither the Labour party or the regional secretary would become involved legally. They had no money, they said. I had been warned earlier by the previous National Agent, now Lord Underhill, that the Militant organisation had formidable financial reserves. They could 'always whistle up a friendly barrister and journalist for free.' My party officers and myself were out on our own once again. We had not shied away hitherto from the sound of gunfire. We were not prepared to surrender at this

---

205   I always thought Eric a very strange person. His primary strength lay in the support of his wife, Doris, both in Liverpool and at Westminster. With the exception of Simon Mahon MP – in my experience – most of Liverpool's MPs failed to match the leadership of the city's outstanding Church leaders.

206   *The Star*. 11 April 1986.

207   *The Star*. 11 April 1986.

late stage. I told my officers not to be deterred and to go ahead. I would undertake the legal and financial responsibility. I entered into such a commitment despite warnings from colleagues at Westminster that my liability might ultimately exceed £100,000. Like my brave councillors the year before whose homes were at risk during the rates crisis, my mother and I kept the city of Sheffield on the right lines by putting our own home on the line.

Chapter Thirteen

A New Realism

The 1980s were years of unrelieved gloom for the Labour party electorally. It went down to defeat at general elections in 1979, 1983 and 1987. In 1987 it avoided the disastrous result of 1983, but it was a third successive reverse. Its share of the UK vote was below that of 1979. More disturbingly, Labour's share of the skilled manual working-class vote declined even from its 1983 low. Labour had lost ground since 1974 with every group and sub-group except the middle classes and the Scots.

Defeat in 1979 was probably inevitable following the 'Winter of Discontent'. Defeat in 1983 was popularly ascribed to the excesses of the NEC, to a controversial defence policy, to the party's extreme election manifesto and to the failure of leadership. The Labour party was burdening itself with self-inflicted wounds and plainly in danger of becoming unelectable. Yet the NEC, which was ultimately responsible, remained impervious to the need for change in the run-up to the election in 1987. By which time the party was further burdened with the Militant Tendency and the antics of certain Labour councils. Did the NEC and those notorious councils not want Labour to win? They were often cited as desperate for the return of a Labour government. Why were they hampering the best efforts of their own party Leader? What were they about? Why were they so indifferent, moreover, to the trend of reforming socialism in Europe?

I was working closely in the early Eighties with defence ministers and parliamentarians within the Western alliance. Those contacts brought home to me the changing mood among Europe's left-of-centre parties towards slimmer government, lower taxation and privatisation. The Social Democrats in Germany apart, such parties were now viewing government intervention as damaging economically and more threatening to individual freedom than market failure. In short, most centre-left parties in Europe were becoming aware that they had to modernise and put market economies before the discredited ideology of Eastern European countries, unlike the Labour party's elected representatives in the UK. Nationally and locally, they were reluctant to grasp the implications for working people at home of changing overseas competition and its impact on Britain's industrial structure. They still preferred to plan resource allocation rather than allow for market forces. As for the goal of wealth creation and its redistributive opportunities, the instinct was still to turn to a new political manifesto.

After the failure of Michael Foot in 1983, Neil Kinnock was bound to be aware of the need for change. How far he was prepared to go, or was deterred by NEC opposition would ultimately determine his fate. Would he take on the NEC? He did try to amend Labour's image and policies generally. But could he exercise effective leadership? That could prove to be the key to winning over public opinion. Could he win, indeed, for his credibility had been in doubt from the outset? He had emerged as Leader from the newly installed electoral college, thanks to fellow Welshmen Clive Jenkins of the ASTMS and Moss Evans of the Transport Workers Union. They were good men, but neither would have played a major part, if any, in the discarded electoral role of the PLP, in which Kinnock would probably not have figured prominently. Thus his standing among many of his parliamentary colleagues was always at a discount. Lack of front-bench experience in the House of Commons was quickly evident in poor performances at the despatch box. His brainstorming speeches at left-wing Tribune meetings during the party's annual conferences were no substitute. He now had an enormous responsibility as Leader of the Opposition, but never presented a serious challenge to Margaret Thatcher. His major task now, given the electoral logic, was to reverse the general direction he had been passionately urging Labour to take at those Tribune meetings. He had to confront it with current realities and make it face up to new responsibilities.

Just how difficult a task that would prove to be was daily apparent to me in the conduct of my own local authority in Sheffield. It had become associated with such notorious councils as Lambeth and Liverpool through its foremost stance in the rate-capping campaign. Those councils became commonly described as 'loony' councils, thereby damaging further the Labour party image. They appeared to be unmoved by current realities at home. In the case of Sheffield they were apparently unmoved even by what its own representatives witnessed elsewhere in Europe. The city's council trade delegation to Moscow in 1986 is a case in point. Its members must have seen Russian housewives queuing outside shops for basic household items, including toilet rolls, as I did during my visits to the Soviet Union at the same time. Yet, I heard no mention of this on the delegation's return. They must have known, as I had been left in no doubt by Mr Gorbachev and other Soviet leaders, that the Russians were losing faith in communist economic policies. Why then was the trade delegation so discreet on returning to Sheffield? Georgi Arbatov, a prominent member of the Politburo, with whom I had become acquainted, raised with me the visit and its report. I had to admit that 'somehow it had not reached me', which amused him. He dismissed Sheffield's mission as 'tourism', and described its members as 'more useful idiots' – a contempt he would repeat when referring to certain members of Labour's NEC.

Concern about the effect on Labour's general standing of such unfavourable images of Labour councils as that cast by Sheffield had become widespread. I became anxious therefore about Labour's prospects in the run-up to the 1987 election. I was not alone, as I encountered near-despair on the doorstep during the disastrous Greenwich by-election when I canvassed for Labour's left–wing candidate. That was the feeling in Kinnock's private office.[208] It led to

---

208   According to a leaked letter to the *Sun* newspaper.

calls generally for him to 'crack down on the loony left.'[209] I urged him publicly to act now, 'before it's too late' when I addressed the Attercliffe GMC the same week. 'The time has come when people like me need to speak out for a return to traditional values and policies which affect working people (who are) worried about the loony left,' I declared. 'We need to get back to fundamentals like the importance of marriage, the family, faithfulness and the proper upbringing of children.'[210] A large swing to the Alliance party in a recent council by-election in our own constituency was a warning, I reminded the meeting.

There was general support from a full attendance, and not one member present demurred. The only complaint I received came in a letter from David Blunkett, who felt the term 'loony left' in the press report inappropriate.[211] However, in his autobiography *Inside Left*, published in 1988, his former friend Derek Hatton accused Blunkett and his supporters of 'behaving like middle class intellectuals – the true Loony Left.' Perhaps that explained Blunkett's sensitivity.

It moved me to pay a special visit to the Mosborough ward party, which had nurtured the Militant Tendency. In my address I contrasted very unfavourably the service I received from their secretary Dave

---

209   *London Evening Standard* 24 March 1987.

210   *The Star.* 25 March 1987.

211   He also felt obliged to copy the letter to Neil Kinnock. This was precisely what Councillor Barton, secretary of the Trades council, did shortly afterwards over an interview I had on Radio Sheffield. His was a single complaint also, and not sub-stantiated by the transcript. Unbelievably, he had not actually heard the interview. That confession was wrung from him only through protracted correspondence. Sim-ilarly with Blunkett in 1981, when he secretly, and in denial afterwards, breached the conventional Westminster practice by separately briefing the press on a ministerial visit arranged by the Sheffield MPs The confusing result was two different reports: the agreed one presented by Fred Mulley, MP, in the press lobby, and a second that Blunkett privately organised with Martin Flannery and the *Sheffield Morning Telegraph*. That had also given rise to much correspondence. It ended with me informing Blun-kett by letter that I found his conduct unacceptable and unethical.

Hutchinson with that I enjoyed with every other ward party secretary. I was not blaming Hutchinson, I pointed out, but those present who had elected him. I received a cringing apology from Hutchinson afterwards. I was not surprised to learn subsequently that he had opposed the removal of Clause Four from the party constitution. As I looked at the changing membership present that evening, I was mentally comparing them with the pioneering stalwarts they were replacing. I recalled also an observation of Kim Beazley senior, a former Australian Labour party leader: 'When I joined the Labour party it contained the cream of the working class, now it has the dross of the middle class.'

During the 1987 election campaign, Kinnock told the Wales TUC in conference that 'we are not going to be kicked around, jeered at by our enemies, and misrepresented by the fringes, the tendencies, the sections and other tassels that hang on to the tail of the Labour party.'[212] Some Sheffield councillors were not listening. For at that critical time three women were allowed to visit a school in my constituency and give a talk on female sexuality. Literature that they distributed was described afterwards as 'recruitment advertisement' for Sheffield's Young Lesbian Group.[213] I was swamped with angry protests, especially from horrified Asian community parent groups. Councillor Mrs Barton, education committee chairperson, assured me of a review of current procedures, but her own officials later defended the displaying of such posters.[214] Otherwise there was no expressed concern by Mrs Barton. Yet she must have known that the council was actually funding the local Young Lesbian Group at a time of education funding cutbacks. As a matter of fact there was a funding

---

212   *Financial Times*. 2 May 1987.

213   *The Star*. 29 June 1987.

214   'The gay and lesbian lobby,' declared *The Star* (13 April 1990) 'should not be allowed a prominent platform in youth clubs'. It called upon the city council to 're-vise its ideas on this misplaced example of liberal thinking.'

crisis in the schools in Sheffield within three years.[215] I had to make an appeal in Parliament by way of tabling an early day motion. By that time jobs and services had come under threat once again along with education. Fears were voiced that 'Sheffield will go the way of Liverpool.'[216]

Despite the extraordinary indulgence granted by the Audit Commissioner,[217] there still remained a view by early 1987 that the 'Sheffield council has many of the hallmarks of a left-wing dominated local authority, apparently out of touch with reality, saturated with political dogma and hopelessly overstaffed.'[218] The Council was desperately awaiting a Labour government to release it, as they saw it, from the straitjacket of rate capping, from financial penalties and from capital spending restrictions. Yet it was not helping to bring that about by going out of its way to assist Kinnock. On the contrary, under its present Council the city of Sheffield, which was once among the best governed in Britain, was now in a crisis situation and a poor advertisement for Labour.

The economic upheaval brought about by the contraction of steel had been shattering. Unemployment had trebled from 1979. To drivers on the M1 as they crossed the Tinsley Viaduct, the vision of Sheffield was one of dereliction. Yet this was just the bottom end of the Lower Don Valley, one third of which was now vacant or underused. The Council had reacted with a variety of initiatives, mostly environmental, consultative and providing help for the surviving businesses. But its high-spending style of community politics designed to protect public sector services and jobs continued to bring it into conflict with the Government The refusal to rein in spending – despite rate capping

---

215   'What a pathetic performance on education by Sheffield Labour councillors' was how they were viewed locally. *The Star.* 5 July 1990.

216   *The Star.* 4 July 1991.

217   *The Star.* 6 September 1987.

218   *Financial Times.* 24 February 1987.

– had had a dramatic impact on the rates and must have discouraged inward investment.

The kind of help extended to Trafford Park, Manchester, in the form of an urban development corporation (UDC) was available, and Blunkett conceded that the financial help given so far to the Merseyside Development Corporation would, if spent on the Lower Don Valley, 'completely transform the nature not just of Sheffield but of the sub-region.' However, a UDC was anathema to the Labour group. To them it represented a centralist and 'grossly undemocratic' approach to development. So, the *Financial Times* concluded, in place of the hundreds of millions of pounds potentially available under a UDC, Sheffield's hard-working officer teams struggled on with a few hundred thousand.[219] Such political and ideological stubbornness at the Town Hall had been confirmed by the extraordinary appointment by the Council of the controversial Dan Sequerra as director of employment and economic development. Like Mick Elliot, Attercliffe's short-lived constituency secretary, he did not last long. Neither really fitted in.

On the other hand, as I pleaded in Parliament, local authorities such as Sheffield and Liverpool were entitled to more understanding. They were in a difficult position. They had lost many tasks to Whitehall over the years. Yet the question remained, how helpfully were they using their residual powers to promote Labour or Neil Kinnock? Their performances in relation to finance – the setting of the rate and the government's response – were well known. But how far were they meeting the basic needs of their local communities? Far from adequately in Liverpool, according to Archbishop Derek Worlock and Bishop Dick Sheppard. And I was far from satisfied myself with the attention being given in Sheffield to the many concerns which dominated my post bag – still preserved – and which I always conveyed to the Town Hall or to a responsible minister or both.

---

219   *Financial Times.* 13 March 1987.

Economic security, unemployment and race relations, which were prominent in my mail, were not neglected at the Town Hall. But matters affecting the home, the family and the quality of life were also prominent in my post. I was never satisfied with the treatment they received. From the home stemmed concerns relating to schools, child abuse, abortion and council-house sales. All of them issues that I pursued in Whitehall as well as in Sheffield. The quality of life gave rise to an abundance of correspondence. For it touched on library hours, buses, trams, drugs,[220] binge drinking, vandalism and opening hours for shops on Sunday. That was the stuff of politics in Sheffield at that time. As were the strong feelings expressed to me by deputations at constituency 'clinics' on Saturday mornings about lesbian intrusion into schools. They were the issues that troubled my constituents. Not the posturing of the Labour group over rates and its ongoing conflict with government ministers. The matters raised with me would have constituted a more purposeful agenda for the Labour group, instead of the gesture politics to which it had become prone. They were needs that were central to 'socialism', moreover, as opposed to its inclination to 'control-ism'. Under its regime, the Town Hall had now taken the place of the employer in my mail as the popular hate-figure. Unfairly, for it was a major stakeholder in only a few of the provisions affecting the quality of life. But it did have a commitment to regulate some, had an interest in all, and should have shown more deference to grassroots concerns, to bread-and-butter politics – to 'social-ism'.

For Sheffield's Left to probe the common good at that level plainly called for more than just a change of direction. Instead of trying to steer the district party to the loftier ideological level of how best to manage the local economy, for example, they would have to try and meet domestic need through a genuine bottoms-up approach, But that would call for a change of character, which would have been

---

220   I raised repeatedly throughout the Eighties with the Home Office and the South Yorkshire Police the impending arrival of class A drugs in Sheffield.

248

unwelcome to some on the Left, for it would smack of the thinking of Anthony Crosland. It might have helped others, however, recall some traditional threads of socialist thinking – redolent of R.H. Tawney. It might have inclined all to a little more compromise and pragmatism – just like Aneurin Bevan. Above all, it might have disposed certain members of the Labour group to approach their duties more humbly, just like their predecessors, the old guard of Labour councillors. Such as Councillor Harry Firth, a blue-collar worker, who walked his Darnall ward constantly in the Seventies. He would knock on doors just to check on some rumoured problem, and not just at election time. He was once flattened to the ground one Saturday afternoon by a resident angered by his interruption of wrestling on television.

The stance of Sheffield's Left had been ultimately unhelpful to Kinnock. It would be totally at variance with that of the expected successor to Kinnock as party leader, the much-lamented John Smith. John Smith stood not only for changes in defence policy, the reselection of MPs, the voting strength of trade union delegates at party conference and the deletion of Clause Four in the constitution, but above all for the common good – for socialism. That is to say, he offered a new direction, the prospect of a changed ethos and a new image that would have more appeal for the centre-ground of British politics. John Smith's funeral took place, significantly, at Iona, associated with the arrival of Irish monks bringing Christianity to Scotland. His leadership would have been tinged with his Christian social idealism, which has a much longer history in Britain than Marxism. It goes back to Wesley, to Wilberforce and, more recently, William Temple, an Archbishop of Canterbury and a paid–up member of the Labour party. It marked, I hoped, my approach and preferred political role in Attercliffe. A stance that also characterised the outlook of my officers and many of my party workers. It gave them strength when the Attercliffe party became politically isolated in the Eighties. But Attercliffe folk had had to overcome much worse, they assured me, reminding me of the unique ministry in Sheffield of Alf Green.[221] Its objective, he has recorded, was to 'liaise or synthesise, Christian faith and social activity.' He extended his appointment as a full-time Congregational Minister into the Sheffield Inner City Ecumenical Mission and beyond into politics, education and civic life as a councillor. Even those more secularly disposed, such as the National Council of British Socialist Sunday Schools, emphasised that the principles on which socialism rested were 'Love, Justice and Truth'. I was not surprised to find literature describing its 'Aims, Objects and Organisation' among the records of the Attercliffe party.

I never wavered in the belief that my work in Attercliffe and its representation locally and nationally should always be infused with those early beliefs. Always demonstrating, that is to say, the spiritual, moral and cultural dimensions, as well as the political. I never lost sight of the moral imperative of caring for those most in need. I attached the greatest importance to the regular and, apparently, single visits I made to St Luke's Hospice in its early days. Those solitary visits stood in contrast at that time to some prevailing attitudes among members of the Labour group. They objected, I was given to understand, to the private status of St Luke – it was outside the National Health Service. Alf Green, who witnessed and experienced unimaginable hardship in Attercliffe, would have found it difficult to understand such ideological purity. Although a 'young Labourite, keenly antagonistic to all Tory enterprise', he admits in his published account that he always enjoyed the 'annual children's party at the Conservative Working Men's Club', for he 'was remarkably open-minded and fair on these occasions.'

Along with the conduct of such Labour councils as Sheffield's, and the lurking Militant Tendency, there was renewed concern about Labour's defence posture as the election loomed in 1987. It had become a crucial factor once again, as in 1983. I had been left in no

---

221   See Alfred Green. *Growing up in Attercliffe*. 1981.

doubt at the time, whilst a shadow defence minister, that Labour's adoption of a one-sided, one-way or unilateral renunciation of nuclear weapons would never be publicly acceptable. Certainly not by trade unionists, whatever the posturing of some of their officials. And never in Sheffield, which had been the nation's armoury in two world wars. I learned from snatched exchanges at weekends in clubs and pubs that my constituents felt that as long as the Warsaw Pact powers had nuclear weapons, Britain should have them too. Would Neil Kinnock carry more conviction than Michael Foot with the same unilateral nuclear policy? He had never filled any kind of office under the Crown. Or held a job that attested to the requisite business skills and intellectual calls required of modern leadership, though he was very intelligent. Crucially, how far had he endured fire, combat or the challenge of command and control in the armed services, like most prime ministers since WWII? Again, how far would he carry conviction in his handling of policies affecting the nation's security? In the absence of personal experience of conflict, there is always the temptation to give war a chance, which has been demonstrated, unhappily, more than once recently.

From WWII, when Clement Attlee led the Labour party, to 1980 when Jim Callaghan handed on the leadership to Michael Foot, there had been a broad bipartisanship in Parliament on defence, and especially on the issue of the nuclear deterrent. Britain had been well served by that consensus. So had the Labour party, despite the rise of CND. Michael Foot and Tony Benn had known how to handle the matter in Cabinet in the Seventies, as I would expect of both.[222] Michael Foot stood back from the business of the Cabinet's defence and overseas policy sub-committee when nuclear issues arose. I respected and admired them, despite taking different views otherwise. Where the nation's security was at stake, individual political stance

---

222   See Barbara Castle. *The Castle Diaries*. 1974–76 (Weidenfeld & Nicolson 1980). Lord Owen. *The Guardian*. 9 December 1980.

could no longer remain a political factor, a view that was held further afield than among my constituents. The defence of the realm had long been seen as a basic social service which it was the first duty of all governments to provide. Whatever the constant change in weapon systems. It was not an ideological issue. How would Kinnock handle it now, at a time when the defence of the UK – it was generally perceived – could only be secured by membership of an alliance of the Atlantic community which relied on a combination of conventional and nuclear weapons? At a time, furthermore, when there was broad agreement on the part of such powerful allies as America and France that that security depended on a balanced array of conventional and nuclear forces? After all, it was during the socialist government of President Mitterand that France began a modernisation of its own nuclear 'force de frappe'.

Since WWII Britain's defence policy had been a success. Her armed forces were served entirely by volunteers. There had been no serious threat of war in Europe. An outstanding record, indeed a success story. Would the British people put it at risk? As Kinnock threatened to unravel it, the issue of a convincing defence policy increasingly became one of the party leader's own credibility. Leader-like qualities and experience in the field of combat apart, was Kinnock a fit person to be put in charge of Britain's national security? Would he be a trustworthy and realistic partner was a question raised also within the Alliance. Such anxiety was heightened following Labour's annual conference in Blackpool in 1986, when Kinnock confirmed not only the abolition of Britain's nuclear deterrent, but disturbingly called for the closure of American bases in Britain. This was a woefully ill-thought out departure in defence policy, with grave implications for industry at home and the deployment of British forces within the Alliance. How far had those favouring it considered the possible consequences? Once we had scrapped our nuclear weapons, did they not realise that we would have to compensate with conventional weapons? Yet members of the NEC were still trying to reduce defence spending overall. What did they mean, therefore, by 'nuclear' and how far would our nuclear-powered submarines be affected, along with the shipyard and dockyard workers who make and service them? And what effect would such a change in Labour party policy have on Britain's key role in the Alliance: second only to the US, sharing its special engagement capabilities, providing deputies to American commanders-in-chief in Brussels, Naples, Norfolk Virginia and prominent always in the Northern command at its Oslo headquarters?

The policy change was riddled with such contradictions. They were bound to surface before polling day in 1987, exactly as they did during the 1983 campaign. The policy was losing support among Labour's own supporters, according to a MORI poll conducted in February. It was not only politically questionable, it was not practical militarily. The NATO policy of escalatory response to the threat of aggression was intended to keep conflict well short of the critical nuclear threshold. That policy would remain, irrespective of the policy of a Labour government in London. But General Bernard Rogers confided to me whilst he was Supreme Commander, if a conventional attack by Soviet forces threatened to break through on the north German plain he did not doubt that his divisional commanders would be screaming for tactical nuclear support. Such a flexible response could invoke first use of nuclear weaponry and inextricably involve locally based British regiments. Leaving them exposed was unthinkable, for they would be very vulnerable to known Soviet 'second echelon' battlefield strategy. That was based on superior conventional capacity, notably in armoured warfare and strategic manpower reserves, which would enable the Warsaw Pact forces to quickly absorb initial losses. The Labour party's defence policy in 1986 had become neither politically nor militarily sustainable.

In Casper Weinberger, the American defence secretary at the time, Britain had a very good friend. He had made it clear to me, however, that America's commitment to the defence of Western Europe and

Britain's continuing participation in NATO, would be jeopardised by Labour's proposed change in policy. Crucially, it would undermine the balance of risk for the US in Europe. Dick Cheney, then vice president, also expressed to me the fear that Labour's defence policy would risk unravelling an alliance of democracies that had kept the peace for a generation. Al Gore and Joe Biden, close colleagues in the NATO Assembly, subsequently US vice presidents, shared with me the same fear. The change did not even meet with favour in Moscow, where the leadership told me during a visit that they did not want any changes in British policy that would affect their current arms negotiations with the US.

Denis Healy did his best at that party conference in 1986, as he had done so earlier in talks with Mr Gorbachev in Moscow, when he tried to dispose of unilateralism by exchanging something for something.[223] He tried to allay American criticism after the party conference when he accompanied Neil Kinnock on his visit to the US to meet President Reagan. By now the real issue at the heart of defence policy was neither the unilateral nor the multilateral approach. It was the crucially important question of how effectively could a non-nuclear UK function within a nuclear-based alliance. Although I sympathised with Neil Kinnock following his second visit to Washington to spell out the details of Labour's new policy, I knew what he was up against, whatever the courtesies involved. As vice-president and soon to become President of the NATO assembly, I was acquainted with successive heads of the State and Defence departments in Washington. As someone 'cleared' for classified information during my former tenure as defence minister, I continued to receive in-depth briefings

---

223   It would have been more telling if instead of promising a marginal reduction of Russia's vast arsenal of nuclear weapons in exchange for Britain's Polaris system, Mr Gorbachev had offered one of his two new intercontinental ballistic missiles (the mobile SS24 and SS.25) which were in breach of SALT2 or surrendered the massive early-warning radar station at Krasnoyarsk, which was a violation of the 1972 anti-ballistic missile treaty.

at the Pentagon. I was accustomed to annual sessions with the armed services and appropriation committees of Congress. I regularly visited commanders- in- chief all around the alliance. I was well aware that Kinnock's policy change was viewed as impractical and unacceptable. Wherever possible, however, I never hesitated to explain and reinforce that policy as a matter of duty.[224] My own differing personal position was well known.[225]

In the run–up to the election in June 1987, others prominent within the ranks of Labour were less restrained. Richard Heller, advisor to Labour's shadow cabinet, published a bombshell indictment of Labour's ramshackle 'defence' policy.[226] Bill Jordan, newly elected president of the engineering workers and Eric Hammond, leader of the electricians union, cited defence as a crippling election issue. They went to see Neil Kinnock and argued unsuccessfully that unilateralism be put to the test of a referendum under a future Labour government. Not surprisingly, Labour suffered a third successive defeat in 1987.

Labour controlled local authorities such as Sheffield were held responsible to varying extents for Labour's defeat. The inflexibility of Kinnock hitherto on nuclear armaments, reinforced astonishingly by the announced policy changes at the 1986 party conference, was

---

224   Neil Kinnock never wanted for formal support and personal sympathy from those who were in private disagreement. At the first Manifesto group meeting following his election as deputy-leader, Roy Hattersley announced his intention to leave, for his exclusive duty lay now with the Leader. Unlike my defeat as chairman of Labour's back-bench Defence committee by one vote, when the Leader's PPS attended for the first time to vote against me.

225   I never allowed that to affect my handling of Labour defence policy. With all its contradictions and inadequacies, I was clear as to where my duty lay from the Front Bench in relevant debates and statements throughout the Eighties.

226   He called on the 'Labour leadership to adopt a new defence policy that does not require the British people to believe six impossible things before breakfast.' Existing defence policy and posture are 'continuing to harm its election prospects', he believed. *The Times.* 10 March 1987.

probably a more potent factor. In accordance with a long standing generosity towards its leadership, the Labour party – unthinkingly in the light of events – gave him another chance.

Nevertheless, the mood of the party began to change after the 1987 election. Out of the defeat of Scargillism there had appeared a willingness to think again. For the first time for a decade or more there also appeared a readiness to scrap old ideological baggage and address the modern world as it is rather than as it is supposed to be. Even hard-line councils, with no prospect of relief from an incoming Labour government, began to consider a 'new realism' instead of a new socialism. The 'gesture politics' of the early 1980s were a thing of the past, said the leader of the Islington council. 'There is a new realism in Haringey Labour politics,' admitted one of its left-wing councillors.[227] The effect of rate capping, the surcharging and subsequent disqualification from public office of Ted 'Red Ted' Knight, former Lambeth council leader, and events leading to the fall of Derek Hatton and fellow Militants in Liverpool, had a salutary effect on Sheffield's Labour group. It went so far, commendably, to initiate exploratory steps to attract private capital. The Labour party was back in business in Sheffield.

Within two years the 'cold war' in Sheffield between the Council and the local business community was over. Collaboration took place to shape a new future. BSC(Industry), the job creation company formed by British Steel to ease the socioeconomic shock of steel closures, opened a regional office in the city. Welcoming it, John Hambridge, stated: 'They tried to run a siege economy and failed. The development office is an acknowledgement that they cannot act alone,' and the council's acceptance soon afterwards of its own UDC was an acknowledgement of past failure. The Minister of inner cities, David Trippier, told me in a private exchange in Parliament that it was time to 'bury the hatchet'.

---

227   *The Daily Telegraph*. 24 October 1988.

The new spirit of partnership was borne out in his widely welcomed appointments of Sir Hugh Sykes as chairman and Lord Mulley as deputy chairman of the new UDC for the Lower Don Valley. The emphasis of each in long and distinguished careers had always been to put 'Sheffield first and foremost'. Why had the spirit of partnership that had been fashioned in the Seventies been so lightly discarded at such cost to the city, was the question heard on all sides. Why did Councillor Heslop, Conservative leader on Sheffield council, have to remind councillors later that the 'way forward is ... to establish a proper partnership with the Government'?[228]

The Council sought to restore Sheffield's tarnished image when it made a bid in July 1987 to stage the World Student Games in 1991. It was intended to signal a renaissance for the city. Misconceived, miscalculated and mismanaged, however, it ended in a considerable financial loss and put ratepayers on the financial rack for a generation, though the debt was subsequently renegotiated.[229] 'When you talk to people in Government about the games,' reported David Heslop, 'they shake their heads and say 'Typical'.'[230]

'But we were desperate to re-establish people's interest in Sheffield,' pleaded Councillor Peter Price, chairman of the Games operating company, 'because no-one wanted to come to this city.' Just as disappointing was the decision regarding the location of the Royal Armouries new museum. Why did Sheffield, with its outstanding claims, have to lose to Leeds? It not only had the historical links, but also an excellent city site, which Lord Eden, who was handling the

---

228   *The Star.* 20 February 1991.

229   Despite the recent sturdy defence of its handling by Howard A. Knight, former councillor, (*The Star.* 23 March 2011)and his claim that 'All three parties on the council agreed', there was, typically, no consultation of the city's MPs. 'Certainly a staggering degree of naïveté appears to have accompanied Sheffield's bid for the Games' was the judgement of *The Sunday Times* (25 February 1990).

230   *The Star.* 20 February 1991.

matter, acknowledged to me personally. But canvassing the cause of Sheffield in London had become very unproductive by the close of the Eighties.

Neil Kinnock had said in his first interview after the defeat in 1987 that defence policy would not be changed. But he was persuaded by Roy Hattersley, John Smith and others at the party conference that followed to include defence in the proposed radical review of policies. Within two years the Labour party had become seriously political once again.

A resounding by-election win in the Vale of Glamorgan on a high turn-out in early May 1989, together with good county elections, were encouraging. As were the fruits of the revisionist policy review, which now had a working majority support on the NEC. There was also a promise at long last of a coherent defence policy. In an impassioned speech to the NEC on 9 March 1989, Neil Kinnock said many in the room had marched for unilateralism. He had done more than that. He had 'gone to the White House, the Kremlin and the Elysee, and argued down the line for it. They had been totally uncomprehending.' Never again. 'I will not do it,' he said. 'The majority of the party and the majority of the country don't expect me to do so.' Most of the twenty-nine executive members broke into applause – an event unknown for years.

'Neil has been bursting to make that speech for two years,' said one Shadow cabinet minister present.[231] He had heard him make it two or three times in private, he added. Could he have said it sooner? Or was the damage to his political credibility now irreparable?

The historic summit in Iceland between President Reagan and Mr Gorbachev in October 1986, had offered him the opportunity of a turning point. The meeting had indicated the extent of Gorbachev's bargaining posture and the magnitude of the possible breakthrough. His espousal of Glasnost and Perestroika and the possible end to the

---

231 *The Sunday Times.* 14 May 1989.

Cold War had opened the way for a much lower nuclear balance between the super-powers. 'Everything has changed: the world has changed,' Kinnock told a close colleague. Kinnock's second meeting with Reagan could have had a quite different outcome had he been free to seize the opportunity and not been saddled with such a binding commitment to unilateralism. He could have pursued nuclear arms control generally, for it was now wide open. For there could be little doubt that the most dramatic and immediate challenge facing the Alliance lay in the area of arms control. Reagan had run out of patience with SALT2, and was contemplating a move towards a new arms-control deal with the Russians.

There was in any event a need to revise basic thinking as new technologies emerged and old defence positions eroded. It was not only the substantive issues that were involved, but also the political dimension and the reaction of public opinion to each new development. This had been most dramatically illustrated at Reykjavik, where it was obvious that questions on arms control needed to be measured not only in military but also in political terms. With a little freedom Neil Kinnock could have seized the opportunity to initiate, at least, a policy of mutual and progressive disarmament. Mr Gorbachev appeared to be ready, and President Reagan was in need of encouragement. Such a heaven-sent exploration and flexibility were presumably denied Kinnock because of the intransigence on unilateralism of the NEC and CND and, in particular, the naiveté of individuals like Ron Todd, of the TGW,[232] and others with their limited grasp of global affairs. Should he, could he, have taken them on, especially in the summer of 1988 when he had made a half-hearted attempt at reform?

The startling U-turn in 1957 of Aneurin Bevan, an early unilateralist, was ample precedent for an appeal beyond the confines

---

232   Whose members were shifting over their anti-nuclear stand. Other trade unionists in general were now two to one in favour of keeping a nuclear deterrent, according to a poll by MORI for *The Sunday Times*. 2 October 1988.

of the NEC. As was that of Hugh Gaitskell when he took on not only the unilateralists at Scarborough in 1960, but party conference itself. It did not end in Labour fratricide. And the Left was altogether more formidable in those days. Neither Bevan or Gaitskell were saddled with the new procedures of the electoral college, of course. Thus Kinnock would be stepping into unknown territory. But Tony Blair ventured into more dangerous territory later when he amended the party constitution at the expense of its famous Clause Four. And Blair could not rely afterwards in its justification on the personal eloquence such as Kinnock possessed. Kinnock would have been at his best appealing in Tribune-speech style to the party membership after exercising the 'Nelson Touch'. At Trafalgar in 1805 Admiral Nelson was Commander-in-Chief and thus wholly responsible for the action's success or failure. Fully aware of the paramount strategic importance to Britain of victory, he nonetheless put his career on the line by disregarding established doctrine as he took on the combined Fleets of France and Spain.[233] Could anything less dramatic have enabled Neil Kinnock meet the challenge of public credibility and win the next election? Or was he incapable of taking tough decisions? Or were those among his parliamentary colleagues right when they described him as 'just a good old Welsh boyo. He wants to be popular all the time'?[234]

He had made tentative moves towards a policy change in the spring of 1988. On 9 May the parliamentary staff of *The Independent* took Neil Kinnock out to lunch. A lead story appeared in the newspaper

233 The manner in which sea-battles should be fought by the Royal Navy in Admiral Nelson's day was clearly laid down by the Admiralty Board and woe betide the unsuccessful sea officer who had not conformed. Off the Portuguese headland of Cape St. Vincent in 1797, contrary to doctrine and without the Admiral's orders, a junior Commodore Nelson broke away from the line and engaged the Spanish rear – with outstanding success.

234 *Observer.* 26 June 1988.

the following day under the headline, 'Kinnock set to modify nuclear weapons policy'. On a BBC programme three weeks later, he stated, 'There is now no need for something from nothing unilateralism.' That served to confirm the original *Independent* story. It was seized upon by the Press as evidence of a major shift in policy. But Kinnock soon came under pressure from the unilateralists.

The TGW executive unofficially withheld its nomination to party conference of the Kinnock-Hattersley leadership ticket pending 'clarification' of the defence policy'. The party's defence spokesman, Denzil Davies, who had not even been informed in advance, much else consulted, resigned. There were reports of Neil Kinnock coming under personal pressure from Robin Cook, joint chairman of the re-election campaign, together with Joan Ruddock, former chairwoman of CND, and David Blunkett, neither of whom I could recall ever making a considered public statement on defence, much less one that examined the complexities of nuclear policy. Kinnock soon wilted, went into retreat and proceeded to make a fresh public statement. He was hosted at lunch once again by *The Independent* and its report appeared on 21 June. In it Kinnock reaffirmed his commitment to unilateralism though attaching much importance to a trade-off with the Soviets. But he must have known, as I was certainly aware, that Russia was not interested.

In a careful examination of the crisis that had overtaken Kinnock's leadership, Robert Harris, Political Editor of the *Observer* found that his 'confused handling of the issue of nuclear defence [had] caused it to explode in his face.'[235] He reported the comment of John (now Lord) Gilbert: 'He danced a jig when the party was captured for unilateralism. Now he finds it has become his scaffold.'

An *Observer* poll revealed: 'Almost twice as many non-Labour voters as a month ago now cite disunity and indecisiveness as reasons

---

235   *Observer.* 26 June 1988.

for not voting Labour.' An editorial in the *Daily Mirror* demanded to know, 'What the hell are you doing, Neil?'

A year ago Neil Kinnock had backed off from firmly supporting a move for one member, one vote in the selection of parliamentary candidates. Now he yielded once more to pressure and allowed himself to be hampered again with a defence policy that had lost Labour two general elections. Worse, it was a policy that was being taken no more seriously in Moscow than in Washington. Ron Todd[236] was told in Moscow early in 1989, along with other members of a Labour party delegation, that while unilateralism was an 'imaginative gesture' it was neither realistic nor a serious option for a major power. General Vladimir Lobov, the next Warsaw Pact forces chief, whom I was also meeting at the same time, told them – and myself – that the best approach was for Britain to throw its Polaris and Trident nuclear defence systems into world disarmament talks. So much for the 'trade-off with the Soviets' on which Kinnock's defence policy now hinged.

When delegates assembled in Blackpool in 1990 for the Labour party conference, they welcomed the policy review 'Looking to the Future'. A comparison with the party's election manifesto of 1983 indicated how far Labour had at long last rethought its policies. It had jettisoned so-called socialist policies that had been articles of faith for a generation for left-wing activists. It had made substantial shifts on Europe and taxation as well as defence that would have been inconceivable a few years earlier. John Smith and Gordon Brown, notably, had proposed an economic and industrial strategy geared to make the country internationally competitive. Not by overriding market forces, but by making them work better. 'Socialism,' the report read, 'is about diffusing power and giving people more control over their lives.' A socialism, it was stressed, that is not about state or local authority control: social-ism, in another word, not control-ism.

---

236   Described by Georgi Arbatov as 'another useful idiot'.

Labour had reassuringly returned to the mainstream of politics. It was about to follow the German social democrats in their historic shift of ideology thirty years earlier. Rejecting Marxism and broadening its base, the party was now prepared to become a centre-left party of the social-market economy. The Germans had summed it up in a phrase: 'markets as far as possible, planning as few as necessary'.

This new realism still stopped short of a credible defence posture, however. Unlike the Germans, who were manning NATO's front line of defence, the Labour party was not ready to adapt to its realities. Unilateral nuclear disarmament had cost Labour dearly at two general elections. During that time events had exposed its futility and underlined the credibility of multilateral disarmament. Unilateralism was no longer credible politically. It was not even practical militarily. Kinnock had done his best and had tried to shift the emphasis on nuclear arms, but could he yet present a defence policy which the public would buy? Would defence prove to be Labour's Achilles heel as in the past? Or, was there still a credibility gap? After all, calls for cuts to Britain's defence spending were defeated by only one vote at an NEC executive meeting during the 1990 party conference.

Yet Neil deserved to be taken on trust. He had taken on the Left, the Militant Tendency, the reform of the party constitution, the modernisation of the party's publicity machine and the revision of policy. He had reacted positively to the Anglo-Irish Agreement in 1985. Following briefings by Dick Spring, Irish Labour party leader, and consultations with his newly-appointed shadow secretary of state for Northern Ireland, Kevin McNamara, he introduced an approach that helped to pave the way later for the peace process. In authorising the document *Towards a United Ireland* on behalf of the Front Bench and offering the prospect – however briefly – of Labour becoming a 'persuader' of Irish unity, he displayed a greater courage and a surer touch on Northern Ireland affairs than any other Labour Leader, before or since. He had assembled, furthermore, a good shadow cabinet, a sound private office and, in Charles Clarke, he had a very good chief-of-staff. Together they built the foundations of Labour's 1997 election win. Did the controversial eve-of-poll rally in Sheffield – an unfortunate choice of location – affect Neil Kinnock's public standing?[237] Or were crucial reservations still lingering among the general public about whether he was a prime minister in waiting or someone into whose hands they hesitated to put the nation's security? Would the 'Nelson Touch' have saved him?

---

237   The pollster Bob Worcester insists that it did.

Chapter Fourteen
Demonising of the Irish in Britain

The Seventies were difficult times for the Irish in Britain because of bombs in Birmingham, Guildford, Woolwich and elsewhere. Entire Irish communities came under suspicion. Feeling bordering on hysteria was whipped up by certain sections of the press. It was in that atmosphere that Parliament considered the Prevention of Terrorism Bill. It was obliged to take action against such acts of subversion, needless to say. But the Prevention of Terrorism Act (PTA) went a good deal further than that in practice. It was used to intimidate Irish people generally. It was used to harass Irish travellers at Holyhead, as I was well aware, personally. Letters to me claimed that in the prevailing ethos the PTA had become anti-Irish rather than anti-terrorist. In its first five years 5,500 people, mainly Irish, were held under the Act and only seventy-eight convicted.

Much more seriously the PTA was used to stifle legitimate political debate. It was also used vindictively, even to the point of injustice. Thus calling into question the hitherto irreproachable British judicial establishment. There was a marked reluctance on the part of some of its members, notably Lord Denning and Lord Lane – at the appeal stage – to bring themselves to admit the mistakes that had led to the miscarriages of justice involving Irish people such as the Birmingham Six, the Guildford Four and the Maguire Seven. Those arrested in Balcombe Street, London, in 1975, told the police that they had carried out the Guildford and Woolwich bombings in 1974, and that the wrong people had been imprisoned. Nevertheless, the Guildford Four were kept in prison for another fifteen years. Along with the others falsely imprisoned, they were tried and condemned by some of the media long before sentencing. The role of sections of the media as well as the PTA contributed to the demonising of the

Irish in Britain in the Seventies and Eighties. Such treatment affected not only justifiable political debate but, arguably, delayed the peace process in Northern Ireland.

The media in England and Ireland has been responsible for certain misunderstanding and protest in each country for a long time. Some cartoons published in England from the eighteenth century are openly racist, portraying the Irish as ignorant peasants – barefoot, ragged and thick.[238] There were few Irish retaliatory cartoons before the 1860s, but they appeared regularly afterwards in magazines in Belfast and Dublin. John Bull was depicted as a bully and Britannia as a murderess – causing evictions and executions. Some of those vituperative exchanges may well have been stirred by the Great Famine. Britain had emerged from it in a very poor light because of its want of sympathy and lack of effective help. The Famine was not widely mentioned, nor did it become an issue during the general election that took place simultaneously in August 1847. The media was much more interested in the current 'Railway mania'.

Charles Trevelyan, an assistant secretary to the Treasurer, was content to allow the Famine to be resolved by laissez–faire market forces. In the dreadful outcome he found a convenient alibi in the Irish people themselves. The 'great evil' was not the Famine, but the 'selfish, perverse and turbulent character of the people'. Thus the colonial mind, despite the immense Irish contribution to the manpower of the British Army at that time,[239] was apparently justifying its conquest by dehumanising the conquered race. Trevelyan was not without support, for the Irish were currently caricatured as stupid, lazy and drunken. When they fought back, they were condemned as disloyal

---

238   Gilray was notorious, as was the *Punch* magazine, according to *Drawing Con-clusions. A Cartoon history of Anglo-Irish Relations, 1798–1988* by Roy Douglas, Liam Hart and Jim O'Hara. 1998.

239   Yet many units at Waterloo were one-third Catholic Irish, and by the 1820s made up more than forty per cent of the Army's rank-and-file.

and clearly in need of a firm British hand. That is how they were portrayed all over again, incredibly, by cartoonists, journalists and public entertainers a century later – in the 1970s and the 1980s.

The belittling Irish 'joke' became the staple diet of radio and television comedians from the 1970s. Even the 'soaps' moved Irish Ambassador Ted Barrington to protest. The appalling racist slurs at that time of Sir John Junor, the former editor of the *Sunday Express*, and Jak, the *London Evening Standard* cartoonist, brought widespread complaints. 'Wouldn't you prefer to be a pig than be Irish?' asked Junor.[240] And shortly afterwards Jak's cartoon conveyed the Irish as 'the ultimate in psychopathic horror'. Along with other Labour MPs I made representations both to the Commission for Racial Equality and the Press Commission. The offences of Junor and Jak proved counterproductive, however, as Irish companies withdrew advertising revenue, notably from the *Sunday Express*. The Greater London Council (GLC) – thanks to Ken Livingstone – withdrew also its huge advertising allocations to the *Evening Standard*. But more watchfulness was clearly called for in aid of balanced reporting.[241]

I did not believe Julie Burchill, the *Guardian* columnist, or Robert Kilroy-Silk, a chat-show host, or a weightier Bruce Anderson merited the publicity their anti-Irish invective received. Nor did I view them as worthy of personal protest. But a comment on Anderson indicates just how venomous a journalist even of his standing could be on Irish affairs. In the *Daily Mail* in November 1996 he attacked Padraig Flynn,

240   I engaged Sir John Junor in correspondence, to which he responded in the friendliest and most courteous manner. I was not surprised to learn later that he had developed a taste for Irish holidays.

241   I raised with the MOD a reported blasphemous interruption by a soldier within the Greenham Common Air Base of an open-air Mass taking place outside the fence. Despite extensive inquiries, I was assured, the identity of the soldier had not been established. Given the stereotypes then rife, I suspected the solder had perceived some Irish link with that Mass.

the European Commissioner for Social Affairs, who was undeniably targetable. But I could not recognise his portrayal of Castlebar, Mr. Flynn's constituency. It happens to be the county town of Co. Mayo, with which I have been personally acquainted for over sixty years. He described its economy as 'pre-twentieth century ... based on the pig and potato', located within an 'enclosed world of cattle markets, farm subsidies and generally tolerated rural corruption.' Ireland then had the highest economic growth rate in the industrialised world, would soon be rated as having a higher standard of living than the UK and rated among those countries with the highest quality of life in the world. Moves were afoot also at the time to commemorate in Castlebar in a memorial beyond compare in most parts of the UK, the men from the county who died in WWI, and the constituency would soon return a taoiseach, or prime minister. But I could not muster a protest against Anderson. I presumed he was too set in his ways. But I remained vigilant and active otherwise.

I challenged always press reports of robbers described as having Irish accents. Some newspapers and police forces cooperated, some not so.[242] The Metropolitan Police were invariably resentful of my enquiries. Significantly, however, in the follow-up of such cases, I realised how far newspapers could be at fault. I never once encountered in a single case validation of the initial report of an 'Irish accent'. Even the BBC became involved. I raised with Alasdair Milne, its director-general in the Eighties, Irish slurs made by Derek Jameson, then occupying Terry Wogan's early-morning slot, by David Jacobs and the *Two Ronnies* programme. 'No such offence was intended,' I was assured. A 'quizzical view of life' was offered as explanation for Jameson and a departmental slip-up for Jacobs.

---

242   The following case fairly illustrates my approach. I wrote to a newspaper in South Yorkshire in the early 1990s enquiring as to what evidence it had that a reported would-be robber, still unapprehended, was Irish. The newspaper replied promptly, saying that their information had been supplied by the local police. I raised this briefing with the Chief Constable of South Yorkshire. I referred also to another local incident involving a fatal shooting, when the media indicated that the man sought had a Dublin accent. When caught, that man turned out to be from north Yorkshire. In his reply the Chief Constable said, 'It is almost becoming a standard practice for armed robbers, bogus officials, etc., to adopt some form of accent during the course of their offences and one can well understand why.' In a follow-up letter the head of the regional police press and public relations department said, 'I fully share your concern about making assumptions of nationality, a practice I would agree to be both racist and detrimental to police investigations.' What had been said was, 'The demands [for cash] were made with an Irish accent.' It was not said that the offender was Irish. Clearly it was the newspaper that put the spin on it. The letter went on: 'We regularly make the point to reporters that any regional accent may not be genuine and that whilst we might mention it as a potentially relevant part of the description, undue weight should not be given to it. Clearly, there is a need to make this point on every occasion when accents are mentioned and I will ask my staff to do so in future.' A welcome exchange that was courteous throughout, and had a mutually helpful outcome. That, unhappily, was not the case when the newspaper in question, the Doncaster Free Press, repeated its Irish racism reportage in September, 2012. A polite request for clarification, and several courteous reminders, were wholly ignored. This was in marked contrast to the newspaper's earlier helpfulness, when it apologised to readers.

Yet, repeats of the *Two Ronnies* have obviously been cleansed. I was moved to complain even to the BBC's local Radio Sheffield about its compere trying to 'raise a laugh at the expense of the Irish', during the annual Feast of Brass and Voices – of all programmes.[243] The BBC had a reputation at that time for journalistic competence and integrity second to none. It was listened to and believed by millions around the world. It was nominated by a group of all-party MPs for a Nobel Peace prize, which I supported. But I was not alone in my complaints, for its own chairman, Marmaduke Hussey, charged it at about the same time with being guilty of 'complacency, arrogance and a reluctance to acknowledge public criticism'. The commendable depiction of Irish people and cultural identity by the BBC to mark St. Patrick's Day, like the televising of Midnight Mass on Christmas Eve, has shrunk since the 1930s.

I raised with British Airways the 'Irish jokes', an item in its *High Life* magazine, and enquired as to the absence of jokes about the English, Scots, Jews, Pakistanis and so on. I received two courteous and sympathetic replies, one from David Burnside, later an Ulster Unionist MP. But neither met the crucial points of timing and even-handedness. Unhappily, some Irish comedians such as Frank Carson perpetuated the 'stupid Irish persona'. Many of his gags were so-called 'Irish' jokes. Some saw them as merely poking gentle fun at his own people, even when they were of the 'thick Mick' variety. Others complained to me that his brand of humour reinforced the derogatory view of the Irish, and put their children on the receiving end of taunts in the school playground. After he was booed off stage at a Sheffield working men's club in 1987, constituents complained that he should change his catchphrase, 'It's the way I tell 'em', to, 'It's where I tell 'em'. Did he use the anti-Irish material he thought appropriate in Sheffield on the Falls Road in Belfast or in the Bogside in Derry, they asked? Did it never occur to Carson that he was now a recruit of the contemporary

---

243   A letter to Nigel Kay. 19 December 1988.

campaign in Britain to demonise the Irish, his own people, I asked myself. A second area of concern, as a spill-over or actually linked, was its possible effect on much-needed political discussion.

It was enough to have an Irish name to be exposed to hostile barbs in Parliament. Thus Kevin McNamara, Martin Flannery and myself were always vulnerable, No matter how objective we were in probing security and policy in Northern Ireland – and our records bear the severest scrutiny – ministers were sometimes disposed to cast us in an unpatriotic light. Whilst some of our own parliamentary colleagues sitting alongside us would be scowling, and ready to pounce if a soldier from a particular constituency was shot on active duty. Andrew Alexander of all people, whose journalistic prowess I have always admired, resented our interventions from the parliamentary press gallery, and asked, 'Why do they not go off and be Irish nationalists in Ireland?'[244] Such parliamentary interventions invariably triggered further threatening letters, and my mother's home would come under discreet police surveillance. I was subject to Special Branch protection in Britain because of threat assessments, and came in for close protection in the Irish Republic for many years. The homes of Kevin McNamara and Martin Flannery were under constant threat. The windows of Kevin's home were stoned on the night of the Birmingham bombing; he and Nora were threatened: 'The next time a soldier is killed, one of your children will be …'. A half-brick thrown through my mother's front window narrowly missed her head. We were all subject to letter-threats for years. All this was nothing compared to the experience of the Catholics in Northern Ireland, of course. But it might have influenced some similarly-placed MPs to 'keep their heads down'. We never allowed it to divert us, however, from what we perceived to be our duty in relation to the plight of Catholics in the province. We could not but probe reported incidents arising from the Falls Curfew, internment, Ballymurphy, Bloody

---

244   *Daily Mail.* 9 November 1983.

Sunday and such controversial developments as the Widgery report whitewash, the behaviour of the Paras, the notorious Castlereagh detention centre, the Stalker and Stevens reports,[245] the assassination of human-rights lawyer, Pat Finucane, as well as London's repeated mishandling of extradition policy.[246] Along with the physical threat to us for doing so, there was the ever-present risk of damaging media reaction. The Gibraltar killings constitute a case in point.

Gibraltar was the scene in February 1988 of a notorious excess by the British Government that simply cried out for questioning from its first official announcement. The SAS shot dead three unarmed members of the IRA, and unleashed an appalling spiral of violence which ended in the deaths of two unfortunate British Army corporals. When the three IRA members were buried in Belfast's Milltown cemetery, a loyalist called Michael Stone threw hand grenades among the mourners, killing three and injuring many. A few days later when one of those killed was being buried, the two corporals, no doubt confused, drove into the cortege. They were beaten to death by a frenzied crowd who believed, it was reported, that they were loyalists intent on another attack. When the Northern Ireland secretary made a statement in Parliament on the violence, Martin Flannery and I mildly reminded him of its link with the questionable violence in Gibraltar. The following day *The Times* newspaper published a scurrilous cartoon depicting Martin and myself worshipping knees-down at an IRA martyrs' shrine.[247]

---

245   Questions remain about prosecutions as a result of the Stalker report, despite assurances given to the Garrett Fitzgerald government at the end of 1986, it was reported.

246   London has been wrong again and again in implementation of extradition arrangements, notably in 'provision of evidence to back up warrants for terrorist suspects. Britain requires such evidence from other countries, so it is hardly surprising if the Republic expects it from us.' *The Daily Telegraph*. 22 February 1988.

247   Far from complaining or seeking legal redress – for I had been advised that it was libellous – I decided a greater contempt was to purchase the original and treat it as a trophy.

Just how questionable also was the reporting by other British newspapers, ranging from *The Sunday Times* to the *Sun*, can be gauged from the number of successful libel cases directed at them. How differently others also viewed the Gibraltar killings was amply illustrated subsequently by the reaction at the inquest in Gibraltar, and at the European Court of Human Rights. The most celebrated case that arose involved Thames Television. In 1989 it asked Lord Windlesham, a former Conservative government minister, to conduct with Richard Rampton, QC, what Windlesham himself called 'the most rigorous examination of a single current affairs programme in the history of British television.' When broadcast, the programme incensed ministers by casting doubt on the military's account of events and suggesting that the IRA members might have been unlawfully killed. The broadcasters said they were simply reporting the facts. *Private Eye*'s report 'Rock Bottom', sold separately, brought together the entire depressing story. Its conclusion, no longer disputed, was that the three were shot down in cold blood on the Sunday instead of on the following Tuesday, as had been planned. Everyone involved knew that there was no bomb on the Sunday, but feared that the three had spotted that they were under surveillance and were about to abandon their plan. Rather than let them escape, or arrest them on charges which might not stand up, they were summarily executed. Martin Flannery and I got off lightly. But our penalty illustrates the lengths to which some newspapers were prepared to go to inhibit justifiable enquiry. I remained puzzled that a newspaper such as *The Times* had fallen into such media company, when other organs, journalists and writers were courageously presenting different pictures.

In an outstanding work Liz Curtis describes how the whole machinery of information was effectively manipulated by a combination of government, the military and a small hierarchy within the media itself.[248] The objective was to ensure that a picture demonising republicans was conveyed to the British public. A serious casualty of the process, she claims, was the truth. Thus the press would take Army briefings as true, even when invariably they were proved to be false.[249] She provides a number of examples of how the failure of the media to report what was going on in the north of Ireland perpetuated injustice. Complaints of torture by British troops were continually put aside until the Irish Government took the issues to the European Court of Human Rights. Failure to report loyalist violence, she stated, such as the bombing of McGurks bar in 1971, stemmed from the need to focus on the IRA. Such selective amnesia meant that all 2,000 deaths arising from the conflict up to the time of the hunger strikes in 1981 were being attributed to the IRA. The reality was that 600 of the deaths, nearly all civilians, were due to the loyalists, with another 200 due to the police and the Army, she points out. 'The books, in short, were being cooked in order to establish the IRA not as a product of the conflict, but as the cause,' says Curtis.

Paul Donovan, who has also given close attention of the media coverage in Northern Ireland, raises the third area of concern.[250] He points out that the approach adopted all too often restricted any constructive discussion as to the real causes of the conflict. More

---

248   In *Ireland. The Propaganda War*, later republished, she shows in some detail how the events of Bloody Sunday were news managed. Amongst the early reports from official sources was the version that the paras had more than 200 bullets fired at them. Such reports filled the column inches with little room being given to alternative viewpoints, even from some reporters on the ground. The Widgery Report exonerated the soldiers involved, and was leaked to Defence correspondents on the eve of publication.

249   One striking example comes from Simon Winchester of *The Guardian* who, in July 1970, was told by the Army that just fifteen shots had been fired during the curfew in Belfast, when the true figure was 1,454.

250   *The Universe*. 17 January 1999.

than two-thirds of all coverage, as Curtis had established, focused on violence and death reported in isolation. The application of any type of historical context was lacking; media coverage was giving a false image and that has 'been a sorry reflection on British journalism', concludes Donovan.[251] Roy Gleenslade, who was editor of the *Daily Mirror* and has worked for most of the national press titles, went further and slammed such British newspaper coverage as 'distorted'. 'If you look to the *Mail, Sun, Express, Telegraph, Times* and their Sunday equivalents,' he writes, what you have is a 'massive preponderance of papers that have distorted, misreported, accepted the word of the authorities without checking and written single source stories.' There was great sympathy for the Catholic population in the late 1960s, he declares, but as soon as the Army went in, the papers fell in behind the troops, whose only mission was to hold the ring and impartially separate two feuding tribes.

I warned the House of Commons in April 1973, when speaking from the Opposition front bench in the annual debate on the Army, of how the media war would be fought in future.[252] It was important to restate the warring tribes model because it exonerates on the one hand any wrongdoing by Crown forces and, on the other hand, demonises the republicans. Massive resources were devoted to this media machine, not only in the UK, but also in Europe and especially in the US. Thus, events such as the Gibraltar killings and the shooting of nine people by the SAS in Loughall in 1987 were effectively legitimised by sections of the media in the UK. When I questioned the official explanations regarding Gibraltar in Parliament, I was

---

251   *The Universe.* 26 October 2003.

252   I explained how Brigadier Frank Kitson in his 1969 book, *Low Intensity Operations*, envisaged the use of psychological operations and disinformation. He wrote that the government must 'promote its cause and undermine that of the enemy ... and this involves a carefully planned and coordinated campaign ... psychological operations.' *Hansard*. Cols. 722–732. 5 April 1973.

publicly and libellously besmirched. When Thames Television's *Death on the Rock* programme presented a different version to the official explanation, the government turned on Windlesham.[253] It pursued a vindictive campaign against the company, which ended when the company lost its franchise.

The Channel Four documentary *The Committee* alleged links between loyalist paramilitaries and the security forces, which was also vigorously contested. Sir John Stephens, when deputy chief constable of Cambridgeshire, was asked in 1989 to investigate such allegations of RUC links with loyalist assassins. An earlier inquiry by another English police chief, John Stalker, had become mired in controversy and his report was never published, nor was that of his successor, Colin Sampson. Most people were unwilling to believe that the RUC or the Army would collude with the loyalist paramilitaries. However, Sir John discovered that the allegations were by and large, true. While he did not conclude that there was a web of conspiracy, he did establish that the Forces Research Unit (FRU), a covert Army intelligence group, had links with the paramilitaries through a double agent. He believed also that his inquiry was deliberately obstructed in its early stages by the RUC and the Army.

But following the report in 2012 by Sir Desmond de Silva of the murder in 1989 of Patrick Finucane, Prime Minister David Cameron – as with the Bloody Sunday killings – made no attempt, as *The Economist* [254] put it, to 'defend the indefensible'. In a statement in the House of Commons in December 2012, he described the report as 'shocking' at least four times. 'It is really shocking,' he said, 'that this happened in our country.' He was speaking about the murder of Pat Finucane, a Catholic solicitor gunned down in 1989 by assassins who

---

253   The Foreign Office and the Ministry of Defence complained of thirty-nine serious inaccuracies. After a three-month investigation, Windlesham found only three minor flaws.

254   *The Economist*. 15 December 2012.

resented his effectiveness in representing republicans. The gunmen were members of the loyalist UDA.

The report by Sir Desmond de Silva, lays out in meticulous detail how senior army and police intelligence officers colluded in the killings of Finucane and other republican sympathisers. This included helping to identify, target and murder the lawyer, supplying a weapon, facilitating its later disappearance and deliberately obstructing subsequent investigations. On three occasions Finucane was known to be on UDA death lists. But the police, with the approval of the Army and MI5, Britain's domestic intelligence service, gave him no warning. The very idea of killing him was probably suggested to a UDA member by a police officer, Sir Desmond concluded. There was a flow of security-force information to the UDA: perhaps eighty per cent of its intelligence came from official sources.

Sir Menzies Campbell MP, speaking after the statement, told fellow MPs that, 'In the more than twenty-five years for which I have been a Member of this House, I cannot remember a statement from the Dispatch Box that has filled me with more revulsion and horror.'

Sir Desmond concluded that both the Army and the RUC actively obstructed the first major investigation of the episode by Lord Stevens, the former Metropolitan Police Commissioner. One of his most damning findings is that the 'system appears to have facilitated political deniability in relation to such operations.' If so, the question of who knew what and when about this murder remains unanswered, concluded *The Economist*.

Yet at this time, when rumours were already freely circulating that the UDA was being directed by British security personnel, there were calls in leading newspapers from the late Eighties for a harder line in Northern Ireland, but confined to republicans. The calls ranged from 'time for an iron hand', by T.E. Utley;[255] for the reintroduction of internment, by Lord Chalfont, then deputy chairman of the

---

255   *The Times*. 16 November 1987.

Independent Broadcasting Authority;[256] and 'Time to get tough in Ulster', by Conor Cruise O'Brien.[257] There were calls in editorials in *The Sunday Times* for the full integration of Ulster's six counties with the UK, though two of them have a majority of Catholics. There was even a renewed call from within the ranks of the Conservative party by Tim Smith MP for the Irish in Britain to be disenfranchised.

Bishop Cahal Dal had learned by now that it was not possible to appease such a mood. His diocese included Belfast and he had often issued statements denouncing the IRA. They made headline news. But they went down badly in Catholic communities, as certain newspapers still continued to call for 'positive action' against the IRA by the Church. And such denunciations in any event were only infrequently matched by Protestant Church leaders in respect of loyalist killings of Catholic civilians. Inevitably, Bishop Daly came in for criticism from some of his own priests, who accused him of calling 'on Catholics to be reconciled to injustice'. Ten years later, by which time he had become Cardinal Cahal Daly, Primate of All Ireland, he was calling on Britain's churches to dispel the 'simplistic assumptions and inherited prejudices about Ireland' that are common in the media. He urged them to promote a greater acceptance among the British public that the complex problems of Northern Ireland are, in part, a residual consequence of Britain's colonial history.[258] He said people should not accept 'hand-washing dismissals of the problems as though it were due to Irish perversities.'

'In particular,' the Cardinal said, 'the churches should protest against the anti-Irish reporting and feature-writing in some of the mass circulation British newspapers.'

---

256   *The Daily Telegraph*. Early August, 1990.

257   *The Times*. 15 April 1992.

258   *The Catholic Times*. 6 December 1998.

The Economist, The Independent, The Guardian, The Irish Times, The Irish Post and *The Star* in Sheffield were honourable exceptions in my own personal coverage. As were many journalists, whose professional skills I envied. Such Ulster Protestant journalists as Barry White, of *The Belfast Telegraph*, Susan McKay, Joan Lingard and David McKittrick were valued sources of insightful commentary on the northern Protestants. I admired them for their courage and objectivity, along with Douglas Gageby, editor of *The Irish Times*, and Brendan MacLua, co-founder of *The Irish Post*. They were invaluable in exploring questionable covert operations by the RUC and the Army. I would recommend all of them as appropriate authorities to those Labour colleagues at Westminster who raised with me editorials and feature articles by such as T.E. Utley and Conor Cruise O'Brien in *The Times* and *The Daily Telegraph*.

Mrs Nuala O'Loan, a prominent Catholic lay-person and married to a SDLP member, was appointed Police Ombudsman for the north of Ireland. In January 2007, she exposed how the RUC and the UVF in one area of Belfast alone colluded in up to fifteen deaths right up to 2003. Her report found that the RUC Special Branch had effectively become a force operating within a force. Furthermore, she believed that her enquiries were obstructed by serving and retired police officers, and slowed by inadequate funding. It is very difficult not to see such collusion in north Belfast alone as part of an often-alleged pattern. It was strongly suggestive therefore of a collusion elsewhere that never escaped the attention of some journalists. They never lost sight of their duty and that of their newspapers to preserve liberties. Why were certain Right-of-centre and tabloid newspapers shy of that traditional responsibility? In their persistent demonising of the Irish instead, they were failing to offer the public an overall and objective picture in the Seventies and Eighties of what was really going on in Northern Ireland. It is very difficult not to see such partiality as unhelpful to the ongoing peace settlement.

Chapter Fifteen

The Hunger Strikes

Of the many events in the Seventies and Eighties that affected the Irish in Britain, one event stood out – the hunger strikes in Northern Ireland. They became news all round the world. They sharpened old antagonisms in the south as well as in the north of Ireland. But they were also a watershed moment in the strife in Northern Ireland and marked the start of Sinn Féin's political involvement and electoral success. Republicans now had a non-violent avenue, and the British could no longer pretend that the North was simply a security situation that only needed enough police and soldiers on the streets. The hunger strikes led also to the Anglo-Irish Agreement in 1985, which conferred on the Irish Government for the first time a say in the affairs of Northern Ireland. That enabled an improved dialogue between Dublin and London, which led to an emerging peace process.

Because of the anomalies affecting 'criminalisation' policy, many republican prisoners being held at Long Kesh had political status. They had been sentenced before March 1976. But some who were sentenced afterwards claimed the same status. The hunger strikers in 1981 were essentially seeking clarification and confirmation of the status of those earlier republican prisoners. Their leader and the most advanced in his fasting was Bobby Sands. One of thousands forced from their homes years before, and with a working-class background, he had not had much of a life. He was arrested at eighteen years for carrying an unloaded pistol and spent his next nine years in jail. Charismatic, poetic and talented as a writer, he did not regard himself as a common criminal, nor was regarded as such by those who knew him. Yet he was accused of being in prison for 'proved serious criminal offences'.[259] It seemed inconceivable to many that the Prime Minister would allow Bobby Sands to do himself to death, while some of his colleagues were walking around in the same prison enjoying the very privileges and rights for which he may yet die. Especially, as the narrowness that separated the government's position and that of the prisoners was mainly on the clothing question. In fact all that was required to resolve the crisis was a small relaxation of the prison regime, for which there were ample precedents elsewhere.

Women prisoners in British and in Northern Ireland jails were allowed to wear their own clothes. A similar confrontation in Portlaoise Prison in the Republic was defused by the prisoners being allowed to wear their own clothes and to associate freely, though not formally being given any particular status. Clearly it was not beyond the power of a government that genuinely wished to ease tension to bridge the very narrow gap that separated both sides. But Margaret Thatcher kept going on about 'political status' though it had not been specifically set out in the demands of the hunger strikers since the previous December.[260]

Bobby Sands MP died on 5 May 1981. On my way into the chamber of the House of Commons that afternoon for prime minister's questions, I looked for Kevin McNamara and said to him, 'They are not going to get away with this.' We agreed that each of us would do our utmost to catch the eye of the Speaker so that we could be called upon to speak and protest. We knew that it would not be easy, given the mood and apparent blood lust among some on the Conservative benches that afternoon. They were not prepared to respect at all the death of a fellow MP. Neither were they helped to do so by the Speaker when he departed from his usual procedure in

---

259   *The Times*. 6 May 1981.

260   *The Irish Times* reported that Bobby Sands asked one of the three European MPs who visited him on 20 April to note that he had not once used the term 'political status'.

announcing the death of a Member. In the most formal and briefest of statements, he said, 'I regret to have to inform the House of the death of Robert Sands Esquire, the member for Fermanagh and South Tyrone.' The normal formula was for the Speaker to express also on behalf of the House, the sense of loss sustained, and then express sympathy.

Mrs Thatcher's approach in Question Time to this hyper-charged issue was even less diplomatic. In a reference to the issue of political status in relation to Bobby Sands and others held in Ulster jails, she said that granting such status would be 'to give a licence to kill'. She came in for immediate support from one of her own members and two Ulster Unionist members. Michael Foot then rose as Leader of the Opposition and strongly supported Mrs Thatcher. He said that political status could not be given to a nationalist prisoner 'without the government itself giving aid to the recruitment of terrorists' in Ulster. He regretfully overlooked the 'aid to the recruitment of terrorists' that had stemmed from the Falls Road curfew, internment, Ballymurphy and Bloody Sunday long before the hunger strikes. Unsurprisingly, he was rewarded with thanks from Mrs Thatcher and a huge cheer from the Tories, but an ominous silence from his own side.[261] Then I was called upon to speak, determined to shatter the complacency of the House of Commons.

Denouncing 'too much me-tooism in this House', in as gentle a tilt at Michael Foot as I could manage, given my rising temper, I then moved to neutralise him. In the face of a rising barrage of Tory protests I reminded Mrs Thatcher of the views that day of the *New York Times*, until recently a staunch ally, which felt that Bobby Sands' death was

---

261   Michael Foot, Leader, had gone a long way since he described the Unionist party in the Commons as the 'Parliamentary B Specials', records Dr Kevin Mc-Namara. As a member of Callaghan's Cabinet, Foot had agreed to the Ulsterisation Policy of Merlyn Rees and the ending of special category status. He had also negotiated with Enoch Powell the unionist demand of extra seats in the Commons to prolong the life of the dying Labour administration.

due to her intransigence. I had to shout in order to make myself heard above the personal abuse that included, inevitably, the epithet 'pig' – according to tape recordings. I went on to say that by appearing hard and unfeeling she had spectacularly illuminated for growing bodies of opinion in neighbouring and allied countries, whose comments were flowing in by the hour, the government's moral bankruptcy and the colossal and criminal incompetence of Conservative governments at all times in their dealings with Ireland. After an angered response from Mrs Thatcher, the Speaker ended Question Time with an obvious haste.

Where were the humanitarianism and the compromise, I had already asked myself. Where were the well-known negotiators? Where was the honest brokering? Where was the formula of words? Governments undoubtedly have to win in any trial of wills and strengths. But the wise government does not seek, or move to confrontation, without leaving some small room for manoeuvre, not only for itself but for the other party. And in this situation, Mrs Thatcher should have been made well aware of the historic significance of the strike of Terence McSwiney, Lord Mayor of Cork in Brixton prison in 1920. He passed away after seventy-four days without food, leaving behind the words, 'It is not those who can inflict the most, but those that can suffer the most who will conquer.'

By April 1981, such awareness should have clearly sounded the need for some flexibility. And some recognition, moreover, of the 30,000 people who had elected Bobby Sands to Westminster, mostly in the hope of saving his life. Were they to be ignored? Instead, Mrs Thatcher was giving the impression of 'No Surrender': an attitude that lay behind much of the North's troubles, I reminded myself. A total lack of respect by the ascendancy of the minority they dominated seemingly still lingered in London. Where were those Labour MPs who were always sensitive to the victims of oppression in other countries, I also asked myself. But the Labour party was still sticking to its bipartisan approach. That gave Mrs Thatcher moral support, despite a growing condemnation of her stance outside parliament. Worse was the dispatch of Don Concannon, to tell Bobby Sands a week before his death, that Labour stood four-square behind Mrs Thatcher.[262]

I received personal compliments and congratulatory notes from many Labour MPs afterwards. The only one who sought me out for reproach for 'supporting terrorists', as he put it, was, of all people, Greville (now Lord) Janner, secretary of the Labour Friends of Israel, of which I was a longstanding member. He condemned the hunger-strikers as 'terrorists', overlooking the ruthless activities of the Irgun gang who hanged British soldiers in Palestine between 1946 and 1948.[263]

In an address to a Sinn Féin conference on 18 June 2011, Kevin McNamara pointed out that it is frequently forgotten that the policy that Mrs Thatcher was implementing, was introduced by Merlyn Rees, as Secretary of State, after the downfall of the power-sharing executive. The cancellation of special category status was a quid pro quo to the unionists for the phasing out of internment. It was upheld, furthermore, by shadow ministers such as Stan Orme and Don Concannon.

Mrs Thatcher had come to regard the issue of special category as one of principle, on which she was therefore not prepared to yield. But she was conveniently overlooking the 'special status' that had long been meted out to Catholics in Northern Ireland. Such as the exclusive attacks by the B-specials and the British Army in

---

262   Rejected in many quarters associated with Labour, and by the National Organisation of Labour Students.

263   Lord Jakobovits, then Chief Rabbi, was just as selective in his approach to human rights in 1988. When the Bishop of Manchester objected in the House of Lords to the broadcasting ban on Sinn Féin, he was opposed by the Chief Rabbi, who was clearly overlooking the much criticised treatment of the people of the West Bank and Gaza.

1969 on their homes in the Falls Road. The policy of internment in 1971 was particularly special, for it was almost confined to Catholics. Indeed, it conferred on them a form of political status, argued *The Observer* at the time.[264] Everything was special about the prisoners in Long Kesh, whether they were IRA or UDA. Bobby Sands got very special treatment from the moment of his arrest – which had always struck me as doubtful – until he entered Long Kesh. He was not tried under regular British Law, but under the Diplock rules. These almost presumed guilt. They denied Habeus Corpus. They denied jury trials. They permitted seven days of interrogation without a lawyer, and then allowed the confession that emerged. The European Commission on Human Rights had criticised the system. The conviction rate was very high, for 90% were based solely on confessions obtained under the interrogation system, with no other evidence required. The Northern Ireland statelet itself was special.

Mrs Thatcher failed to anticipate the wave of public sympathy unleashed by the death of Bobby Sands. I received hundreds of letters from all over the world. Sympathy was quietly evident among many European colleagues in NATO circles. There were protests, some violent, across America and Europe. The US Longshoremen's Union boycotted British ships. The Queen was heckled on a visit to Norway. The Soviet Union and Cuba denounced British oppression. Les Walesa of Poland paid tribute to Bobby Sands as 'a great man who sacrificed his life for his struggle'. Thousands marched through the streets of Paris in protest. Tory Euro MPs failed to block a debate on his death in the European parliament, where the Socialist group condemned Britain. While in India, Opposition MPs in the upper house stood for a minute in tribute. The hunger-strikers had focussed international attention on the administration of the Six Counties. And in Ireland more than 100,000 mourners turned out for Bobby Sands' funeral, which was attended by 300 photographers. Owen

---

264   *The Observer.* 3 May 1981.

Carron, Sands' election agent, retained the seat at a by-election on 20 August, with an increased majority.

The Sunday Times carried out a special survey of sixty-four newspapers in twenty-five countries to find out what the outside world thought about Britain's role.[265] The results were bad news for the British Government. The survey found that the hunger strikers' campaign had rekindled flagging interest in Northern Ireland and its problems. Editors around the world believed it was time for Mrs Thatcher to begin negotiations with the Irish Republic over the unification of Ireland. There was growing bewilderment in many countries that Britain was able to find an imaginative solution to the problems of Rhodesia, but had failed to achieve anything in Ulster – 'her own backyard'.

Ken Livingstone gave considerable moral support to the hunger strikers during his campaign for leadership of the GLC. He boycotted the wedding of Prince Charles and Diana, saying it was no time for the country to hold a 'bean feast' while men were dying in the H Blocks. In an *Irish Post* phone poll, Livingstone garnered an astonishing 95% of promised votes from its readers. He was elected a few days later, despite opposition from his own party, the Labour party.

The PLP was clearly upset by the hunger strikes and the bipartisan support of Mrs Thatcher by its shadow ministers. Martin Flannery and Kevin McNamara, senior officers of the Northern Ireland group, called an urgent meeting. During a lengthy meeting, with a record turn-out, Michael Foot encountered outspoken criticism. One MP present pointed out that no-one had spoken in support of existing Labour policy. Foot, taken aback by such hostility, then accepted the need for a new policy, and the party's executive study group on the matter was charged with drawing up an 'outline'. At the autumn conference Labour overwhelmingly became the first British party to adopt the policy of unity by consent.

---

265   *The Sunday Times.* 31 May 1981.

I was obliged to miss the meeting with Michael Foot because I had been summoned by my constituency party in Sheffield to explain my position. The meeting was called by a new secretary and former communist, Mick Elliot, who would soon oppose my readoption under new rules governing reselection. He reported that he was being stopped in the street by complaining constituents. Strangely, not one of them ever got in touch with me. I told the meeting that I had received only one complaint – from a trade union official, close friend and a Catholic. Typically, I also came in for criticism from the ever hostile *Morning Telegraph*.[266] I told the meeting that I had written to Michael Foot explaining my absence from his meeting, and reiterated the view that I still held strongly, 'that it was not beyond the power of a government that genuinely wished to ease tension, to bridge the gap, the narrow gap, that separated both sides in last week's crisis.' I called therefore 'for the government's handling of the issue to be probed critically and publicly, with the party taking up a more and more detached position on Northern Ireland.' That was agreed by the meeting.

Meanwhile, Margaret Thatcher, it was later revealed, had been secretly offering substantial concessions to end the hunger strike, according to documents obtained later by *The Sunday Times* under the Freedom of Information Act.[267] In July 1981, halfway through the hunger strike, she not only authorised secret communications with the IRA, but was also willing to agree to key demands that she had publicly rejected. Those talks faltered, but two of the hunger-strikers' five demands – for their own clothing and the right to more visits – were met within days of the strike's end.

The hunger strikes had left Mrs Thatcher with a major political crisis. Yet, within three or so years London and Dublin had moved sufficiently to be able to sign in 1985 the Anglo-Irish Agreement.

266   *Morning Telegraph*. 7 May 1981.

267   *The Sunday Times*. 5 April 2009.

For the first time, a British government recognised the right of the Irish government to have a say in the affairs of Northern Ireland. Without it there almost certainly would have been no Downing Street Declaration nor the ceasefire that led eventually to the Good Friday Agreement (GFA). How did this come about?

The death of Bobby Sands had led to widespread civil unrest in both parts of Ireland. The posters bearing protests or inscriptions on the roads of the counties with which I was most familiar, Mayo, Roscommon and Sligo, all focussed on the intransigence of Mrs Thatcher. The support shown at the polls for Bobby Sands and his successor, Owen Carron, and the election of H Block candidates in the Republic, demonstrated growing electoral support for the republican movement. Charles Haughey's government had fallen in Dublin and the new Taoiseach, Garret FitzGerald, was fearful that the IRA now posed a threat to national security. He was alarmed by the increasing electoral support for the IRA, resulting in it winning 10.1% of the vote for the new Assembly in Northern Ireland. He feared also the sidelining of the constitutional nationalist party, the SDLP. On the advice of John Hume, its leader, he decided to call a conference of all the constitutional parties on the island of Ireland. As a result, the New Ireland Forum was set up to examine ways by which the different communities could accommodate and be reconciled to one another. The unionist parties did not attend and Sinn Féin was not invited.

The Forum report recommended three possible constitutional arrangements for the future of the island: joint authority, a federal state and unitary state. At the Chequers summit with FitzGerald in November 1984, however – after the Brighton bombing of the Conservative party conference in October – Mrs Thatcher notoriously dismissed all three options: 'Out! Out! Out!' They had suggested a derogation from British sovereignty, and she was not going to have that. Despite this contemptuous rejection of the Forum's proposals, FitzGerald was determined to press on and he had support from within Mrs Thatcher's own administration. The Foreign Secretary,

Geoffrey Howe, and the Cabinet Secretary, Sir Robert (now Lord) Armstrong pressed for further discussion.[268] They realised that the IRA , as was said later on another occasion, 'had not gone away'. That had been the assessment in the MoD in the Seventies. It was regarded now as a continuing threat to stability in both parts of Ireland that could conceivably spread to Britain. The Northern Ireland civil service was deliberately excluded from the discussions that followed, presumably for fear of leaks. Discussion documents were headed 'For UK Eyes Only'. Likewise, the unionists were excluded, and had no knowledge of the detailed contents of what was agreed – the Anglo-Irish Agreement – until shortly before it was published.

For Mrs Thatcher, like Edward Heath before her, had had enough. As the 1981 State Papers published under the thirty-year rule reveal, her position had slowly changed as she realised the intransigence of the unionists. She was also subject to increasing pressure from President Reagan, Tip O Neill, Speaker of the House of Representatives, and the increasingly vocal Irish-American lobby. She must have been aware also of the feelings of many of her European allies. Furthermore, and at long last, two effective British ministers in Jim Prior (later Lord Prior) and Lord Gowrie had arrived in Ulster. According to Maurice Hayes, who was made chairman of the Community Relations Commission in Northern Ireland after Jim Callaghan's visit in 1969, and then went on to hold the highest office in its civil service, they 'did much to lance the boil of the hunger strikes'.[269]

When – 'after a decent interval' – most of the prisoners' demands were conceded without collapse of the prison system, wrote Hayes, 'it made me wonder why ten men had to die to achieve them.' At a meeting with the Taoiseach, Garret FitzGerald in November 1984, Mrs Thatcher agreed to set up a steering committee for Anglo-Irish

---

268   See his memoir *Conflict of Loyalty*. (Macmillain 1994)

269   *Minority verdict: experiences of a Catholic public servant.* (1995)

relations. It was jointly chaired by Sir Robert Armstrong and Dermot Nally, of comparable status in Dublin.[270]

A key advantage of this approach, Lord Armstrong has recalled, was that it removed the problem both from the Foreign Office and from the Northern Ireland Office. Lord Armstrong has also said that he found Nally to be 'one of the most admirable public servants' he had ever encountered. Thus was formed what was undoubtedly one of the most effective partnerships in the history of Anglo-Irish relations. It developed mutual trust to a remarkable degree. Mrs Thatcher became very much aware of Nally's role, and developed 'a high regard for him' based on the fact that he was 'reliable, trustworthy and had great integrity and skills.'

The deal was intended to set up a framework by which the Republic could collaborate in establishing peace and security. It accepted the principle of unity by consent, but it also recognised the legitimacy of Irish nationalism. This represented an enormous shift by London. It was a carefully constructed deal, with fewer of the pitfalls which had made power-sharing so fragile after Sunningdale in 1974. This intergovernmental arrangement set out to be deliberate and not executive. It did not need Ulster men to make it work, only British and Irish ministers and officials. It meant that as long as Margaret Thatcher was prepared to face down the unionist politicians, the mob and the paramilitaries – and she was – it would not suffer the fate of Sunningdale.

---

270   It established a ministerial council, which would meet regularly, and a standing secretariat of civil servants in both jurisdictions. The Irish government would be consulted on all legislation, and could propose candidates for public appointments affecting the interests of nationalists in the North. It could raise any political social and economic issue affecting Northern nationalists, including policing, security and discrimination. The agreement was registered as an international treaty at the UN. There was no derogation of British sovereignty in the North, but British government had conceded what might be termed the equivalent of joint sovereignty.

The leaders of Ulster's Protestant community reacted in traditional style to this latest attempt to bring peace to the province. They whipped their followers into self-righteous indignation, despite every possible reassurance. They called the deal treachery. They could speak of it only in terms of despair, which contrasted with the constructive reaction of John Hume, who had close ties with Dublin. The speech in the House of Commons by Harold McCusker (Upper Bann) in the debate on the Agreement is a case in point.[271] During that debate Roy Mason and I sat alongside each other, with Michael Foot immediately behind. Jim Callaghan sat across the aisle from us with Harold McCusker behind him. Roy Mason saw the Agreement in his speech as a progressive and historic step. But in the manner in which he then dwelt on 'the wrath of the unionists, and the difficulties ahead relating to security and the rising political success of provisional Sinn Féin', it was a speech that could more appropriately have come from McCusker. Whereas McCusker made a long rambling and bitter speech, in which he complained of lack of consultation. He expressed distrust of the people of the South, and their institutions, as well as a lack of respect for those of his fellow citizens in the north who identified with them. They would now have the power to interfere in every aspect of life in Northern Ireland, he charged. Loyalism to him still implied the right to Britain's loyalty, with no corresponding obligation of tolerance and mutual respect in return for the majority of the people on the island of Ireland or, indeed, respect for his own Parliament and its laws at Westminster.

Throughout his speech I could distinctly hear Michael Foot sympathising sotto voce. Nor was there any inclination on the part of my other neighbours and friends, Jim Callaghan and Roy Mason, to intervene constructively and ask McCusker to explain his despair now of a former ally, Margaret Thatcher. Why her dramatic change of policy? After all, she is described by her biographer as 'the most Orange

---

271   *Hansard.* 27 November 1985, cols 914–920.

leader ever to occupy Downing Street'. Nor was there any attempt by any one of them to enquire of McCusker why – quoting from the current issue of *The Economist* – 'Protestant Ulster has refused to share power with the Catholic minority: refused not just at the ballot box but by gerrymandering, corruption, violence, terrorism and (most notably in 1974) industrial mayhem.'[272] Nor was there any mention by Roy Mason in his reference to the 'difficulties that lay ahead' of the other 'difficulties' long suffered by a considerable Catholic minority and which I had often brought to his attention.

Some arose from my own wartime background in the province, which he always rejected. But some of them had come up in my own classified briefings whilst a defence minister with a degree of responsibility in Northern Ireland. Some, significantly, arose in briefings in Army outposts. Even they roused him to little concern. Yet more acknowledgement earlier of the complaints he had received officially from Catholics would have illuminated the need for the further channel of communication now made available in the 1985 Agreement, whatever his reservations. Those complaints had been widely publicised. They constituted a growing list. They now included the shoot-to-kill policy, the beatings, the threats and various forms of ill-treatment said to be taking place in the Castlereagh Holding Centre, of which Gerry Adams subsequently gave a horrifying description when detailing his own torture at the hands of the RUC and Army.[273] They are tellingly similar to some of the stories that have since come out of Guantanamo Bay. Roy Mason was well aware, as I was, given their openly-expressed feelings to both of us, of the growing concern of parliamentary colleagues about the lies told to order in Ulster courts, notably in the notorious Constable Robinson case, the lack of juries, the strip searches of women prisoners and the lack of trust in the RUC. The growing resentment over Mason's

272   *The Economist*. 23 November 1985.

273   *The Irish Post*. 19 June 2004.

attitude was inevitably transferred to myself. Why did Catholics have to bear, I was often asked, by some fellow MPs, those Orange marches in predominantly Catholic neighbourhoods whilst Republican marches were restricted, and the display of the tri-colour banned, though the Union Jack was waved regardless.

The reneging by State-owned Short Brothers in Belfast of its Catholic jobs pledge was the final straw for some Labour MPs. Mason shared eventually my concern in respect of some of those issues. But not all of them. In any event, he insisted, they could only be addressed once he had smashed the IRA. He paid for that in the Shadow-cabinet poll following the fall of the Callaghan government in 1979, when I was his campaign manager. It was hard work mustering support for him. He came last among all those elected, which was quite undeserved.

Some authorities thought Mason should have topped the poll for the shadow cabinet. He would have certainly fared altogether better than Michael Foot in the 1984 general election. He would have projected quite a different image at the Cenotaph on Remembrance Sunday. I easily envisaged him as a popular 'Labour Stanley Baldwin', constantly photographed pipe in hand against the background of one of the surviving colliery head-gears in his Barnsley constituency. Yet he did not speak to me for two years following my parliamentary intervention on the day Bobby Sands died. Our old friendship was never properly restored, for the PLP under the leadership of Neil Kinnock soon moved away from his policies on Northern Ireland and voted overwhelmingly in support of the Anglo-Irish Agreement. It was passed with the biggest majority achieved for any measure during Mrs Thatcher's long period in power. After talks with Dick Spring, deputy Taoiseach, who flew over especially from Dublin, Neil Kinnock briefed Kevin McNamara and initiated significant steps towards a change of Labour policy on Northern Ireland.[274] They were contained in 'Towards a United Ireland', which was published by the Front Bench. It was mainly Kevin's work after he was appointed Shadow Secretary of State.

Ted Heath had deprived the unionists of Stormont. Margaret Thatcher was now allowing the Irish government to share a secretariat at Maryfield, halfway between Belfast and Bangor, and apparently share in the government of Northern Ireland. And they themselves had not even been consulted. The unionists were not going to accept it, they declared. The government would not be allowed to get away with this insult to Ulster. The power-sharing executive had been brought down earlier by political pressure and by mobs on the street. Subject to the same treatment the unionists expected the new agreement to go the same way. Maryfield was exposed to unionist picketing, and became reliant on the helicopter for the daily supply of milk and newspapers. It was besieged by mobs from all shades of unionism, including loyalist paramilitaries. To demonstrate their control of the community, all the unionist MPs with the exception of Enoch Powell resigned their seats to fight a mini-general election. It was a pyrrhic victory. They lost a seat as Seamus Mallon of the SDLP won the South Armagh and Newry seat. Margaret Thatcher was not Merlyn Rees, however, and would not bow to their pressure. The great gesture had failed. The crowds outside Maryfield dwindled away. It was a turning point for unionism. The unionist absolute veto was gone, and with it the status quo.

---

274 When Neil Kinnock became party leader he was far more sympathetic to the aspirations of constitutional nationalism. He welcomed the report of the New Ireland Forum because it had accepted the principle of unity by consent. This change of policy was underlined in the publication of the front page document *Towards a United Ireland* to which Kinnock contributed a powerful introduction. Seeking to achieve 'Unity by Consent' ceased to be a mere slogan, and exploring how to achieve it had become a positive policy goal.

The Anglo-Irish Agreement changed utterly the relationship between unionists and loyalists and the rest of Britain. First, it forced the British government to confront nationalist concerns in a way not seen before. Because, second, it provided formal acknowledgement of a role in northern affairs for Dublin through a secretariat permanently based in Belfast and the intergovernmental conference it served. Third, it set up a framework that addressed the problem of interlocking relationships between Belfast, Dublin and London and offered a prospect of a progressive building of British-Irish 'real politick'. It may not have produced the early improvement in security expected by some. Neither did it serve to divert support from Sinn Féin to the SDLP. But it represented the most significant step since Sunningdale, and some saw it as the most important move since partition in 1922.

The unionists were in a difficult position. The old certainties were gone. To try and clarify their new position, Jim Molyneux MP and Ian Paisley MP appointed a small committee comprising Frank Miller, secretary of the Unionist Party, Harold McCusker MP, and Peter Robinson MP, respectively deputy leaders of the Official Unionists and the DUP, to examine the state of unionism within the Six Counties and to make recommendations of how they would be rid of Dublin's interference and the Hillsborough agreement. The report was never published. Presumably because they concluded that to get rid of Maryfield they would have to come to the table and negotiate.

The unionists never forgave Thatcher for their humiliation. At her last Question Time in the House of Commons, Martin Smyth MP, former Grandmaster of the Orange Order, in expressing sympathy also reminded her, 'For we too know what it is to be betrayed.'

For all the objections of unionists, Tom King, Secretary of State for Northern Ireland, (who had to face violent street protests and the refusal of unionist leaders to talk to him) commended it to the House of Commons in a review statement in 1989. Thus reaffirming the full commitment of both governments 'to all the provisions of the agreement and to its shared understanding and purposes.' This was warmly welcomed by Kevin McNamara, Opposition spokesman, who commented that its greatest achievement 'has been its survival.' It eventually caused unionists and republicans to assess their positions and accept much of what they had so vehemently rejected in 1985. By the Nineties it had become very much prized in Dublin, though still resented by unionists. It was seen by Dick Spring, then Irish Foreign Minister, as perhaps the true beginning of the 'equality of esteem' that came to pervade Anglo- Irish relations.

Chapter Sixteen

Changing Perceptions of the Irish

An important section of the British media had persisted in casting the Irish people in a bad light in the Seventies. However, the many complaints I received both in Parliament and in my constituency about the peddling of so-called Irish 'jokes' and racist slurs were offset by important developments. The *Irish Post* and its distinguished editor, Brendan McLua, with his fearless news presentation, had become a source of strength. The Federation of Irish Societies (FIS) began to function as a nationwide organisation. The hurt felt by many Irish in Britain actually forged a common loyalty and created a sense of community that, for some, was consolidated by the hunger strikes, and legitimised by the Anglo-Irish Agreement.

The Irish people in Britain were comforted also by the success of personalities who remained unashamedly Irish, like Eamon Andrews and Terry Wogan. They were helped personally by the community building of brave and resourceful Irishmen at grass-roots level. Canon Gerald Rodgers in Bristol, Father Joe Taffe in Birmingham and Pat McCabe in Leeds are outstanding examples, though far from alone in their local initiatives. Canon Rodgers helped launch the Catholic Housing Aid Society in the post-war years – still going as an interdenominational housing advisory service – which led to the formation of the Bristol Family Housing Association. Despite severe tensions in Birmingham in the Seventies, Father Joe Taffe emerged as a legendary figure in service to Irish people in difficulties, to the Birmingham Irish Centre and to the wider community. Pat McCabe was similarly unsparing in his personal support of the Irish in Yorkshire through his promotion of the Gaelic Athletic Association, his executive work on behalf of Irish Ferries and as a trustee of the Leeds Irish Centre.

Many Irish clubs emerged elsewhere. Irish bank branches appeared on high streets throughout Britain. The Irish in Britain were showing a remarkable resilience in surviving the many dramas affecting them. Such welcome developments were accompanied by the emergence in Britain of a new breed of Irish emigrant, who were a far cry from the wandering dispossessed Irish of old. In a fitting memorial, Ultan Crowley describes the pioneers who constructed Britain's canals, railways, roads and reservoirs. His account destroys long-standing anti-Irish stereotypes. It is also a reminder of how much Britain owes to those early Irish workers, whose sweat and toil made possible its modern infrastructure and still dominate its renewal. Britain has always had a plentiful supply of shopkeepers and market stallholders, as Napoleon observed. But one has only to look around to be further reminded of the continuing need for irreplaceable Irish workers. Current projects such as the Channel Tunnel, the Victoria Line, the Thames Barrier and the British Library represent only a small sample of that 'special relationship'. Those projects reflect also the changing skills as well as the hard work of the Irish workers. According to Sir William McAlpine, writes Ultan Crowley, their contribution has been immeasurable. He recalls other memorable tributes.[275] Father Owen Sweeney, chaplain, Llanwern Steelworks, 1959–1962, testified to the inestimable value of their contribution to human wellbeing: 'I came to regard them as the true nobility of society, humble, hard-working men who rarely complained about their lot.' John Cox, former chairman, Tarmac Construction, testified: 'I have worked all my life with Irishmen, several of whom, had they completed their education, could have been behind the Chairman's desk instead of me.'[276]

---

275   *The men who built Britain: A History of the Irish Navvy.* Ultan Crowley. (Merlin Publishing 2001).

276   Ultan Crowley quotes McAlpine's death-bed wish: 'If the men wish to honour my death, allow them two minutes silence, but keep the big mixer going, and keep Paddy behind it.'

If the Irish have traditionally provided the labour for big building contractors in Britain, they have become big building contractors themselves since WWII. Clancy, Kennedy, McNicolas, Murphy and many others are now household names. They made vital contributions to post-war reconstruction. They were to the forefront in the introduction or development of services and utilities such as water, sewage, gas, electricity and telecoms. It would be hard to point to any important structure or utility with which Kerry man John Murphy and Mayo men John and Joseph Kennedy, among many others, were not associated. These men also distinguished themselves socially and academically, and achieved eminence as public benefactors. From modest beginnings, their individual business careers illustrate remarkable entrepreneurial leadership and great determination. Each fashioned multi-disciplined design and build services across a range of sectors that developed into a wide range of civil engineering and infrastructural projects. John Murphy was recognised academically for his unique contribution to Britain's business life and received a Kerry person of the Year award. Likewise, John and Joseph Kennedy continue to foster university development and have received individually the Mayo person of the Year award as well as the rare distinctions of papal Knights of St. Gregory. Together with John Murphy, who passed away in 2009, they were each an uplifting and invigorating presence to their workers, to their customers and suppliers. Incomparable benefactors on both sides of the Irish Sea, they have deservedly received many awards and accolades. None more so, in my personal acquaintance, than much admired John Kennedy, CBE, KSG and one of Her Majesty's deputy Lord-lieutenants in Greater Manchester.

Other Irish men and women have become prominent in the professions. They are to be found in Parliament, the armed forces command structure, the judiciary, the police, the universities and the trade unions. They have grown in number as doctors and nurses, Lord mayors and councillors. They are now appearing in the boardrooms of British companies and head some of them. They are more numerous as company directors than any other nationality after the British. All testifying to the strength of Ireland's education system. All contributing to the changing image of the Irish in Britain. Memories of those Saturday-night dances for Irish workers in Catholic parish halls in the Thirties have been replaced by the image of *Riverdance* – the biggest touring show in the world. I was increasingly reminded during my assigned visits around the Western Alliance of that particular triumph. I noted how much the Irish were valued overseas, notably in Germany, for their skills and strong work ethic. They were appreciated also for their warmth and hospitality. I came across 'Irish pubs' everywhere, and spotted one newly opened in Moscow immediately after the fall of the Berlin wall. A far cry from the experience of a cousin in the Queen's Head in Heddon outside Hull in 1946: 'We don't serve Irish here.'

Ireland had always been outward-looking culturally as well as politically and socially. Irish missionaries had spread the gospel and education around the world. They made communities in some of the poorest countries. They widened their vocations as priests and nuns to become aid workers and human rights' defenders. They greatly enhanced Ireland's international reputation, as borne out at the United Nations (UN). Thanks to the energy and fluent French of Foreign Minister Garrett FitzGerald, Ireland soon distinguished itself within the European Community. He ensured that the first Irish Presidency in 1975 was very successful: quite singular, indeed, among the smaller member-nations. Thus the Irish in Britain survived the anti-Irishness of the 1970s and the 1980s.

The emergence in Ireland of a vibrant economy and domestic transformation characterised the 1990s. The EU's structural funds after the Maastricht Treaty of 1992 were helpful. But the EU subsidies made only a modest contribution to economic growth as Ireland proceeded to win big Foreign Direct Investment projects in such businesses as software, semiconductors, personal computers, pharmaceutical and medical devices. The IDA was now competing globally in landing such valuable projects. In 1997 Ireland featured on *The Economist's* cover as 'Europe's Shining Light'. Irishness had become a remarkable commodity. It had become fashionable to be Irish otherwise as well.

The Irish were also seen as the guardians of the 'craic' – the quintessential, spontaneous music and good time popularly identified by many with the 'Irish pub'. The Atticus column in *The Sunday Times* in early February 1993 was most complimentary about the previous week's luncheon at London's Guildhall in honour of the Lord Mayor of Dublin. 'It was a splendid occasion that did a power of good for Anglo-Irish relations', the column said. It was the first time in history that the city of London hosted Dublin's Lord Mayor. Atticus also speculated that it was the first time that the Irish national anthem was played at an official British function. The Lord Mayor of London paid a warm tribute to the contribution of the Irish community in Britain.

The city of London occasion was a significant reminder that Northern Ireland was now drifting away from British consciousness. Instead there was a growing realisation that it was the Republic that counted because of its membership of the EU and its status at the UN. For centuries, reflected Brendan MacLua – who was present in the Guildhall – Dublin was subservient to London. In international terms it had now become a capital of equal rank. That was emphasised at the Guildhall luncheon, he believed, by the attendance of quite a number of ambassadors as well as high commissioners.

A few weeks previously, Robert McCrum mused in an article in *The Guardian*: 'What is this extraordinary hold that Ireland and its people continue to exercise over our collective imaginations? Partly it's because the Irish seem to the grim, colonising English altogether wittier, more charming and yes, more likeable. We are the oppressor, yet we envy the oppressed. They have been invaded, yet they remain, maddeningly free. Internationally, the Irish have acquired the popularity of the under-dog ...'

Simultaneously, published reports exploded two of Britain's most pernicious national myths – the stupid Irishman and the drunken Irishman. The first report, published by one of Britain's largest trade unions, the GMB, found Irish emigrants had a better academic record than the British average. The second report, written by Professor Roy Carr Hill and Larry Harrison of Hull University and jointly backed by the FIS and the British government agency Alcohol Concern, concluded that Irish people are no more likely to abuse alcohol than their British neighbours. Indeed a further survey revealed a special relationship between the Irish and the British. The Irish born in Britain are held in high regard by their hosts. They are not considered foreigners and the English prefer them to the Welsh. The Welsh and the Scots, on the other hand, prefer the Irish to the English. These were some of the fascinating findings in the first-ever nationwide survey of British attitudes to the Irish and to Ireland. The survey was commissioned by the University of Bradford in 1994.[277]

The British in great majority said they had more affinity with the Irish than they had with Americans or Europeans and that, price and quality being equal, they would buy Irish agricultural produce ahead of Danish or French. Four-fifths of Britons associate the Irish with folk music and singing as against 37% who associated them with literary activity. Throughout the findings there emerged a much greater affection for the Irish than could previously have been imagined. Asked about the long term future of Northern Ireland, 38% favoured a reunited Ireland, 25% said that Northern Ireland should remain part of the UK, while 20% opted for an independent Northern Ireland. The rest did not know.

In essence, that important survey confirmed a rather special relationship between the Irish and the British. Despite all the historical and contemporary problems, the British held positive images of the Irish. They overwhelmingly rejected the idea that the Irish who come to Britain are foreigners and, whether by intermarriage or descent, the

---

277   It was carried out by the IMC Research on 24 and 25 June 1994, in 103 randomly selected constituencies where 1,396 adults were interviewed face-to-face. The Irish-born were excluded so as to concentrate on British public opinion.

survey found that a surprising number of Britons have Irish relatives. Such changes in popular perception, accompanied by other cultural as well as economic changes, were altering the perception each of the other and affecting British-Irish relations. They would gradually evolve to a more mature, more balanced and equal relationship between the two countries.

Chapter Seventeen

The Peace Process

Such progressive developments enabled the British and Irish governments to remain steadfast in support of the Anglo-Irish Agreement and in their belief that the governing of Northern Ireland now required an Irish dimension – a role for Dublin. Protestant unionist leaders remained implacably opposed, but Tom King sturdily defended it as Secretary of State. He was succeeded by Peter Brooke in 1989. Peter Brooke bravely attempted to transcend the 1985 Hillsborough agreement by offering the vision of a political settlement based on the entire range of relationships between Britain and Ireland and within Ireland. Despite misgivings, the Ulster Unionist party (UUP), the traditional unionists, agreed in mid-1991 to talks with the nationalist SDLP. The DUP had announced, however, that they would never share a conference table with Sinn Féin. It was planned that a 'second strand' of talks with the Irish Government would follow. The prospect of further change to the status quo was poor, however. It had taken so long to devise the formula that would simply enable the parties to talk. Monsignor Denis Faul, who had worked tirelessly for peace – despite his harsh treatment by sections of the British media – cautioned in January 1988, 'There is a law of history in Northern Ireland which says that wherever the Catholics show any sign of advancing in legal, political or civil rights, they are assassinated and burned out – 1921, 1969, 1972, 1974, 1981 … and that these attacks are assented to at a high level is a common belief. All to preserve the status quo.' There were still huge obstacles to overcome. So it was no surprise when the brave efforts of Brooke went the way of previous British initiatives. Nevertheless, he had accomplished much. He had affected somewhat the intransigence of the leaders of the traditional Unionists.

Realistically, they had no option now but to start talking, for that was what public opinion was demanding of them at home. Popular radio programmes were inundated with calls from people protesting their unionist loyalties, but complaining about the attitude of their leaders. A joint statement in the spring of 1991 by churchmen, businessmen and trade union leaders demanded that Unionist leaders avoid getting bogged down in needless detail. Effective leadership at such an opportune time could have carved out such a good deal for them, for London and Dublin would have still felt beholden. Whereas the London and Dublin governments were about to move once again to the point, as in 1985, of working together without them.

'Peter Brooke may be exasperated,' wrote Walter Ellis at the time, but 'he can hardly be shocked … Dealing with Ulster Unionists in particular is always a thankless task. They talk repeatedly of their willingness to make concessions, but never actually make one.'[278] Marvelling at what was unfolding currently in South Africa, Labour colleagues commented also on the poverty of leadership in the ranks of unionism. They had always been well disposed to John Hume and were now stirred by the arrival at Westminster of his SDLP colleagues, Seamus Mallon, Eddie McGready and Jo Hendron. They found Unionist MPs mediocre for the most part, with the exception of James Molineux. There appeared to be little affection for them either among members of the other parties. By contrast, the SDLP was sending to London from the Eighties onward MPs who struck me as brighter, better educated, more sophisticated politically and more appealing than the Unionist MPs.

I continued to brief members of the Manifesto group of moderate Labour MPs on John Hume's vital role, whilst Kevin McNamara was similarly active in the Tribune group. We stressed the importance of his continuing attempts to convince Gerry Adams of the need to halt violence and enter mainstream constitutional politics. We

---

278 *London Evening Standard.* 16 May 1991.

had supported that campaign from its outset. Kevin and I also kept members of the Northern Ireland group abreast of John Hume's objective of mobilising the broader nationalist family in the US as well as in Ireland and the UK. We issued reminders of its potential, whenever appropriate. We challenged London and Dublin to make more imaginative use of the Anglo-Irish Agreement, despite the poor response it received in certain quarters. We were immensely helped by such colleagues as Alf Dubs, Martin Flannery and Clive Soley. Together with Kevin they were prominent in changing Labour's policy to act henceforth as 'persuaders'. The arrival of Neil Kinnock as Leader, and his appointment in 1986 of Kevin McNamara as shadow spokesman on Northern Ireland, constituted a significant breakthrough.

None of us were prepared for the emergence on the Northern Ireland scene, however, of Taoiseach Albert Reynolds. Although I had long been aware of his county Roscommon background and early business success through the pages of the weekly *Western People*, published in County Mayo. Instead of seeking peace through structural change like all previous initiatives and proposals, he reversed the process and sought peace first and foremost in the belief that the political solution would follow. Astonishingly, he had to defend such an appealing notion against doubters and even hostile elements in Dublin as well as in Belfast. Although Charles Haughey did brief him on the Northern issue.[279] Like John Hume to some extent before him, Albert Reynolds was now thought to be keeping doubtful company. The IRA had been officially an enemy in Dublin since 1922. Presumably, therefore, John Bruton of Fine Gael, Labour's Dick Spring, Mary Harney of the Progressive Democrats and, even SDLP Seamus Mallon, were insisting on conditions such as a permanent ceasefire and decommissioning that were leaving Albert Reynolds almost isolated. The international reaction I encountered during my

---

279   This was the only issue on which Haughey did brief him, according to John Hume.

contemporary NATO assignments was surprise at the insistence on such stringencies in a simple bid for peace. I was reminded in more than one quarter of the contrasting flexibility of President Reagan and Mr Gorbachev in Reykjavik in 1986 – where the stakes were higher – that characterised their historic agreement. Yet the ceasefire, which was Albert Reynolds' mission, proved to be the right approach. It eventually gave peace a chance, if a short-lived one, for it was universally welcomed and ultimately helpful for all its brevity.

That was not the only major positive achievement of Albert Reynolds. He cajoled Prime Minister John Major into the Downing Street Declaration, later clarified it through the Framework Document and thus laid the foundations of the Good Friday Agreement. He entered, moreover, into a personal relationship of mutual trust with Major that was advantageous to both. He built relationships of trust also with the Church of Ireland primate, Archbishop Robert Eames, and with the Rev Roy Magee, who faithfully reported loyalist opinion. This enabled Major to keep the unionists in the peace process. Whilst it was plainly up to Reynolds to do the same with the nationalists and thus facilitate the IRA ceasefire. Reynolds delivered, but Major could not do so. Major was unable, therefore, to take full advantage of the seventeen months' ceasefire that started in the autumn of 1994. The time-wasting and delaying of all-party talks also robbed the peace movement of momentum. With the Euro-sceptics in his parliamentary party threatening his small parliamentary majority, Major was in a difficult position. He needed the nine UUP votes to cover his back. By this time, however, he only needed them politically. For there remained no longer any strategic or financial reasons for a continued UK presence in Northern Ireland, as he publicly acknowledged. Furthermore, its problems had become embarrassing internationally, as I had been long aware through my work in NATO. It really was time for Major to lay such realities on the line to the unionists, and otherwise stiffen the general policy of persuasion. If only he could do so. Nevertheless, Reynolds was convinced of his sincerity. He knew he was not prejudiced – he had an Irish grandmother – and was similarly bent on a just solution so far as parliamentary alignments allowed. But Major had to keep looking to the UUP for survival in Parliament, which explains his treatment of the ceasefire. His objection to the granting of a US visa to Gerry Adams resulted in the unfortunate 'Washington 3' condition that there could be no negotiation without decommissioning.[280] After brushing aside the Mitchell Commission Report and yielding to further UUP election threats, he was clearly putting the ceasefire at risk. Kevin McNamara was alone in protesting in Parliament, and was shamefully heckled by some New Labour colleagues.

By this time the Ulster unionists were becoming isolated politically as the focus of interest changed. Orange displays were hardly noted in 1993 by either the *Guardian* or the *Daily Express*. The MoD was looking for a reduction of troops – then 19,000 – by half, on grounds of cost now rather than NATO assignment. Neither of the unionist parties could any longer count on the UDA and UVF, as some of their members formed their own party, the Progressive Unionists, with David Ervine as leader. David Ervine and Billy Hutchinson had now recognised that they had much in common with the republicans: the same mean streets, suffering, exploitation and for many on both sides, prolonged imprisonment. They were no longer at the beck and call of David Trimble when he became leader of the UUP, or Ian Paisley and the DUP.

Meanwhile, the republicans had taken the high road in entering negotiations of such historic scope, however brief the ceasefire allowed. For it had given them international status, notably in the US, where the Sinn Féin leaders were well received by President Clinton. It helped them rally Irish–Americans in support of President Clinton's bid for a second term. It strengthened a growing nationalist

---

280   This was to prove a major barrier to progress before Tony Blair let it drop – having supported it originally.

consensus in Ireland. Much else flowed from the ceasefire, despite the violations and eventual breakdown. It had made possible the loyalist ceasefire of October 1994, and enabled George Mitchell to act as mediator. It was hugely popular in Belfast, where President Clinton received the warmest welcome in late 1996. A peace process was now unfolding, no matter how long and tortuous. 'Patience is the key weapon in winning the Northern Ireland game,' wrote Brendan MacLua at the time.[281] London's talks with Sinn Féin, the London-Dublin Framework Document, Albert Reynolds' forum for Peace and Reconciliation and, finally, the expected arrival of the unionists, were bringing agreement in sight. But John Major continued to be hampered in the House of Commons. David Trimble became leader of the UUP in 1995, and significantly broadened his agenda.

Erasing the Anglo-Irish Agreement – an international treaty – Trimble declared in interviews, was a foremost objective of his party. Given the Downing Street Declaration, the Framework document and all else, Trimble was going backward, not forward. He was not without encouragement. *The Daily Telegraph* was still calling for its scrapping as late as July 1996. And that was at precisely the time that Trimble was being exposed at Drumcree, where he danced in the street hand in hand with Paisley. Incredibly, the *Sunday Telegraph* also said in a leader that Enoch Powell was right, and that Northern Ireland should be assimilated within the UK.[282] In doing so, it contrived somehow to invoke a 'Moral principle'. But it managed to overlook reporting the dilemma of the RUC at Drumcree: penning Catholics in their homes with force, though absent when Catholic homes elsewhere were torched after the families had fled, and leaving the RUC open to the taunt of acting yet again as the armed wing of the Orange Order. Whilst the 'most ominous thing of all about

---

281   Quoting Michael Jones of *The Sunday Times*, 'It is but the opening of a door into a room.' *Irish Post.* 30 April 1994.

282   *The Sunday Telegraph.* 14 July 1996.

Drumcree', according to a leader in *The Economist* at the time, 'is that it has confirmed the political bankruptcy of unionism.' Andrew Marr, editor of the *Independent*, also wrote of the unionists then that 'their lack of an alternative political strategy has made them the naysayers, the immovable object, in modern Europe.' In contrast, the SDLP and Sinn Féin had addressed the ceasefire and peace process positively and benefited immensely. Many people were now talking to Sinn Féin, and it featured increasingly on radio and television.

None of this would have been lost on John Major. Although many British commentators thought his quick reaction was prompted by the unfortunate bombing in London's dockyards in early February 1996. It was a force option with which Northern Ireland Loyalists were familiar, of course. They had threatened it themselves in defiance of the will of parliament and constitutional settlements. Mindful of the force option, the same commentators had been indicating the growing capabilities of the IRA since the early Nineties. They were astonished at how close the IRA's audacious mortar bomb attack on 10 Downing Street in February 1991 came to striking a Cabinet meeting. In an article in *The Times* in January 1992, Edward Gorman described the IRA as a 'highly disciplined and politically motivated guerrilla army'.[283] Neil Ascherson pursued the same theme the next day in *The Independent on Sunday*. Conor Cruise O'Brien was more fearful shortly afterwards.[284] John Taylor, the Ulster Unionist MP, went even further the following summer after the IRA succeeded in smuggling two large car-bombs into Army headquarters in Lisburn. That was echoed in a leader in *The Sunday Times*. Whilst Simon Jenkins later expressed concern in *The Times* in July 1993 that London had been reduced 'to such inanities as … 'ring of steel' road blocks,' and concluded, 'The IRA is one foe that Britain has yet to vanquish.'

---

283   *The Times*. 11 January 1992.

284   *The Times*. 15 April 1992.

David Trimble may have succeeded in persuading Labour's new Leader, Tony Blair, to drop Kevin McNamara as his shadow spokesman on Northern Ireland, but that was a last throw of the dice for old-style unionism. Further delay and prevarication was no longer possible. For London and Dublin, wielding their big sticks in the background, were now committed to impose what was contained in the Framework Document. For all its complexity, the peace process was the only viable road ahead. There remained only the inevitable exchanges between the concerned parties: the ambiguities challenged, the clarifications sought and the dwindling obfuscation of unionism. They would end in an unavoidable fudge that was The Good Friday Agreement.

But as well as the patience that Brendan MacLua often stressed was vital in the handling of the peace process, skilful brokering by the Irish and British governments was also required. The election of new governments with clear majorities in the mid-Nineties in Dublin and London was a big help. But given the continuing nervousness in Dublin, would the incoming Fianna Fail government be up to it? A personal discussion in the Leeds Irish Centre with Bertie Aherne prior to his election as Taoiseach about the stalled peace process left me in no doubt as to his strong sense of purpose. The only question that remained was whether the incoming Labour government was up to it. It had the necessary majority in Parliament. But given the Labour party's lamentable record on Ireland and suspect leadership currently, would it rise to the occasion? For Kevin McNamara was not alone in the neglect by the new Prime Minister, Tony Blair – whatever his self-proclaimed Irish connection – of those in his party who had long laboured on behalf of Anglo-Irish relations. Thanks to Bertie Aherne, and his Secretary of State, Mo Mowlam, during lengthy summits at Stormont, Hillsborough and St Andrews, together with many meetings in London, Dublin and Belfast, Tony Blair nevertheless exhibited a remarkable diligence and work-rate in helping bring the prolonged peace process to a successful conclusion.

The deal was carefully threaded into three strands. Strand one, establishing an assembly, met the wishes of the unionists. Strand two set up a North-South ministerial council, which appealed to the nationalists. Strand three, the British-Irish council, was intended to reassure the unionists. But the relentless drive of the Scottish National party must have worried them. Only the first two strands were organic. But the first, the Assembly, was prone to reflecting a changing electorate – 'The Melting Pot' is how *The Economist* described it[285] – and thereby tending toward an undermining of traditional unionism. Whilst the second could establish a positive cross border role, as yet under-developed.

David Trimble was reduced to whimpering about his border and Britishness. The IRA, on the other hand, could afford satisfactorily to view the outcome essentially as 'transitional arrangements' and only amounting therefore to an interim deal. Its leaders were well aware that the all-important status quo, which had been compromised by the Hillsborough agreement of 1985, had now been fatally breached. At the very least, they could look forward to a sharing of power. How they handled it, and the scope also available to colleagues on the ministerial council, together with a changing North-South ethos, enabling a choice of passports, for example, and a significant Sinn Féin parliamentary presence in Dublin as well as Belfast, could yet yield the greater potential. A comparison of the relative positions and public standing of all parties several years on, south and north, and the accomplishments of certain individuals is already most illuminating.

Along with the basic shift in status of the two communities in Northern Ireland, London and Dublin moved also into a new power relationship. The Good Friday Agreement brought to an end London's customary talking-down and occasional patronising towards Dublin. The parity of esteem that followed made more difficult the demonising of the Irish in Britain ... Indeed, Prime Minister Blair

---

285   *The Economist.* 9 March 2013.

was enabled shortly afterwards in an address to the Irish Parliament to specifically pay tribute to the contribution that the Irish people had made over many generations to the political, economic, social and cultural life of Britain.

Chapter Eighteen
The NATO Assembly

The Callaghan administration never had a stable majority, therefore its fall in 1979 was not unexpected. Although I was retained by Jim Callaghan as a shadow defence minister, I found myself switched, on his insistence, to Brussels and membership of the NATO Assembly. I protested, for a defence portfolio had become 'a bed of nails' for a Labour MP given the contentious issue of nuclear disarmament. The newly arrived Labour group in my own city of Sheffield had already proclaimed it a nuclear-free zone. Jim expressed a wish to retain close defence links, however, and wanted me to keep him well briefed. Thus I remained active in the Western Alliance from the late Seventies onwards as it faced major military and political challenges. I was briefed on or became involved in some of the historic issues that arose. Eventually I was party to the closure of the Cold War, to which the fall of the Berlin Wall was the historic prelude.

The NATO Assembly was the interparliamentary assembly of member countries of the North Atlantic alliance.[286] It provided a forum where West Europeans and North American parliamentarians met regularly to analyse, discuss, voice their opinion on issues and developments and act as a link between NATO's military and political authorities. Its members were then in a position to report meaningfully to plenary sessions of the Assembly and to their own national parliaments and individual political parties. It worked surprisingly well. Composed of nearly 200 members nominated by their political

---

286 Other parliamentary organisations in the West included the Assembly of the Council of Europe, the European Parliament and the Assembly of the Western European Union. Each with an important role to play, not least in fostering greater understanding, good faith and good will as representatives of democratic assemblies.

parties, the Assembly operated through five committees: Military, Political, Economic, Cultural Affairs, Scientific and Technical. These committees met regularly to consider current problems affecting the Atlantic community and form sub-committees or working groups to analyse specific subjects in greater detail.

I was assigned to the Military committee, and quickly became rapporteur of its sub-committee on cooperation in the procurement of defence equipment. I was soon appointed chairman. That was a most engaging start, given my select committee work on trade and industry in the UK. It quickly exposed me to the challenges the Alliance faced in the early Eighties. My horizon of activity was now international, of course. Our remit invited us to probe the potential for cooperation and savings in new weapons systems by major corporations throughout the Alliance, particularly in the US. Much of our briefing was necessarily confidential, and some skirted the classification category. By the mid-Eighties I was regularly invited by Brussels to lead the annual tour of members around the Atlantic community. Then in Hamburg in 1988, after briefly serving as vice-president, I was elected President of the NATO Assembly. It was a great honour, and one conferred significantly for the first time in twenty years on one of its members who was politically left of centre.

NATO was formed after WWII to give a weak and war devastated Western Europe the protection of the nuclear power of the US, whilst it built a counterforce to the vast conventional arms superiority of a threatening Soviet Union. The post-war Foreign Secretary, Ernest Bevin, former general secretary of the TGW, played a vital role in its formation. His toughest battles it seemed to me – then a student at the LSE – were with his own party's left wing. Such ideological protests were not the only difficulty that confronted him. Overcoming nationalism among its members sufficiently to induce some sense of commonality was another challenge. Many of them had fought each other in past European wars, whilst the US had long looked askance at joining alliances. The new structure faced unique problems of geography and the vastness of the territory it embraced. It had to accommodate a whole range of pluralistic democracies, and its objectives could not be confined to military purposes. Though plainly dedicated, if necessary, to the policy of nuclear-deterrence, it had to maintain a high level of public acceptability. It fell, therefore, to Assembly members to brief not only their party colleagues, but explain also to their electorates and local parties as best they could, Alliance policies at varying levels of technical and political sophistication. Not easy at any time, but it became profoundly difficult in the early Eighties to explain and justify the policy of the nuclear deterrent. It was never free of controversy. Neither was spending on defence. Its funding was always inadequate. As a result, NATO never succeeded in building a conventional counterforce to the Warsaw Pact nations. Its superior technology did enable it to narrow the gap, but it remained crucially dependent on nuclear arms.

As long as NATO had a monopoly, or near monopoly of nuclear forces, some inferiority in conventional forces did not matter too much. But sooner or later this situation had to change, which was always conveniently overlooked by members of CND. It was inevitable that the Soviet Union would acquire its own intercontinental nuclear capability, though not as early nor in the numbers that alarmists were falsely reporting during the late Fifties.[287] By the late Seventies, however, the Soviet Union did acquire the edge in short and intermediate-range nuclear forces, or INF. It introduced for example, the mobile, multi-headed SS20 missile system with a capability beyond the reach of our western systems. What was to be the response?

---

287   This contributed to the disastrous mission of U2 pilot Gary Powers who was shot down over the Soviet Union on 1 May 1960. It caused the abandonment of the imminent summit meeting between President Eisenhower and Secretary-general Khrushchev. It also persuaded John Kennedy – misled by CIA members according to Giles Wittel (*Bridge of Spies: A true story of the Cold War*, Simon and Schuster, 2011) – to campaign in 1960 against a threatening 'missile gap'.

The strategic superiority of the west was now threatened and its key policy of forward defence was in question. Its security and cohesion were also affected by economic stringency. For the OECD forecast for some member nations in 1980 was that they would suffer zero growth with record current account deficits, record unemployment and an inflation rate of 10%. This led them to an increased preoccupation with domestic politics. In some member nations it led to policy clashes over budgets and challenges to defence spending. However, the logic of alliance strategy still pointed inexorably to the need for increased spending, given the new INF threat. For the longstanding gap in conventional arms between the Warsaw Treaty Organisation (WTO) and NATO remained. That was when the public relations function of some Assembly MPs became extremely difficult and politically dangerous. But it was a duty that could not be shirked, no matter how thankless it became when trying to explain some controversial development to the man and woman in the street. It was politically perilous when attempting it in your own party at home, of course. For political choices at constituency level are rarely simple and clear cut, especially in defence matters. The conflict between rising living standards and our way of life on the one hand, and preserving both in a rough and tumble world on the other, could not be neatly solved by any government. Trying to explain and justify it as a defence minister at Westminster in those days was not a job for the faint-hearted. When replying to hostile questions in Parliament in the Seventies about the costs of nuclear weapons, I would point out that they were the most cost-effective systems, absorbing about 3% only of the defence budget spread over a number of years. That was met sometimes with increased hostility.

Happily, there was a stout defence team in place under Jim Callaghan. Fred Mulley had succeeded Roy Mason as Secretary of State, John (later Lord) Gilbert had followed Bill Rodgers at defence procurement, and Robert Brown and James Wellbeloved were Army and RAF ministers respectively. So I was blessed with very good colleagues whilst Navy Minister. Nevertheless, our ministerial steadfastness served to put each one of us at risk in our constituencies. This was due not only to the increasing waywardness of our own party's NEC. We had to contend also with a wider electorate which was fragmenting into special interest groups – such as the protest presented at Greenham Common – cutting across traditional party lines, increasingly strident, sceptical and critical. The solidarity of NATO was also affected. This was all too clear, unhappily in 1976, when Britain received the IMF loan. Two of the principal subscribers were the US and West Germany. Neither wanted to see further cuts in Britain's defence expenditure, of course. Yet at no stage did either formally recognise the connection between the need of such a loan by Britain and her maintenance of the defence contribution on which they counted.[288]

Indeed, the question now for all member nations was how to find sufficient defence funds to meet the growing needs of their military commanders. For those needs had become strategic as the Soviet Union moved from a position of inferiority in the nuclear field to one of strategic parity and, actual superiority, in the case of the INF. In the conventional field, the Warsaw Pact land and air postures had significantly improved, and the Soviet Navy had moved out of its coastal waters into the oceans of the world.

Calls for change were not new to the Alliance. Its history is a record of change. Over its first forty years it had faced a number of challenges and experienced difficult periods. But it had emerged with

288   There was no link between alliance forward planning and the forward planning of national defence budgets. Nor was there formal NATO authority. It was denied by the sovereignty of national governments. They were all agreed, for example, on standardisation of defence equipment in principle, but not in practice, if it affected their own industry. Despite constant calls for a two-way street in procurement, there was an inequitable trade in arms across the Atlantic, with a ratio of ten to one in favour of the US. Whilst there existed such an inequitable sale of arms, there had also developed, inevitably, a disproportionate burden sharing by the US.

increased vigour and determination. Once again it was being called upon to adapt its structures and policies to changing requirements. In the mid–1960s, when the Soviet Union emerged as a major nuclear power, the NATO strategy of massive retaliation was replaced by one of flexible response. In the search for improved relations with the East, however, it adopted the Harmel doctrine and a policy of dialogue based on adequate defences.

NATO now faced further challenges. First, to undertake a modernisation of its forces that would restore a reasonable balance with the Warsaw Pact forces, bearing in mind the warning of Sir Michael Carver that peace depended on the balance of risk rather than the balance of forces in Europe. Second, to re-shape the partnership between America and Europe so as to dispel the growing impression in the US that the Europeans were not carrying a fair share of the burden. Third, to maintain public support for the Atlantic partnership and its changing policies, especially on INF, at a time of increased support for less nuclear-reliant policies. Such a development called notably on the resources and expertise of the NATO Assembly.

The search for the first two objectives – more value for money from a better balance in resource allocations, and more equitable burden sharing – fell within the remit of my committee on defence cooperation. Thus my committee members were all too familiar with the measures frequently proposed to alleviate apparent waste, such as standardisation, interoperability, the avoidance of duplication and excessive specialisation. But they were also well aware that the economies achieved were unlikely to be anything like as great as the enthusiast claimed. Something else was needed: preferably a fundamental change. It was provided by Sir Frank Cooper, when permanent under-secretary at the MoD in London, who called for a new strategic concept. It must be a 'clear and unambiguous definition of defence strategy and objectives,' he declared. In short, as Colonel Anthony King Harman, OBE, a member of the international NATO staff pointed out to my defence cooperation committee in Brussels, one way to 'maintain adequate forces with limited budgets is to know exactly what your forces are trying to do and what objectives your military posture is designed to carry out.'[289] Furthermore, such a new and strategic concept, he reminded us, needs to be global, recalling the previous warning of Supreme Atlantic Commander, Admiral Ike Kidd. The enormous dependences of the West, and particularly Europe, on the shipping of raw materials from the Gulf around southern Africa, together with the defence needs of Australia and New Zealand, called for reassessment in the light of the emerging Soviet maritime presence in the southern Atlantic and Indian Ocean. 'The threat in this area may well be as serious to Western survival as the military confrontation in Central Europe,' he had often reminded me.

In tackling such major challenges every government in NATO had to contend by the early Eighties, as noted, with serious inflationary economic factors and other conflicting claims on national budgets. They were sorely pressed also by rising real costs in the defence sectors due to the lengthening time-span of defence programmes. Increasing real costs arose as each generation of new equipment

---

289   Central to the whole issue of how to implement the strategic concept in a way that will be both credible in terms of deterrence and affordability was the length of time NATO conventional forces can or should be able to hold the line in the event of a Soviet attack. Once a politically acceptable level of threshold – both conventional and nuclear – had been established, using a sensible worst-case scenario, then it would be possible to establish some realistic general priorities. They covered the ratio of ready forces to reinforcements and reserves, timing of reinforcement and mobilisation programmes, stock levels, and, of course, a reassured public opinion.

became progressively more costly.[290] Thomas A. Callaghan Jr, a former US navy official, deemed it structural disarmament, and warned my committee that, 'trying to produce everything ourselves means nothing can be produced at affordable prices.' He called for more cooperation in the defence market: 'not small, protected national defence markets, but a two-pillar North Atlantic defence market; a

---

290   In an address in June 1986, at the Royal Union Services for Defence Studies (RUSI) in London, General Bernard W. Rogers, then Supreme Allied Commander Europe (SACEUR), explained that:'Every time we replace an older system, the cost of the newer one has increased by a factor of from three to five. Consequently, we procure fewer and fewer systems as replacements each time. Contributing to what was now known as 'structural disarmament'.' In May 1987, NATO's Secretary-general, Lord Carrington, told a Washington Capitol Hill seminar sponsored by the Euro Group and the Centre for Strategic and International Studies that: 'National parochialism in the development and procurement of weapon systems has resulted in situations, such as four different national main battle tanks in Europe that cannot even fire the same ammunition, or a host of different national tactical battlefield communication systems that cannot speak to each other or even to NATO's own communication system. The critical fact is that the alliance today is spending more and more money to buy less and less equipment, and the spiralling costs of our small, inefficient production runs are threatening to overwhelm defence budgets.'

Two-Way Street,' joining the two pillars; not bearing burdens but sharing burdens and benefits, equitably and efficiently.[291]

There was an urgent need from the late Seventies, therefore, to move towards a more effective harmonisation of the military and economic dimensions of security. The immediate issue, however, was the INF threat, given the Soviet's introduction of the SS20 missile system. How to respond moved the Alliance sharply into the political dimension of security. Yielding to domestic political pressure, Assembly members called for a much more thorough dialogue between the US and the Soviet Union. Talks had begun between them in the 1960s to find ways of slowing down the arms race and limiting the size of their arsenals. Yet the US and the Soviet Union now held more than 30,000 nuclear warheads each. The US secretly deployed thousands of nuclear weapons in twenty-seven countries. In some cases this global deployment took place without the knowledge of the governments involved, according to a study based on newly declassified documents.[292] Did the US, asked some European Assembly members, need to maintain so large an arsenal? They called for

---

291 Thomas Callaghan briefed my committee on the pooling of resources on both sides of the Atlantic. 'Where is English Electric? Whatever became of Messer Schmitt?' he asked us. 'They and many other once independent European companies,' he explained, 'are long-ago victims of domestic defence markets that were simply too small to sustain them economically, or required subsidies in the vain attempt to preserve the defence industrial base.' Whereas, as we were well aware, the ability of Alliance forces to operate together – to be able to refuel, rearm, repair, reinforce, support, supply, or communicate with one another , or even identify friend from foe – had been only marginally improved, if at all. Meanwhile, the NATO-Warsaw Pact conventional force gap was widening once more, even though NATO nations were now spending more on conventional forces than the Warsaw Pact nations. 'What the American, Canadian, and European defence industrial bases need now is not less cooperation but more', he insisted.

292 The study, published in 1999 in *The Bulletin of the Atomic Scientists*, was based on a secret Defence Department document detailing America's nuclear arsenal overseas between 1945 and 1977.

reduced numbers, a speed-up of negotiations and a scaling back of unnecessary modernisation. Significantly, it was clear that despite the INF crisis there was a strengthening wish for the Alliance to wean itself from over reliance on nuclear policies. That had always been its clear and stated preference, but as its members were only too well aware, it had proved most difficult to achieve given the imbalance in conventional arms.

Between 1969 and 1979 there were a series of negotiations between the US and Soviet Union aimed not at reducing stockpiles, but at limiting the growth of their arsenals. The Strategic Arms Limitation talks (START or SALT) had begun in 1969 between President Lyndon B. Johnson and Soviet leader Leonid Brezhnev. Neither the SALT accord, which was effective between 1972 and 1977, nor its successor, the SALT2 pact, called for reductions, but merely a limit on their expansion.[293] Such negotiations were always at risk because of the sensitivities surrounding intercontinental missiles. The fear of retaliation always posed a nightmare scenario of first-strike potential and, therefore, pre-emptiveness. Strategic stability went to the heart of reducing the danger of the outbreak of war. Arms control was vital to preserve balance and stability.

But, as I was well aware from my own attendance at the SALT talks in Vienna, the constant search for it gave rise to difficulties on both sides that were rarely grasped by those bent on a one-sided disarmament of nuclear arms, such as members of Labour's NEC. They ranged from the calculation of an agreed balance, subject to agreed technical definitions, to the offsetting of similar categories (of different generations) of systems and weapons and, finally, mutually acceptable verification. My acquaintance later with the Soviet record suggested

---

293   SALT2 was never fully ratified because of the Soviet invasion of Afghanistan, although its terms were respected by both sides until President Reagan exceeded its limitations during his second term. The negotiations had been threatened also by the Soviet invasion of Czechoslovakia and the emergence in Poland of the Solidarity movement.

genuine difficulties on their part, rather than actual cheating. Yet it left NATO with no choice in 1979 but to deploy its own INF as a deterrent while seeking to negotiate with the Soviet Union a formula for mutual restraint. An attempt by Secretary-general Brezhnev to impose a precondition to such dual-track talks was dropped on the intervention of Chancellor Schmidt during a visit to Moscow in 1980. It was a further reminder of the complexities that surrounded negotiations on arms control.

To the relief of its allies, the US provided the new response capabilities. They were ground-launched cruise missiles with nuclear warheads. The decision had been bravely taken earlier by President Jimmy Carter, Prime Minister Jim Callaghan and Chancellor Helmut Schmidt of Germany at a meeting in Whitehall, which I was privileged to attend at the express invitation of the Prime Minister. It was agreed to locate them in Germany, Belgium, the Netherlands, Italy and the UK. Along with the cruise missiles, Germany would also deploy Pershing 2 missiles. All systems would be under American command and control, though their allies would contribute to their general support and infrastructure. Yet there was serious political opposition within all the affected countries to their deployment. In Germany, Chancellor Schmidt experienced difficulty with members of his own party. Belgium and the Netherlands reserved their own deployment date, pending progress on arms control. However, the Christian Democrat government in Italy adopted a positive position, as did the UK.

Despite demonstrations, including those notoriously mounted at Greenham Common, Margaret Thatcher, like Jim Callaghan, consistently adopted actions running closely parallel to American policy, notably within NATO's nuclear planning group, which was restricted in its membership. Both invited me to brief them on the NATO Assembly. They were anxious that its proceedings reflected the rapport of the UK with the US. That close relationship ranged from intelligence gathering to military appointments within the alliance.

The key military appointments of Supreme Allied Commander in Europe, Supreme Atlantic Commander in Norfolk, Virginia, and at Allied Forces South headquarters in Naples were always filled at that time by Americans, with British deputy commanders, whilst Allied Forces North headquarters in Oslo sometimes had a British commander-in-chief. British parliamentarians, however, wielded a quite disproportionate reverse of power and influence in the NATO Assembly.

Sir Patrick Wall MP, Sir Peter Emery MP, Sir Geoffrey Johnson-Smith MP, and Bruce George MP chaired three or four of its senior committees consistently in the Eighties. Together with Lord (Michael) Jopling and Sir Menzies Campbell MP, they also distinguished themselves otherwise in Assembly proceedings and related activities. They worked closely with other prominent members such as Loic Bouvard of France, Senator William Roth of Delaware, and Robert Hicks of Canada. All of us were dependent on the effective support of an outstanding secretary-general in Dr Peter Corterier, a former Minister of State in the German Foreign Office, and his talented staff in Brussels.

Thus the beginning of the Eighties was a particularly crucial time in the life of the Western Alliance. NATO ministers reaffirmed in Rome in 1981 the earlier dual-track decision to proceed simultaneously to the modernisation of its own INF and engage in arms control negotiations. There was a new President in the US in the person of Ronald Reagan. President Brezhnev signalled that he was keen for an early summit meeting to ease the growing tension. The hint that Moscow might be ready for new negotiations on a second START came in his report to the Soviet Communist Party's twenty-sixth congress. The following day Opposition party leaders at Westminster in Michael Foot and David Steele pressed Prime Minister Thatcher to urge President Reagan – whom she was about to visit – to make a positive response to Mr Brezhnev. Ronald Reagan's response, however, and that of Margaret Thatcher, was to call on their NATO colleagues to boost defence spending. That historic decision eventually imposed too great a strain on the economy of the Soviet Union, and crucially heralded the end of the Cold War.

In collaboration with his newly appointed Defence secretary, Casper Willard Weinberger, Reagan had endorsed a plan to revitalise America's strategic nuclear deterrent. Some aspects of the plan proved controversial, notably a Strategic Defence Initiative (SDI), nicknamed 'Star Wars', for it was feared that it would prejudice the balance between America and the Soviet Union on arms control negotiations. Despite several briefings I seriously doubted whether it would work. Six former secretaries of defence argued that, in any event, it would violate the Anti-Ballistic Missile Treaty. As a result the administration did not proceed with testing. The six tests Weinberger listed coincidentally in November 1984 entitled 'The Uses of Military Power' were, I thought at the time, a model for the use of combat forces abroad. If they had been observed in the years that followed, the US and the UK would have been spared much pain and bloodshed. After several meetings, I judged him to be a very competent defence secretary. Margaret Thatcher wrote of him in her memoirs: 'America never had a wiser patriot, nor Britain a truer friend.'

Worried at the nuclear risk, Reagan announced a constructive diplomatic policy initiative in January 1984.[294] But it was the Reagan-Thatcher alliance and their joint resolve to increase defence spending that was about to have a crucial effect on arms control negotiations. For the increased defence budget was making possible the development of significant new systems such as the 'Stealth' aircraft and the Airborne Warning and Control Systems (AWACS) planes as well as the SDI. Such a package soon paid dividends, forcing the near-bankrupt Soviet Union back to the negotiating table. Furthermore, the Soviet Union

---

294   He offered the Soviet Union a challenge to begin building a more constructive relationship. 'Our challenge is peaceful. It will bring out the best in us. It also
calls for the best from the Soviet Union … if the Soviet government wants peace,
there will be peace.'

now had a new leader in Mikhail Gorbachev. Following the death of the ailing Konstantin Chernenko in March 1985, he was selected as Communist Party boss by the military element in the Kremlin, who believed he would maintain Soviet power and imperial glory.[295] But Gorbachev displayed a new brand of leadership. It began in his private office and his choice of advisers – always, in my experience, the key element in the equipment of a new leader. Among his advisers were some who were well acquainted with the West. They included Georgi Arbatov, whom I came to know and who I believed would assure him that the West posed no immediate military threats.

I was quick to follow up later in the year therefore at the NATO Assembly's annual congress in San Francisco. It was addressed by George F. Schultz, US Secretary of State, who delivered the routine platitudinous assurances about ongoing arms control negotiations. He struck a new note however, in his assertion that a 'positive relationship' between the NATO alliance and the WTO would be a major goal of President Reagan when he met Gorbachev the following year. In a public exchange, caught on national television, I urged the Secretary of State to advise the President to 'go that extra mile'. George Shultz was markedly cautious in his reply, but we were assured that the President would be 'giving new impetus' to this entire agenda. Mr Reagan and Mr Gorbachev held meetings in August and September 1986. They culminated in the historic Reykjavik summit, where President Reagan had encountered an entirely different Soviet leader.

For Mikhail Gorbachev was making it clear by this time that he was about to embark on a fundamental restructuring of the Soviet economy. His soon to be declared policies of Glasnost, or 'openness', and Perestroika spelt 'change', and offered a degree of debate not seen

---

295   C.N. Donnelly explained in October 1988 in *Soviet Military Developments under Gorbachev*, that because Gorbachev came to power on a 'party ticket' and not by the machinations of the Army or the KGB, unlike his predecessors, Secretary-generals Andropov and Chernenko, as well as Brezhnev, he was remarkably independent of the military lobby.

since the early days of the Soviet Union. He proceeded to launch a series of diplomatic ventures also that stunned onlookers throughout the world. At home he turned out to be a genuine reformer who imagined he could revive communism. He achieved remarkable things between 1985 and his fall from power in 1991, if not always to his satisfaction. He introduced a semi-free press and relatively free parliamentary elections in which anti-communist candidates stood for the first time. From these emerged a genuine opposition and a rival for power in the person of Boris Yeltsin.

Thus the Reykjavik summit ushered in the most profound consequences, for which – I was led to understand during a visit to Iceland shortly afterwards – the Americans were largely unprepared. The Americans could not bring themselves to believe that Gorbachev meant what he said. His readiness to enter into far reaching mutual nuclear disarmament found the Americans unprepared. They were not alone. The extreme cautiousness of the Defence secretary, Dick Cheney, in Washington, was shared by Marshall Sergei Akhromeyev, Chief of the General Staff in Moscow, as I learned during one-to-one meetings with both subsequently. In a personal exchange in Bonn in 1989, Marshall Akhromeyev went further, despite the valuable cover he had extended to Gorbachev. In the presence of Rita Sussmith, President of the German Bundestag, during a dinner, he vehemently denounced the oppressive hostility of NATO and declared: 'NATO will launch a first strike on the Soviet Union.' I could not believe it. Although I was well aware by this time of the implacable hostility of the senior Soviet military, who were now viewing western technology generally and, in particular the SDI, as serious threats.

Mr Gorbachev was also very mindful of the SDI, when I met him, though from a different perspective. Even if it could not be made to work as an umbrella against intercontinental missiles, he recognised that its scientific ingenuity and technological spin-off were so great as to enable the West to render obsolete the vast Soviet fleets of tanks and aircraft, and to give the domestic economy of the US a huge advantage. The answer, he now believed, was to develop Soviet science and technology as fast as possible across the whole board, and not just the military. As he was to admit to me again, personally, in conversation in 1989 and 1990 in Moscow and London, it is no use a nation creating a massive military machine, if in the process it so distorts its economy and weakens its social cohesion that it risks stagnation and lack of commercial competitiveness.

The summit meeting in Reykjavik left the two participants in reverse roles. Now it was the West that was being challenged: not just to react to changes in Soviet rhetoric, policy and behaviour, but also to redefine its own short- and long-term purposes.[296] Happily, the President had sensed, well ahead of many in official Washington, that he was now engaged with a completely different scenario, domestically as well as internationally – and proceeded accordingly. As a result, under the much-maligned leadership of Ronald Reagan and Margaret Thatcher, the conditions and prospects of the NATO Alliance were transformed in the 1980s.

---

296   This led to the 1987 Intermediate-Range Nuclear Forces Treaty. This elim-
inated nuclear and conventional ground launched ballistic and cruise missiles with
intermediate ranges of between 300–3400 miles. One of the key aspects of this treaty
was the mutual inspection and verification process, which I was invited to observe
in the US. It significantly improved trust between the two countries over the reduction of their nuclear stockpiles. Agreement 'in principle' between Washington and
Moscow in 1990, eliminating the last obstacles to the treaty reducing conventional
forces in Europe (CFE), removed the danger of surprise land attack in Europe. The
imaginative 1992 Nunn-Lugar Act provided American cash to fund the safe disposal
of Russia's redundant nuclear inventory.

Chapter Nineteen

Missions to Moscow, Rome, Westminster and Sydney

The NATO Assembly was a forum which brought together legislators from all the member nations of the North Atlantic alliance in order to discuss issues of common concern. It was a touchstone of parliamentary and public opinion. It was the only interparliamentary forum that united European and North American parliamentarians in this fashion. It was swift to react to the profound changes taking place in the nations of Eastern Europe in the mid-Eighties, and established a monitoring sub-committee as early as 1986. Over the next two years its members visited Hungary, Czechoslovakia and Poland, and were received with every courtesy. Rt. Hon Bruce George former British MP, and Loic Bouvard of France, leaders of the Political committee, initiated the early visits and continued to take the lead in developing parliamentary ties.

As President, I led delegations of senior western parliamentarians, including US senators and congressmen, to Czechoslovakia, Poland and the Soviet Union. At the end of October 1989, I hosted the first East-West Parliamentary Round Table in Bonn. In the following February, I presided in Brussels over the first meetings between NATO and the WTO at military as well as at parliamentary levels. We were anxious in the West to exchange practical experience and ideas on the role of legislatures in shaping and overseeing foreign policy and defence budgets.

The coolness and political orthodoxy of the leaders we met initially in Czechoslovakia contrasted sharply with the friendliness and accommodation of the military. Our reception in Poland was more varied. It was prior to the elections of June 1989, when the Communist party was displaced by Solidarity as the country's dominant political force. Mr Rakowski, as premier, was not yet ready for Perestroika and the market economy. 'We don't want a Volkswagen culture here,' he firmly declared. I found Cardinal Jozef Glemp, leader of the country's Catholic Church, just as unbending. I pleaded with him personally on behalf of German colleagues for a little more tolerance and friendliness towards former displaced Germans visiting their old parish churches and graveyards, now within Poland's new boundaries. I cited the 'Polish mass' that had been celebrated every Sunday in my own St. Peter's church in Doncaster since WWII. He was unmoved.

I found the former premier and Communist party leader, now President, General Wojcioch Jaruzolski, much more welcoming. He was polite and friendly throughout a prolonged private meeting. But he stoutly defended his imposition of martial law in 1981, following months of strikes and protests by the Solidarity movement. Would the Soviet Union have intervened otherwise, I asked? He could not take that risk with Leonid Brezhnev in control in Moscow, he replied. A repeat of the Hungarian uprising of 1956 was out of the question. He claimed that his Government, with the help of the Catholic Church, had tried to reach agreement with the leaders of Solidarity. The 'interference', he alleged – despite many disclaimers – of the US and the UK, was 'unhelpful'. 'We never ventured to tell London how to handle Northern Ireland,' he reminded me.

Meanwhile the US intensified his domestic difficulties by cutting credit assistance before the imposition of martial law. Which, he also reminded me, was publicly approved, by a margin of 69% to 20%, according to opinion polls. He insisted that he was compelled to act against Solidarity. It did not prevent him from later working with its leaders in power. Furthermore, he had ensured a peaceful transition from communist rule to democracy. Now he had been elected to the revised office of President. Briefed no doubt on my own background, he recalled his Catholic upbringing. Pointing to his dark glasses, he explained how his impaired eyesight came about after he was deported to Siberia as a teenager. He clearly retained considerable warmth for the Church, and singled out certain of its leaders for praise. He paid warm tribute to Pope John Paul.

I laid a wreath on the Unknown Soldier's Monument in central
Warsaw. I was deeply moved also when I laid a wreath on the
'Monument to British Airmen' in the Skaryszewski Park in Warsaw.
This is the actual place where a British bomber came down on 14
August, 1944. The crew were killed whilst attempting to deliver arms
during the Warsaw uprising. Meanwhile, the Soviet army remained
immobile on the other side of the nearby Vistula River.

The first visit to the Soviet Union by the NATO Assembly, which
I led, began on 2 July in Moscow. The delegation comprised nineteen
parliamentarians from twelve of the sixteen NATO nations, and Peter
Corterier, Secretary–general.[297] Along with Mikhail Gorbachev, I was
looking forward to meeting one adviser in particular, Georgi Arbatov,
whom I had already met in Vienna. I was struck then by his command
of the English language and grasp of western affairs. He had been an
important adviser of successive general secretaries of the Communist
party. He played a key role in the Brezhnev years when he was a pro-
détente voice within the Soviet establishment, and was known to be
anti-Stalinist.[298]

---

297   The delegation to Moscow included Robert Hicks of Canada, Loic Bouvard
of France, Lothar Ibrugger of the Federal Republic of Germany, Luigi Poli and Sen-
ator Mariano Rumor of Italy, Mrs Viviane Reding of Luxemburg, Ton Frinking and
Thijs van Vlijmen of the Netherlands, Jan Petersen of Norway, Jose Lello of Portugal,
Rafael Estrella of Spain, Seki Yavuzturk of Turkey, Bruce George and Sir Geoffrey
Johnson-Smith of the UK, Senators William Roth, Barbara Mikulski and Charles
Robb of the US.

298   He quickly told me how he had become engaged in the making of Soviet foreign policy in the early days of Perestroika. He became also a deputy to the Supreme
Soviet, and a member of the Communist Party Central Committee. He was critical
of the size of the defence budget, and showed courage in his willingness to take on
the military and the influence of the military-industrial complex. He reminded me
again and again of his conviction that the Soviet Union could only be secure on the
basis of a 'common security' for both East and West. That understanding did appear
to become part and parcel of the Gorbachev era.

As guests of the Supreme Soviet, the delegation was greeted and briefed first of all by its chairman, Tevgeny Primakov. During our stay we had meetings with the Committees on International Affairs and Defence and State Security, with the Academy of Sciences, with the Chairman of the Council of Ministers, with Prime Minister Nikolai Ryshkov and at the Defence and Foreign ministries. The discussions explored Glasnost and Perestroika at length. They ranged over security and domestic issues, from nuclear armaments to the regulation of the market economy. We probed their published *New Thinking in Foreign Policy*, and they responded reassuringly about German reunification, Eastern Europe and the presence of US and Canadian forces in Europe, within their notion of a 'Common European Home'. They were also cooperative about arms control negotiations and the joint pursuit of greater stability and security, asking whether a compromise was not possible around minimum nuclear deterrence.

The Supreme Soviet's scrutinising of the Defence budget and the Government's accountability of their military/industrial complex surfaced at most meetings. When deputies were present, we noted their resolve to play a major role in overseeing the promised reduction on spending, the conversion of military to civilian production, greater transparency in military procurement and the ongoing arms negotiations between East and West. The overall objective was the maximum politicisation of domestic and military matters, they declared. 'We must fight your and our military/industrial complex,' commented one deputy. Another remarked that their success in doing this would depend 'on how well we all work together.'

Our first meeting on the morning of Monday 3 July took place in the Kremlin, where – in the absence of Mr Gorbachev, who was committed to address the Council of Europe – we met members of the International Affairs and Defence committees. Those present, along with their officers, included Georgi Arbatov, Director of the Institute for the US and Canada, Vladimir Kravets, Foreign Minister of Latvia, General Vladimir Lobov, now a deputy as well as the Warsaw Treaty Organisation (WTO) military commander, and Roy Medvedev, author. Early discussions focussed on the Supreme Soviet's role in scrutinising the Defence budget. Searching questions concerning security generally were raised by both sides. Apart from murmurings from General Lobov about the introduction by NATO of certain new strategic military concepts, the only serious clash came later, at the Defence ministry.

Thanks largely to the energising presence of Georgi Arbatov, many other interesting points arose. He nettled some members of our delegation by arguing that the absence of war in Europe and the presence of nuclear weapons 'may just be coincidence'. Quite apart from the risk of accidental war, he insisted 'that nuclear weapons cannot be regarded as a universal means of preventing war.' Short-range weapons were the most dangerous because they are considered 'useable', he pointed out. He was asked why, if short-range nuclear weapons were considered so dangerous, the Soviet Union by its own data had deployed over fifteen times as many ground-launched missile launches as NATO. Without hesitation, he declared it 'a dumb and stupid mistake'. We replied that our experience had persuaded us that nuclear weapons were a stabilising influence, and would therefore remain an essential part of NATO strategy. Arbatov reminded us that the Soviet Union was now intent on depriving the West of its enemy. 'That game is over. Now you must prepare your own concept; do not preserve an image that is not there.'

General Lobov stressed the active role played by the Soviet military in arms control negotiations. He cautioned against getting bogged down in 'old facts and fears' concerning which side had more forces. Noting the importance of military doctrine, he criticised certain NATO concepts, notably air-land battle. He regarded them as aggressive, with the potential for surprise and pre-emptive strikes. He contrasted such concepts with the new WTO doctrine of 'preventing wars'. Whilst 'the offensive potential of NATO strike aircraft now posed a greater threat than tanks,' he went on. 'Together with increased range, they could conduct pre-emptive attacks against ground forces.'

Lobov praised the arms negotiations in Vienna, but was doubtful of early agreement. He commented favourably on the progress made on mutual inspections, but regretted that 'they were not extended to air forces and navies.' Finally he expressed the wish to meet the 'top brass of NATO', Supreme Allied Commander, General John Galvin, 'so that he could look into his eyes.' On the proposal of Sir Geoffrey Johnson-Smith, we proceeded immediately to arrange such a meeting with General Galvin at the forthcoming annual session in Rome. Asked about the rate of tank production in the Soviet Union, deputies were unable to provide an answer, explaining that this was a matter for our meeting at the Defence ministry.

In conclusion, I declared the Assembly's interest in continuing exchanges of this kind between parliamentarians from East and West. We offered our Soviet hosts whatever political help and co-operation was considered appropriate. Our Soviet hosts proclaimed the visit 'as nothing less than historic' and said they looked forward to further such exchanges and constructive dialogue.

The following morning, Tuesday, our group visited the Lenin mausoleum, and I laid a wreath at the tomb of the Unknown Soldier.[299] Afterwards we met Dr Vitally Zhurkin, Director of the Institute of Europe of the USSR Academy of Sciences, Dr Sergei Karaganov, Deputy Director, and their colleagues. Our discussions varied from nuclear armaments to economic policy. While reiterating the Soviet goal of total elimination, Institute officials noted the Soviet acceptance of deterrence as an inevitable evil, at least for the time being. In the pursuit by both sides of greater stability and security, however, they asked whether a compromise was not possible around

---

299   I explained beforehand the preference for a dedication, 'To all who died on both sides in WWII', which was readily agreed and well received. Our German colleagues were deeply moved – one wept.

the notion of minimum deterrence, though recognising again the 'manifest difficulties'. Could not some interim steps be agreed, they asked? They understood NATO's attachment to nuclear systems, but asked how far minimum deterrence could prohibit the elimination of the more destabilising systems. They admitted that considerable work was needed on a definition of what constituted 'minimum deterrence', and did not offer one themselves.

On economic matters, Institute officials regretted the lack of interdependence between the European Community and their own Comecon. Noting that the relationship between central planning and the market varies from country to country, they explained that the Soviet Union was now attempting a new model in which the market would be the driving force, with the state acting as a guiding hand or goal-setter and regulator.

During the afternoon we met Chairman Primakov once again, along with Deputy Yevgeny Velikhov, deputy chairman of the Defence Committee and vice president of the Academy of Sciences. Primakov stressed the significance of the Soviets' current political reform. He contrasted the potential of the new Supreme Soviet with the superficial democracy of the old institution where voting had been 'strictly programmed'. The new chamber would have a decisive role in making the Executive accountable, he claimed. It would hold hearings on the budget, form sub-committees and ad hoc groups to deal with specific issues, whilst ministers would be obliged to provide information. The confirmation of government appointees was now taken seriously; qualifications scrutinised carefully; and, where necessary, appointments refused. He cited the recent example of the Defence minister, who had faced tough questioning before receiving confirmation.

In reply to questions, Primakov emphasised that the Defence budget would be discussed in great detail. There would be no 'sacred cows'. When asked to provide an example, he replied, 'the Navy'. He stressed, however, that such supervision of the military must not undermine the country's defence capabilities. Furthermore, the rate of change would have to depend on world disarmament. But new weapons systems should not replace those being reduced, he reminded us.

To illustrate the new transparency and accountability, Primakov cited the invasion of Afghanistan in 1979. That had been decided behind closed doors: few people had been informed. That would be impossible in today's environment. The Supreme Soviet intended to play a role in arms control, and would be sending a delegation to START negotiations in Geneva in order to monitor progress. The televising of their debates had provoked great interest, he disclosed, so much so that coverage had been switched to the evenings because daytime coverage had seriously affected production.

That meeting was followed by one with the Chairman of the Council of Ministers, Prime Minister Nikolai Ryzhkov. He discussed candidly the economic challenges to Perestroika. Admitting that rejuvenation of the Soviet economy had fallen short of expectations, he explained that 'new principles' had been introduced during 1986/87. It was now recognised that the fundamental issue was the role of the market, along with its regulation. He and his colleagues did not believe in the free market concepts of the nineteenth century. Yet, they asked themselves, by what means should the market be regulated? Any transitional stage, he believed, would have to combine market forces and 'elements of the command style'.

Ryzhkov raised the potential of joint ventures, and claimed that 500 had been created in two years. The main obstacle was rouble convertibility. They hoped to tackle it by 1995, depending on the state of the economy. Price reform, he conceded, was an essential prerequisite. As always, the questions were where and at what time. They were only too well aware of the potential social consequences. Social tension had already caused some postponement. He begged leave to refer questions concerning the Defence budget to our next appointment at the Defence Ministry (Appendix 1).

The paramount goal was an improvement in the general standard of living. There were 'too many distortions and disproportions in production; structural changes were urgently needed.' A major problem was food production. Up to one third of all crops were lost 'on the way', he admitted. He was more optimistic about the production of consumer goods. Although that depended on a speedy conversion of military industries to civilian use. However, it would take longer for certain consumer goods, like cars, to be available in sufficient quantity.

On Wednesday morning we presented ourselves at the new and resplendent Defence Ministry for our meeting with Defence Minister Yazov, whom we had already met. He was later one of the ill-fated coup leaders. He introduced us to General Lizichev, chief of the Political Directorate of the General Staff, General Kochetov, first Deputy Minister, Colonel General Omelichev, first Deputy chief of Staff, Admiral Tolupov, a ministerial aide, and Colonel General Nikolai F. Chernov, Chief of the Arms Control directorate of the General Staff. General Yazov made early reference to the adoption of the defensive doctrine by the WTO in May 1987. This constituted an official guideline for their armed forces. Its underlying principle was that no state should threaten another, and that all issues should be resolved through political dialogue.

He described the unilateral reductions now underway and the restructuring of the remaining units. He offered, as an example, the changes in armoured divisions so as to give tanks a more defensive character. He indicated how forces used in attack operations, such as air and assault troops, were being withdrawn. That this was being done unilaterally, however, did not rule out a readiness to talk and undertake further reductions.[300] On the question of short-range nuclear forces, he was surprised that NATO was modernising the Lance system to bring its range up to 500km whilst the Soviet Union had taken steps to destroy the OKRA missile, with a range just below 500km. Yazov rejected with feeling the Western belief that the Soviet Union had too many arms, and consequently must be dealt with from a position of strength. In his view each side had its strengths and weaknesses. He quoted, as an example, the US Marine corps with 220,000 men as against an equivalent Soviet force of 60,000. When all forces from both states were counted, he insisted that a situation of rough parity existed.[301]

Yazov expressed the belief that visits such as ours demonstrated a new openness on the part of the Soviet Union. This could be the foundation for trust and confidence. In the light of an intervention by one of our delegates that NATO's INF did not threaten the

---

300   Defence Minister Yazov referred to Soviet willingness to discuss the elimination of chemical weapons; to ban nuclear weapons tests (provided all nuclear powers agree); and to proceed to a START agreement within the existing framework. He reiterated Soviet opposition to a militarisation of space and said that if the US did not deploy anti-satellite weapons (ASAT), the USSR was prepared to eliminate them also, along with the tracking stations.

301   Concerning the force levels on both sides, Yazov set out WTO assessments of 2,250,000 for themselves as against 2,650,000 for NATO; 7,242 aircraft as against 5,103 for NATO (but stressed NATO's superiority in strike aircraft) and 3,147 helicopters as against 4,300 for NATO.

Soviet Union, he asked why then did we need these weapons.[302] He echoed the opinion of Arbatov that one should not count on nuclear weapons to keep the peace. The use of battlefield nuclear weapons, in his view, would lead to an escalation. However, if NATO wanted to keep their nuclear weapons, 'it is for you to decide'. But he warned against the menace of nuclear proliferation. Whatever the arms, he said, 'the fewer the stronger our chances for security', indicating the sizable reduction in Soviet Union hardware.

When pressed on the new role of the Supreme Soviet, he confirmed that his future Defence budget would be discussed and adopted by that body. Asked about conscription, he replied that considerable sections of the Soviet armed forces were already semi-professionals. For example, all pilots and submariners were professionals. Conscripts were mainly used where high skills were not called for. Surprisingly, the issue of aircraft carriers was brought up once again by the generals. It was clear that they had not accepted our earlier corrections of their figures and were prepared for confrontation. Angry words were directed at the ever-gentle and courteous US Senator William Roth (Delaware), until suddenly, one general rushed to the Minister and slammed down a note in front of him. I thought it prudent then to propose thanks to the Minister, and suggest that we adjourn for lunch.

In the afternoon, we had a meeting with Deputy Foreign Minister Vladimir Petrovsky in the Foreign Ministry. The Minister explained the key elements of *New Thinking in Foreign Policy*. 'It was based,' he explained, 'on comprehensive security,' and the goal was 'to restructure

---

302   Asked what elements of NATO's capabilities the Soviet Union found most threatening, Yazov mentioned first of all NATO's thirty aircraft carriers – the US twenty, UK five and France five. Following strong protestations from our members about the accuracy of those numbers, he admitted that they could be in error. Second, he returned to the offensive nature of the US marine corps. Finally he referred to the upgrading of NATO's Clear, Thule and Fylingdales Moor early warning systems, and tried to equate it with their new system at Krasnyorsk, which actually was in violation of the Anti-Ballistic Missile (ABM) treaty.

and humanise international relations.' He reviewed the various areas we had already discussed with Supreme Soviet Deputies, concluding that 'Congress had settled the principles that will serve as a guideline for Foreign policy.' The goal, he announced, was the elimination of all nuclear weapons, reasonable arms sufficiency for defence, non-use of force and the solution of problems through political means. As for the recurring issue of the 'Common European Home', Petrovsky allowed that 'the United States and Canada can have good apartments, and this was in our interest.' The all-European House should be a united space with the same legal standards for all. Indeed, the standards in the European process need to be of the highest, he pointed out, and would be applied in our political reform. 'We take them as guidelines,' he declared.

The newly elected Supreme Soviet illustrated how deep Glasnost and openness in government had gone, he added. The elections had demonstrated support from the bottom, whilst the opposition had become weaker and was more transparent. Pessimism was prevalent, of course, so the issue was one of 'optimism of the will versus pessimism of the mind.' Finally, he stated that the USSR was ready to mediate on the situation of the Turkish Muslim minority in Bulgaria, recognised that the humanitarian aspect of the Conference on Security and Co-operation in Europe will be 'one of the most important things for us', asserted that all military supplies should be cut off to Latin America, and assured us that the dialogue with Japan would include political, geographical, legal and historical dimensions at the level of deputy Foreign ministers.

On Thursday, the delegation flew to Leningrad, now St Petersburg, where we were received most warmly by Mr Vladimir Khodirev, Chairman of the city Soviet, and his colleagues. I laid a wreath in the Piskryovskoye Memorial Centre where the famine victims of the city's wartime siege are buried. Then we had a fascinating meeting with naval officials at the Grechka Academy. The commandant stated that this was the first ever visit by such a group. The Academy was the equivalent of a Western senior staff college and catered for middle to senior officers, he explained. All commanders in the Soviet Fleet graduated from this Academy. The Commandant stressed the effects of Perestroika on the armed forces. The new defensive doctrine, for example, required a revision in the approach to education and training. All military problems had to be solved within its framework.[303] He contrasted the new doctrine with the continuing offensive maritime strategy in the US. Whereas the Academy implemented the policy laid down by the political leadership of the Soviet Union. The official programme then came to an end.

It had been an amazing experience for the members of the delegation. Quite without precedent on either side, of course. We judged it a success, not least because of the warmth of our reception – the clash in the Defence ministry apart – and the candour under relentless questioning of our hosts everywhere, In letters of thanks I expressed the gratitude of the entire delegation for the opportunity to visit at such a time of change. The exchange had been most useful, I said, and my colleagues would be seeking ways to carry forward this unique dialogue. They had been struck by the zealousness and the confidence of the newly-elected Supreme Soviet deputies.

On the other hand, we wondered privately how far they would be able to exercise their new powers of scrutiny and oversight, especially on defence matters and, in particular, nuclear negotiations. We were intrigued by the dual role of General Lobov as WTO military commander and also a Supreme Soviet deputy. Georgi Arbatov caught the eye, as did Yevgeny Primakov. As for the purported new economic model, we wondered how far the new deputies could reconcile the market economy with Marxism–Leninism. How

---

303   Asked to provide specific examples where training courses had actually changed as a result of this new doctrine, the Admiral was unable to go beyond the use of a general analogy. It was that of two boxers where one had the declared intention of not throwing the first punch; after being knocked down he must therefore get up and start fighting.

far could they engage in price reforms and rouble convertibility, for example, without at least questioning the exclusive claims of that ideology? Would reforms prove acceptable to all members of the Politburo, such as the KGB? Still shadowy, we thought it was continuing to fill a key role, though I was unable to elicit any detailed information, despite much questioning. Could Mr Gorbachev keep this last great land empire together, we asked ourselves? Could he preserve the unity of the USSR with its many different republics? Or would the Baltic or the Muslim republics push down the road to secession? Most important, could Gorbachev change the Communist party where it had seemed to us there was still a strong residual loyalty to Stalin? Could he keep the support of the Army? Indeed, could he survive?

It seemed to us that Mr Gorbachev's biggest weakness was that there was not the slightest chance that he could restore prosperity overnight. Apart from the magic of Red Square, my deepest impression of the visit to Moscow was of the deprivation, the long queues, the empty shops and the reality all too often of no meat, no sugar, no tea, no coffee and, possibly, no soap. Senator William Roth told me Moscow was the first city he had visited where he found himself looking for a McDonalds.

We came to realise that the bright façade of a homogenous and progressive society had also hidden a multitude of social as well as political and economic problems. They could not even begin to be addressed, because they could not be acknowledged. They covered corruption, crime and family breakdown. Time, we agreed, may turn out to be Gorbachev's greatest need. What could any of us do to help him? I took early steps to help him in my own city of Sheffield.

Prime Minister Ryzhkov had stressed to me the potential of joint ventures, for he was anxious to acquire western-type entrepreneurial and management skills. I brought this to the notice of the city council and the Sheffield Development Corporation (Appendix 2). The response was positive and helpful, and I reported it to Prime Minister Thatcher.

Then there was the possibility of help at Westminster on the parliamentary front, which had become the preoccupation of some members of the delegation. Chairman Primakov had told me that he intended that the new Supreme Soviet would be effective and 'not a rubber stamp Assembly'. Thus, I raised with Mr Speaker in the House of Commons the possibility of developing a practical relationship with the Supreme Soviet. Finally, I wondered personally, if it might yet be the spiritual mettle of the ordinary people of Mother Russia and the resurgent Christianity that I glimpsed during my visit to the famous Sogarsky monastery,[304] rather than Glasnost or Perestroika that would eventually prevail within its borders.

Such spiritual musings on the completion of my mission to Moscow was almost a preliminary for my next mission – to Rome. For I received an unexpected call from the Vatican. Before departing for Rome in October for the thirty-fifth annual session of the Assembly, I had attended the first day of the Labour party annual conference in Brighton. Whilst sitting alongside Jim Callaghan and Roy Mason, I was summoned urgently in the late afternoon to take a message outside. Then I learned of special arrangements in hand to whisk me to Heathrow to catch an evening Italia flight to Rome. Only then did I learn that the Holy Father, John Paul, wished to see me the next day before he had to leave for South Korea. Jim Callaghan, though a former prime minister, was so impressed that he broadcast the news that 'Pat Duffy has been called to Rome to see the Pope', of which I was favourably reminded long afterwards.

I presented myself at the Vatican the next morning, accompanied by Peter Corterier and the Italian Prime Minister. John Paul only wished to speak to me, however, and not in audience but at his desk

---

304   The monastery was so thronged with pilgrims – mostly women – that very long queues were formed for personal dedication with a lighted candle before the shrine to the Virgin Mary. On being invited to sign the visitor's book, I noted that I had been assigned a special page which contained two other signatures – those of President Jimmy Carter and Prime Minister Margaret Thatcher.

in his small private study. It quickly became evident that it was not a courtesy visit. In fact it turned out to be an occasion for a hard-hitting exchange of views around his desk that neither of us were able to bridge. In uncompromising style, the Pope condemned current spending on arms. He described it as wanton and wasteful of scarce resources, much of which should be going to the Third World. 'We must get rid of these military blocs', he added, which put me firmly on the defensive, of course. Finally, he pointed out that the Cold War was over, and that it was no longer the duty of either the Western Alliance or the Soviet bloc to maintain the status quo. 'They must both change,' he said, adding 'such stuttering and reluctance'. When was NATO going to undertake changes that would bring order, stability and hope to a new Europe, he demanded?

My pleas of progress through lowered East–West tensions and more harmonious relationships, to which I was currently witness and even participatory, and which promised further reduced military resource allocations, I explained, he brushed aside. 'Too slow, too little, typical of power blocs,' he said. Soothingly, I tried to establish some progress by playing the 'Polish card', referring to my own recent visit and the success of the Solidarity movement. He saw it coming and deftly shunted it to one side. He was clearly not to be reconciled with any measure or level of military spending, whatever my protestations. He rubbed it in by calling after me as I was leaving, 'Don't forget the Third world, Mr Duffy. Don't forget the Third World.' In a personal aside he had already asked where I came from. When I replied Yorkshire, he said he knew that, but what about my family? When I replied 'the West of Ireland – Co. Mayo', he said, 'I thought so.' Like some of my schoolteachers, the Holy Father was probing my Irishness rather than my Englishness.[305]

People all over the world were puzzled by the extraordinary response to the death of John Paul. 'We shall not see his like again' was one tribute paid to 'a titan of the twentieth century'.[306] 'His careful, pivotal intervention in Eastern Europe proved to many,' it went on, 'that moral and spiritual forms of power can win out against political tyranny.' He certainly left me with the impression that it would be extremely difficult to match in leadership anywhere his moral, physical and intellectual strength.

A highlight of the annual conference of the NATO Assembly that started later in the week was the joint appearance of the WTO's General Vladimir Lobov and NATO's General John Galvin. It was the first time a Soviet military commander had addressed a formal NATO gathering of this type, and the first time the two military leaders had come together in this fashion. Socially it was a success. But militarily it was disturbing. Their positions were still too far apart, recalling the fears of John Paul. On the other hand, General Lobov

---

305   However much we had clashed, I consoled myself afterwards that at least the Pope had got my name right, unlike others. On a ministerial visit to San Diego in the mid-Seventies, the Admiral commanding locally arranged for me to attend Mass on Sunday in the lovely small church of St Agnes down by the harbour. In his formal welcome from the altar, the priest referred to me as Patrick Murphy. He was inconsolable over breakfast afterwards, despite my well meant assurance that the name of Murphy was most welcome to me. After all, I had a dearly-loved first cousin in Co. Mayo called John P. Murphy. Remarkably, the same confusion of name arose on another formal visit in the mid-Eighties. I was leading a NATO Assembly delegation to Naples, where I was welcomed officially by Admiral William Crowe (later US Ambassador in London), Commander-in-Chief of Allied forces, Southern Europe. He also referred to me as Patrick Murphy, and persisted in doing so throughout the ceremony and subsequent proceedings. He was rather put out afterwards because I had made no attempt to correct him, whilst it gave rise to growing amusement, especially on the part of his wife.

306   *The Economist.* 9 April 2005.

eventually discarded his written text and described how Perestroika was improving social conditions. 'We need that the resources we are now applying for our military forces should be used for the interest of people's lives', he said. Both the structure and the doctrine of the Soviet armed forces were also changing – not just in words, but actions as well. The unilateral reductions – 50% of which had been completed, he insisted, including the removal of three tank divisions from East European territory – constituted the most visible indicator of the change in doctrine. He was often asked, however, by his electorate what reciprocal actions NATO was carrying out, and pointed out that, 'We are expecting something from you.'

General Galvin welcomed the promising developments that had occurred since he addressed us the previous year. Nevertheless, despite Soviet statements of intent, he had seen 'little decrease yet in the level of combat power available to the East.' Although the unilateral withdrawals were proceeding, the parallel reorganisation of Soviet divisions had resulted in the retention in Eastern Europe of some of the capabilities of 'withdrawn' units. Soviet military output remained unnecessarily high. He was optimistic, however, about the ongoing Conventional Forces in Europe negotiations. But the most important thing was to remove the Soviet 'blitz' capability in all its manifestations.

In the question and answer period, General Lobov insisted that the new defensive doctrine was being implemented already in military exercises and training. But General Galvin was cautious about the definition of 'defensive'. The burden of proof lay ultimately with the Soviet Union, he declared. General Lobov reminded us of the ever-changing technology, and its impact on modernisation. He was confident, however, that changing force levels could still be confined to defensive purposes and brought under parliamentary control. Both men agreed that that particular exchange illustrated the need for much more dialogue to help reduce misunderstanding in a time of rapid change. They both commented finally on the formidable logistical challenges confronting their respective armed forces in an era of diminishing East–West tensions, arising from decreasing resource allocations, changing professional roles and responsibilities and their affect on personnel.

The historic meeting in Rome of the NATO and WTO military commanders was just one of the monumental and fast-moving political changes taking place during 1989. By the autumn the political landscape of Europe was undergoing a transformation of seismic proportions as a result of developments in Eastern and Central Europe and the Soviet Union. The Warsaw pact grouping literally disintegrated as an effective military entity. The Berlin Wall was swept away in a peaceful populist revolt. Germany would soon attain unity and secure the right to remain in NATO with the blessing of the Soviet Union. For the first time in history, all the twenty-two member nations of NATO and the Warsaw Pact were committed to reduce their conventional armouries on a basis of East-West parity following the signing of the Conventional Forces in Europe Treaty.

At the end of October, I hosted in Bonn the first East-West parliamentary Round Table. In Brussels in February 1990 I presided over the first meeting between NATO and the WTO at military as well as parliamentary level.

We were anxious throughout 1990 to take full advantage of this new era of institution-building, and proceed as best as possible towards closer ties. We extended warm invitations therefore to members of the old WTO to attend our annual conference in London in November. They were quickly accepted by Bulgaria, Czechoslovakia, Hungary, Poland and the Soviet Union, whilst ultimately the German delegation represented the East and the West for the first time.

I felt obliged to include Ireland along with those countries I wished to invite, though they were not members of NATO. Accordingly, I invited the House of the Oireachtas to attend. In a courteous reply, Mr Sean Tracey, TD., said the executive of the Irish Parliamentary

Association had considered the invitation, but 'it will not be possible to accept.'

Conscious that a new era of cooperation was now upon us, we viewed our annual conference in November 1990 as the most momentous in the history of the NATO Assembly. It was held in London, and the opening ceremony took place in the unique surroundings of Westminster Hall. 'This great hall of Westminster is nearly a thousand years old,' I declared in my opening address. 'All that time it has been a focus of our national life. Within its walls, and under its hammer beams, it enshrines the whole history of Britain. In 1941 these same beams above us were set alight by bombing. Here, in the centre, the body of Winston Churchill rested in state. We are greatly honoured to return to this magnificent hall – the cradle of parliamentary democracy – for our opening ceremony.'

For nearly three years, I claimed, we had played a 'significant role in helping to build bridges with the new democracies of Central and Eastern Europe.' Now we are being joined at our conference by parliamentary delegations from Czechoslovakia, Bulgaria, Germany, Hungary, Poland and the Soviet Union. I welcomed also as associated delegations the return of old and trusted friends in the parliamentary delegations from Australia and Japan. We have all shared the good fortune 'to witness our continent take leave of the tragic paralysis of the Cold War … remarkable for our Alliance, for all of Europe, and for the entire world.' By the early afternoon I had received by special messenger a personal note of congratulations from the US Ambassador.

I should have been followed in my address by Mrs Margaret Thatcher, but to my disappointment she was actually on her way to Buckingham Palace to tender to the Queen her resignation as Prime

Minister.[307] Senior colleagues who constituted the Assembly's Bureau also expressed acute disappointment. They asked me to convey to her 'their deep and unanimous regret that at the opening ceremony of the North Atlantic Assembly held here in our own unrivalled Westminster Hall, that everyone sensed formally marked the end of the Cold War, it was not possible for you – who had played such an historic and distinguished role – to address them. Congressman Jack Brooks from Texas, a former President, asks me to write that had you been present, he would have led a standing ovation.'

The Queen kindly consented to a reception of delegates and their consorts at Buckingham Palace, despite the huge numbers involved, several hundreds strong. It was my honour to personally introduce the heads of twenty-four national delegations to Her Majesty. The Queen complimented me afterwards on remembering every name. I dare not reveal that I had fluffed one name. She lingered to discuss the composition and variety of the many national delegations. She was clearly intrigued by the presence of one delegation and one member of another delegation.

---

307   My Russian hosts in the 1980s frequently referred to Margaret Thatcher as the 'Iron Lady'. I found her to be a complex figure. After a late-night debate on Education in the early 1970s, when she was Secretary of State, I saw her in the Members' tea-room of the House of Commons organising refreshments for her staff. She insisted on carrying two trays herself on successive journeys back to the rear of the Chamber. I never witnessed such thoughtfulness on the part of any other Minister. On the other hand, when a former Commons secretary tried to hang herself from a lamppost outside the London home of Scottish Solicitor-General, Nicholas Fairbairn in December 1981, there was a widely held expectation of early dismissal (*Daily Mirror*, 24 December 1981). His private life had become the subject of intense gossip among back-benchers, to the embarrassment of his party colleagues. I had realised, whilst Navy Minister, that he was a deeply unpleasant man. He was reported later to be as grotesque in behaviour as in appearance. Yet, Margaret kept him in office as long as possible. Why did she waver, despite pressure, when she was already exhibiting such a direct and leader-like style in the Cold War?

I was disappointed that Ireland was not among the twenty-four countries represented at such a memorable conference, but not surprised. I presumed the House of the Oireachtas decided that the time had not yet arrived for the acceptance of such an invitation. Nevertheless, I believed, with the warm support of senior colleagues within the Alliance and at Westminster, that the time had certainly arrived for the issue of NATO membership or association by Ireland to be raised. It was hardly unreal of me to do so. Nor was I setting a precedent. Two years earlier a senior member of the Irish military, Commandant Martin Lohan (Retired) had said, 'It is common sense to do so.'[308] Like myself he would know that it was now an appropriate time to discuss at least the concept of joining NATO. He was aware, as I was, that despite its commendable fulfilment of UN peacekeeping Ireland was now facing new security challenges without a defence budget to match. Ireland, no less than the UK, now had to create modern, mobile military forces. However modest, they still had to be equipped and trained to operate in any environment, and to deal with a widening range of threats. Moreover, they could not be prepared in isolation. They needed to be trained in culture cooperation and acquire the ability and equipment to engage in multi-national force projects. For the only viable project now, even in peace-keeping, was the acquisition of a modern military capability and one appropriate for operating with allies or partners or associates. But its attainment had become too expensive for any one of them – even the US – to deliver alone. Where Ireland could look for this new role, other than to this new peace-dedicated NATO, either in membership or as a partner, was self-evident.

---

308   In a letter published in the *Irish Independent* (30 March 1988), he suggested in the light of the ongoing review of the Defence forces that the question be put to the 'people in the form of a referendum. Over the years we have heard arguments why we should not join NATO: national independence, the nuclear dilemma and the division of our country were the obsessions thrown at us by our politicians. It is common sense to join NATO.'

I had been closely following press coverage of such new security developments, including a restructured NATO, quite apart from my own private briefings. Editorials had appeared in *The Irish Times* concerning Ireland's future security relationships, prompted perhaps by the visit of the Taoiseach, Charles Haughey, to Washington. I thought the opportunity at least, to stir comment in its correspondence columns had arrived. I was also prompted by a certain underlying reality. For I knew, as very, very few were aware at the time in either Dublin or London, of their changed relationship: that should a like emergency to the events of June 1940, have occurred during the Cold War, there would have been a better response in both cities. So NATO involvement had not been entirely out of the question for Ireland for some time.

Accordingly, I dispatched a letter to Conor Brady, editor of *The Irish Times*, dated 8 March 1990. In the light of recent attention to security structures 'and given that Ireland holds the presidency of the European Community – which is increasingly taking on more political functions vis-a-vis Eastern Europe – has not the time arrived to open up a debate in Ireland about the desirability of Ireland joining a more politicised NATO entity?' I asked. There was no reply. I had kindled no interest in the new NATO on the part of Pope John Paul either. But there had been an honest exchange of views during which we had both valiantly stood our corners. For all his rough handling of me, there was no want of courtesy either. Would I get no response from *The Irish Times*, I wondered after a while. My letter did eventually appear. But only after I had reminded the Editor several weeks later. It had clearly evoked no interest. Nor did any published evidence of concern appear in the paper's correspondence columns, which really did surprise me.

I had witnessed our continent take leave of the tragic paralysis of the Cold War. The geopolitical and military changes in Eastern Europe had opened the way to broader assessments of security. NATO's essential task, like Ireland's had been in keeping the peace:

collectively with colleagues, exercising nuclear deterrence, but always seeking dialogue. Now the challenge was to build peace from San Francisco to Dublin and on to Vladivostock without nuclear confrontation. It appeared inconceivable to some that Ireland could remain detached from such a process. Especially after NATO affirmed its intention in June 1990, to be 'the keystone of efforts to build a new European order of peace.' Any more than Ireland could have escaped conflict – geographically – in the event of the breakdown of peace during the Cold War.

Much discussion had taken place at the first East–West parliamentary Round Table in Bonn the previous October on how far NATO could proceed towards closer ties with Eastern Europe, given the constraints of the Washington Treaty. The need for relaxation in the maritime sphere had been evident since the mid–Seventies when I was Navy Minister. But references to maritime strategy were almost absent in NATO policy documents at that time, other than by the occasional mention of the growing Soviet threat. The continental role was always favoured over the maritime, in my experience. Yet the Cold War had intensified and the Soviets now had twice the number of warships at sea as NATO, from the Atlantic to the Pacific. Soviet submarines had grown into the largest such force in the world, and had become deeper and quieter. Detecting and tracking them could no longer be confined to the Atlantic Ocean.

It had become a global problem and needed to be addressed in the broader context of Alliance strategic policy. That was the abiding concern of Admiral Ike Kidd, in the regular briefings I received from him in Norfolk, Virginia. He firmly believed that effective deterrence required not only a Fleet able to act as a conventional deterrent to the Soviet Fleet. It now called for a maritime capability to convoy raw material and oil from the rest of the world, particularly from the Gulf and around southern Africa. That raised the out-of–area issue, however, and how far such an extended capability would be in breach of NATO's framework. If NATO was to face up to its strategic responsibilities, he insisted, it now needed a naval capability directed towards the Indian and Pacific Oceans, and geared operationally with the Anzus Pact nations, Australia, New Zealand and the US.

Such a contingency received special attention in the deliberations of the Admiralty Board when I chaired its proceedings. My second Sea Lord, Admiral Sir Gordon Tait, was a New Zealander, who returned home on retirement. After joining the NATO Assembly I constantly stressed the importance of consultations, cooperation and naval manoeuvres outside the Treaty area. By the mid-Eighties, happily, Australian and Japanese parliamentarians were accorded observer status at the formal gatherings of the NATO Assembly. A similar interest was soon demonstrated by some of their neighbours. By the late Eighties I was attending the Pacific Caucus, which brought together annually parliamentary representatives of the Western Alliance – Australia, New Zealand, Japan, South Korea, Taiwan, the Phillipines, and a growing number of the Pacific rim nations. As a result, the NATO Assembly became better apprised of Soviet and China force levels in South-East Asia and the implications for security in the Pacific theatre.

The first Gulf crisis was a further reminder that NATO stood at a critical juncture in maritime affairs. As its Assembly President I questioned whether the Alliance should not now move beyond merely consulting on out-of area matters. There was no longer a role for an inward looking NATO, I pointed out; an out-of-area commitment was one nettle that had to be grasped. I made such a declaration in August 1990, while leading a delegation to Turkey. In association with Senator Bill Roth of the US and the former Turkish Defence Minister, Seki Yavuzturk, my two vice-presidents, I called for the amendment of the Washington Treaty 'in order that NATO take on a broadened role, deterring conflict not only in Europe, but wherever else conflict may threaten the security of Alliance members.'

Earlier in the year, I had received an invitation from the Hon Leo McLeahy, Speaker of the House of Representatives and the Hon

Kerry W. Sibraa, President of the Senate, to visit Australia as guests of the Parliament of Australia. They believed that my visit of 16–23 September 1990 'will enhance the close relationship which has been built up between the North Atlantic Assembly and the Australian Parliament, and comes at a time of enormous economic and political change in Europe.' It was a timely invitation, which I gladly accepted. I was accompanied by David Hobbs, Senior Director of the Assembly. We were honoured to find awaiting us the most comprehensive and meaningful programme.

It provided for discussions with the Maritime Commander in Sydney; a visit to Williamstown Airport for briefings and a tour of no. 77 squadron; calls on the Secretary of the Department of Defence and the Chief of the Defence Force in Canberra; and discussions with the Chiefs of Staff committee. I missed the newly-elected Prime Minister Paul Keating, who was engaged in Olympic Games talks in Tokyo. I had very useful meetings in Parliament House, however, with the Minister of Defence, the Leader of the Opposition and with various shadow Ministers. I was received most warmly by the Speaker of the House of Representatives, Leo McLeahy, as I was later in the week in Sydney by the Presiding Officers of the New South Wales Parliament.

I had been well briefed in Brussels before departure. My mission was simply to look and listen, of course, and report back accordingly. Yet the depth of discussion that I encountered on all sides, along with the exposure to weapon systems and their manning skills had quickly suggested an incipient relationship entirely suited to the more intensive consultation, exchange of information and harmonisation of policy of an extended NATO framework. The service spirit and political resolve firmly displayed throughout – and clearly reflected already in Australia's naval deployments to the Gulf – compared more than favourably with the hesitant response of some NATO members during the INF crisis in Western Europe in the early Eighties. Australian ships, incidentally, were the first non-American forces to fire warning shots in the enforcement of the naval blockade.

Another major topic which emerged during my meetings was the coordination of arms exports. It was repeatedly pointed out that companies from NATO nations were attempting to sell highly sophisticated defence equipment to nations in the Pacific region and such sales would inevitably have an effect on Australia's security interests.

Concern was also expressed about the future balance of power in the Pacific. Essentially, it was pointed out that a reduced American presence resulting, for instance, from the closure of bases in the Philippines, would create a 'power vacuum' which might be filled by certain specified nations. Precise predictions were not possible but it was clear that there could in the long-term be major changes in the Pacific/Indian Ocean strategic equation that NATO could not ignore. An associated matter raised was the creation of a Conference on Security and Cooperation in Asia along the lines of the Conference on Security and Cooperation in Europe. It was felt that this subject could be very usefully discussed by Atlantic and Pacific policy makers.

Other items raised included pending negotiations concerning the status of Antarctica, the need of the West to attempt to gain a deeper understanding of the Islamic nations and the problems of resolving sea boundary disputes. They illustrated yet again Australia's unique position brought about by its history and geography which have combined to form a political 'bridge' between the Atlantic and Pacific communities of nations and cultures. It clearly indicated, I was reminded again and again, that the NATO nations and Australia have an enormous array of convergent interests and goals.

During visits to air force and naval bases, I received briefings on the ways in which Australia's armed forces and military posture must take account of the country's geography. The nation's sheer size – approximately the same area as the United States – and distance from many of its principle armaments suppliers pose formidable problems for operating and maintaining the weapons inventory. Considerable importance was clearly attached by Australia to opportunities to operate and train alongside Western forces and to exchange personnel. Naturally, there was considerable interest in recent developments in the Soviet Union and Eastern Europe and in the ways that the NATO Assembly was already evolving in this new strategic environment. I described how the Assembly's relationships with Warsaw Treaty Organisation countries were developing following the first contacts with Hungary and then expanding into contacts and dialogue with other Warsaw Treaty Organisation countries.

I had been well prepared for the sight of Sydney's legendary Opera House, its instantly recognisable Harbour Bridge and the harbour itself. And if Canberra was the focus of my visit, I was not unaware of its vast hinterland, unique terrain and challenging climate. Nor was I unaware of the magnificent achievements of successive generations of Australians in transforming such a varied landscape and its people into a very successful country, predicted since to 'become a model nation' – after California – 'The Golden State'. I was certainly aware of the role of the Irish, but not prepared for the strong lingering sense of Irish heritage that I encountered on the part of so many even during a brief stay. I was accustomed to its gathering strength in England and long familiar with its presence in the US. But in neither country did it strike me that it was as far-reaching and embedded in its influence as in Australia or was being handled with the same pride, comfort and confidence.

The Irish influence in the higher reaches of politics and society was exemplified for me by Leo McLeahy, parliamentary Speaker in Canberra, and Kevin Rozzoli, Speaker in the Legislative Assembly in Sydney. The personal warmth of their reception of me on many occasions remained memorable. When seated in the public gallery of the House of Representatives during Question Time awaiting a public introduction by Mr Speaker Leahy, I noticed that the Attorney-General, who was seated on the Front Bench, was Michael Duffy. Just one of many reminders that if the Irish in Britain have made an impact in religion, in literature, in music and dance, they are only now becoming prominent in industry and have yet to fully express themselves in politics. Whereas the Irish in Australia have distinguished themselves in all areas. When I conceded as much to Leo McLeahy, he was quite quick to remind me, 'Yes, and you are not descended from convicts like us.'

Saturday morning was free for me to reflect and pursue individual interests, prior to departure. I had satisfied one immediately on arrival at Sydney Airport early on the Sunday morning when I asked for directions to Australia's oldest Catholic church, St Patrick's on Grosvenor Street, to attend Mass – if that wasn't too singular a request, I asked. Not at all, was the reaction of the escort officer who met me, introducing herself as Ms Siobhán Ni Fhaoláin, originally from Co. Cork.

My programme provided for another special interest when I visited the national War Memorial and laid a wreath. It was a ceremony that I had performed in many cities during my ministerial days, and in Moscow, Leningrad and Warsaw only the year before. None left me so deeply moved as that occasion in Canberra, and the sight of the preserved Avro Lancaster bomber aircraft. It was so evocative of my wartime awareness of the many courageous Australian servicemen who flew with such distinction in those aircraft from airfields in Yorkshire and Lincolnshire quite close to my home. My father would later describe the gathering and ever-ascending circling of the bomb-laden Lancasters in the evening sky over Doncaster, a favoured assembly point, as they sought formation prior to departure on night raids. Now I was anxious to renew another similar personal war memory and visit the harbour in Sydney where a former ship, *HMS Formidable*, had berthed during assignment to the British Pacific Fleet. I wished to pay tribute to casualties among my former ship mates during operations, including my replacement.

My next call was to St Andrew's Cathedral, which I found closed. St Mary's Cathedral, where I had hoped to attend Mass, was open but seemingly full of ladies preparing for a major flower festival and obliged therefore to refer me to the 'No Visitors' notice. My final visit did bring fulfilment, however. It was essentially romantic: to the railway station to witness the departure just after 1pm of the world-renowned Sydney-to-Perth transcontinental train. I felt enormously privileged as I completed my morning walk around the central area of such an interesting and beautiful city.

I noted sadly two years afterwards the reports in a leading Sydney newspaper, the Telegraph-Mirror, on 12 December 1992, of a venomous attack on the Irish by its London-based columnist Bruce Wilson. So they are at it down there as well, I mused. Like Sir John Junor, former editor of the *Sunday Express*, with whom I had personally raised his appalling racist slurs, Wilson even claimed to enjoy Irish holidays. Yet his portrayal of Ireland bore no resemblance to a country already promising at that time high global economic growth and a higher standard of living than the UK. A similar unrecognisable Irish feature by Bruce Anderson appeared in London's *Daily Mail* in November 1996. Intriguingly, it took the same slant as the feature by Wilson, even to the choice of phrasing. Both were of a piece, in my view, with the earlier demonisation of the Irish in Britain. Why journalists like Wilson and Anderson were persisting in that early anti-Irish invective was puzzling, given the peace process in Northern Ireland. At a time, moreover, when Ireland and Britain were becoming increasingly entwined economically, culturally, socially and politically. The Irish in Britain had demonstrated that the most effective counters to such grotesque attacks were their own impressive creativity, achievements and appealing lifestyle, which were ever more-widely appreciated. The same values, if expressed otherwise, had contributed to NATO's success in bringing the Cold War to a peaceful close.

Appendix 1

When pressed, Prime Minister Ryzhkov did reveal that military expenditure amounted to 77.3 billion roubles. He broke this down to 32.6 billion for the purchase/procurement of hardware, 15 billion for the upkeep of the armed services, and 4.5 billion for military construction, with 2.23 billion, finally, for pensions. The relative share of the national income as distinguished from gross national product, for military spending, was 12.8%, whilst the comparable figure for the US, he conceded was 7.8%. The goal, he insisted, was to reduce the Soviet figure by 1995 to 6.2%. More had had to be spent, he explained, in order to maintain parity with the US. But substantial reductions were now being sought, and he was confident of their achievement if arms control talks were successful. The conversion from military to civilian use programmes were most important. Some industries currently were at sixty per cent military to forty per cent civilian production. The goal was to reverse this ratio by 1995 and, hopefully, attain an equal ratio as early as 1991. He offered as an example, however unbelievably, the case of a factory in which spaghetti was now being produced alongside aircraft.

Appendix 2

I wrote letters (27 November 1989) to Councillor Clive Betts, Leader of Sheffield's Labour group, and Sir Hugh Sykes, Chairman of the Sheffield Development Corporation (SDC) describing the wider interest in joint ventures that I had encountered in Eastern Europe and in the Soviet Union. Poland's Prime Minister Rakowski had stressed their importance to me in the spring, as did Trade Minister Jiri Nemec in Czechoslovakia. To each of them I presented brochures detailing Sheffield's vision: the strategy of the City Council, its current links with the Chamber of Commerce, and the role of the SDC. I related how I had explained to the Soviet Prime Minister Ryzgkov, the current programmes of restructuring and regeneration in Sheffield and the challenge it was presenting to the Sheffield Partnership. I hoped therefore the Labour group would consider how far Sheffield could be of assistance. I asked if the SDC was in a position to promote some form of economic partnership with Eastern Europe. Would it be possible to promote a pilot scheme in Sheffield with the view to a cultivation of such joint ventures further afield within the Yorkshire regional economy and the national economy?

Chapter Twenty
Reflections

The earliest memoirs I have come across in this genre take me back to the 1940s and the 1950s. I retain much earlier memories of childhood in the Lancashire and Yorkshire coalfields. An early taste of industrial warfare during the General Strike of 1926 and personal experience in WWII set one foot on a political path that eventually led to the House of Commons. The other foot stayed rooted in academe, for I had been enormously stimulated following WWII by vintage-year fellow students at the LSE and Columbia University, New York.

I have tried to confine my narrative to actual presence, involvement and primary sources, and concern myself with facts rather than myths. I have recalled and reviewed certain events, not as a historian but as someone who was there. A persistent question, as with many second-generation Irish, has been identity. Am I British or Irish? It was an ever-changing question, for I moved from an early awareness of my Irishness to an actual connection as I made my first visit to Ireland, before becoming involved politically and acquiring some understanding after arriving at Westminster. Mam and Dad never shared that anxiety. Whenever they dwelt on the relationship between Britain and Ireland they were guided simply by their sense of obligation and duty to Britain. President Rwame Nkruma of Ghana viewed identity differently. His US Ambassador, Judge Bill Mahoney, told me of his leave-taking of the president prior to going on vacation. He explained apologetically that his immediate destination would not be to Washington or his home in Phoenix, Arizona, but to Dublin. 'I understand,' said Nkruma, 'You must first of all visit your tribe.' However, Mam and Dad's abiding concern was that Irish men and women should retain their traditional values and conduct themselves decently at all times.

I have met people like them all around the world whilst engaged on ministerial and NATO Assembly business. No matter how prolonged the separation, they still felt a profound sense of connection and inclusivity with Ireland. When I entered Parliament I received letters of congratulations from Irish people in the UK, the US, Canada and Australia, as well as from nuns and priests serving the African missions. I started to wonder then how much the widespread Irish were valued by the Dublin establishment. I wondered whether the hard-earned remittances sent home by my father and grandfather and many others a century earlier were any longer remembered, and was grateful for the reminders of President Mary Robinson. During my early years at Westminster I was warned by Brendan McLua that 'successive Irish governments viewed the Irish in Britain through dark glasses and often with suspicion.' He believed that those, such as myself, who had had their Irishness thrust upon them, though responding dutifully in search of improved relationships on all sides – despite occasional discrimination and even violent threats – were especially at risk. Such discrimination presented an early personal challenge, notably at the constituency selection stage.

As a Member of Parliament, I was involved essentially in the communication and exchange of ideas, opinions and information. Naturally, mine were probed when I was being considered for selection, especially my views on cultural and ethical issues as well as political and social problems.

I never shirked the moral and ethical questions that were raised, as I made clear when selected in Attercliffe. My constituency officers appreciated my principled stand when we were seriously threatened by the Militant Tendency. They saw also how it infused my attempts at even-handedness in Northern Ireland. Conscious though I was of the plight of the Catholics burnt out and left in fear of death on occasions, I always pointed out that in an all-Ireland population of five millions, a million respectable hard-working, God-fearing folk were concentrated in the North-East. Yes, we must do our best to ease

Ireland's wrongs, I would often say, but how are we going to fairly handle the Protestants, irrespective of how they arrived?

As a further demonstration of my ecumenism, I marked the centenary of the death of Cardinal Newman in 1990 by tabling an early-day motion in Parliament recalling that 'of his ninety years, he spent forty-five an Anglican and forty-five a Catholic ... brought the two Churches closer ... and is uniquely qualified to become the first ecumenical saint.' It received significant all-party support. It attracted the attention of Lord (Frank) Longford, who had long since appealed to me because of his early work for the Workers Educational Association. Practice as well as precepts and personal example along with public exhortation, it seemed to me, strikingly marked his public life. So I felt particularly privileged to succeed him as President of Labour Life in its steadfast defence of the unborn child.

My early membership of the House of Commons enabled me to pursue some troubling questions relating to identity that had arisen during WWII. One was the foundation of the state of Northern Ireland and the fragile peace that followed. Another arose from personal experience during active service in ship and squadron in the province. A growing recognition of Britain's ultimate responsibility became a growing concern. My Britishness gradually gave way to my Irishness as I acquired a greater understanding. Both were much affected by the challenges, disappointments, encouragements and inspirations that were encountered in a deepening political involvement. Until WWII, my Irishness was no stronger than an 'Irish connection' arising from parental influence, faith and early visits to Ireland. I was firm in my Britishness and its obligations. I was very disappointed in the Irish government's declaration of neutrality on the outbreak of WWII, for example. I was wholly admiring of the Royal Navy in which I served. I remained devoted to the memory of school friends lost on active service.

Like my parents, I came to admire Britain's institutions: its parliamentary system, political parties, constitutional monarchy, commercial practice and its civil service. But I became disappointed subsequently in the judiciary, sections of the media and the handling of the Army in Northern Ireland. The disastrous involvement of the Army in certain tragic events dismayed me, and I was shocked by disclosures pointing to its collusion with the ugliest elements in Northern Ireland. Such developments stimulated my sense of Irishness and taxed my Britishness. However, my parliamentary presence introduced me later to international security during the Cold War, in which I participated at ministerial level in London and as President of the NATO Assembly in Brussels. If I had grown up Irish in Britain I was eventually exercising with pride, a British presence and authority on missions to such varied capitals as Washington, Moscow, Rome and Sydney as well as during an earlier visit to Dublin.

I remained disappointed therefore in Irish neutrality in WWII. My father believed at the outset that it would entrench partition and damage relations with Britain and the United States. It also exposed the Irish in Britain to exaggerated claims regarding the denial of Irish ports, unfounded reports of U-boat operations in Irish coastal waters and, later, an intemperate attack by Winston Churchill during his victory speech in May 1945. Why did Churchill single out Ireland for attack from among the other western neutrals? None, with honour, were as helpful to Britain throughout the war as Ireland. She shared valuable assets such as manpower and meteorological services; granted over-land access to the Atlantic by the RAF; facilitated the return of Allied airmen; and readily allowed border access to servicemen for leisure, for which my 822 squadron colleagues and I – then working up over Lough Foyle – were grateful when we travelled from Derry to Buncrana at week-ends.

Why did Churchill think the southern Irish ports would remain immune to German air attacks from France, when Portsmouth and Plymouth had become scarcely viable? As I was personally aware from operations to the seawards the port of Liverpool and the unrivalled anchorages of the Clyde further north were more realistic havens.

Whilst unreported inshore U-boat operations were highly unlikely given the presence of British Intelligence – already a prime tool – along Ireland's southern and western shores. There could hardly have been a village in those districts where the locals could not have readily identified their very own friendly British agent. Churchill was well aware of how advantageous Irish neutrality had become by the end of hostilities. I could only view his attack on the Irish in his victory broadcast as another 'rush of blood to the head', like his horrific judgment in December 1941, in deploying in the South China Sea my old ship *Repulse,* together with the *Prince of Wales,* without their aircraft carrier. That he was prone to bursts of anger was confirmed, personally, when I occupied his desk at the Admiralty. Immediately behind me was the damaged cabinet that he was known to kick on receiving bad news. I have often wondered therefore how far Eamonn De Valera was responsible for the outcome of his exchanges with Churchill in June 1940.

Informally rejecting the British offer of Irish unity in exchange for active support, de Valera had indicated concern about the 'abandonment of our neutrality' with no guarantee of a united Ireland unless 'concessions were made to Lord Craigavon', who was Prime Minister in Northern Ireland. Such a packaged offer hinging on Craigavon's conditions, given his record, simply invited question. In Belfast in 1912, Craigavon, then James Craig, had inspired with Edward Carson, the threat of a mass defiance of constitutional authority 'using all means which may be found necessary'. It led to the founding and arming a year later of the Ulster Volunteer Force. It decisively brought the gun back centre stage to Irish politics, as was freely warned at the time. It also kindled the oft-proclaimed intransigence later of 'what we have we hold'. Would Craigavon have presented the same hard-line resistance to Churchill's proposed Irish unity? It is well known that after the fall of France Craigavon strongly urged on Churchill military intervention in the south of Ireland, the occupation of certain ports and the appointment of a military governor with headquarters in Dublin. It is difficult to imagine any concessions by de Valera that would have modified such hostility.

At a time of such complexities, insecurities and uncertainties, de Valera was nevertheless authorising contingency arrangements. Was he not entitled to question further the ambiguity of Churchill's offer and a more sensitive handling of the issues involved? Instead of sending Malcolm MacDonald to Dublin as emissary with improved terms, why did Churchill not send his confidante and right-hand man, Brendan Bracken? That remarkable Irishman could conceivably have explored more feelingly the steps under consideration should Ireland become involved in conflict. De Valera had already significantly authorised secret talks between British and Irish staff officers concerning a possible German invasion of Ireland, when 'allied assistance' would be immediately sought and expected.

Nevertheless, whatever the complexities involved, should Ireland have sided with a beleaguered Britain in 1940? My father certainly thought so, whilst his brother Patrick at home in Co. Mayo, disagreed. With nearly one million first-born Irish in Britain, like myself, my father believed Ireland had a plain duty to rally in support. With two million second-generation Irish in Britain, like myself, I agreed. An increasing number of young people in Ireland clearly thought so as well. Throughout the war they travelled to Belfast to enlist, along with 5,000 members of Ireland's own Defence Forces. They had formally recognised, however varied their motives, that no two nations and no two peoples have closer ties of history, of geography and of family, if not of friendship, and one was now in mortal danger.

Many people in the South of Ireland in 1940 no doubt entertained a quite different perspective. It was only twenty years after their War of Independence and the Civil War that followed. Neutrality for them had less to do with the German threat than with the partition of their country by the British. After all, they were the same people, they recalled , who had failed to stand by agreed Home Rule in 1918 and sent over instead the terrorising Black and Tans and the auxiliaries.

Yet they had never taken on militarily or politically the unionists and the Protestants north and south, whilst never hesitating historically to take on republicans and Catholics. They would no doubt have remained mindful that the Irish still had to wait fifty years for their objective of a united Ireland to be even recognised as a legitimate political aspiration when it was codified in the Downing Street Declaration, which formed part of the bedrock on which the Good Friday Agreement was finally laid. It is difficult not to conclude that the momentous issue that arose for Dublin in June, 1940, could and should have been better handled in London.

That must have been the view of some who continued to shape Irish non-military alignment and neutrality after WWII, which confined Irish military operations overseas to United Nations mandates. Irish troops have established a proud record on such mandated missions – which are governed by a 'triple lock' mechanism in Dublin – and eighty-nine soldiers and gardai have given their lives. It is a policy that left Ireland exposed as the only militarily unattached member of the EU. Although keeping Ireland outside NATO during the Cold War, it nevertheless remained contingency-based as in June 1940. It was sharply questioned as NATO moved to the same United Nations mandated peacekeeping policy after the end of the Cold War. Was it any longer serving the best interests of Ireland's armed services, as more perilous peace-keeping called for modern communications and weapons systems not available to Ireland as well as necessary training in allied co-operation? Consequently, Ireland has gradually begun to enter into ties with NATO through the Partnership for Peace programme. Ireland should get more involved in such NATO projects to develop its defence forces, said NATO's secretary-general, Anders Fogh Rasmussen, during a visit to Dublin – the first by a NATO secretary-general – in February 2013. Shortly afterwards, it was announced that Irish and British troops would be teaming up for the first time in Mali on an EU training mission. The mission would not require Dail approval, as fewer than twelve Irish personnel would be involved. But Ireland does now appear to be edging into the military alignments that she has long avoided.

The disappointment I felt over Ireland's insistent neutrality was accompanied by disappointment in certain sections of the British media. Such as related to their treatment of the Irish in Britain, their reporting of events in Northern Ireland and my own personal experience. Their coverage in Northern Ireland was balanced, however, by the courage and objectivity of other journalists. But Cardinal Cahal Daly was eventually moved to complain that the feature-writing in some of the mass-circulation British newspapers reporting what was going on in Ireland often took on a 'nasty racial tinge'. The scurrilous cartoon of me published in the *Times* reminded me of an earlier personal encounter with the press. It arose from a complaint by a Tory MP based on a report in the *Sunday Express* of 14 February 1965. I was then MP for the Colne Valley and it was claimed that I had said some Conservative MPs were 'half-drunk'.

It was the way in which a reply to a question at a private gathering came to public light that disappointed me. For as well as the intrusion, it led to the setting up of a Committee of Privileges which exposed me to parliamentary sanctions. In reply to the Committee's questions, I explained that I made the reported remark at the annual dinner of one of my local Labour parties. I did so in reply to questions by someone present who had been seated in the Public Gallery of the House of Commons during the closing stages of a recent debate. I was not aware of the presence of a local journalist until afterwards, for he had no right to be there. When this was brought to my attention, I quickly located him in the public bar downstairs and reminded him that I had already submitted my speech to the local press and everything else therefore was private and off the record. I saw no reason , I explained to the Committee, why the remark in question should be 'reported until a reporter from the *Sunday Express* gained access to my constituency surgery in the guise of a constituent the following day.' He had no right to be there either, for one of my officers was actually checking credentials at the door, but the reporter had falsely represented himself as a constituent. He had clearly been briefed by the local reporter who had unofficially gained access the previous evening.

I agreed broadly with his report, but I pointed out to the Committee that it was 'incomplete' and not 'representative of my comments'. It had been sensationalised, of course. Given the precedents that astonishingly went back to 1701, according to its report (Session 1964–65), the Committee reported a 'breach of its privileges', but recommended 'that the House should take no further action in the matter'. Michael Foot was quick to inform me that any offence lay in the mention of the pejorative term 'drunk', instead of suggesting that some Honourable Members had only been 'half-sober'. I had made it clear in answering the Committees questions that no criticism of the Press was intended. But personally, I felt badly let down by the two journalists involved. I did not complain or deny anything, though I was strongly urged to do so by a member of Labour's NEC in an urgent telephone call.

I was left with the same feeling in 1981 when I was MP for Sheffield (Attercliffe) and was the victim of phone hacking. During the course of an industrial dispute in the constituency, as already described, a tape of a conversation with management was produced. Despite the reaction of certain trade unions, it was quickly agreed that a particular charge that had been levelled at me was without foundation. But such an intrusion of my privacy is still a mystery to me. I never saw the tape that was often cited and knew nothing of its circulation. Yet the hacked phone conversation was speedily published in the local *Morning Telegraph* by a Jonathan Foster, whom I had never heard of before. He simply rang me the day before seeking a comment. Otherwise he never made any attempt at any time to see me. Contrary to the wishes of the trade unions that the matter be 'buried' in the interests of the Labour movement in Sheffield, he continued to revive it at every opportunity, no matter how tortuous the innuendo, before leaving the *Morning Telegraph*. My constituency party officers thought Foster's unremitting hostility seriously compromised his newspaper's editorial claim at the time that its staff 'go to a great deal of trouble to be ... accurate, fair and balanced'. They remained unshaken in their belief that more than anyone else, Foster's sole publication of the tape — if it ever existed — enabled him to shed some light on those responsible for the phone hacking.

In view of Lord Leveson's judicial inquiry into the 'culture, practices and ethics of the press', I wrote to him on 13 September 2011. I referred to Part 1 of his terms of reference — 'contacts and the relationships between national newspapers and politicians and the conduct of each ... ' and asked him in the light of my own personal experiences to call in Foster for questions. Not only because of his suspected role in 1981, and subsequently. But also, I explained, because I understand that he is currently employed In the Department of Journalism Studies at Sheffield University as a senior lecturer, and therefore responsible for the cultivation of impressionable young people in the 'culture, practices and ethics of the press' — which is central to the inquiry, of course.

A year later I was informed by the Inquiry that because it was 'limited ... to investigate individual cases in which specific criminal activity is alleged', and had 'heard evidence from a large number of individuals and organisations in relation to culture, practices and ethics of the press, it was not considered necessary to hear from Mr Foster.' So I am still left in the dark as to how, why and by whom my phone-call was hacked. I was prevented from pursuing the matter earlier by the sudden demise of the *Morning Telegraph*. Whilst the continuing harassment by Foster at the time has left me puzzled as to his motivation and private agenda. He could not clam to be acting in the public interest, when no wrongdoing had been exposed.

I have not allowed the conduct of individual journalists to affect a longstanding belief in the freedom of the press, however. It was strengthened during the turbulent Seventies and Eighties in Sheffield as I witnessed the critical role of its evening daily, *The Star*. Under distinguished editors and the courageous news-gathering of some of their colleagues, it was a beacon during the transformation of the city. It survived a formal complaint in Parliament by a Sheffield MP because of an impressive presentation at Westminster by its editor, Colin Brannigan. In the light of the Leveson Inquiry and its disclosure of unethical and unlawful behaviour by some journalists, there has been an inevitable clamour for a tougher oversight of the press. I was not concerned so much for the national titles as for the hundreds of possibly cash-strapped local newspapers. I could not see in any event how the worst abuses could not be dealt with by existing law, and why any new regulation needed to be underpinned by statute, however attired and presented. Despite my personal experience, I still recall the greater security I always felt as a Member of Parliament in the integrity of Lobby correspondents and local journalists than I did in the company of supine parliamentary colleagues. All too many remain easy prey, I fear, for the MP seeking their signature for an early-day motion or other sanction in pursuit of some grievance, as was directed at Colin Brannigan. In any parliament there are likely to be all too few MP s with the courage and integrity of Tam Dalyell.

At that time also there were all too few Labour MPs who worried about Ireland and its deprived Catholic communities in Ulster – apart from a few attentive and conscientious Members. I once questioned Stan Orme about such indifference, contrasting it with the continuing agitation by some Labour MPs with the colonialism that was fast disappearing in any event with the 'wind of change'. 'It's too near home,' he explained. By 1973 Ireland had officially disappeared as an issue within the Labour movement. Its bipartisan policy was only terminated by a revolt of Labour backbenchers during the Hunger Strikes. Yet Labour has continued to take for granted its Irish Catholic vote, the most faithful of its historic constituencies. From 1938 when Neville Chamberlain ceded control of certain Irish ports, Conservative administrations have a much better record on Ireland.

As a former Lancashire Hussar, my father would have been most concerned about the misconduct of certain of the security forces which have prompted repeated apologies by Prime Minister Cameron in the House of Commons. He could not have foreseen the complexity of the operations, but he would not have been deceived by the euphemism 'Troubles' which conveniently disguised their scale and depth. For they actually covered thirty-eight years of continuing operations, with 651 fatalities and 6,307 casualties of service personnel, and around 3,000 civilian deaths. That was about the same number of people who were killed in the Irish Civil War in 1922–23. 'That bloody war', was how Defence Secretary Fred Mulley always referred to Operation 'Banner', when driven to find yet more and more troops for Northern Ireland out of NATO assigned forces.

The blunderings of successive governments in London had placed the Army in an invidious position. For the Falls curfew, Ballymurphy, internment and Bloody Sunday, together with the freer use of firearms by the Army clearly pointed to unsatisfactory political control. It indicated the need to rewrite the rules of engagement for urban conflict. It illustrated the failure in London to recognise that the continued denial of basic rights to the Catholic community was leading whole districts to move outside the law as they provided safe havens for those defending them. Whilst London's preferred option was to 'smash the IRA', as epitomised by Jim Callaghan and Roy Mason, these communities looked more and more to the IRA for protection rather than to the constitutional SDLP. When they started to elect its leaders, the security forces appeared to resort to desperate measures, leading to rumours of collusion by the Army and the RUC with the UDA in the targeting of Catholics. Reports of covert operations by the Army and the RUC involving links with loyalist assassins prompted the raising of questions in Parliament. The apparent self-interested role of different security agencies in covert operations raised other important and, as yet, unanswered questions: under whose or what authority did they operate, and whether they did so in unison? And did those covert operations, like the role of sections of the media ease or prolong the conflict? I was left to ponder, because I was no longer in the loop on the role of intelligence and the military in Northern Ireland from the early Eighties. The official papers will not be available for many years. It was apparent from the early Eighties, however, that the conflict had become a dirty war. By the early Nineties, it was suspected that certain Army units and the RUC were deep in the mire. The dreadful disclosures concerning the murder of the solicitor Paddy Finucane unhappily acknowledged officially the involvement of some security forces.

Yet within twenty years a peace agreement had been reached in Belfast. Queen Elizabeth had paid a visit to Dublin and personally reminded all that the ties that unite the Irish and the British are stronger than their historical animosities. She came wearing green with the harp on her breast, she addressed the Irish in their own language, listened to their music, tread their hallowed sporting ground and bowed her head in honour of those who fought for Irish freedom. It was a personal triumph, perhaps her greatest achievement. But great credit was due to the Irish and British governments, who rose so well to the challenge. None more so than Ambassador Bobby McDonagh in London and Ambassador Julian King in Dublin. A newspaper poll a week after the visit showed that an overwhelming majority of the Irish people had taken the Queen to their hearts, and most want her to come back soon.

The people I wish to credit for this transformation include, first, John Hume, who risked all trying to convince Gerry Adams and his colleagues to call a halt to the violence and enter mainstream constitutional politics. Second, I nominate Kevin McNamara. No-one in Britain, to my knowledge, strove longer, more strenuously, assiduously and honourably for justice in Northern Ireland. Third and fourth, I think of two women: the first is the one I challenged in the House of Commons on the day Bobby Sands died and charged with intransigence – Margaret Thatcher – the lady who was not for turning. Yet she soon changed direction on Northern Ireland, took on the Orangemen, signed the Anglo-Irish Agreement with Garret FitzGerald and fashioned the first building block in the peace process. The second is President Mary McAleese who, with husband Martin, strengthened the peace process through charm at Stormont and hospitality at her official residence in Dublin.

Five, I recall the political flair of Albert Reynolds that enabled him to evade much of a hostile Dublin establishment and six, John Major who did his best to elude the clutches of Unionist MPs in the House of Commons. Together they produced the Downing Street Declaration and the Framework Document, which kept on course the unfolding peace process. Seven, I have to mention, with the deepest affection, Brendan McLua of the *Irish Post*, who bolstered morale and helped create a sense of community among the Irish in Britain during the darkest days. Eight, I am still left somewhat in awe of the audacity of the man who reinforced that support, whilst leading the Greater London Council – Ken Livingstone. Nine, I still marvel also at the courage and skill of the man who took up the cause of the Birmingham Six – Chris Mullins, MP. I can never forget the outstanding support of certain Jewish MPs, notably Paul Rose and John Silkin, ten. Unlike Welsh MPs, who were surprisingly unmoved by the plight of their fellow Celts, until Neil Kinnock amply compensated, eleven. Twelve, I recall the contributions of the Irish Ambassadors in London I came to know, notably Joe Small, Ted Barrington, Daithi O Ceallaigh and David Cooney. In difficult times the Embassy maintained a remarkable standing with MPs of the three major parties for its warmth, its conviviality and its briefings, quite unmatched elsewhere. Finally, the courage and objectivity of certain Northern Irish Protestant journalists, such as Walter Ellis and Susan McKay, furnished Labour MPs with valuable and insightful reports.

The economic management of Irish governments and the various inputs of the Irish diaspora have been critical factors, and are ongoing. Structural changes initiated by Sean Lemass and Dr

Ken Whitaker ushered in a changed and more productive economic relationship with the UK economy. The Irish economy continues to impress, despite its severe indebtedness – compared with like-situated countries – as it claws its way back to market credibility. If it can overcome its present precarious and apparently unsustainable fiscal position, maintain an export-led recovery from austerity, and shrug off unjustifiable sniping, it could once again become the Eurozone's poster-child when it outperformed the rest of Europe.

The spread and composition of Irish exports is illuminating. Such growth could well be stimulated nowadays by the global endorsement of the Irish and their national saint. A host of venues, concerts, parades and parties now mark St Patrick's Day festivities annually in Britain. They are spreading as famed sites and symbols are also going green around the world, ranging from the Leaning Tower of Pisa, to the Pyramids and to the Sidney Opera House. It is a unique development and of incalculable benefit to the Irish Government, which is responding appropriately. It must owe something to the Irish overseas. None more praiseworthy in Britain in my view, than such disparate figures as Tim O'Leary and Joe Gormley on the one hand, and John Kennedy and Andy Rogers on the other.

Tim O'Leary was formerly the national docks secretary of the Transport Workers' Union. He led Britain's dockers through a period of exceptional turbulence, when he had to contend with a formidable agitator in Jack Dash – whom I knew personally. In contrast, Tim O Leary was a moderate. But his quiet and effective negotiating manner gained for the dockers better conditions than any other union official was able to do before or since. The Lancashire Miner's leader, Joe Gormley, was also of Irish descent. I invited him to an Admiralty Board lunch early in my ministerial career. He had a similar negotiating style to Tim O'Leary. Had he succeeded to the presidency of the Miner's Federation instead of Arthur Scargill, he would have negotiated also the best possible deal for his members during a similar period of turbulence. John Kennedy and Andy Rogers, on the other hand, were successful in business and finance before retirement. Like Tim O'Leary and Joe Gormley, who preceded them, they are also distinguishing themselves in the public interest. But they are undertaking innovative, charitable and cultural work on both sides of the Irish Sea and further afield. In addition to his public duties in Greater Manchester, John Kennedy is active in university development and other voluntary activities on three continents.

Andy Rogers, formerly of Co. Sligo, is using his experience as a career banker to help a new generation of ambitious young Irish people succeed in the world of business. As co-chair of the Irish International Business Network, he is involved in a formal mentoring programme for such aspirants. In November 2012, he received a Presidential Distinguished Service Award for the Irish Abroad at a ceremony attended by President Michael D. Higgins, the Taoiseach and the Tanaiste. The awards, which were presented for the first time, honoured the members of the Irish diaspora that have made the biggest contribution to Ireland away from home. A much and widely welcomed acknowledgement, its recipients also came from the US, Canada, Australia, France and Zambia. It appears to me, however, that Andy Rogers' focus is still Britain's Sligo Business Network, which he heads. Thanks to his drive and the enlistment of Mayo friends such as John Kennedy and myself, it has achieved a membership of more than 300. Its purpose is to assist Enterprise Ireland, the IDA and the Western Development Commission in advising anyone in Britain who is interested in either investing or setting up business in Connaught.

Such are the various Irish inputs that are helping to shape modern Britain. They contributed initially to its infrastructure, more recently to its culture and nowadays to its economic development. How far they were nurtured by the Catholic Church we are reminded by the stoical faith of the Irishmen building the Woodhead Tunnel linking Lancashire and Yorkshire in the mid-nineteenth century. Their tramp across the moors in search of a Christmas Mass is commemorated by Ashley Jackson in a mural at St. Ann's Church, Deepcar, on the outskirts of Sheffield. St Vincent's church under construction in Sheffield was too far even for such redoubtable men. But they were grateful for the promise of a Mass at Easter. Successive generations such as Tim O'Leary's community in London's docklands have also needed the consoling role of the Church: priests and nuns – as well as the example of men like Tim O Leary, spartan in food and drink – who tended to their material as well as their spiritual needs.

Irish priests acted not only as fundraisers for the building of the churches, schools and parish centres now officially commended in many towns and cities. They sustained the Irish traditional music and dancing, which are now eagerly sought by today's younger generation. Along with the other Irish inputs, they have also fostered the public interest and their legacy continues to enhance modern Britain. The late Father Gerard Harney from Co. Mayo and the late Monsignor Donal Banbury from Co. Kerry, were honoured as Freemen by the Doncaster Metropolitan Borough.

I might have helped marginally to maintain that unique tradition. After I retired from Parliament, my local Deanery asked me to consider a late vocation for the priesthood, in which the Diocese had already achieved success. It was with the utmost reluctance that I felt unable to pursue such a privileged role because of a prior commitment to John Smith, soon to be leader of the Labour party. I narrowly missed another rare distinction, for I was proposed to succeed the Earl of Scarbrough as Lord Lieutenant of South Yorkshire, until the Cabinet Office intervened, pointing out that I was above the mandatory retiring age. Otherwise, my retirement was marked memorably at Westminster and in my constituency.

Mr Speaker hosted a reception for retiring MPs prior to the dissolution of Parliament in March 1992. I was standing alongside Michael Foot, Merlyn Rees and Peter Archer, when Margaret Thatcher, accompanied by a TV crew, spotted me and approached. Pointing her finger at me and addressing Michael Foot, she told him that, 'Patrick

Duffy was the only member of your party who understood defence and was prepared to do something about it,' before she swept away with her entourage. Happily, Michael took it all in good spirits, and I overheard him telling others about it at the Irish Embassy the next night.

I had already been involved in arranging a dinner in Mr Speaker's apartments for members who had served in WWII. It was recognised that it would be the last such gathering, and was a happy all-party occasion. Still at Westminster, and together with Sir David Price, DL MP, I helped to arrange a Mass of Thanksgiving for retiring members in the Chapel of St Mary-Undercroft, adjacent to Westminster Hall, each of us made a brief address. In recalling the sacrifice of wives and families and expressing thanks to parliamentary colleagues and staff for their support, David conveyed our thoughts so well in the lines of Hillaire Belloc: 'There's nothing worth the wear of winning but the laughter and the love of friends ... Deo Gratias.'

I ventured to suggest that those parliamentary colleagues present who knew active wartime service – 'and we are almost the last – will recall an even more precious brand of comradeship. So evocative, with echoes of action stations, dawn bombardments, commands to start engines, both on airfields and the heaving decks of carriers turning into wind, of private terror, from which the only release was prayer. To have been preserved, like the Great Hall of Westminster, which was set alight by enemy action in 1941, and then later to tread its historic flagstones and to walk within walls which enshrine the whole history of the peoples of these islands, is not only to be privileged, but to be blessed and blessed again.'

The occasion was matched by a similar Thanksgiving Mass in my Attercliffe constituency. I had requested my party executive that I be allowed to arrange my own farewell. I was conscious of how much I owed to each of the four friends who had acted as agent and chairman whilst I represented the constituency. All had suffered untimely deaths in their late fifties, and I was anxious to pay public tribute to their widows – who were present – as well as to party members and all who had supported me over the years. I requested a memorial Mass for them, which was conducted on an ecumenical basis in a packed St. Joseph's Church, Handsworth, followed by a worthy reception. A dinner was arranged separately in honour of the wives of my late officers, and presided over joyfully by the Bishop of Hallam late into the night. Seating and accommodation were severely strained by the numbers of fellow MPs and friends who were anxious to be present and doubled the numbers.

I have constantly renewed the friendship of those loyal constituents in the following years and have been able to do so entirely free in conscience. I held a brief for a short period for the Newsagent's Federation in my early days at Westminster, because my brother-in-law was a member. I resolved afterwards that I would never make any money out of politics, as opposed to my academic profession.[309] Neither did I need to do so, despite the absence then of salary levels, second homes and all manner of allowances that MPs receive today, though spending much less time in Parliament.

For example, I continued to receive £6,500 as an MP, whilst Navy Minister, plus a ministerial allowance of £3,000. That made me the poorest paid member of the Board of Admiralty, which I chaired. But I never felt disadvantaged. I was filled with pride. After all, I was still receiving my 40% wartime disability pension of £4,000, even though it had remained unchanged structurally in sixty years.

Nor did I ever feel at any time that my select committee chairmanship and NATO Assembly presidency called for remuneration. My close

---

309   On being elected to Parliament for Attercliffe I took steps to terminate a visiting professorship with Drew University in the United States. I accepted a visiting professorship, also in economic studies, with the American Graduate School of International Management in the Eighties, which I confined to the Christmas recess. I declared it in the House when the Register of Members' Interests was established. Before the doubt that was entertained about its relevance to the Register's then terms was resolved, I retired from Parliament.

involvement in economic affairs and defence procurement gave rise inevitably to consultancy proposals, however. I received one which would have put me squarely inside the very lucrative world arms trade. It was Washington-based and addressed also to Sir Patrick Wall, who was leading the Conservative party delegation to the NATO Assembly. 'We don't want to do this kind of thing, do we?' asked Patrick as he brandished his letter. That was as far as it was considered. Since those days the division between public duty and private gain has become increasingly blurred. Retired MPs appear now to be prone to accept opaque and even questionable consultancies as they seem to have less and less regard for the old ethical guidelines. How former Parliamentary colleagues can any longer maintain the old ties with their party workers, and preserve the camaraderie that bound them all into the traditional belief in a mass movement, even a cause, is puzzling. It must be quite impossible for some nowadays to look into the eyes of those crusading working-class folk whose past self-sacrifice put them into Parliament, and dispel any suspicion that in the end it has all come down to money-making.

As well as staying close to those to whom I owe so much, I was anxious to put something back into the constituency where I could properly do so. I became president of a restored Lower Don Valley Forum, which had been dedicated earlier to industrial renewal and community relations. As its founders, Lord (Fred) Mulley and Sir Hugh Sykes had learned, it was a difficult project. All the Sheffield MPs were most supportive. David Blunkett generously found some money for our work. But lack of resources was a severely limiting factor.

If all that reflects continuing concern for the east end of Sheffield, it was matched by concern for the future of the Fleet Air Arm following the end of the Cold War. I soon became engaged in defence matters generally, university conferences and periodic presentations at the Defence Academy at Shrivenham. I never met a Labour MP. I was particularly active through consultations and published articles in the promotion of a new generation of aircraft carriers. Together with Admiral Sir Raymond Lygo, I co-chaired the Carrier Conclave Group which came together after the Strategic Defence Review of 1997. Admiral of the Fleet Sir Benjamin Bathurst, Rear- Admiral Colin Cooke-Priest, Rear-Admiral Richard Phillips, Professors Martin Edmonds and Eric Grove were unsparing in their involvement.

Ten years later, after signing the manufacture contract for the new carriers, Prime Minister Gordon Brown in a letter to me paid handsome tribute to the Group and 'Acknowledged the valuable assistance that the group has provided to the Government in the development of defence policy in this field.' He had been steadfast in his close interest in and support of our work, as was Lord (John) Prescott, who chaired the relevant Cabinet committee and received presentations. They understood and appreciated the longstanding commitment of my colleagues to the public interest, and deeply shared it.

I had been an ever-present member of the annual all-party parliamentary pilgrimage to Walsingham in Norfolk. I had been climbing the pilgrim mountain of Croagh Patrick in Co. Mayo as long as I could remember. Come the holy days of spring, wrote Geoffrey Chaucer, 'people long to go on pilgrimage'. Thus in retirement and until I was well into my mid-eighties, I would still take up my pilgrim's hat and staff and head for Northern Spain and the Camino Santiago de Compostela. My main route began in the watershed of the Pyrenees and then wound its way for 800kms to the cathedral of St. James in Santiago. I usually set off in late April to avoid a baking sun as I trekked the vast plain between Burgos and Leon. But even in May the weather can vary enormously, and I often encountered rain and storms as I climbed the mountains and hills between Pamplona and Burgos. Yet it was always a magical experience.

My fellow-pilgrims came from all over the western world, including Australia and New Zealand, and represented the entire range of Christian beliefs. The two countries that I found consistently under-represented in its pilgrims were Britain and Ireland. I would always tackle the pilgrimage alone and on foot. I usually dedicated it to my mother and all those other wonderful mothers who sustained their families through the difficult years between the two world wars. I never forgot my lost school friends. Remaining mindful of Chaucer, I came to appreciate how far the modern worshipper can adapt to medieval aspects of the pilgrimage. The comradeship and generosity, as well as the spiritual force, still provide new insights into life and human relationships and enduring friendships.

Britain and Ireland share an 800-year history of conflict and distrust. Beneath the fractured politics, however there had developed in my lifetime a relationship of partnership rather than friction. It was shaped culturally in my teenage years by the Irish tenor, the popular Irish melodies of the 1930s, the compelling Guinness advertisement and the success of Ireland in horse-racing and its gifted horsemanship. Despite the shadow cast on the evolving relationship by events in Northern Ireland, it was gradually strengthened by Ireland's unrivalled literature, music and dance. It was the economic performance of the Irish Republic, however, that indicated a significant dimension to its newly arrived interdependence with the economy of the United Kingdom. The new economic relationship indicated that the pick and shovel contribution of Irishmen was giving way to their actual presence in company boardrooms. Parity of esteem was confirmed in the Good Friday Agreement and the manner of its public presentation. 'The historical, cultural, linguistic, economic and racial links between Britain and Ireland,' Sir David Goodall, former British Ambassador in Dublin, reminded us in *The Times*, 'makes it illusory for Britain and Ireland to regard one another as foreign countries.'

New relationships between Britain and the island of Ireland were specified in the Agreement. Within a new unified civic and economic space, there was now ample scope for practical co-operation within the island of Ireland. Greater mobility within the European Community of people, goods, money and ideas, along with technological change, have shifted the onus on to Belfast rather than London and Dublin in the defining of its future relationships. The need of new trading patterns by Northern Ireland – internal and external – if it is to meet such challenges, as well as sustain its public sector, rather than rely on the all too familiar transfer payments, will appear more relevant and become more pressing than historic myths.

Ireland and Britain have emerged as equal nations. The political relationship has never been better or closer. Our personal connections are also interwoven in ways that few if any other countries are. They will become closer, for significant developments in Castlebar, the county town of Mayo indicate the inauguration of a two-way process involving the diaspora. One is the emergence of an outreach through the Mayo Emigrants Liaison Committee. The drive of Kevin Bourke, Joe O'Dea and admirable colleagues, has already facilitated homeward-bound travel by Mayo men and women in Britain. It has led to successful and happy visits by the Lord Mayors of Manchester and Leeds and the Mayor of Wigan, which point to closer ties. The other development at the inspiration of Michael Feeney MBE, is the construction of a Garden of Remembrance to honour the WWI dead of Co. Mayo. Of outstanding design and decoration, it was recently opened by President Mary McAleese. The names of the fallen are inscribed parish by parish on its pillars, and include a family member.

Largely because of those whose self-sacrifice I honoured, when I laid my wreath a year later, I felt my allegiance to Britain to be immovable. But I have become exceptionally proud of my Irish background. For me, therefore, identity has become more and more a matter of balance. I live in Roscommon west of the Shannon, and also in Doncaster in Yorkshire. I divide my travel between air flights and the car ferry. On clear days in the middle of the Irish Sea I can actually see both the Wicklow and the Welsh mountains. I always feel part of the reality that lies behind them and know that I am blessed to feel part of both. I still recall how honoured and blessed I felt during the Queen's visit to Ireland to be represented by Queen Elizabeth and

President Mary McAleese – whom I have been privileged to meet. Thanks to being brought up Irish in Britain and British in Ireland I can proudly identify with and would unhesitatingly serve both.

Index

Adams, Gerry, 293, 308, 311, 377
Aherne, Bertie, 314
Aikin, Alan, 231
Aitken, Ian, 81
Akhromeyev, Sergei, 331
Alexander, Andrew, 76–7, 271
Allaun, Frank, 128, 222, 228
Ambler, Cyril, 225
Ames, Aldrich, 138
Anderson, Bruce, 267, 268, 362
Andrews, Eamon, 299
Arbatov, Georgi, 243, 262, 330, 335, 336, 337, 343, 345
Archer, Peter, 381
Armstrong, Robert, 290, 291
Ascherson, Neil, 313
Ashmore, Edward, 125, 127, 130, 131, 132, 133, 134, 135, 136, 138, 139, 142, *211*
Ashton, Joe, 177
Asquith, Herbert, 65
Atkinson, Norman, 91
Attlee, Clement, 72, 251

Baker-Falkner, Roy, 49, 51–4
Baldwin, Stanley, 21, 294
Banbury, Donal, 381
Bankhead, Tallulah, 21

Barnet, Joel, 83
Barrington, Ted, 267, 378
Barton, Mrs, 245
Barton, Roger, 166, 244
Bathurst, Benjamin, 385
Beaton, Cecil, 21
Beazley, Kim, 245
Beevor, Anthony, 39
Benn, Tony, 89, 222, 223, 224, 251
Bennell, David, 71
Bergman, Ingrid, 38
Bermingham, Gerry, 189
Berry, Alan, 36, 37
Betts, Clive, 166, 177, 364
Bevan, Aneurin, 174, 177, 249, 259, 260
Bevin, Ernest, 318
Bevir, Mr & Mrs, 72
Biden, Joe, 254
Bigg-Wither, Tony, 51, 53
Billings, Alan, 163, 177
Birch, Reg, 89
Blair, Tony, 99, 260, 311, 314, 315
Blundy, Frank, 211
Blunkett, David, 159, 164, 165, 166, 177–8, 235–9, 244, 247, 261, 384

Blunt, Anthony, 138
Boston, Terence, 78
Bourke, Charles, 36
Bourke, Eoin, 63
Bourke, Kevin, 387
Bouvard, Loic, 328, 333, 335
Bower, Mike, 177
Bracken, Brendan, 370
Brady, Conor, 355
Bramley, Mr, 30
Brannigan, Colin, 197, 375
Brearley, John, 196
Brezhnev, Leonid, 326, 327, 328, 330, 334, 335
Bright, Geoff, 228, 233–4
Brooke, Basil, 72
Brooke, Peter, 307, 308
Brooks, Jack, 353
Brown, Gordon, 262, 385
Brown, Robert, 320
Browne, D. A. S., 72
Bruton, John, 309
Burchill, Julie, 267
Burford, Ron, 8, 188, 190, 199, 231, 232, 234
Burgess, Guy, 138
Burnside, David, 270
Butler, Arthur, 72, 73
Byng, Geoffrey, 72

Caborn, George, 185, 186, 188, 195, 198, 226
Caborn, Richard, 187, 199

Cagney, Jimmy, 38
Callaghan, Jim, 91, 95, 97, 122, 125, 127, 128, 129, 133, 141, 175, *210*, *215*, 223, 224, 251, 290, 292, 317, 320, 327, 347, 376
Callaghan Jr, Thomas A., 324, 325
Cameron, David, 85, 101, 276, 376
Campbell, Menzies, 277, 328
Capelin, Howard, 234
Carlton, Nurse, 21
Carney, Sean, 17
Carr, William, 179
Carr-Hill, Roy, 304
Carrington, Lord, 324
Carron, Owen, 286–7, 289
Carson, Frank, 270
Carter, Jimmy, 141, 327, 347
Carver, Michael, 139, 322
Castle, Barbara, 251
Catlin, Shirley, later Baroness Williams, 73
Cecil, Nigel, 144
Chalfont, Lord, 277
Chamberlain, Neville, 40, 375
Charles, Prince, 147, 287
Cheney, Dick, 254, 331
Chernenko, Konstantin, 330
Chernov, Nikolai, 341
Churchill, Randolph, 65
Churchill, Winston, 21, 26, 41, 50, 63, 352, 368, 369, 370

Clark, David (politician), 74, 78
Clark, David (Hadfields), 163
Clark, Gilbert, 51
Clarke, Bobby, 98
Clarke, Charles, 263
Clayton, Richard, 126
Claytor, Graham, *218*
Clinton, Bill, 311, 312
Concannon, Don, 122, 285
Connolly, Amy, 29
Connolly, Joan, 98
Conti, Mario, 148, *212*
Conway, Cardinal, 107
Cook, Miss, 29, 30
Cook, Robin, 261
Cooke-Priest, Colin, 385
Cooney, David, 378
Cooney, Patrick, 92
Cooper, Frank, 322
Cooper, Gladys, 21
Cooper, Ivan, 86, 116
Corby, Paul, 234
Corner, Michael, 197
Corterier, Peter, 8, 328, 335, 347
Cosgrave, Liam, 92, 108, *211*
Cox, John, 300
Craig, William, 97, 110
Crosby, Bing, 38
Crossley, Len, 198
Crowe, William, 349
Crowley, Ultan, 300
Cunnane, Helen (Ellen),
    grandmother, 14, *201*

Curran, Ken, 187, 199
Currie, Austin, 86
Curtis, Liz, 273–5
Curtis, Robert, 96

Daly, Cahal, 278, 372
Daly, Lawrence, 180
Darling, Peter, 188, 197
Dash, Jack, 379
Davey, Michael, 225
Delargy, Hugh, 72, 100
Dell, Edmund, 83
Denning, Lord, 265
Devlin, Bernadette, 100
Devlin, Paddy, 86, 116
Dickinson, Reverend, 103
Donovan, Paul, 274–5
Dootson, Sheila, 234
Douglas, Roy, 266
Drucker, Graham Roy, 54
Dubs, Alf, 309
Duffy, Bernard, 35, *204*
Duffy, James, brother, 31, 47, 61,
    201, 211
Duffy, James, father, 7, 11–20,
    22–6, 31, 35, 46, 47, 96, 101,
    106, 114, 147, 148, 153, 176,
    181, 182, 190, 225, 361, 365,
    366, 368, 370, 376
Duffy, Margaret, mother, 11, 14,
    15, 18, 20–24, 29–30, 31, 32,
    35, 43, 128, 147, 148, *212,*
    218, 219, 240, 365, 386

Duffy, Patricia, cousin, 8
Duffy, Patricia, sister, 7, 8, 35, 37, 147, *204*
Duffy, Patrick, grandfather, 12, 33, 366
Duffy, Patrick, victim of the Maypole Colliery disaster, 15
Duffy, Terry, 188, 226
Dunleavy, Brian, 13
Dunleavy, Julia, 12
Dunlop, John, 115
Durkin, Jimmy, 23
Dyson, Cyril, 193
Dyson, Mary, 192–3, *213*
Dyson, Sidney, 8, 140, 177, 190, 192–3, *213*, 230, 232

Eames, Robert, 310
Eberle, James, 126
Edmonds, Martin, 385
Edward, Prince, 147
Elizabeth, the Queen Mother, 148
Elizabeth II, Queen, 127, 147, 286, 352, 353, 377, 387
Elliott, Mick, 185, 187, 233, 247, 288
Ellis, Walter, 308, 378
Emery, Peter, 328
Ervine, David, 107, 311
Esmonde, Eugene, 59
Evans, Moss, 242
Eyre, Muriel, 26

Farrar, Bill, 229, 234
Farren, Sean, 111, 115
Faul, Denis, 307
Faulkner, Brian, 85, 92, 109–11, 114, 115, 117
Fawcett, Mr, 38
Feeney, Michael, 387
Finn, Martin, 33
Finn, Owen, 33
Finnegan, Miss, 30
Finucane, Brendan 'Paddy', 59
Finucane, Pat, 272, 276–7, 377
First Sea Lord, *see* Ashmore, Edmund
Firth, Harry, 249
Fisher, George, 237
Fitt, Gerry, 86, 103, 118
FitzGerald, Garret, 92, 109, 113–14, 117, 272, 289, 290, 302, 378
Flannery, Blanche, 185
Flannery, Martin, 92, 94, 104, 171, 174, 194, 197, 199, 244, 271, 272, 273, 287, 309
Flynn, David, 188, 197
Flynn, Father Charles, 29–30, 40
Flynn, Padraig, 267–8
Foley, Maurice, 83
Foot, Michael, 224, 225, 235, 242, 251, 283, 287, 288, 292, 294, 328, 373, 381
Ford, Peter, 158, 165
Ford, Tennessee Ernie, 19

Foster, Jonathan, 187–8, 189, 196, 373–4
Foulds, George, 231
Franklin, Gloria, 8
Fraser, Bruce, 48, 50

Gageby, Douglas, 279
Gaitskell, Hugh, 183, 260
Galsworthy, Arthur, 92, 113
Galvin, John, 338, 349, 350
Garland, Judy, 38
George, Bruce, 328, 333, 335
Gilbert, John, 261, 320
Gillies, Harold, 54, 55, 71
Gladstone, William Ewart, 34, 65
Glemp, Jozef, *218*, 334
Glover, Major, 103
Godwin, Kelvin, 186, 190, 232
Goodall, David, 386
Gorbachev, Mikhail, 189, 243, 254, 258, 259, 310, 330, 331, 335, 336, 346
Gordon-Walker, Patrick, 77
Gore, Al, 254
Gorman, Edward, 313
Gormley, Joe, 379, 380
Gow, Ian, 92
Gowrie, Grey, 85, 290
Grayson, Victor, 74
Green, Alfred, 250
Green, Paul, 228, 233–34, 235, 236–37, 239
Greenslade, Roy, 275

Griffith, Arthur, 81
Griffiths, Eddie, 173
Grocott, Bruce, 92
Grogan, John, 26
Grogan, Kate, 18
Grove, Eric, 385

Habberjam, Jeff, 234
Hall, Glenvil, 73
Hambridge, John, 158, 160, 256
Hammond, Eric, 255
Hardy, Peter, 92
Harman, Anthony King, 322
Harney, Gerard, 381
Harney, Mary, 309
Harper, Joseph, 182
Harris, Arthur, 147
Harris, Robert, 261
Harrison, Larry, 304
Harrison, Royden, 179
Hart, Liam, 266
Hartley, Alan, 228, 233
Hartley, Jane, 233–34
Hattersley, Roy, 83, 92, 95, 177, 224, 225, 226, 255, 258, 261
Hattersley, Roy & Enid, 177
Hatton, Derek, 235, 239, 244, 256
Haughey, Charles, 289, 309, 355
Haydon, Robin, 146
Hayes, Maurice, 290
Healey, Denis, 129, 130, 307
Healings, Harry, 229, 234

Heath, Edward, 85, 86, 100, 101, 107, 110, 161, 223, 226, 290, 295

Heathcote-Amery, Derek, 73

Heffer, Doris, 239

Heffer, Eric, 222, 228, 238

Heller, Richard, 255

Henderson, Neville, 40

Hendron, Jo, 308

Heseltine, Michael, 160

Heslop, David, 257

Hicks, Robert, 328, 335

Higgins, John, grandfather, 14, 33

Higgins, Michael D., 380

Hitler, Adolf, 39, 40

Hobbs, David, 358

Holland, Margaret, 146

Holland, Tony, 146

Holloway, Michael, 143

Holt, Councilor, 78

Hooley, Frank, 185, 186, 227

Howe, Geoffrey, 290

Howland, Geoffrey, 8

Hughes, David, 239

Hume, John, 86, 108, 113, 115, 120, 289, 292, 308, 309, 377

Hussey, Marmaduke, 270

Hutchinson, Billy, 311

Hutchinson, Dave, 230, 234, 244–5

Hynd, John, 153

Ironmonger, Ron, 85, 158, 160, 173, 177

Jackson, Ashley, 8, 74, 381

Jackson, Mike, 101

Jacobs, David, 269

Jak (cartoonist), 267

Jakobovits, Lord, 285

James, Robert Rhodes, 126

Jameson, Derek, 269

Janner, Greville, 285

Jaruzolski, Wojcioch, 334

Jenkin, Patrick, 164, 179

Jenkins, Clive, 188, 242

Jenkins, Roy, 118, 119

Jenkins, Simon, 313

John Paul II, Pope, *219*, 334, 347–8, 349, 355

Johnson, Ernest, 195, 198

Johnson, Lyndon B., 326

Johnson-Smith, Geoffrey, 328, 335, 338

Jones, Ernest, 21, 22, 182

Jones, Michael, 312

Jopling, Michael, 328

Jordan, Bill, 226, 227, 255

Junor, John, 267, 362

Kane, Doctor, 21

Karaganov, Sergei, 338

Keating, Paul, 358

Kelly, Gene, 38

Kelly, John, 63

Kennedy, John, CBE, 8, 301, 379, 380
Kennedy, John, US President, 132, 319
Kennedy, Joseph, 301
Kerr, Russell, 101, 103, *207*
Keynes, John Maynard, 180, 181
Keys, Eddie, 184, 185, 186, 194, 195, 196, 197, 198, 199
Khodirev, Vladimir, 344
Kidd, Ike, 135, 136, 137, 138, 323, 356
Kilroy-Silk, Robert, 267
Kimberley, Arthur, 52
Kimm, Captain P. R. D., 8
Kimmins, Anthony, 52
King, Julian, 377
King, Tom, 296, 307
Kingdon, Richard, 53
Kinnock, Neil, 224–5, 235, 236, 242, 243, 244, 245, 246, 247, 249, 251, 252, 254, 255, 258, 259, 260–2, 263–4, 294, 295, 309, 378
Kitson, Frank, 275
Knight, Howard A., 257
Knight, Ted 'Red Ted', 256
Kochetov, General, 341
Kravets, Vladimir, 336

Lambert, *nee* Deehan, Sharon, 14
Lane, Lord, 265
Laski, Harold, 39, 180
Le Bailly, Louis, 126

Leach, Henry, 135
Lello, Jose, *220*, 335
Leslie, Shane, 63
Lewis, Isidore, 160, 177
Lingard, Joan, 62, 279
Littlejohn, Kenneth, 100–101
Livingstone, Ken, 232, 267, 287, 378
Lizichev, General, 341
Llewellyn, Mr, 30
Lobov, Vladimir, *218*, 262, 336–7, 338, 345, 349, 350
Lockwood, Betty, 77
Lofthouse, Geoffrey, 13, 182, 225
Lohan, Martin, 354
Long, Captain, 85, 100, 116, 197
Longford, Frank, 367
Lygo, Raymond, 125, 385
Lynch, Jack, 92
Lynn, Vera, 47

MacDonald, Malcolm, 370
MacDonnell, Mary, great-grandmother, 35
MacGregor, Ian, 155–7
Maclean, Donald, 138
MacLua, Brendan, 99, 100, 279, 303, 312, 314
Macready, Neville, 64
Magee, Roy, 310
Magennis, J. J., 59, 61
Mahoney, Bill, 365
Maine, John, 130

Major, John, 310–11, 312, 313, 378

Mallalieu, J. P. W., 72

Mallon, Seamus, 65, 111, 295, 308, 309

Marr, Andrew, 313

Marshall, Beverley, 234

Marshall, Edmund, 116

Marshall, Gerald, 167, 199

Mason, Roy, 81–2, 116, 117–18, 119, 120, 121–2, 125, 127, 130, 134, 140, *208*, *217*, 225, 292, 293, 294, 320, 347, 376

Mates, Michael, 92

Mattholie, Harold, 53–4

Maudling, Reginald, 97, 100, 101

Maynard, Joan, 166, 171, 174, 175, 176, 194, 197, 222

McAleese, Martin, 378

McAleese, Mary, 378, 387, 388

McAlpine, William, 300

McAteer, Brian, 195

McBride, Vonla, *215*

McCabe, Pat, 299

McCrum, Robert, 303

McCusker, Harold, 292–3, 296

McDermott, Sharron, 228, 233–34

McDonagh, Bobby, 377

McDonald, Sheila, 193

McGready, Eddie, 308

McGrigor, Rhoderick, 52, 53, 54

McIndoe, Archibald, 55

McKavanagh, Billy, 98

McKay, Susan, 113, 115, 279, 378

McKee, Billie, 105

McKittrick, David, 279

McLachlan, Donald, 51–2

McLeahy, Leo, 357, 358, 360, 361

McLoughlin, Bid, great-grandmother, 14, 63

McMahon, Inspector, 146–7

McNamara, Kevin, 8, 79, 83, 86, 99, 101, 103, 104, 105, 115, *207*, 263, 271, 282, 285, 287, 294, 296, 308, 309, 311, 314, 377

McSwiney, Terence, 119, 284

Medvedev, Roy, 337

Melchett, Lord, 122

Mellett, Mark, *212*

Mellish, Bob, 99

Messer, Oliver, 21

Michie, Bill, 186, 228

Micklem, Guy, 52, 53, 54

Millan, Bruce, 95

Miller, Frank, 296

Miller, Maurice, 104

Milne, Alan, 71

Milne, Alasdair, 269

Milsom, David, 199, 228, 233–34

Mintoff, Moyra, 144

Mintoff, Dom, 144

Mirfin, Bill, 229
Miscampbell, Norman, 92
Mitchell, George, 312
Mitchell, James, 112–13
Molyneaux, James, 296, 308
Montgomery, Bernard, 64
Moore, Henry, 50
Morris, Patricia, 8
Morton, Andrew, 125
Morton, Roy, 225
Mosley, Oswald, 40
Mountbatten, Lord, 127, 146, 147, *210*, *217*
Mowlam, Mo, 314
Mulhern, Tony, 238
Mullan, Hugh, 98
Mulley, Fred, 140, 172, 185, 186, 187, 192, *213*, 227, 244, 257, 320, 376, 384
Mullins, Chris, 378
Munday, Nurse, 21
Munn, Meg, 177
Munn, Reg & Roy, 177
Murphy, John, 301
Murray, Len, 104
Murray, Rob, 8, 171, 190, 198, 229, 232, 233, 234, 236, 238, 239
Myers, Kevin, 111

Nally, Dermot, 291
Nellist, David, 238
Nelson, Tony, 92

Nemec, Jiri, 364
Newton, Harry, 183
Nicholas, David, 224
Nkruma, Rwame, 365
Norton, Derek, 162
Novello, Ivor, 21

O Ceallaigh, Daithi, 378
O Muraile, Nollaig, 34
O Neill, Tip, 290
O'Brien, Conor Cruise, 92, 278, 279, 313
O'Brien, Jimmy, 12
O'Brien, Margaret, 12
O'Brien, Pat, 38
O'Brien, William, 182
O'Dea, Joe, 387
O'Duffy, Eoin, 30
O'Farrall, Basil, 127
O'Halloran, Michael, 99, 167
O'Hara, Jim, 266
O'Hara, Maureen, 38
O'Leary, Tim, 379, 380, 381
O'Loan, Nuala, 279
O'Malley, Brian, 21, 75
O'Malley, Jack, 21
Omelichev, Colonel, 341
Orme, Stan, 101, 103, 104, 111, 285, 375
Orwell, George, 14, 39
O'Sullivan, Maureen, 38
Owen, Will, 172–2, 199

Paisley, Ian, 82, 97, 110, 115, 296, 311, 312
Percival, Arthur, 64
Petrovsky, Vladimir, 343–4
Peysner, John, 239
Philby, Kim, 138
Phillips, Richard, 385
Pickard, Ben, 75
Powell, Enoch, 283, 295, 312
Power, Tom, 26
Power, Tyrone, 38
Powers, Gary, 319
Prescott, John, 385
Price, David, 382
Price, Dolores, 118–9
Price, Marion, 118–9
Price, Peter, 257
Primakov, Yevgeny, 336, 339–40, 345, 347
Prime, Geoffrey, 140
Prior, Jim, 85, 290

Quinlan, Michael, 141

Rakowski, Mieczysław, 333–4, 364
Rampton, Richard, 273
Rasmussen, Anders Fogh, 371
Reagan, Ronald, 149, 254, 258, 259, 290, 310, 326, 328, 329, 330, 332
Rees, Merlyn, 75, 83, 86, 95, 116, 117, 120, 130, 283, 285, 295, 381

Reid, Jimmy, 226
Reynolds, Albert, 309, 310, 312, 378
Rhys, D. G., 91
Richardson, Jo, 129, 175, 176
Ritchie, Doctor, 21
Roberts, Mrs, 14
Robertson, David, 232, 234
Robinson, Derek 'Red Robbo', 87, 88, 89, 173
Robinson, Mary, 366
Robinson, Peter, 15, 296
Rodgers, Bill, 87, 221, 320
Rodgers, Gerald, 299
Rogers, Andy, 8, 379, 380
Rogers, Bernard, 253
Rogers, Robert, 91
Rose, Paul, 79, 378
Ross, Stephen, 92
Roth, William, 328, 335, 343, 346, 357
Rozzoli, Kevin, 360
Ruck-Keene, Captain, 52–4
Ruddock, Joan, 261
Ryan, Ritchie, 102
Ryder, Don, 89–90
Ryzhkov, Nikolai, 336, 340, 346, 363

Sampson, Colin, 276
Sands, Bobby, 281–7, 289, 294, 377
Savory, D. L., 79

Scanlon, Hugh, 89
Schmidt, Helmut, 141, 327
Schultz, George F., 330
Scott, Sandy, 104
Sedgwick, Fred, 183
Sequerra, Dan, 167, 188, 195, 196, 230, 247
Sheedy, Joe, 8, 190, 231, 232
Sheldon, Robert, 83
Sheppard, David, 238
Sheppard, Dick, 247
Sibraa, Kerry W., 358
Silkin, John, 78, 224, 225, 378
de Silva, Desmond, 276, 277
Simpson, Derek, 188, 227
Sims, Harold, 77
Small, Joe, 378
Smart, Jack, 182
Smith, Jessie, 75
Smith, John, Conservative MP, 51
Smith, John, Labour MP and leader, 99, 249, 258, 262, 381
Smyth, Martin, 296
Soley, Clive, 309
Spence, Gusty, 106, 107, 123–4
Spring, Dick, 263, 294, 297, 309
Stalker, John, 276
Stallard, Jock, 99, 101, 105, 118, 119
Steel, David, 223, 328
Stephens, John, 276
Sterland, Jim, 177

Stevens, Lord, 277
Stillington, Graham, 101
Sussmith, Rita, 331
Swain, Tom, 172
Sweeney, Owen, 300
Sykes, Hugh, 257, 364, 384

Taafe, Peter, 239
Taffe, Joe, 299
Tait, Gordon, 126, 357
Taylor, John, 313
Tebbutt, Grace, 177
Tennant, W.G. (Bill), 44
Thatcher, Margaret, 78, 92, 114, 137, 138, 149, 161, 189, 223, 242, 282, 283–5, 286, 287, 288, 289, 290–1, 292, 294, 295, 296, 327, 328, 329, 332, 346, 347, 352–3, 377, 381–2
Thompson, Edward, 179
Thorne, Stan, *207*
Todd, Ron, 91, 259, 262
Tolupov, Admiral, 341
Tracey, Sean, 351
Tracey, Spencer, 38
Trevelyan, Charles, 266
Trimble, David, 311, 312, 314, 315
Trippier, David, 256
Tuzo, General, 101, 102, 118

Underhill, Reg, 227, 228, 239
Utley, T. E., 277, 279

de Valera, Eamon, 30, 33, 72, 369, 370

Velikhov, Yevgeny, 339

Von Hayek, Friedrich, 180, 181

Wade, Alan, 8, 190, 195, *213*, 230, 231, 232, 233, 234

Wainwright, Richard, 76–7

Walden, Brian, 95

Walesa, Lech, 286

Walker, John, 137–8

Wall, Patrick, 143, 328, 384

Walmsley, Francis, 145

Walton, Dorothy (Dot), 172, 229

Walton, Jim, 229, 230

Watkins, Admiral J. D., 137

Wealthall, Mr, 37

Wedgwood-Benn, Tony *see* Benn, Tony

Weinberger, Casper, 253, 329

Weiner, Tim, 138

Wellbeloved, James, 320

West, Harry, 110

Whitaker, Kenneth, 83, 84, 379

White, Barry, 279

White, Michael, 143

White, Peter, 125–6, 127

Whitehead, Anne, 35–6, 37

Whitelaw, William, 85, 86, 100, 102, 103, 107, 108, 109, 116

Whitely, Peter, 127

Wigfield, Alan, 177, 234

Wilkinson, Frank, 225

Williams, Baroness, *see* Catlin, Shirley

Williams, David, 126, *210*

Williams, John, 8

Williams, Vin, 179

Wilson, Bruce, 362

Wilson, George, 158

Wilson, Harold, 77, 78, 86, 99, 110, 122, 192, 222, 224

Wilson, Patricia, 8

Winchester, Simon, 274

Windlesham, Lord, 273, 276

Wisher, Steve, 233–4

Wogan, Terry, 269, 299

Woodall, Alec, 92, 182, 208

Woodham-Smith, Cecil, 63

Woodley, Tony, 227

Worlock, Derek, 238, 247

Wynn, Bert, 179, 180, 182

Yavuzturk, Seki, *220*, 335, 357

Yazov, Dmitry, 341, 342, 343

Zhurkin, Vitally, 338